BUSINESS
BUSINESS
BUSINESS
BUSINESS
THESAURUS
BUSINESS
BUSINESS
BUSINESS
BUSINESS
BUSINESS
BUSINESS
BUSINESS

BUSINESS
BUSINESS
BUSINESS
BUSINESS

BARRON'S

Mary A. De Vries

THESAURUS

BUSINESS
BUSINESS
BUSINESS
BUSINESS
BUSINESS
BUSINESS
BUSINESS

All inquiries should be addressed to:
Barron's Educational Series, Inc.
250 Wireless Boulevard
Hauppauge, New York 11788

Library of Congress Catalog Card No. 95-43483
International Standard Book No. 0-8120-9327-5

Library of Congress Cataloging-in-Publication Data
De Vries, Mary Ann.
    Business thesaurus / Mary A. De Vries.
        p.   cm.
    ISBN 0-8120-9327-5
    I. Title.
    Z697.B9D4   1996
    025.4'965—dc20   95-43483
                                                       CIP

PRINTED IN THE UNITED STATES OF AMERICA

6789   8800   987654321

Preface

A rich and varied vocabulary is a major asset in business. Although expert writers and speakers sometimes use repetition intentionally for effect, most of the time it is indicative of a limited vocabulary. Those who learn to use a wide selection of words are leading candidates for success. Educators and business leaders alike often point to studies that show how articulate, word-wise businesspeople have enhanced their careers—and paychecks. One way to use an impressive vocabulary and avoid the monotony of boring repetition is to have at your command appropriate synonyms that add interest and vitality to your messages.

Considering the extent and types of communication that businesspeople use to carry out their daily tasks, the *Business Thesaurus* is long overdue. Although numerous general thesauruses are available, businesspeople need a thesaurus of their own, one that is tailored specifically to their professional language needs. Providing such a collection in a convenient size, both for desk use and as a travel companion, the *Business Thesaurus* is small enough to fit in a briefcase but large enough to serve most needs, with nearly 3,500 entries and 75,000 synonyms.

Thousands of business documents were scrutinized to select the best entries and synonyms for the *Business Thesaurus*. The samples included conventional letters and memos, electronic messages, business reports, proposals, news releases, meeting minutes, conference proceedings, and a wide array of other business material. Careful examination of these models revealed that certain words—both technical and nontechnical—were used over and over in business; those words form the core of entries for this book. Other essential terms were then drawn from business magazines and journals, the business section of newspapers, and numerous specialized dictionaries (accounting, information processing, finance, insurance, real estate, law, and so forth). Finally, business associates from across the country suggested many useful entries.

Generally, words having five or more synonyms appropriate for business usage were retained; specialized terms with few or no acceptable synonyms were eliminated. A key objective in compiling this reference tool was to create a well-rounded collection that people in different positions could use; therefore, terms were also selected or rejected on that basis.

Because the book is intended to be an easy-to-use portable reference work, it was not possible to include every synonym that could be found for each entry. Rather, a useful selection of the most important synonyms was included. Neither was it possible to give all parts of speech for each term. In some cases, based on an evaluation of sample business documents, only the most widely used form was selected: for example, the noun form of *plant*; in other cases, research indicated that two or more forms were used extensively, such as the noun and verb forms of *plan.*

Synonyms are generally the same part of speech as the entry term. However, synonyms for noun entry terms may include "-ing" forms that could be used as nouns in a sentence. Hence the entry term "outlay," a noun, includes among the synonyms the "-ing" form "spending," for example. "Outlay/spending increased dramatically last month."

The requirement that a term be useful to businesspeople resulted in many entries, such as *flowchart,* that are not found in general thesauruses. The choice of synonyms also differs. In a general thesaurus, for instance, the entry *complaint* might have synonyms such as *squawk, stink,* and *bellyache.* But such language is inappropriate in business and will not be found in the *Business Thesaurus.*

Because this book is designed for individuals in any business or professional capacity, it includes a variety of entries that will be helpful to anyone in any size or type of office, including those in management, personnel, accounting, training, word processing, and national and international sales.

Entries are listed in a dictionary format, with both the entries and associated synonyms arranged alphabetically. The main term is printed in a bold face, and an abbreviation of the associated part of speech is given in an italic face. Most of the entries are in either noun (*n.*), verb (*v.*), or adjective (*adj.*) form; other forms used less frequently are the adverb (*adv.*) and preposition (*prep.*).

Occasionally, the synonyms in an entry pertain only to a technical definition or a very narrow meaning, although the entry term itself may be more commonly used according to another definition. When it is helpful in such cases, an explanatory word is added. The synonyms in the entry *down,* for example, refer only to equipment operations; therefore, the italicized word *equipment* follows the entry term *down* to alert you to this restricted usage.

Each entry includes a group of synonyms that are organized in one of two ways. Most groups are simply alphabetical listings—a variety of synonyms having various shades of meaning. With some entries, however, it was practical to arrange the synonyms in two or more groups that were easily segregated by general definition. *Value,* for example, clearly has one group of synonyms pertaining to financial worth and another group pertaining to nonfinancial worth. The group listed first in any entry is usually the one that our research indicated is most widely used in business (rather than the one given first in a general dictionary).

In spite of efforts to orient the entries to the needs of businesspeople, readers are urged to consult a dictionary to determine subtle differences in meaning. Rarely do synonyms mean *precisely* the same thing, even though many may appear very similar. Often writers and speakers don't want an exact synonym, and slight differences in meaning among synonyms are helpful, because they increase the options for users. Regardless of the variation in meaning that is desired, it is always necessary for a communicator to select judiciously from those words that appear to fit a particular context.

I appreciate the advice and help of those who supplied innumerable sample business documents to examine for possible entries, and I'm grateful to those who recommended additional entries and offered other valuable information. I especially want to thank Judith Grisham, a noted language expert and administrator at Harvard University, for her intensive, word-by-word review of the *Business Thesaurus* and detailed lists of suggested entries. An earnest language aficionado with an impressive command of the English language, Judith has often been called on to review important reference works dealing with business communication, word usage, and vocabulary.

abandon *v.* abdicate, back out, cancel, cease, cede, clear, clear from computer memory, depart, desert, discard, discontinue, disown, drop, drop out, end, evacuate, forfeit, forsake, give up, leave, leave behind, let go, neglect, quit, reject, relinquish, renounce, repudiate, stop, surrender, vacate, waive, walk out, withdraw from, yield

abandonment *n.* **1.** abdication, abnegation, relinquishment, resignation **2.** defection, departure, desertion, evacuation, neglect, rejection

abate *v.* allay, alleviate, assuage, calm, cease, cool, decline, decrease, diminish, dwindle, ebb, lessen, let go, let up, lower, moderate, quiet, recede, reduce, slacken, slow, subdue, subside, taper off, wane, weaken

abbreviate *v.* abridge, abstract, compress, condense, curtail, cut, digest, pare, prune, reduce, restrict, shorten, summarize, synopsize, take out, trim

abdicate *v.* abandon, abjure, abnegate, cede, demit, drop, forgo, forsake, give up, leave, quit, refuse, reject, relinquish, renounce, repudiate, resign, retire, step down, surrender, vacate, waive, withdraw, yield

abeyance *n.* cessation, delay, deferral, discontinuation, dormancy, inaction, inactivity, intermission, interruption, latency, postponement, quiescence, recess, remission, suspension, waiting period

ability *n.* adeptness, adequacy, adroitness, aptitude, brilliance, capability, capacity, cleverness, command, competence, competency, comprehension, deftness, dexterity, endowment, expertise, expertness, facility, faculty, genius, gift, handiness, inclination, ingenuity, intelligence, know-how, knowledge, means, might, mind for, potential, potentiality, power, proclivity, proficiency, propensity, prowess, qualification, readiness, resources, resourcefulness, scope, skill, skillfulness, strength, sufficiency, talent, training, understanding

able *adj.* accomplished, adept, adroit, agile, alert, apt, bright, brilliant, capable, clever, competent, deft, dexterous, effective, effectual, efficient, endowed, equal to, equipped, experienced, expert, facile, fit, gifted, good, handy, ingenious, intelligent, knowing, knowledgeable, learned, powerful, practiced, prepared, proficient, qualified, ready, responsible, skilled, skillful, smart, talented, trained

able-bodied *adj.* firm, fit, hardy, healthy, hearty, physically fit, powerful, robust, sound, staunch, stout, strong, sturdy, vigorous

abnormal *adj.* aberrant, anomalistic, anomalous, atypical, bizarre, curious, deformed, deviant, deviating, distorted, divergent, eccentric, erratic, exceptional, extraordinary, idiosyncratic, irregular, malformed, odd, peculiar, perverse, perverted, preternatural, rare, singular, strange, uncharacteristic, uncommon, unexpected, unnatural, unorthodox, unrepresentative, unusual, variable

abolish *v.* **1.** abate, abrogate, annul, call off, cancel, delete, disestablish, dispense with, dissolve, do away with, eliminate, end, erase, finish, invalidate, negate, nullify, overturn, prohibit, put an end to, repeal, remove, repudiate, rescind, retract, revoke, set aside, supersede, terminate, undo, vacate, vitiate, void, withdraw **2.** annihilate, demolish, destroy, eradicate, expunge, exterminate, extinguish, extirpate, get rid of, kill, liquidate, obliterate, overthrow, subvert, suppress

abort *v.* arrest, break off, call off, cancel, cease, check, circumvent, contravene, cut off, cut short, drop, end, fail, frustrate, fall short, halt, inhibit, intercept, interfere, interrupt, miscarry, nullify, obstruct, preclude, prevent, stop, terminate, thwart

aboveboard *adj.* creditable, direct, fair, forthright, frank, honest, honorable, legitimate, open, overt, public, respectable, straight, straightforward, true, trustworthy, truthful, veracious

abridge *v.* abbreviate, abstract, compress, concentrate, condense, contract, curtail, cut, decrease, digest, diminish, edit, lessen, limit, narrow, précis, reduce, restrict, shorten, summarize, synopsize, trim

abridgment *n.* abbreviation, abstract, brief, compendium, condensation, contraction, curtailment, decrease, digest, epitome, lessening, outline, précis, prospectus, reduction, restriction, summary, syllabus, synopsis

abrogate *v.* abate, abolish, annul, cancel, discharge, discontinue, dissolve, end, invalidate, make void, negate, nullify, reject, renege, repeal, rescind, retract, reverse, revoke, terminate, undo, vacate, vitiate, void, withdraw

absence *n.* **1.** absenteeism, nonappearance, nonattendance, nonresidence, truancy, unavailability, vacancy **2.** dearth, deficiency, drought, inadequacy, insufficiency, lack, need, omission, privation, unavailability, void, want

absent *adj.* **1.** astray, away, missing, removed, unavailable, vanished **2.** bare, blank, devoid, hollow, lacking, minus, missing, nonexistent, omitted, unavailable, vacant, vacuous, wanting

absenteeism *n.* absence, absence frequency, absence from work, absence from school, avoidance, chronic absence, delinquency, dereliction, desertion, evasion, habitual absence, malingering, neglect, truancy

absentee owner *n.* absent owner, nonmanaging owner, nonresident owner, off-premise owner, out-of-state owner, out-of-town owner

abstain *v.* abjure, abnegate, avoid, cease, constrain, control, curb, decline, deny, desist, discontinue, do without, evade, forgo, give up, keep from, pass, pass up, quit, refrain, refuse, renounce, resist, stop, suppress, withhold

abstract *n.* abbreviation, abridgment, brief, compendium, condensation, digest, epitome, outline, précis, résumé, summary, synopsis

abstract *adj.* abstruse, academic, complex, conceptual, deep, hypothetical, ideal, ideational, indefinite, intangible, intellectual, metaphysical, nonconcrete, obscure, philosophical, recondite, theoretical, transcendent, transcendental, unreal, unrealistic, visionary

abundance *n.* affluence, ampleness, bounty, copiousness, endless supply, excess, fortune, luxuriance, opulence, oversupply, plenitude, plenty, profusion, prosperity, prosperousness, riches, richness, surplus, wealth

abundant *adj.* abounding, ample, big, bounteous, bountiful, copious, excessive, extravagant, exuberant, filled, flourishing, fruitful, full, generous, great, heavy, huge, large, lavish, liberal, luxuriant, numerous, overflowing, plenteous, plentiful, plenty, profuse, proliferous, rampant, rich, sufficient, teeming, well-supplied

accede *v.* accept, acquiesce, admit, allow, assent, comply, concede, concur, consent, cooperate, endorse, enter into, grant, let, permit, submit, subscribe, yield

accelerate *v.* advance, change velocity, facilitate, further, go faster, hasten, help onward, hurry, hustle, increase, increase speed, increase velocity, intensify, move faster, move forward, precipitate, progress more quickly, promote, quicken, speed up

acceleration *n.* advancement, dispatch, expediting, facilitation, hastening, precipitation, quickening, speeding up

accent *n.* **1.** accent mark, character, diacritic, diacritical mark, stress mark, syllable stress, symbol **2.** accentuation, articulation, beat, cadence, dialect, emphasis, enunciation, force, inflection, intonation, meter, modulation, mood, pitch, prominence, pronunciation, pulse, rhythm, significance, sound, speech pattern, stress, stroke, tenor, timbre, tonality, tone, vocalization, voice, weight

accent *v.* accentuate, draw attention to, emphasize, feature, give emphasis to, heighten, highlight, intensify, punctuate, spotlight, stress, underline, underscore

acceptable *adj.* adequate, admissible, agreeable, all right, appropriate, average, befitting, common, competent, creditable, decent, delightful, deserving, fair, fitting, mediocre, meritorious, passable, pleasant, pleasing, presentable, proper, respectable, right, satisfactory, satisfying, standard, sufficient, suitable, tolerable, unexceptional, unobjectionable, welcome, worthy

acceptance *n.* accepting, acknowledgment, affirmation, acquisition, agreement, agreement to an offer, approval, assent, bill, certification, consent, consent to terms, draft, endorsement, order, ratification, signed contract, voluntary receipt

access *n.* accessibility, admission, admittance, approach, avenue, connection, course, door, entrance, entry, highway, ingress, inlet, introduction, key, means, passage, path, right of entry, road, route, street, way

access [*computer*]: *v.* call out, call up, enter, exit, find, make use of, obtain access to, open, retrieve, search

accessory *n.* **1.** accent, accompaniment, addition, adjunct, adornment, appendage, appendix, appliance, attachment, component, decoration, detail, embroidery, extension, extra, frill, ornament, ornamentation, supplement, trim, trimming **2.** accomplice, aide, assistant, ally, associate, auxiliary, adjunct, coconspirator, cohort, collaborator, colleague, confederate, conspirator, contributor, cooperator, helper, insider, partner, participant, subsidiary, subordinate

accident *n.*　adventure, adversity, affliction, blow, blunder, calamity, casualty, catastrophe, chance, circumstance, coincidence, collision, contingency, crash, derailment, disaster, fate, fortuity, fortune, happening, hazard, luck, misadventure, miscarriage, mischance, misfortune, mishap, mistake, occasion, occurrence, setback, wreck

acclaim *n.*　acclamation, acknowledgment, admiration, applause, approbation, approval, celebration, cheering, citation, clapping, commendation, congratulation, endorsement, eulogy, exaltation, extolment, laudation, ovation, plaudits, praise, rave, recognition, salutation, standing ovation

acclimate *v.*　acclimatize, accommodate, acculturate, accustom, adapt to, become accustomed to, become familiar with, conform to, familiarize, get used to, habituate, harden, season, toughen

accommodations *n.*　apartment, arrangement, board, boardinghouse, domicile, dwelling, home, hotel, lodging, motel, living arrangement, prearrangement, provision, quarters, residence, room and board, rooming house, rooms, shelter, sleeping arrangement

accompany *v.*　**1.** attend with, be with, chaperon, come along with, come with, escort, go along with, go with, lead, look after, take out, travel with　**2.** add to, appear with, append to, be associated with, be connected to, belong to, belong with, coexist with, coincide with, complement, complete, co-occur with, go together with, go with, happen with, join with, occur with, send with, supplement, take place with, transmit with

accomplish *v.*　achieve, arrive at, attain, bring about, carry out, complete, conclude, consummate, discharge, do, effect, execute, finish, fulfill, gain, make, make happen, manage, perform, produce, reach, realize, succeed in, take care of, win

accomplishment *n.*　achievement, attainment, completion, conclusion, consummation, deed, effect, effort, end, execution, expertise, exploitation, feat, finish, fulfillment, perfection, performance, production, proficiency, realization, skill, success, triumph

accord *n.*　accordance, agreement, concert, concord, concordance, concurrence, conformity, congruence, consensus, consonance, correspondence, deal, harmony, mutual understanding, pact, rapport, reconciliation, sympathy, treaty, unanimity, understanding, unison

account [*accounting*]: *n.* balance, bill, book(s), calculation, charge, check, computation, enumeration, inventory, invoice, ledger, receipt, record, register, report, statement

accountable *adj.* answerable, chargeable, culpable, liable, obligated, obliged, responsible

accrue *v.* accumulate, add up, amass, build up, collect, compound, enlarge, expand, gather, grow, increase

accumulate *v.* accrete, accrue, acquire, add to, agglomerate, aggregate, amalgamate, amass, assemble, bring together, build up, cache, collect, compile, concentrate, cumulate, expand, gain, gather, grow, incorporate, increase, multiply, procure, profit, stockpile, store, unite

accumulation *n.* accretion, accruement, accumulated profits, aggregation, amassment, collection, growth, increase, purchase of shares, regular investment

accuracy *n.* accordance, accurateness, actuality, agreement, carefulness, certainty, closeness, conformity, correctness, definiteness, definitiveness, exactitude, exactness, factuality, faithfulness, faultlessness, fidelity, flawlessness, incisiveness, literalness, meticulousness, perfection, preciseness, precision, rectitude, rightness, sharpness, skill, skillfulness, soundness, strictness, sureness, thoroughness, truth, truthfulness, validity, veracity, verity

accurate *adj.* absolute, actual, authentic, authoritative, careful, certain, conclusive, concrete, conscientious, correct, definite, definitive, discriminating, discriminative, error-free, errorless, exact, explicit, factual, faithful, faultless, flawless, genuine, infallible, irrefutable, judicious, just, literal, matter-of-fact, methodical, meticulous, official, particular, perfect, precise, proper, punctual, regular, reliable, right, rigid, rigorous, scientific, scrupulous, skillful, sound, specific, thorough, true, truthful, undeniable, unerring, undisputed, unimpeachable, unmistakable, unquestionable, unrefuted, valid, veracious

accusation *n.* allegation, arraignment, blame, censure, charge, citation, complaint, condemnation, criticism, denunciation, implication, imputation, incrimination, inculpation, indictment, insinuation, prosecution, recrimination, rebuke, summons

accuse *v.* allege, arraign, attack, attribute, betray, blame, brand, bring charges, cast aspersions on, censure, charge, charge formally, cite, complain, condemn, criticize, impugn, impute, incriminate, inculpate, indict, malign, prosecute, serve summons

achieve *v.* accomplish, acquire, actualize, arrive at, attain, bring about, carry out, complete, conclude, consummate, deliver, discharge, dispose of, do, do successfully, earn, effect, effectuate, end, execute, finish, fulfill, gain, get, manage, negotiate, obtain, perfect, perform, procure, produce, reach, realize, resolve, settle, solve, succeed in, terminate, win, work out

achievement *n.* accomplishment, acquisition, actualization, attainment, completion, conclusion, conquest, consummation, creation, deed, effectuation, enactment, end, execution, exploitation, feat, fruition, fulfillment, masterpiece, perfection, realization, resolution, settlement, solution, success, termination, triumph, victory

acknowledge *v.* accept, address, admit, affirm, allow, answer, attest to, avow, compensate, concede, confess, confirm, endorse, express gratitude, give thanks, go along with, grant, greet, notice, recognize, reply to, respond to, reward, salute, show appreciation, signal to, support, take an oath, thank

acknowledgment *n.* acknowledging, admission, avowal, certification, declaration, favorable notice, legal declaration, recognition, response, salutation, verification

acquaint *v.* accustom, advise, apprise, brief, disclose, divulge, enlighten, familiarize, fill in, habituate, inform, introduce, make aware, make familiar, make known, notify, reveal, tell

acquaintance *n.* **1.** associate, business associate, colleague, companion, comrade, contact, coworker, friend, neighbor, peer, teammate **2.** affinity, association, awareness, cognizance, companionship, conversance, conversancy, familiarity, friendship, grasp, intimacy, knowledge, relationship, understanding

acquiesce *v.* accede, accept, acknowledge, admit, agree, allow, assent, comply with, concede, concur, conform to, consent, give in, recognize, reconcile, submit, subscribe to, yield

acquire *v.* achieve, amass, annex, appropriate, assume, attain, bring in, buy, capture, collect, earn, gain, garner, gather, get, grasp, harvest, inherit, obtain, possess, procure, purchase, realize, receive, recover, retrieve, salvage, secure, seize, take, take possession of, win

acquisition *n.* accretion, achievement, addition, annexation, appropriation, assumption, attainment, award, bonus, capture, collection, earnings, fortune, gain, gift, grant, harvest, inheritance, possession, prize, procurement, property, purchase, realization, receipt, recovery, retrieval, reward, salvage, seizure, takeover, winnings

acquit *v.* absolve, clear, declare innocent, declare not guilty, discharge, dismiss, exculpate, excuse, exonerate, find innocent, forgive, free, let go, liberate, pardon, pronounce not guilty, release, relieve, reprieve, set free, vindicate

acquittal *n.* absolution, amnesty, clearance, declaration of innocence, deliverance, discharge, dismissal, exculpation, exemption, exoneration, finding of innocence, forgiveness, freedom, freeing, liberation, liberty, pardon, release, relief from, remission, reprieve, respite, vindication

act *v.* **1.** accomplish, achieve, begin, carry out, consummate, create, decide, determine, develop, do, enact, enforce, execute, exert, function, intrude, judge, labor, make progress, manage, maneuver, move, officiate, operate, perform, perpetrate, persevere, persist, practice, preside, proceed, pursue, resolve, respond, take effect, take part, take steps, take up, transport, undertake, work out **2.** appear, behave, carry oneself, comport, conduct oneself, deport, do, feign, function, give the appearance, impress as, make believe, perform, play part, pretend, react, represent oneself, seem, serve, simulate

action *n.* **1.** activity, agility, alacrity, alertness, animation, commotion, drama, energy, events, excitement, force, functioning, game, haste, incident, life, liveliness, measure, motion, movement, operation, plan, power, process, proposition, reaction, response, rush, scene, spirit, stir, stunt, trip, turmoil, vigor, vitality, vivacity **2.** accomplishment, achievement, act, adventure, commission, dealings, deed, effort, endeavor, enterprise, execution, exertion, exploitation, feat, handiwork, initiative, maneuver, manipulation, move, step, transaction, undertaking **3.** case, cause, claim, lawsuit, litigation, proceeding, suit

activate *v.* actuate, animate, arouse, awaken, begin, commence, compel, drive, energize, enliven, excite, fire, force, fuel, galvanize, impel, ignite, incite, induce, initiate, invigorate, kindle, light, mobilize, motivate, move, prompt, propel, push, rouse, set in motion, set off, start, stimulate, stir, switch on, trigger, turn on

active *adj.* **1.** alive, effective, effectual, efficacious, employed, exertive, explosive, flowing, functioning, going, impelling, laborious, mobile, movable, moving, ongoing, operating, operative, progressive, pushing, rapid, restless, rolling, running, rushing, shifting, simmering, speeding, streaming, swarming, ticking, traveling, turning, volatile, walking, working **2.** aggressive, agile, alert, alive, animated, assiduous, bold, brisk, busy, committed, creative, daring, dedicated, determined, devoted, diligent, dynamic, eager, effective, efficacious, employed, energetic, engaged, enlivened, enterprising, enthusiastic, eventful, exertive, forceful, forcible, fresh, hard-working, high-spirited, hyperactive, industrious, intense, inventive, involved, lively, militant, nimble, occupied, persevering, productive, prolific, prompt, purposeful, quick, rapid, ready, resolute, robust, spirited, spry, strenuous, swift, vibrant, vigorous, vital, vivacious, well-coordinated, zealous

activity *n.* **1.** action, activeness, animation, commotion, effort, energy, excitement, exercise, exertion, industriousness, interest, life, liveliness, motion, movement, performance, tumult **2.** act, affair, avocation, deed, endeavor, engagement, enterprise, entertainment, event, game, hobby, job, labor, occupation, occurrence, operation, pastime, project, pursuit, scheme, service, stunt, task, trip, undertaking, venture, work

actual *adj.* **1.** absolute, categorical, certain, concrete, corporeal, definite, indisputable, indubitable, material, physical, positive, real, substantial, substantive, sure, tangible, true, truthful, undeniable, unquestionable, verifiable **2.** current, existent, existing, extant, live, living, original, present, prevailing

adage *n.* aphorism, epigram, folk wisdom, maxim, motto, old saying, proverb, saying

adamant *adj.* determined, firm, fixed, immovable, impenetrable, inexorable, inflexible, insistent, intractable, intransigent, inured, obdurate, relentless, resolute, rigid, set, stubborn, unbendable, unbending, unbreakable, uncompromising, unrelenting, unshakable, unswayable, unyielding

adapt *v.* acclimate, acclimatize, accommodate, accustom, adjust, amend, assimilate, attune, become accustomed to, become adapted to, become conditioned to, become familiar with, conform, familiarize, fit, habituate, harmonize, limit, make suitable, match, moderate, modify, naturalize, orient, orientate, prepare, process, qualify, readjust, rearrange, rebuild, reconcile, reconstruct, refashion, remake, reorganize, reshape, revise, season, tailor, temper

add *v.* **1.** calculate, charge up, compute, count, count up, do addition, enumerate, figure, foot, number, sum, summate, total **2.** adjoin, affix, amplify, annex, append, attach, augment, boost, build up, combine, complement, connect, continue, include, increase, integrate, intensify, join, join together, put together, reinforce, subjoin, superimpose, supplement, unite

addendum *n.* addition, adjunct, appendage, appendix, attachment, augmentation, codicil, epilog, extension, extra, postscript, rider, supplement

addition *n.* **1.** accretion, accrual, adding up, calculation, computation, counting, enlargement, enumeration, expansion, increase, summation, summing up, tabulation, totaling **2.** accession, adding to, adjoining, admixing, affixing, amplifying, annexing, boosting, combining, enlarging, extending, including, increasing, joining, uniting **3.** accessory, addendum, additive, adjunct, affix, afterthought, aggrandizement, annex, appendage, appendix, attachment, augmentation, bonus, commission, continuation, dividend, enhancement, enlargement, expansion, extension, extra, gain, increase, increment, insertion, interjection, option, postscript, profit, raise, reinforcement, suffix, supplement, wing

address *n.* **1.** box number, computer memory address, domicile, dwelling, headquarters, home, house, identification, identification label, living quarters, location, lodging, memory address, number, office, place, place of business, place of residence, street, zip code **2.** declamation, discourse, eulogy, lecture, oration, sermon, speech, talk

address *v.* approach, call, deliver address, deliver speech, discourse, discuss, engage in conversation, give speech, give talk, greet, label, lecture, make speech, memorialize, orate, postmark, route, salute, send, sermonize, speak to, take the floor, talk to, transmit

ad infinitum *adv.* ceaselessly, continuously, endlessly, forever, perpetually, relentlessly

adjourn *v.* break off, defer, delay, discontinue, dissolve, hold off, hold over, interrupt, lay aside, postpone, prorogue, put off, recess, reserve, shelve, stay, stop, suspend, table

adjournment *n.* break, continuance, deferment, deferral, delay, discontinuation, dissolution, intermission, interruption, pause, postponement, prorogation, recess, stay, stoppage, suspension

adjudicate *v.* adjudge, arbitrate, decide, decree, determine, hear, judge, mediate, order, pronounce, referee, rule, settle, try, umpire

adjunct *n.* accessory, accompaniment, addendum, annex, appendage, appendix, attachment, auxiliary, codicil, complement, corollary, epilog, postscript, supplement

adjust *v.* **1.** acclimatize, accommodate, accustom, adapt, alter, arrange, change, compose, conform, coordinate, dispose, fashion, fit, fix, habituate, harmonize, make conform, modify, order, proportion, reconcile, rectify, redress, regulate, remodel, settle, shape, tailor **2.** accommodate, accord, agree, align, allocate, arbitrate, arrange, clarify, compose, compromise, conclude, conform, coordinate, grade, harmonize, heal, make peace, mediate, mend, modify, negotiate, organize, reconcile, rectify, redress, regulate, resolve, satisfy, settle, sort, standardize, systematize **3.** accommodate, align, attune, balance, calibrate, connect, correct, fine-tune, fit, fix, focus, grind, improve, mend, overhaul, readjust, rectify, regulate, renovate, repair, service, set, sharpen, straighten, synchronize, tighten, troubleshoot, tune up

ad lib *v.* create, extemporize, improvise, invent, make up, originate, speak impromptu

administer *v.* **1.** administrate, arrange, carry out, command, conduct, control, direct, effectuate, execute, fulfill, govern, head, implement, lead, manage, officiate, organize, oversee, preside over, prosecute, regulate, reign, render, rule, run, settle, superintend, supervise, **2.** allot, apply, apportion, assign, authorize, contribute, deliver, disburse, discharge, dispense, distribute, dole out, extend, furnish, give, hand out, impose, inflict, issue, measure out, mete out, offer, parcel out, perform, portion, proffer, provide, regulate, serve, supply, tender

administration *n.* **1.** administering of, application, authority, charge, command, conduct, control, direction, dispensation, disposition, distribution, enforcement, execution, governance, guidance, handling of, jurisdiction, legislation, management, order, organization, oversight, performance, policy, power, provision, regulation, rule, running of, strategy, superintendence, supervision, surveillance **2.** admiral, advisors, agency, board, boss, bureau, cabinet, chamber, chair, chairman/woman/person, chargé d'affaires, commander, committee, congress, consulate, controller, council, department, directors, directorship, dominion, dynasty, embassy, executive(s), general, governing body, government, head, headquarters, incumbency, leadership, legislature, managers, management, ministry, officers, officials, organizer, parliament, presidency, president, presidium, regime, reign, senate, stewards, superintendents, supervisors

administrative *adj.* authoritative, bureaucratic, commanding, controlling, deciding, decisive, departmental, directive, directorial, executive, executory, governing, governmental, jurisdictional, legislative, managerial, official, organizational, policy-making, presiding, regulative, regulatory, ruling, superintending, supervising, supervisory

administrator *n.* authority, boss, bureaucrat, CEO, chair, chairman/woman/person, chief, chief executive officer, civil servant, commander, comptroller, controller, curator, custodian, dean, director, executive, governor, head, judge, leader, manager, managing director, minister, officer, official, organizer, overseer, president, presiding officer, proctor, producer, regent, ruler, steward, superintendent, supervisor, trustee

admission *n.* **1.** accession, acknowledgment, admittance, affidavit, affirmation, agreement, allowance, assent, assertion, attestation, averment, avowal, concession, confession, confirmation, declaration, deposition, disclosure, divulgence, exposure, profession, revelation, statement, testimonial, testimony **2.** acceptance, access, admittance, door, entrance, entry, ingress, initiation, introduction, permission, passage, reception, recognition, right of entry, way, welcome

admit *v.* **1.** accept, acknowledge, acquiesce, adopt, affirm, agree, allow, approve, avow, concede, concur, confess, confide, confirm, consent, credit, declare, disclose, divulge, expose, express, grant, indicate, make known, proclaim, profess, recite, recognize, relate, reveal, say reluctantly, subscribe to, tell, unveil, yield **2.** accept, allow to enter, give access to, give right of entry to, grant, harbor, house, include, initiate, let, let in, lodge, open door to, permit, receive, shelter, take in, welcome, yield passage to

adopt *v.* **1.** accept, acquire, affirm, appropriate, approve, assent, assume, back, champion, choose, confirm, embrace, endorse, espouse, follow, imitate, maintain, mimic, patronize, ratify, sanction, select, stand by, support, sustain, uphold, use **2.** befriend, choose, foster, naturalize, raise, rear, select, take in

adroit *adj.* adept, agile, apt, artful, astute, clever, cunning, deft, dexterous, expert, handy, ingenious, inventive, neat, nimble, proficient, quick, quick-witted, resourceful, shrewd, skilled, skillful, smart, subtle, talented

advance *n.* **1.** advancement, amelioration, betterment, breakthrough, development, enhancement, enrichment, evolution, forward movement, furtherance, gain, growth, headway, improvement, increase, movement forward, progress, promotion, prosperity, step forward, upgrade **2.** accommodation, allowance, credit, deposit, down payment, loan, prepayment, retainer

advantage *n.* asset, avail, blessing, boon, break, comfort, convenience, dominance, edge, eminence, expediency, favor, gain, good, gratification, help, improvement, influence, leeway, leverage, luck, odds, power, precedence, preeminence, preference, prestige, profit, protection, recognition, resources, return, superiority, support, supremacy, utility, usefulness, wealth

adversary *n.* antagonist, assailant, attacker, competitor, contestant, enemy, foe, opponent, opposer, rival

adversity *n.* affliction, calamity, casualty, catastrophe, difficulty, disaster, distress, hardship, misadventure, misery, misfortune, mishap, reversal, reversal of fortune, ruin, ruination, setback, suffering

advertise *v.* acquaint, advance, announce, bill, broadcast, build up, circularize, circulate, communicate, declare, disclose, display, disseminate, distribute, divulge, endorse, exhibit, expose, flaunt, herald, inform, make known, market, merchandise, notify, proclaim, promote, promulgate, propagandize, publicize, publish, push, reveal, show off, sponsor, spotlight, spread, uncover, unmask

advertisement *n.* ad, announcement, bill, blurb, broadcast, broadside, bulletin, circular, circulation, classified ad, commercial, communication, declaration, display, display ad, endorsement, exhibit, exhibition, flier, handbill, handout, leaflet, literature, notice, notification, placard, poster, proclamation, promotion, promulgation, propaganda, publication, publicity, spot, spot announcement, statement, want ad

advice *n.* admonition, advisement, advocacy, aid, caution, consultation, counsel, directions, dissuasion, encouragement, enlightenment, exhortation, forewarning, guidance, help, hint, idea, information, injunction, insight, instruction, judgment, lesson, opinion, persuasion, prescription, proposal, proposition, recommendation, suggestion, teaching, tip, view, warning, wisdom

advise *v.* acquaint, admonish, advocate, appeal to, apprise, caution, command, communicate, counsel, direct, dissuade, encourage, enjoin, enlighten, exhort, fill in, forewarn, guide, impart, inform, instruct, make known, notify, offer opinion, persuade, point out, prepare, prescribe, prompt, recommend, relate, report, suggest, teach, tell, update, urge, warn

advisor(er) *n.* arbiter, authority, coach, confidant, consultant, counsel, counselor, director, expert, guide, helper, instructor, mentor, monitor, preceptor, professional, referee, teacher, therapist, tutor, umpire

advocate *n.* apologist, apostle, attorney, backer, campaigner, champion, counsel, defender, exponent, expounder, intercessor, lawyer, patron, promoter, proponent, spokesperson, supporter

advocate *v.* advance, argue for, associate with, back, build up, campaign for, champion, countenance, defend, encourage, endorse, espouse, favor, further, maintain, patronize, plead for, promote, propagate, propose, push, recommend, side with, speak for, support, sustain, uphold, urge

affidavit *n.* affirmation, deposition, oath, pledge, sworn statement, testimony, written declaration

affiliate *n.* ally, arm, associate, branch, division, member, offshoot, partner, subdivision, subsidiary

affiliation *n.* alliance, amalgamation, association, bond, coalition, combination, confederation, connection, cooperation, league, link, membership, partnership, relationship, tie, union

affirm *v.* acknowledge, allege, announce, assert, attest, aver, avow, certify, claim, confirm, contend, declare, depose, endorse, guarantee, insist, maintain, make known, proclaim, profess, promulgate, pronounce, propound, ratify, say, say positively, state, state positively, swear, testify, vouch for, warrant, witness

affirmation *n.* acknowledgment, affidavit, allegation, announcement, assertion, attestation, averment, avowal, certification, confirmation, contention, declaration, deposition, guarantee, oath, positive statement, proclamation, profession, promise, promulgation, pronouncement, ratification, statement, sworn statement, testimonial, testimony, warranty

affix *v.*   add, add to, adjoin, annex, append, attach, bind, conjoin, connect, fasten, fix, glue, hook, join, nail, paste, pin, put on, rivet, staple, subjoin, tie, unite

afford *v.*   **1.** allow, be able to, bear, be rich enough for, find enough for, have enough for, have the means for, manage, manage to give, sacrifice, spare, stand, support, sustain   **2.** accord, award, bestow, bring forth, confer upon, furnish, generate, give, grant, impart, offer, provide, render, supply, yield

age *n.*   **1.** adolescence, adulthood, advancing years, agedness, anility, boyhood, childhood, declining years, elderly, generation, girlhood, infancy, life, lifetime, majority, maturity, middle age, milestone, old age, senescence, senility, seniority, stage of life, youth   **2.** aeon, century, cycle, date, day(s), decade, duration, epoch, era, generation, interim, interval, life, lifetime, long time, millennium, period, span, time, year

agency *n.*   **1.** bureau, business, company, concern, corporation, enterprise, firm, house, institution, office, organization   **2.** action, activity, auspices, channel, consequences, effect, efficiency, force, good offices, influence, instrument, instrumentality, intercession, intervention, means, mechanism, mediation, medium, operation, organ, potency, power, result, vehicle, ways and means, work

agenda *n.*   calendar, docket, itinerary, lineup, list, outline, plan, program, schedule, timetable

agent *n.*   **1.** advocate, ambassador, assistant, attorney, broker, commissary, commissioner, delegate, deputy, diplomat, emissary, envoy, executor, functionary, handler, lawyer, mediator, messenger, minister, officer, operative, operator, proctor, procurator, promoter, representative, salesperson, steward, surrogate, trustee   **2.** cause, channel, factor, force, means, medium, moving force, organ, power, vehicle

aggregate *n.*   accumulation, agglomerate, agglomeration, all, amount, assemblage, body, bulk, collection, combination, composite, compound, conglomerate, conglomeration, cumulation, entirety, gross, group, mass, mixture, net, quantity, sum, summation, total, totality, whole

agitator *n.*   agent provocateur, anarchist, demagogue, disrupter, dissident, fighter, fomenter, incendiary, inciter, instigator, insurgent, insurrectionist, malcontent, mover, partisan, propagandist, provocateur, rabble-rouser, radical, reactionary, rebel, revisionist, revolutionary, troublemaker, zealot

agrarian *adj.* agricultural, agronomic, country, cultivated, landed, natural, nonurban, pastoral, peasant, rural, rustic, uncultivated, undeveloped, undomesticated

agree *v.* **1.** abide by, accede, accept, acknowledge, acquiesce, admit, allow, approve, assent, be in accord with, be in concert with, be in harmony with, be unanimous with, comply, concede, concur, consent, grant, make a contract, permit, pledge, promise, recognize, side with, think alike, yield **2.** be consistent with, be the same, blend, cohere, coincide, conform, correspond, equal, go together, harmonize, match, synchronize

agreement *n.* **1.** acceptance, acknowledgment, adjudication, affidavit, approval, armistice, arrangement, assent, authorization, avowal, bargain, bond, cartel, charter, codicil, compact, compromise, concordat, confirmation, contract, convention, covenant, deal, endorsement, entente, guarantee, indenture, lease, memorandum of intent, memorandum of understanding, negotiation, note, oath, pact, pledge, promise, proposal, protocol, recognition, settlement, stipulation, transaction, treaty, truce, understanding, warranty, word, writ **2.** acceptance, accession, accommodation, accord, accordance, acknowledgment, adjustment, affiliation, affinity, alliance, amity, approval, arbitration, arrangement, assent, mutual assent, authorization, communion, compatibility, compliance, compromise, concert, concession, concord, concordance, concurrence, conformity, congruence, congruity, consensus, consent, consistency, correspondence, endorsement, harmony, mediation, mutual understanding, pledge, rapport, ratification, reconciliation, similarity, suitableness, sympathy, unanimity, union, unison, unity, verification

aid *n.* advancement, advocacy, allowance, assistance, avail, backing, backup, benefaction, benefit, benevolence, care, charity, collaboration, comfort, compensation, contribution, cooperation, countenance, deliverance, donation, encouragement, endowment, facilitation, favor, funding, furtherance, gift, grant, guidance, handout, help, humanitarianism, loan, maintenance, ministration, ministry, patronage, philanthropy, promotion, reinforcement, relief, rescue, salvation, service, sponsorship, subsidy, succor, support, sustenance, treatment

aid *v.* accommodate, advance, alleviate, assist, back, befriend, benefit, bolster, collaborate with, comfort, contribute to, cooperate with, encourage, enhance, expedite, facilitate, further, help, improve, maintain, make easier, mitigate, promote, relieve, subsidize, support, sustain, uphold

aide/aid *n.* adjutant, adviser, aide-de-camp, assistant, attaché, attendant, coadjutant, coadjutor, devotee, helper, staff, subordinate, supporter

aim *n.* ambition, aspiration, attempt, design, desire, destination, determination, direction, dream, effort, end, endeavor, focus, goal, hope, intent, intention, mark, object, objective, plan, purpose, scheme, target, understanding, wish

aim *v.* **1.** aspire, attempt, concentrate on, contemplate, covet, endeavor, intend, mean, plan, propose, strive toward, try, want, wish for, work toward **2.** direct, fire at, focus, point, prepare to fire, sight, take aim, target, train

airport *n.* airdrome, airfield, airstation, facility, field, hangar, helipad, heliport, installation, landing strip, runway, strip

alarm [*device*]: *n.* alarm bell, alert, bell, buzzer, caution, drum, forewarning, horn, sign, siren, trumpet, warning, whistle

album *n.* anthology, book, collection, compilation, depository, file, folder, memento, memory book, notebook, organizer, portfolio, record-keeper, register, registry, scrapbook

algorithm *n.* computational procedure, computer program, logical procedure, mathematical procedure, method of problem solving, predetermined instructions, problem-solving approach, problem-solving procedure, sequence of instructions, set of instructions, set of rules, solution

alias *n.* AKA, anonym, assumed name, false name, fictitious name, nom de plume, pen name, pseudonym, stage name

alibi *n.* account, affirmation, allegation, answer, argument, assertion, assurance, avowal, case, cover, declaration, defense, excuse, explanation, justification, plea, pretext, proof, reason, reply, retort, statement, vindication

alien *n.* displaced person, emigrant, extraterrestrial, foreigner, foreignness, guest, illegal alien, immigrant, intruder, invader, migrant, newcomer, noncitizen, outlandishness, outsider, refugee, stateless person, settler, strangeness, stranger, unnaturalized citizen, visitor

alkaline *adj.* acrid, alkalescent, alkali-based, antacid, bitter, caustic, salty, soluble

allegation *n.* accusation, affirmation, assertion, attestation, averment, avowal, charge, claim, complaint, declaration, deposition, implication, imputation, insinuation, plea, profession, statement, statement of facts, testimony

allegiance *n.* adherence, constancy, dedication, deference, devotion, faithfulness, fealty, fidelity, loyalty, obedience, subjugation

alliance *n.* accord, affiliation, affinity, agreement, bloc, bond, cartel, coalition, coherence, collaboration, collusion, combine, communion, compact, concord, concordat, confederacy, confederation, connection, consortium, contract, covenant, entente, enterprise, federation, friendship, interrelationship, league, membership, pact, partnership, pool, relationship, syndicate, treaty, trust, union

allotment *n.* allocation, allowance, apportionment, appropriation, assignment, budget, dispensation, distribution, division, grant, lot, measure, part, percentage, piece, portion, provision, quota, ration, share

allowance *n.* **1.** addition, aid, alimony, allocation, allotment, amount, annuity, apportionment, assistantship, bequest, commission, contribution, deduction, discount, donation, endowment, fee, gift, grant, gratuity, help, increase, inheritance, interest, legacy, lot, maintenance, margin, measure, part, pay, payment, pension, percentage, piece, portion, present, prize, quantity, quota, ration, rebate, recompense, reduction, relief, remittance, remuneration, reward, salary, scholarship, share, stipend, subsidy, subsistence, sum, support, tip, wages **2.** accommodation, acknowledgment, acquiescence, adaptation, adjustment, admission, admittance, advantage, agreement, approval, assent, authorization, consent, concession, concurrence, support, tolerance

alloy *n.* admixture, adulteration, agglomeration, aggregation, amalgam, amalgamation, blend, coalescence, combination, combine, commixture, composite, compound, conglomeration, debasement, fusion, hybrid, intermixture, mix, mixture, union

ally *n.* accessory, accomplice, adjutant, associate, backer, coadjutant, colleague, companion, comrade, confederate, consociate, helper, partner, supporter

alma mater *n.* academy, college, institution, place of graduation, place of matriculation, school, university

almanac *n.* annual, calendar, chronicle, journal, record, register, registry, yearbook

alphabet *n.* ABCs, basics, characters, fundamentals, hieroglyphs, ideographs, letters, morphemes, phonemes, pictographs, rudimentary principles, rudiments, runes, signs, syllabary, symbols

alphabetize *v.* arrange, categorize, categorize by letter, codify, file A to Z, index, order, organize, put in alphabetical order, put in order, systematize

alter *v.* adapt, adjust, amend, change, commute, convert, correct, diversify, edit, emend, enlarge, exchange, fix, make different, mend, modify, qualify, recast, reconstruct, refashion, remake, remodel, remold, renovate, reorganize, reshape, revamp, reverse, revise, transfigure, transform, transmute, vary

alternate *n.* backup, fill-in, proxy, replacement, stand-in, substitute, surrogate, understudy

alternative *n.* backup, choice, other choice, preference, recourse, replacement, selection, substitute

altitude *n.* apex, distance, elevation, extent, height, peak, stature, summit, upward measurement

alumnus/alumna *n.* alum, former student, graduate, postgraduate

amalgam *n.* admixture, alloy, amalgamation, blend, coalescence, combination, commixture, composite, compound, cross-breed, fusion, hybrid, mix, mixture, mongrel, union

amateur *n.* apprentice, aspirant, beginner, dilettante, layperson, learner, neophyte, nonprofessional, novice, recruit

ambassador *n.* agent, attaché, commissioner, consul, delegate, dignitary, diplomat, emissary, envoy, legate, minister, nuncio, official, plenipotentiary, representative

ambiguity *n.* abstruseness, ambivalence, circumlocution, deceptiveness, double entendre, double meaning, doubtfulness, dubiousness, equivocality, equivocation, indefiniteness, indeterminateness, indistinctness, obscurity, uncertainty, unclearness, untelligibility, vagueness

ambition *n.* aim, appetite, ardor, aspiration, commitment, craving, design, desire, destination, dream, drive, eagerness, earnestness, end point, energy, enterprise, enthusiasm, goal, hope, hunger, ideal, initiative, intent, intention, longing, object, objective, passion, plan, purpose, scheme, striving, target, wish, yearning, zeal

ambitious *adj.* aggressive, ardent, arduous, aspiring, assertive, avid, bold, challenging, committed, demanding, designing, determined, driving, eager, earnest, elaborate, energetic, enterprising, enthusiastic, far-reaching, fervent, forceful, formidable, goal-oriented, grand, grandiose, hardworking, hopeful, impressive, industrious, large-scale, lofty, power-oriented, pretentious, purposeful, resourceful, scheming, self-motivated, striving, success-oriented, vigorous, zealous

ameliorate *v.* alleviate, amend, advance, assuage, better, ease, heal, help, improve, lessen, lighten, make better, meliorate, mend, mitigate, promote, relieve, remedy, upgrade

amend *v.* adapt, adjust, alter, change, convert, correct, edit, emend, enhance, fix, improve, make different, mend, modify, recast, rectify, remedy, remold, reorganize, repair, reshape, revise, right, transfigure, transform

amendment *n.* **1.** adjustment, alteration, amelioration, change, clarification, conversion, correction, editing, emendation, enhancement, improvement, modification, qualification, recasting, reconstruction, rectification, reform, reformation, remedy, remodeling, remolding, reorganization, repair, revision, transfiguration, transformation, variation **2.** act, addendum, addition, adjunct, appendage, attachment, bill, clause, codicil, measure, motion, postscript, rider, suggestion, supplement

amenity [*real estate*]: *n.* advantage, civility, comfort, convenience, enhancement, enrichment, excellence, extra, extravagance, facility, frill, improvement, luxury, merit, pleasantry, quality, refinement, service, virtue

amnesty *n.* absolution, clemency, condonation, dispensation, excuse, excusal, exemption, forgiveness, immunity, impunity, leniency, mercy, pardon, remission, reprieve

amorphous *adj.* chaotic, characterless, formless, inchoate, indeterminate, irregular, jumbled, nebulous, nondescript, shapeless, structureless, unformed, unorganized, unshaped, unstructured, vague

amortization *n.* cost write-off, debt reduction, gradual extinguishment, installment paying, payment of debt, periodic charges, proration, write-off

amount *n.* **1.** body, bulk, bundle, expanse, load, lot, magnitude, mass, number, quantity, size, supply, volume **2.** addition, aggregate, cost, expense, grand total, net, outlay, output, product, sum, total, value

amplify *v.* add to, augment, boost, broaden, build up, clarify, develop, elaborate, elevate, elongate, enhance, enlarge, exaggerate, expand, expatiate, explain, expound on, extend, heighten, illustrate, increase, inflate, intensify, lengthen, magnify, make greater, make larger, make louder, multiply, prolong, raise the volume, strengthen, stretch, supplement, turn up, widen

anachronism *n.*   archaism, antedate, chronological error, misdate, misplacement, obsolete form, out of proper order, postdate, predate

analogy *n.*   accordance, affinity, alikeness, comparison, correlation, correspondence, equivalence, equivalency, homology, implicit comparison, likeness, metaphor, parallelism, parity, relation, relationship, resemblance, semblance, similarity, simile, similitude

analysis *n.*   **1.** assay, breakdown, clarification, dissection, dissociation, dissolution, division, estimation, evaluation, examination, explanation, inquiry, interpretation, investigation, judgment, partition, postmortem, reasoning, reduction, resolution, review, scrutiny, search, separation, study, subdivision, test   **2.** abstract, critique, finding, judgment, opinion, outline, report, summary, synopsis

analyst *n.*   assayer, evaluator, examiner, inquisitor, investigator, questioner, reviewer

analyze *v.*   **1.** assay, clarify, consider, criticize, critique, determine, estimate, evaluate, examine, examine critically, explain, figure, figure out, inspect, interpret, investigate, judge, ponder, question, reflect on, resolve, scrutinize, spell out, study, test, think through   **2.** anatomize, break down, break up, cut up, decompose, disintegrate, dissect, dissolve, divide, separate out, sort out, take apart

ancestor *n.*   antecedent, ascendant, forebear, forerunner, founder, originator, precursor, primogenitor, progenitor, prototype

ancient *adj.*   aged, age-old, antediluvian, antiquated, antique, archaic, earlier, earliest, early, elderly, fossilized, obsolete, old, olden, older, oldest, old-fashioned, outmoded, out-of-date, past, preadamic, preglacial, prehistoric, primal, primeval, primitive, primordial, pristine, remote, superannuated, timeworn, venerable, very old

ancillary *adj.*   accessory, adjunct, adjuvant, auxiliary, satellite, secondary, subordinate, subservient, subsidiary

anecdote *n.*   allegory, amusing story, entertaining story, episode, fable, funny story, illustration, incident, legend, memoir, myth, narration, narrative, relation, reminiscence, short story, sketch, tale

angle *n.* branch, corner, decline, divergence, division, fork, incline, intersection, notch, point, Y

animation *n.* action, ardor, buoyancy, dynamism, ebullience, effervescence, energy, enthusiasm, esprit, excitement, exhilaration, exuberance, fervor, flair, gaiety, high spirits, intensity, life, liveliness, passion, spirit, verve, vibrancy, vigor, vitality, vivacity, zeal, zest

annals *n.* account, annual report, archive, chronicle, classbook, diary, history, journal, memorial, memoir, record, register, registry, yearbook

annex *n.* addendum, adjunct, affiliate, affix, annexation, appendix, arm, attachment, branch, codicil, division, epilog, part, postscript, section, subdivision, suffix, supplement

annex *v.* acquire, add on to, adjoin, affix, append, appropriate, attach, combine, connect, conquer, consolidate, fasten, include, incorporate, join, link, merge, obtain, occupy, procure, seize, subjoin, take, unite, usurp

anniversary *n.* annual observance, birthday, celebration, ceremony, commemoration, feast day, festival, fete, holiday, jubilee, recurrence, yearly observance

annotation *n.* appendix, commentary, comments, elucidation, exegesis, explanation, footnotes, gloss, glossary, interpretation, illustration, margin comments, notes, remarks

announce *v.* **1.** annunciate, broadcast, call, communicate, declare, divulge, give notice, give out, inform, impart, intimate, introduce, issue, make known, make public, notify, print, proclaim, promulgate, propound, publicize, publish, release, report, state, tell **2.** forecast, forerun, foretell, indicate, introduce, portend, predict, presage, present, signal, signify

announcement *n.* advertisement, briefing, commercial, declaration, decree, disclosure, dissemination, divulgence, edict, exposition, introduction, message, notice, notification, ordinance, presentation, proclamation, promulgation, publication, publicity, recital, recitation, release, revelation, statement

announcer *n.* anchorperson, broadcaster, commentator, disc jockey, host, media commentator, newscaster, reporter, telecaster

annual *n.* annual report, perennial publication, publication issued annually, report, summary, yearbook, yearly publication

annual report *n.* corporate report, financial report, financial statements, fiscal report, shareholders report, year-end report, yearly report

annuity *n.* income, income benefit, insurance contract, payment, periodic payment

annul *v.* abjure, abolish, abrogate, cancel, countermand, disaffirm, disavow, discharge, discontinue, dissolve, erase, expunge, invalidate, negate, neutralize, nullify, recall, recant, renounce, repeal, repudiate, rescind, retract, reverse, revoke, set aside, stop, suspend, terminate, undo, vacate, vitiate, void, withdraw

annulment *n.* abjuration, abolition, abrogation, cancellation, disaffirmation, disavowal, discharge, discontinuation, dissolution, erasure, expunction, invalidation, negation, neutralization, nullification, recall, recantation, renouncement, repeal, repudiation, recision, retraction, reversal, revocation, vitiation, voidance, withdrawal

anomaly *n.* aberration, departure, deviation, digression, divergence, eccentricity, exception, idiosyncrasy, incongruity, inconsistency, nonconformity, oddity, peculiarity, rarity, variance

anonymous *adj.* allonymous, incognito, innominate, nameless, pseudonymous, secret, unacknowledged, unattributed, uncredited, undesignated, undisclosed, unidentified, unknown, unnamed, unsigned, unspecified

answer *v.* acknowledge, argue, clarify, confirm, contest, counter, counterclaim, defend, deny, disprove, dispute, elucidate, explain, interpret, plead, react, rebut, refute, rejoin, remark, reply, respond, retort, say, write

antecedents *n.* ancestors, ancestry, antecessors, family, family tree, forebears, forerunners, genealogy, history, house, lineage, pedigree, precursors, predecessors, primogenitors, progenitors, stock

antedate *v.* antecede, backdate, come before, date back, foredate, forerun, misdate, precede, predate

anthology *n.* album, collection, compendium, compilation, digest, excerpts, extracts, garland, literary collection, miscellany, omnibus, selections, treasury

antidote *n.* antibody, antitoxin, antivenin, corrective, counter-acter, counteraction, counteracting agent, counteragent, countermeasure, counterpoison, counterstep, cure, drug, medication, medicine, neutralizer, neutralizing agent, nullifier, preventive, preventive measure, remedy, vaccination, vaccine

antique *n.* antiquity, artifact, collectible, collector's item, heirloom, monument, old object, rarity, relic, vestige

antique *adj.* aged, age-old, ancient, antiquarian, antiquated, archaic, classic, collectible, earliest, elderly, historic, obsolescent, obsolete, old, oldest, old-fashioned, old-world, original, outdated, out-of-date, prehistoric, primitive, primordial, rare, rustic, superannuated, timeworn, traditional, vintage

antiquity [*time*]: *n.* ancient times, classical times, distant past, early ages, former age, former times, the past, remote time

antiseptic *n.* alcohol, bactericide, chlorine, cleanser, cleansing agent, decontaminant, detergent, disinfectant, germicide, iodine, purifier, sterilizer, sterilizing agent

antithesis *n.* antipode, contra, contradiction, contradictory, contraposition, contrariety, contrary, contrast, converse, counter, diametrical opposition, direct contrast, exact opposite, in contrast, inverse, opposite, opposition, other side, pole, reverse, sharp contrast

antonym *n.* opposite, reverse, word with opposite meaning

aperture *n.* airhole, chink, cleft, crack, cranny, crevice, eye, eyehole, eyelet, fissure, foramen, gash, hole, interstice, opening, peephole, perforation, pinhole, pore, puncture, rift, slit, slot, spiracle, vent

apex *n.* acme, apogee, cap, climax, crest, crown, crowning point, culmination, extreme, head, heights, highest point, loft, maximum, meridian, peak, pinnacle, point, roof, spire, sublimity, summit, tip, top, vertex, zenith

aphorism *n.* adage, apothegm, belief, epigram, gnome, half truth, maxim, moral, motto, opinion, principle, proverb, rule, saying, truism, witticism

apology *n.* acknowledgment of regret, admission, admission of error, apologia, atonement, concession, confession, excuse, expiation, explanation, expression of regret, extenuation, redress, reparation, request for pardon, statement of remorse

apostle *n.* advocate, champion, converter, crusader, disciple, divine, evangelist, follower, herald, messenger, minister, missionary, preacher, priest, propagandist, proponent, proselytizer, reformer, supporter, teacher, witness

apparatus *n.* appliances, bureaucracy, contraption, device, equipment, fixtures, furnishings, gadget, gear, hierarchy, implement, instruments, machines, machinery, means, mechanism, network, organization, outfit, plant, provisions, structure, supplies, system, tools, utensils

appeal *n.* **1.** address, adjuration, application, bid, call, claim, cry, demand, entreaty, imploration, invocation, overture, petition, plea, prayer, proposal, proposition, question, recourse, request, requisition, solicitation, submission, suit, supplication **2.** allure, attraction, attractiveness, beauty, charisma, charm, enticement, fascination, glamour, interest, seductiveness, temptation

appeal *v.* **1.** address, adjure, advance, apply to, ask earnestly, beg, bid, call, call upon, canvass, claim, contest, crave, cry out, demand, engage, entreat, implore, importune, invite, invoke, petition, plead, pray, propose, proposition, question, refer, request, require, resort to, solicit, submit, sue, supplicate, urge **2.** allure, attract, beguile, captivate, charm, entice, fascinate, interest, intrigue, please, tantalize, tempt

appease *v.* abate, accommodate, allay, alleviate, assuage, calm, comfort, compose, conciliate, ease, gratify, humor, lessen, lull, mitigate, moderate, mollify, pacify, placate, propitiate, quiet, reconcile, relieve, satisfy, soften, soothe, temper, tranquilize, win over

append *v.* add, adjoin, affix, annex, attach, fasten to, join to, supplement

appendage *n.* addendum, addition, adjunct, ancillary, annexation, appendix, attachment, auxiliary, branch, codicil, epilog, extension, offshoot, postscript, projection, supplement

appendix *n.* addendum, addition, adjunct, annexation, appendage, attachment, codicil, epilog, excursus, extension, postscript, rider, sample, supplements

appliance *n.* apparatus, contraption, contrivance, device, equipment, furnishing, gadget, implement, instrument, machine, mechanism, tool, utensil

applicant *n.*   appellant, aspirant, candidate, claimant, competitor, entrant, interviewee, job hunter, job seeker, office seeker, participant, petitioner, postulant, suppliant, supplicant

application *n.* **1.** appeal, claim, demand, draft, entreaty, fill-in blank, form, inquiry, letter, order, paper, petition, recourse, request, requisition, solicitation, suit   **2.** appliance, employment, exercise, function, operation, practice, purpose, software program, use, utilization

appointment *n.* **1.** arrangement, consultation, date, engagement, interview, invitation, meeting, rendezvous, session   **2.** assignment, authorization, certification, choice, commission, delegation, deputation, designation, election, employment, empowerment, installation, job, nomination, office, ordainment, ordination, place, position, post, promotion, selection, situation, station

appraisal *n.*   appraising, assessment, calculation, computation, critique, determination of value, estimate, estimate of value, estimated value, estimation, evaluation, judging, opinion, price survey, pricing, rating, surveying, valuation

appraise *v.*   assess, assess value, calculate value, compute value, critique, estimate, evaluate, rate

appreciation *n.* **1.** acknowledgment, gratefulness, gratitude, obligation, recognition, testimonial, thankfulness, thanks, tribute   **2.** admiration, adoration, aesthetic sense, affection, appraisal, assessment, attraction, awareness, cognizance, commendation, comprehension, enjoyment, esteem, estimation, grasp, high regard, honor, knowledge, liking, love, perception, realization, regard, relish, respect, responsiveness, reverence, sensibility, sensitiveness, sensitivity, sympathy, understanding, valuation, veneration   **3.** advance, enhancement, escalation, gain, growth, improvement, increase, inflation, multiplication, raise, rise, spread

apprentice *n.*   amateur, beginner, learner, neophyte, newcomer, novice, novitiate, probationer, pupil, recruit, rookie, starter, student, trainee

approach [*procedure*]: *n.*   course, manner, means, method, mode, plan, procedure, program, steps, style, technique, way

approbation *n.*   acceptance, admiration, adoption, approval, backing, consent, endorsement, esteem, favor, high regard, patronage, permission, praise, recognition, regard, respect, sanction, support

appropriation *n.* allocation, allotment, allowance, apportionment, assignment, budget, budgeting, concession, dispensation, donation, endowment, funding, grant, provision, stipend, stipulation, subsidy

approval *n.* acceptance, acknowledgment, acquiescence, adoption, advocacy, agreement, approbation, assent, authorization, backing, blessing, certification, commendation, compliance, concurrence, confirmation, consent, countenance, endorsement, favor, honor, license, patronage, permission, ratification, recommendation, respect, sanction, support, validation

aptitude *n.* ability, acuity, adequacy, aptness, astuteness, bent, brilliance, capability, capacity, cleverness, competence, competency, disposition, endowment, facility, faculty, fitness, flair, genius, gift, giftedness, inclination, ingenuity, intellect, intelligence, knack, leaning, potential, predilection, proclivity, proficiency, proneness, propensity, qualification, sagacity, sufficiency, suitability, talent, tendency

aqueduct *n.* artificial waterway, canal, channel, conduit, course, ditch, drain, duct, passageway, pipeline, watercourse, water passage, waterway, waterworks

arbiter *n.* adjudicator, arbitrator, authority, decision maker, mediator, moderator, negotiator, ombudsman, peacemaker, referee, troubleshooter, umpire

arbitrate *v.* adjudge, adjudicate, adjust, bargain, conciliate, decide, determine, hear, intercede, intervene, judge, mediate, moderate, negotiate, pass judgment, placate, pronounce judgment, reconcile, referee, settle, troubleshoot, umpire

arbitration *n.* adjudication, agreement, bargaining, compromise, conciliation, conference, conflict resolution, decision making, determination, dispute settlement, hearing, intervention, judgment, mediation, negotiation, peacemaking, reconciliation, settlement, trial, troubleshooting

arbitrator *n.* See **arbiter**

arc *n.* arch, bend, bow, crescent, curvature, curve, curved line, flexure

arch *n.* arc, archway, bend, bow, bridge, camber, curvature, curve, dome, doorway, semicircle, span, vault

archetype *n.* ancestor, exemplar, classic example, example, forerunner, form, ideal, model, mold, original, paradigm, paragon, pattern, precursor, predecessor, prime example, prototype, specimen, standard, typical example

architecture *n.* architectonics, blueprinting, building, composition, construction, design, engineering, formation, framework, planning, structure, structural design, style

archive *n.* annals, chronicles, clippings, collection, compressed file, compressed computer file, documents, excerpts, extracts, files, government papers, historical documents, historical papers, memorabilia, memorials, papers, public papers, records, registers, rolls, scrolls, writings

archives *n.* athenaeum, depository, files, library, memorial, museum, office, place for storage, register office, registry, repository, stack room, stacks, storage, treasury, vault

area *n.* **1.** acreage, belt, block, city, county, department, district, division, domain, dominion, enclosure, environment, field, kingdom, locality, neighborhood, parcel, patch, plot, precinct, principality, province, quarter, range, realm, region, section, sector, sphere, square, state, stretch, territory, township, tract, vicinity, ward, zone **2.** breadth, compass, distance, expanse, extent, range, scope, size, space, sphere, surface, width

arena *n.* amphitheater, auditorium, bowl, building, circus, coliseum, course, enclosure, gridiron, grounds, gymnasium, hippodrome, park, platform, ring, rink, square, stadium, stage

argue *v.* **1.** altercate, battle, clash, contend, controvert, debate, defend, differ, disagree, dispute, dissent, feud, fight, insist, object, protest, quarrel, quibble, remonstrate, squabble **2.** answer, appeal, assert, attest, bargain, claim, clarify, debate, defend, deliberate, demonstrate, denote, discuss, display, dissent, dissuade, elucidate, establish, evince, exhibit, explain, expostulate, illustrate, imply, indicate, justify, maintain, manifest, persuade, plead with, present, prevail upon, prove, question, show, signify, submit, suggest, talk about, talk into, testify, vindicate, warrant, witness

argument *n.* **1.** altercation, battle, clash, contention, controversy, debate, defense, difference, disagreement, dispute, dissension, feud, fight, insistence, objection, protestation, quarrel, quibble, remonstration, squabble **2.** answer, appeal, assertion, attestation, bargain, claim, clarification, debate, defense, deliberation, demonstration, denotation, discussion, display, dissension, dissuasion, elucidation, establishment, exhibition, explanation, expostulation, implication, indication, justification, maintenance, manifestation, persuasion, plea, presentation, proof, question, reason, submission, suggestion, testimony, vindication, warrant

arithmetic *n.*   addition, calculation, computation, counting, division, estimation, mathematics, mathematical operations, multiplication, subtraction

arrange *v.* **1.** accommodate, adjust, agree to, compose, compromise, decide, design, determine, devise, direct, draft, establish, fix, get ready, harmonize, line up, make ready, manage, map out, negotiate, orchestrate, organize, plan, prearrange, prepare, prescribe, prime, project, promote, provide, schedule, settle, tailor, work out   **2.** align, allocate, allot, apportion, array, assign, assort, bracket, categorize, class, classify, codify, collate, coordinate, dispose, distribute, file, form, grade, group, index, line up, methodize, order, organize, position, range, rank, regulate, set up, size, sort, sort out, straighten, systematize, tabulate

array *n.*   agglomeration, arrangement, assemblage, batch, body, bunch, bundle, clump, cluster, collection, components, data structure, design, devices, display, disposition, exhibition, formation, group, grouping, host, large number, lineup, listing, lot, matrix, multitude, numbers, order, panoply, parade, pattern, presentation, series, set, show, supply, unit

arrears *n.*   amount due, amount past due, arrearage, back payment, balance due, claim, debit, debt, deficiency, deficit, financial obligation, late payment, liability, money owed, obligation, payment outstanding, outstanding payment, past-due bill, remaining balance, unpaid bill, unpaid debt

art *n.* **1.** abstraction, artwork, carving, description, design, fine art, illustration, imitation, model, molding, painting, pictorialization, portrayal, representation, sculpture, simulation, sketch, symbol **2.** adroitness, aptitude, artistry, cleverness, craft, craftsmanship, dexterity, expertise, expertness, facility, genius, imagination, ingenuity, inventiveness, know-how, knowledge, method, proficiency, skill, skillfulness, talent, technique

artery *n.*   aqueduct, avenue, boulevard, canal, causeway, channel, concourse, conduit, corridor, course, ditch, duct, expressway, freeway, highway, interstate highway, line, main road, main street, parkway, passage, pathway, pipe, road, route, sewer, strait, street, strip, thoroughfare, track, tube, turnpike, watercourse, waterway, way

article [*document*]: *n.*   chapter, clause, column, commentary, composition, discourse, division, document, editorial, element, essay, exposition, feature, item, magazine article, matter, paper, passage, piece, report, spread, story, treatise

artificial *adj.* **1.** concocted, constructed, fabricated, feigned, imitated, imitation, manufactured, phony, plastic, pseudo, simulated, substitute, synthetic, unauthentic, ungenuine **2.** assumed, contrived, engineered, feigned, forced, labored, phony, pretended, so-called, strained

artist *n.* artisan, artiste, composer, craftsperson, creator, designer, entertainer, expert, genius, handicrafter, illustrator, inventor, musician, painter, performer, sculptor, talent, technician, virtuoso

ascent *n.* **1.** ascendance, ascension, climb, climbing, escalating, lift, mounting, moving upward, rising, scaling, spring, takeoff **2.** acclivity, elevation, grade, gradient, height, hill, incline, ramp, rise, slope, tilt, upgrade

ashamed *adj.* abashed, apologetic, chagrined, chastened, compunctious, conscience-stricken, contrite, debased, demeaned, discomfited, disconcerted, disgraced, dishonored, distressed, embarrassed, guilty, humbled, humiliated, mortified, penitent, regretful, remorseful, repentant, rueful, shamed, sorry

aspect *n.* air, angle, appearance, attitude, attribute, bearing, carriage, cast, character, characteristic, circumstance, complexion, condition, countenance, demeanor, deportment, detail, direction, element, expression, face, facet, features, figure, form, interpretation, look, manner, mien, nature, orientation, outlook, perspective, phase, position, presence, property, prospect, quality, regard, scene, side, situation, slant, standpoint, style, trait, view, viewpoint, visage

aspiration *n.* aim, ambition, craving, design, desire, destination, dream, eagerness, endeavor, enterprise, enthusiasm, goal, hope, ideal, inclination, intent, intention, longing, mark, object, objective, passion, plan, purpose, pursuit, scheme, target, urge, vocation, wish, work, yearning, zeal

aspire *v.* aim for, covet, crave, desire, dream of, endeavor, hope for, hunger for, intend, long for, need, pursue, search for, seek, strive, struggle, try, want, wish for, yearn for

assay *n.* analysis, appraisal, assessment, determination, estimation, evaluation, examination, experimentation, inspection, investigation, measurement, rating, survey, test, trial, valuation

assay *v.* analyze, appraise, assess, check out, consider carefully, determine, estimate, evaluate, examine, experiment with, explore, inquire into, inspect, investigate, judge, look over carefully, measure, pass judgment, probe, prove, put to the test, put to trial, rate, read, scrutinize, search, size, study, survey, test, try, try out, valuate, value, weigh

assemblage *n.* assembly, association, band, body, circle, collection, combination, company, conclave, conference, congregation, congress, convention, crew, crowd, gathering, group, meeting, rally, throng, troop, troupe, union

assemble *v.* **1.** accumulate, agglomerate, amass, bring together, call together, call up, collect, come together, congregate, convene, converge, convoke, draw together, gather together, get together, group together, join together, marshal, meet, mobilize, muster, organize, rally, reunite, round up, summon, unite **2.** build, collate, compile, construct, erect, fabricate, fashion, fit, form, make, manufacture, model, mold, produce, put together, set up, shape

assembly *n.* **1.** accumulation, aggregation, assemblage, association, audience, band, bloc, body, caucus, circle, collection, combination, community, company, conclave, conference, congregation, congress, convention, convocation, council, crew, crowd, faction, gathering, group, host, mass, multitude, meeting, parliament, rally, synod, throng, troop, troupe, union **2.** adjustment, attachment, connection, construction, erection, fabrication, fashioning, fit, formation, manufacture, modeling, molding, production, setup, shaping

assent *n.* acceptance, accession, accord, accordance, acknowledgment, acquiescence, admission, affirmation, agreement, approbation, approval, authorization, compliance, concession, concurrence, conformity, consent, consensus, endorsement, permission, recognition, sanction, submission, unanimity, union

assertion *n.* acknowledgment, affirmation, allegation, announcement, assurance, averment, avowal, contention, declaration, emphasis, expression, defense, guarantee, pledge, predication, proclamation, profession, promise, pronouncement, protestation, statement, word

assessment *n.* **1.** appraisal, assay, calculation, computation, consideration, determination, estimate, estimation, evaluation, gauge, investigation, judgment, measurement, rating, review, valuation **2.** charge, duty, fee, levy, price, rate, surcharge, tariff, tax, taxation, toll

asset *n.* advantage, aid, benefit, blessing, credit, distinction, help, profit, resource, service, strength, treasure

assets *n.* accounts receivable, belongings, bonds, budget, capital, cash, chattel, credit, effects, equitable assets, equity, estate, fixed assets, fixtures, frozen assets, funds, goods, goodwill, holdings, inventories, liquid assets, machinery, means, money, notes, personal assets, possessions, property, real estate, real property, reserves, resources, savings, securities, valuables, wealth

assignment *n.* **1.** appointment, charge, chore, commission, duty, errand, homework, job, mission, obligation, ordination, position, post, project, responsibility, task, work **2.** allocation, allotment, allowance, apportionment, appropriation, ascription, assignation, attribution, authorization, consignment, delegation, designation, determination, dispensation, distribution, grant, nomination, part, selection, share, stipulation, transfer, transfer of rights

assistance *n.* advance, advocacy, aid, backing, benefit, benevolence, care, charity, collaboration, comfort, compensation, consolation, contribution, cooperation, encouragement, facilitation, furtherance, gift, help, humanitarianism, kindness, maintenance, patronage, reinforcement, relief, service, sponsorship, subsidy, support, sustenance, sympathy

assistant *n.* accessory, accomplice, adjunct, adjutant, adjuvant, aide, apprentice, attendant, auxiliary, clerk, coadjutant, coadjutor, collaborator, deputy, helper, secretary, servant, subordinate

associate *n.* accessory, accomplice, affiliate, aide, assistant, auxiliary, coadjutant, coadjutor, collaborator, colleague, companion, comrade, confederate, equal, helper

association *n.* **1.** affiliation, alignment, alliance, amalgamation, assemblage, band, bloc, cartel, circle, clan, clique, club, coalition, combination, combine, community, company, confederation, congress, consortium, cooperative, corporation, crew, federation, group, guild, league, lodge, merger, monopoly, order, organization, partnership, party, society, syndicate, team, tribe, troops, trust, union **2.** acquaintance, acquaintanceship, affiliation, camaraderie, companionship, comradeship, connection, cooperation, familiarity, friendship, friendliness, intimacy, involvement, membership, participation, partnership, patronage, relationship, sodality

assortment *n.* agglomeration, array, batch, category, choice, class, collection, combination, conglomeration, diversity, group, jumble, kind, lot, medley, mélange, miscellany, mixture, potpourri, range, selection, set, sort, type, variety

assumption *n.* axiom, belief, conjecture, deduction, expectation, guess, hunch, hypothesis, inference, postulate, postulation, premise, presumption, presupposition, supposition, surmise, suspicion, theorization, theory, thesis, understanding

assurance *n.* affirmation, assertion, attestation, averment, bond, commitment, contract, declaration, deposition, evidence, guarantee, insurance, oath, pledge, positive statement, profession, promise, proof, reassurance, reassuring statement, security, support, surety, sworn statement, vow, warrant, warranty, word of honor

assure *v.* affirm, assert, assuage, attest, aver, calm, certify, confirm, console, corroborate, declare, encourage, ensure, guarantee, hearten, inform, inspire, insure, make certain, make sure, pacify, pledge, promise, reassure, relieve, secure, solace, soothe, state, tell, vouch for, vow, warrant

asylum *n.* den, harbor, haven, hideaway, hideout, hospice, institution, mental hospital, mental institution, preserve, refuge, retreat, safe house, sanatorium, sanctuary, sanctum, shelter

atmosphere [*mood*]: *n.* ambience, aura, background, character, condition, element, environment, feeling, impression, medium, milieu, mood, quality, scene, semblance, sense, setting, spirit, surroundings, tenor, tone

atom *n.* dyad, electron, molecule, monad, neutron, nucleus, proton, smallest unit, triad, unit of matter

attach *v.* add, affix, anchor, annex, append, bind, bond, cement, combine with, connect, couple, fasten, glue, join, join with, link, pin, rivet, secure, solder, stick on, subjoin, tack, tie, unite, wed, weld

attachment *n.* accessory, addition, adjunct, appendage, auxiliary, binder, binding, bond, clamp, codicil, complement, connection, connector, extension, extra, fastening, holder, joint, junction, link, nexus, ornament, rider, supplement, tie

attain *v.* accomplish, achieve, acquire, actualize, arrive at, be successful, complete, earn, finish, fulfill, gain, get, make real, obtain, procure, reach, realize, reap, secure, succeed in, win, wrest

attainable *adj.* accessible, accomplishable, achievable, acquirable, available, completable, conceivable, doable, feasible, imaginable, likely, manageable, obtainable, possible, potential, practicable, probable, procurable, reachable, realizable, reasonable, securable, surmountable, workable

attainment *n.* accomplishment, achievement, acquisition, completion, consummation, fulfillment, realization, success, termination, victory

attend *v.* appear at, be a guest at, be present at, frequent, go to, make an appearance at, present oneself at, show up at, turn up at, visit

attendance *n.* assemblage, audience, congregation, crowd, gathering, number attending, number present, persons attending, seats filled, tickets sold

attendant *n.* aide, aide-de-camp, assistant, auxiliary, companion, comrade, escort, helper, orderly, page

attention *n.* **1.** amenity, assiduity, attentiveness, awareness, care, civility, compliment, concern, consciousness, consideration, courtesy, deference, heedfulness, kindness, mindfulness, ministration, notice, observation, politeness, recognition, regard, respect, service, thoughtfulness, treatment, urbanity, vigilance, watchfulness **2.** absorption, alertness, application, assiduity, awareness, concentration, consciousness, consideration, contemplation, deliberation, diligence, heedfulness, immersion, industry, intentness, mindfulness, scrutiny, study, thought, vigilance

attest *v.* affirm, allege, assert, assure, authenticate, aver, avow, bear witness, certify, confirm, corroborate, declare formally, declare solemnly, demonstrate, depose, display, endorse, ensure, exhibit, give evidence, give testimony, guarantee, insure, offer evidence, plead, pledge, promise, prove, show, state under oath, substantiate, sustain, swear to, testify, uphold, validate, verify, vindicate, vouch for, vow, warrant, witness

attire *n.* apparel, clothes, clothing, costume, dress, garments, habit, uniform, vestments, wearing apparel

attitude *n.* air, appearance, aspect, bearing, behavior, bias, carriage, countenance, demeanor, deportment, disposition, expression, feeling, frame of mind, idea, impression, inclination, interpretation, leaning, manner, mental state, mien, mindset, mode, mood, opinion, orientation, outlook, personality, philosophy, point of view, pose, position, posture, prejudice, reaction, stance, temperament, tendency, thought, view, viewpoint

attraction *n.* affinity, allure, appeal, attractiveness, bait, captivation, charm, draw, enchantment, endearment, enticement, fascination, gravitation, inclination, inducement, interest, lure, magnetism, pull, seduction, stimulation, temptation, tendency, traction

attribute *n.* ability, capability, characteristic, distinction, eccentricity, endowment, faculty, feature, genius, gift, grace, idiosyncrasy, mark, note, oddity, peculiarity, property, quality, singularity, specialty, talent, trademark, trait, virtue

atypical *adj.* aberrant, abnormal, anomalous, curious, deviant, different, distorted, eccentric, erratic, divergent, exceptional, extraordinary, idiosyncratic, irregular, nonconforming, odd, peculiar, preternatural, singular, strange, uncharacteristic, uncommon, unnatural, unorthodox, unrepresentative, untypical, unusual

audible *adj.* aural, clear, detectable, discernible, distinct, hearable, loud, perceivable, perceptible, plain, recognizable

audience *n.* admirers, aficionados, assemblage, assembly, attendees, attenders, congregation, crowd, devotees, fans, following, gallery, gathering, house, listeners, market, onlookers, public, readers, spectators, viewers, watchers, witnesses

audit *n.* accounting, analysis, attestation, check, examination, inspection, investigation, review, scrutiny, verification, voucher

audit *v.* account, analyze, attest, check, examine, inspect, investigate, review, scrutinize, verify

auditorium *n.* amphitheater, arena, assembly hall, assembly room, coliseum, concert hall, dance hall, field house, gallery, hall, house, lecture hall, meeting room, music hall, opera house, playhouse, reception hall, stadium, theater

augment *v.* add to, aggrandize, amass, amplify, boost, broaden, build, build up, deepen, develop, distend, elevate, enhance, enlarge, escalate, expand, extend, grow, heighten, increase, inflate, intensify, magnify, make greater, make larger, multiply, prolong, protract, raise, reinforce, spread, spread out, strengthen, supplement, swell, thicken, widen

auspices *n.* advocacy, aegis, aid, approval, assistance, authority, backing, care, championship, charge, control, countenance, custody, direction, encouragement, favor, funding, guardianship, guidance, help, oversight, patronage, protection, responsibility, sanction, security, sponsorship, supervision, support, tutelage

authentic *adj.* accurate, actual, authoritative, believable, credible, creditable, dependable, exact, factual, faithful, genuine, honest, indisputable, indubitable, official, precise, real, realistic, reliable, strict, true, trusted, trustworthy, truthful, undisputed, unquestionable, veracious

authenticate *v.* accredit, affirm, assure, attest, aver, certify, confirm, corroborate, countersign, endorse, evidence, guarantee, insure, justify, prove, substantiate, underwrite, uphold, validate, verify, warrant

author *n.* annalist, biographer, chronicler, columnist, comedian, commentator, composer, creator, dramatist, essayist, ghostwriter, historian, journalist, lyricist, narrator, novelist, playwright, poet, reporter, screenwriter, scribe, speechwriter, storyteller, writer

authoritarian *adj.* absolutistic, autocratic, despotic, dictatorial, disciplinarian, dogmatic, doctrinaire, domineering, imperious, overbearing, tyrannical

authority *n.* administration, authorization, control, domination, dominion, force, guidance, hegemony, influence, jurisdiction, leadership, permit, power, predominance, prerogative, regency, reign, right, rule, sanction, sovereignty, sway

authorize *v.* **1.** accede to, accept, acknowledge, agree to, allow, approbate, approve, back up, bind, confirm, consent to, countenance, countersign, endorse, pass, permit, ratify, sanction, support, underwrite, uphold, witness **2.** accredit, certify, commission, constitute, empower, enable, entitle, establish, give authority, give control, give power, institute, invest, legalize, license, make acceptable, make official, notarize, ordain, set up, validate, vest

autograph *n.* endorsement, handwritten signature, inscription, mark, signature

automated *adj.* automatic, automatically controlled, computerized, cybernetic, electrical, electronic, machine-controlled, machine-made, mechanical, mechanized, motorized, programmed, robotistic, self-acting, self-directing, self-moving, self-propelling, self-regulating, self-starting, unmanned

automatic *adj.* **1.** automated, computerized, cybernetic, electrical, electronic, mechanical, mechanized, motorized, programmed, pushbutton, robotistic, self-acting, self-directing, self-moving, self-propelling, self-regulating, self-starting, unmanned **2.** autogenous, conditioned, habitual, impulsive, instinctive, instinctual, intuitive, involuntary, natural, perfunctory, reflex, routine, spontaneous, unavoidable, unconscious, uncontrolled, unforced, unintentional, unthinking, unwilling

automation *n.* automatic control, automatic operation, computerization, control by machine, industrialization, machine control, mechanization

autonomy *n.* freedom, home rule, independence, liberty, self-determination, self-direction, self-government, self-legislation, self-rule, sovereignty

auxiliary *n.* accessory, accomplice, adjuvant, aid, aide, ally, assistant, backer, coadjutor, collaborator, comrade, confederate, employee, help, helper, partner, patron, subordinate, support, supporter

auxiliary *adj.* accessory, additional, adjuvant, aiding, ancillary, assisting, cooperative, extra, helping, helpful, reserve, secondary, subordinate, subservient, subsidiary, supplementary, supporting, supportive

available *adj.* accessible, attainable, convenient, free, handy, obtainable, present, procurable, purchasable, reachable, ready, realizable, securable, serviceable, usable

avenue *n.* approach, boulevard, channel, concourse, corridor, drive, entrance, entry, lane, main road, parkway, passage, passageway, public road, road, roadway, street, strip, thoroughfare, walk, walkway, way

average *n.* arithmetic mean, intermediate position, mean, median, mediocrity, medium, middle, midpoint, norm, normal, normal state, ordinary, rule, standard, usual

average *adj.* **1.** intermediate, mean, median, medium, middle, midpoint **2.** common, commonplace, customary, decent, everyday, fair, familiar, general, mainstream, mediocre, medium, moderate, normal, ordinary, passable, regular, standard, tolerable, typical, undistinguished, unexceptional, usual

average *v.* balance, calculate the average, distribute proportionately, equate, equalize, even out, normalize, standardize

aversion *n.* antagonism, antipathy, disgust, disinclination, distaste, grudge, hate, hatred, hostility, nausea, opposition, prejudice, reluctance, repugnance, repulsion, revulsion, unwillingness

avocation *n.* activity, amusement, distraction, diversion, hobby, interest, pastime, play, pleasure, recreation, relaxation, side interest, sideline, sport, toy

avoid *v.*   abstain from, avert, elude, escape from, eschew, evade, forbear, hide from, recoil from, refrain from, shun, stay away from, ward off, withdraw

avow *v.*   affirm, allege, assert, attest, aver, assure, certify, declare earnestly, declare solemnly, depose, grant, guarantee, maintain, proclaim, predicate, profess, propound, say, state, state emphatically, testify, uphold

award *n.*   allotment, blue ribbon, citation, conferral, decoration, endowment, fellowship, gift, grant, honor, honorarium, medal, payment, premium, present, presentation, prize, recompense, remuneration, reward, scholarship, trophy

award *v.*   allot, bestow, cite, confer, decorate, endow, grant, honor, present, reward

away *adv.*   abroad, afar, apart, aside, beyond, elsewhere, out

awkward *adj.*   **1.** artless, blundering, clumsy, floundering, graceless, incapable, inefficient, inelegant, inept, inexpert, maladroit, uncoordinated, unfit, ungainly, ungraceful, unhandy, unpolished, unrefined, unskilled   **2.** bulky, cumbersome, dangerous, difficult-to-handle, hard-to-use, hazardous, ill-adapted, ill-proportioned, inconvenient, insecure, massive, perilous, ponderous, precarious, risky, threatening, troublesome, uncertain, unfit, unhandy, unmanageable, unsuitable, unwieldy, weighty

axiom *n.*   adage, aphorism, apothegm, assumption, dictum, gnome, maxim, motto, postulate, precept, premise, presupposition, principle, proverb, rule, saying, self-evident truth, theorem, truism

axiomatic *adj.*   absolute, aphoristic, apothegmatic, assumed, certain, generally known, gnomic, granted, incontestable, manifest, presupposed, proverbial, self-evident, understood, universally acknowledged, unquestionable

axis *n.*   arbor, axle, central line, line of rotation, mandrel, pin, pole, rod, shaft, spindle, stem, trunk, vertical

B

back *v.* advocate, affirm, aid, approve, assist, attest, back up, bolster, certify, confirm, corroborate, countenance, countersign, encourage, endorse, ensure, favor, guarantee, help, maintain, patronize, plead for, promote, recommend, reinforce, sanction, second, sponsor, strengthen, subsidize, substantiate, support, sustain, testify for, uphold, validate, vouch for, warrant

backbone *n.* **1.** base, basis, foundation, spine, spinal column, support, vertebrae, vertebral canal, vertebral column **2.** character, courage, determination, endurance, firmness, fortitude, integrity, mettle, principles, quality, resoluteness, resolution, resolve, soundness, stamina, steadfastness, strength, tenacity, toughness, will, willpower

backer *n.* adherent, advocate, benefactor, champion, cosigner, endorser, insurer, guarantor, helper, patron, promoter, proponent, sponsor, subsidizer, supporter, sympathizer, underwriter, upholder, warrantor

background *n.* **1.** accomplishments, attainment, credentials, culture, education, experience, personal history, preparation, qualifications, rearing, training, upbringing, work history **2.** atmosphere, aura, backdrop, circumstances, conditions, context, environment, framework, setting, stage, surroundings

backing *n.* advocacy, aid, approval, assistance, boost, championing, cooperation, collaboration, commendation, encouragement, endorsement, funds, furtherance, grant, help, maintenance, patronage, promotion, reinforcement, relief, sanction, sponsorship, strengthening, subsidy, support

backlog *n.* accumulation, excess, reserve, stock, store, supply, supply on hand, uncompleted work, unfilled orders

backup *n.* accumulation, backlog, backup copy, computer disk copy, copy, disk copy, duplicate, duplicate copy, extra, extra copy, inventory, overflow accumulation, replacement, replacement copy, relief, reserve, reservoir, spare, stock, stockpile, substitute, supply, supply on hand, support, surrogate

bad debt *n.* account receivable, loan receivable, open-account balance, uncollectible amount, uncollectible debt

badge *n.* brand, brassard, button, chevron, coat of arms, crest, device, emblem, ensign, identification, insignia, label, logo, mark, marker, seal, shield, sign, signet, stamp, symbol, trade-mark

bag *n.* attache case, backpack, briefcase, case, duffel bag, handbag, knapsack, luggage, pocketbook, portmanteau, pouch, purse, sack, suitcase, trunk, valise

baggage *n.* bags, effects, luggage, pack, packages, suitcases, trunks, valises

bail *n.* bail bond, bond, collateral, deposit, guarantee, pledge, security, sponsorship, surety, warranty

bait *n.* allurement, decoy, enticement, lure, seduction, snare, tantalization, temptation, trap

balance *n.* **1.** difference, excess, extra, profit, remainder, residue, rest, surplus **2.** counterbalance, counterweight, equality, equilibrium, equalization, equalizer, equity, equivalence, evenness, harmony, par, parity, stabilizer, symmetry, uniformity **3.** assurance, calmness, composure, confidence, consistency, equanimity, evenness, levelheadedness, poise, presence of mind, prudence, self-assurance, self-confidence, self-control, self-possession, stability, steadiness

balance *v.* **1.** add up, calculate, compute, count up, enumerate, equate, figure, settle, sum up, tally, total **2.** accord, adjust, align, arrange, compensate, counteract, counterbalance, countercheck, countervail, equal, equalize, equate, even out, harmonize, level, match, make equal, offset, order, parallel, poise, proportion, square, stabilize, steady, tie **3.** appraise, assess, compare, consider, deliberate, estimate, evaluate, ponder, rate, reflect, valuate, value, weigh

balance sheet *n.* account book, account current, accounting statement, annual report, assets and liabilities, cashbook, debits and credits, financial statement, ledger, register, report, running account, statement

balcony *n.* boxes, gallery, loge, loggia, mezzanine, peanut gallery, piazza, porch, portico, terrace, upper circle, veranda

ballot *n.* **1.** list of candidates, slate, ticket, voting ticket **2.** election, franchise, plebiscite, poll, referendum, vote, voting, voting record

ban *n.* banishment, boycott, censorship, disallowance, embargo, exclusion, excommunication, forbiddance, injunction, interdiction, limitation, moratorium, ostracism, prohibition, proscription, rejection, segregation, stoppage, suppression, veto

ban *v.* declare illegal, disallow, forbid, halt, interdict, make illegal, make impossible, outlaw, preclude, prevent, prohibit, proscribe, reject, restrict, stop, suppress, veto

band *n.* **1.** aggregation, alliance, assemblage, assembly, association, body, bunch, circle, clique, club, company, confederation, corps, coterie, crew, crowd, gang, gathering, group, horde, host, league, mob, multitude, order, outfit, pack, society, sodality, swarm, team, throng, tribe, troop, troupe **2.** combo, ensemble, group, musical group, orchestra, symphony

bank [*finance*]: *n.* commercial bank, commercial house, credit union, depository, Federal Reserve Bank, financial institution, house of finance, repository, reserve, reservoir, savings bank, savings and loan, savings and loan association, savings institution, S & L, storehouse, thrift institution, treasury, trust company, vault

banker *n.* bank manager, bank officer, financier, investment banker, money lender, treasurer

bankrupt *adj.* destitute, financially depleted, financially exhausted, financially ruined, impoverished, insolvent, penniless, poverty-stricken

bankruptcy *n.* exhaustion of resources, financial collapse, financial default, financial depletion, financial failure, financial ruin, indebtedness, insolvency, liquidation, poverty

banner *n.* banderole, burgee, colors, emblem, ensign, flag, gonfalon, heading, headline, insignia, labarum, pennant, pennon, standard, streamer

banquet *n.* feast, formal dinner, meal, repast

bar [*law*]: *n.* advocates, attorneys, attorneys-at-law, bar association, barristers, bench, counsel, counselors, court, judicatory, judiciary, jurists, lawyers, legal fraternity, legal profession, legal system, legists, members of the bar, solicitors, tribunal

bar *v.* ban, banish, barricade, block, blockade, boycott, constrain, debar, deter, disallow, disqualify, eliminate, enjoin, except, exclude, excommunicate, exile, forbid, forestall, frustrate, hinder, impede, interdict, keep out, leave out, lock out, obstruct, obviate, omit, ostracize, outlaw, preclude, prevent, prohibit, refuse, reject, restrain, restrict, rule out, segregate, shut out, stop, thwart

bargain *n.* **1.** budget price, closeout price, discount, good buy, good deal, good value, low price, markdown, nominal

price, reduced item, reduction, special offer, special value
2. agreement, arrangement, bond, cartel, compact, concordat, contract, convention, covenant, deal, deed, entente, indenture, negotiation, settlement, stipulation, transaction, treaty, understanding

bargain *v.* agree, arrange, barter, come to terms, contract, covenant, discuss terms, deal, decide terms, make terms, negotiate, negotiate terms, pledge, promise, settle, stipulate, transact

barricade *n.* bank, bar, barrier, block, blockade, bulwark, dam, fence, hindrance, hurdle, impediment, obstacle, obstruction, palisade, protection, railing, roadblock, wall

barrier *n.* **1.** See **barricade**. **2.** bar, check, difficulty, drawback, encumbrance, handicap, hindrance, hurdle, impediment, limitation, obstacle, obstruction, restraint, restriction

barter *v.* bargain, deal, exchange, haggle, negotiate, swap, trade, traffic, truck

base *n.* **1.** basement, basis, bed, bedrock, bottom, brace, core, foot, footing, foundation, groundwork, infrastructure, pedestal, plinth, prop, rest, root, seat, socle, stand, stay, substratum, substructure, support, underpinning **2.** authority, basis, chief constituent, component, core, element, essence, essentials, foundation, fundamental element, groundwork, heart, important part, key ingredient, main ingredient, origin, primary element, principal, principle, radical, root, source, stem **3.** anchorage, camp, center, depot, dock, field, hangar, harbor, headquarters, home, mooring, point of departure, port, post, settlement, site, starting point, station, strip, terminal

basement *n.* cellar, excavation, furnace room, hold, lower level, storage room, substructure, subterranean room, underground room, vault, wine cellar

basic *adj.* basal, basilar, central, chief, crucial, elemental, elementary, essential, foremost, fundamental, indispensable, inherent, innate, intrinsic, key, main, necessary, primary, principal, radical, rudimentary, substrative, underlying, vital

basin *n.* bay, bed, bowl, cavity, channel, concavity, container, cove, crater, depression, dip, dish, hole, hollow, pan, pool, pond, receptacle, reservoir, sag, saucer, sink, sinkhole, tub, vessel, washbowl

basis *n.* **1.** base, bed, bottom, core, foot, footing, foundation, ground, groundwork, infrastructure, rest, seat, stand, substructure, support   **2.** adjusted cost, antecedent, assumption, authority, chief ingredient, core, cost, essence, essentials, evidence, foundation, fundamental ingredient, fundamental principle, fundamentals, grounds, groundwork, heart, justification, law, postulate, premise, presumption, presupposition, principal element, principle, proof, radical, reason, root, rudiment, soul, source, starting point, substance, support, taxpayer cost, theorem, theory

basket *n.*   bin, box, bucket, bushel basket, case, container, creel, hamper, in-basket, out-basket, pannier, receptacle, vessel, wickerwork

batch *n.*   accumulation, agglomeration, aggregate, aggregation, array, assortment, bunch, bundle, cluster, collection, combination, combine, computer file, conglomeration, crowd, file, group, grouping, lot, mass, mixture, quantity, set

battery *n.*   **1.** chain, cycle, order, progression, ring, sequence, series, set, string, succession, suite   **2.** assault, attack, battering, beating, onslaught, physical violence   **3.** artillery, artillery unit, cannon, gunnery, gunnery unit, guns

battle *n.*   **1.** agitation, altercation, argument, contention, contest, controversy, debate, difference of opinion, disagreement, discord, discussion, dispute, dissension, polemic, quarrel, squabble   **2.** action, assault, attack, barrage, blitzkrieg, bloodshed, campaign, clash, combat, conflict, confrontation, contest, crusade, encounter, engagement, fight, fighting, hostilities, massacre, military campaign, onslaught, scrimmage, skirmish, struggle, uprising, war, warfare

bay *n.*   **1.** arm, basin, bight, cove, estuary, fiord, firth, gulf, harbor, inlet, loch, moorings, mouth, sound, strait   **2.** alcove, bay window, bow window, compartment, cubicle, dormer, enclosure, niche, nook, oriel, recess, window seat

bazaar *n.*   arcade, benefit, charity fair, emporium, exchange, exposition, fair, market, marketplace, mart

beach *n.*   bank, coast, coastline, foreshore, lakeshore, lakeside, littoral, oceanfront, sand, sands, seacoast, seafront, seashore, seaside, shingle, shore, strand, waterfront, water's edge

beacon *n.*   alarm, alert, arrow, beam, beacon light, bonfire, fire, flare, flashlight, guide, guidepost, indicator, mile post, pilot light, pointer, rocket, searchlight, sign, signal, signal fire, signal light, smoke signal, torch, warning light, warning signal, watch fire, watchtower

beautiful *adj.* alluring, appealing, attractive, becoming, captivating, charming, delightful, elegant, enchanting, engaging, enticing, exquisite, fascinating, glamorous, gorgeous, graceful, handsome, lovely, lustrous, magnificent, marvelous, personable, pleasing, pretty, radiant, ravishing, resplendent, seemly, splendid, stunning, superb, unequaled, winsome, wonderful

beautify *v.* adorn, array, decorate, dress up, embellish, emboss, embroider, enhance, enrich, furbish, garnish, gild, glamorize, grace, illuminate, improve, ornament, restore, trim

bedlam *n.* anarchy, chaos, chaotic situation, clamor, commotion, confusion, disarray, disorder, furor, noise, pandemonium, tumult, turmoil, uproar

begin *v.* activate, actuate, bring about, commence, conceive, create, embark, engender, establish, found, generate, go ahead, impel, inaugurate, induce, initiate, instigate, institute, introduce, launch, make a start, mount, open, organize, originate, pioneer, set in motion, set up, start, take initiative, take steps, trigger, undertake

beginner *n.* abecedarian, amateur, apprentice, fledgling, freshman, initiate, learner, neophyte, newcomer, novice, novitiate, probationer, pupil, recruit, rookie, student, trainee

beginning *n.* **1.** actuation, commencement, constitution, creation, establishment, foundation, inauguration, inception, induction, initiation, installation, instigation, institution, introduction, onset, organization, origin, origination, source, starting point, threshold, top **2.** antecedent, birth, conception, egg, embryo, first cause, fountainhead, genesis, infancy, mainspring, origin, root, seed, source

behavior *n.* actions, air, attitude, comportment, conduct, decorum, deeds, demeanor, deportment, expression, form, functioning, mode, operation, performance, reactions, response, style

behest *n.* bidding, charge, choice, command, commandment, decree, demand, desire, dictate, direction, edict, enjoiner, enjoinment, expressed desire, fiat, injunction, instruction, invitation, mandate, order, ordination, petition, precept, prescription, proposal, request, requirement, requisition, rule, ruling, solicitation, summons, urging, volition, will, wish, word, writ

beholden *adj.* answerable, accountable, bound, chargeable, grateful, indebted, liable, obligated, obliged, owing, responsible, thankful

being *n.* **1.** actuality, animation, existence, life, life force, living, omnipresence, presence, reality, ubiquity, vitality **2.** character, entity, essence, essentiality, individuality, nature, personality, principle, quintessence, singularity, soul, spirit, substance, temperament **3.** animal, beast, body, conscious thing, creature, entity, human, human being, individual, living thing, mortal, one, organism, person, personage, sentient, someone, soul, thing

belief *n.* **1.** acceptance, assent, assumption, assurance, attitude, certainty, concept, conclusion, confidence, conjecture, conviction, deduction, divination, expectation, experience, faith, fancy, feeling, guess, idea, impression, intuition, judgment, knowledge, leaning, mind-set, notion, opinion, perception, persuasion, position, postulation, presumption, presupposition, profession, reliance, supposition, surmise, suspicion, trust, understanding, way of thinking **2.** axiom, canon, catechism, credence, credo, creed, declaration, doctrine, dogma, fundamentals, hypothesis, ideology, law, maxim, postulate, precept, principles, religion, rule, teaching, tenet, theorem, theory, thesis

believer *n.* acceptor, adherent, apostle, confirmed believer, convert, devotee, disciple, dogmatist, follower, prophet, proselyte, religious person, supporter, upholder, zealot

belongings *n.* accessories, articles, chattel, chose, chose in action, chose in possession, effects, goods, personal effects, personal possessions, personal property, personalty, possessions, property, things

bench *n.* **1.** adjudicators, advocates, bar, barristers, counsel, court, judges, judiciary, judicature, jurists, lawyers, legists, solicitors, tribunal **2.** bleacher, grandstand seat, long seat, pew, seat, stool **3.** booth, counter, ledge, stall, stand, table, trestle, trestle table, window seat, workbench, work table

benchmark *n.* criterion, example, exemplar, gauge, guideline, ideal, measure, model, pattern, prototype, reference point, requirement, standard, standard unit, touchstone, yardstick

bend *n.* angle, arc, bias, bow, corner, crook, curvature, curve, deflection, deviation, flexion, flexure, hook, skew, turn, twist, warp

benefactor *n.* altruist, backer, contributor, donor, helper, humanitarian, patron, philanthropist, protector, sponsor, subsidizer, supporter, sympathizer, underwriter, well-wisher

beneficiary *n.* assignee, devisee, donee, heir, heir apparent, inheritor, legatee, receiver, recipient, successor

benefit *n.* advantage, assistance, convenience, extras, fringe benefit, fund-raising event, good, interest, payment, perquisite, reward, well-being

benevolence *n.* altruism, charitableness, charity, compassion, considerateness, consideration, friendship, generosity, gift, goodness, goodwill, graciousness, helpfulness, humanitarianism, humanity, kindheartedness, kindness, love, mercy, philanthropy, present, support, sympathy, unselfishness

bequeath *v.* allot, apportion, assign, award, bestow, cede, commit, confer upon, consign, devise, distribute, divide, donate, endow, entrust, gift, give, grant, hand down, hand over, impart, leave, leave to, pass on, pass out, present, render, reward, transfer, transmit, turn over, will

bequest *n.* bequeathal, bequeathment, devise, dower, estate, heritage, inheritance, legacy, patrimony, trust, will

bereavement *n.* adversity, affliction, deprivation, dispossession, distress, grief, hardship, loss, misfortune, mourning, privation, sadness, sorrow, trial, tribulation, trouble

berth *n.* anchorage, bed, billet, breakwater, bunk, compartment, cot, dock, dry dock, floating dock, harbor, haven, jetty, landing space, levee, moorage, pallet, pier, port, quay, quayage, slip, wharf

best *n.* apex, choice, elite, favorite, finest, first, foremost, healthiest, highest, model, most powerful, paragon, peak, pick, prime, prize, select, strongest, top, utmost, zenith

bestow *v.* accord, afford, allot, apportion, assign, award, bequeath, cede, commit, confer, consign, deliver, dispense, dispose, distribute, divide, donate, endow, entrust, expend, gift, give, give away, grant, hand, honor with, impart, pass, present, render, turn over to, yield

bet *n.* ante, collateral, chance, gamble, game of chance, game of fortune, guaranty, lottery, money, pledge, pot, raffle, risk, security, speculation, stake, surety, sweepstakes, venture, wager

bet *v.*   ante, back up, cover, enter the sweepstakes, gamble, make a bet, play the lottery, pledge, put up collateral, risk, speculate, stake, take a chance, venture, wager

beverage *n.*   cocktail, cooler, draft, drink, liquid refreshment, liquor, refreshment, soda, soft drink, thirst quencher

bias *n.*   **1.** bent, bigotry, close-mindedness, disposition, favoritism, fixed idea, imbalance, inclination, intolerance, leaning, narrow-mindedness, one-sidedness, partiality, partisanship, penchant, preconceived notion, preconception, predilection, predisposition, preference, prejudice, prepossession, proclivity, proneness, propensity, racism, sexism, tendency, twist, viewpoint, warp   **2.** angle, bevel, cant, diagonal, incline, list, skew, slant, slope, tilt

bible *n.*   **1.** authority, employee manual, guide, guidebook, handbook, manual, primer, text, textbook   **2.** creed, doctrine, God's word, Gospel, holy book, Holy Scriptures, Holy Writ, New Testament, Old Testament, sacred writ, sacred writings, scripture, testament, word of God

bid *n.*   advance, amount, ante, declaration, earnest effort, invitation, motion, offer, offering, price, proffer, proposal, proposition, request, submission, suggestion, sum, tender

bid *v.*   adjure, advance, charge, command, dictate, extend, offer, order, pay, present, proffer, propose, render, submit, suggest, tender, venture

bigot *n.*   biased person, close-minded person, doctrinaire person, dogmatist, extremist, fanatic, illiberal person, intolerant person, narrow-minded person, prejudiced person, persecutor, sectarian, segregationist, warped person, zealot

bigotry *n.*   bias, close-mindedness, discrimination, dogmatism, fanaticism, intolerance, narrow-mindedness, partiality, prejudice, provincialism, sectarianism

bilateral *adj.*   mutual, reciprocal, two-sided

bill *n.*   **1.** account, account payable, amount due, charges, check, cost, debt, expenditures, expenses, fee, invoice, IOU, itemized account, itemized statement, list of expenditures, record of charges, request for payment, statement, statement of indebtedness, tabulation of charges   **2.** bank note, certificate, currency, legal tender, money, note, paper money, tender, treasury bill, treasury note   **3.** advertisement, agenda, announcement, brochure, bulletin, calendar, card, circular, flier, folder, handout, inventory, leaflet, list, listing, notice, placard, poster, program, prospectus, roster, schedule, summary, syllabus, synopsis, timetable   **4.** act, draft, legislation, measure, proposal, proposed act, proposition, statement

bill *v.* charge, charge for, invoice, list expenses, send a bill to, send an invoice to, send a statement to, tabulate expenditures, total expenditures

bind *n.* crisis, deadlock, difficult situation, difficulty, dilemma, plight, predicament, problem, quandary, tight situation

bind *v.* adhere, attach, bandage, bridle, buckle, bundle, cement, chafe, chain, choke, cinch, clamp, coalesce, cohere, combine, congeal, connect, consolidate, constrict, dress, encase, encircle, entwine, fasten, fetter, fuse, gird, glue, hamper, handcuff, harden, hem, hitch, hobble, hold, hold together, hook, interlace, interlock, join, lace, lash, leash, manacle, moor, muzzle, paste, pin, pinion, plait, restrain, restrict, rope, secure, set, shackle, solidify, stick together, strap, swathe, tape, tether, tie, tie up, trammel, truss, unite, weave, weld, wrap   **2.** assign, burden, compel, confine, constrain, constrict, encumber, enforce, engage, force, hinder, impel, inhibit, obligate, oblige, prescribe, press, require, restrain, restrict, yoke

binder *n.* adhesive, cover, preliminary agreement, temporary contract

binding *adj.* **1.** burdensome, compelling, compulsory, confining, constraining, constricting, controlling, encumbering, enforcing, engaging, forced, impelling, indissoluble, inhibiting, irrevocable, mandatory, necessary, nonelective, obligatory, prescriptive, pressing, required, requisite, restraining, restricting, unalterable   **2.** attached, confined, constricted, coupled, fastened, joined, limiting, restraining, restricting, tied

biography *n.* account, adventures, autobiography, biographical account, confessions, diary, experiences, fortunes, history, journal, life, life history, life story, memoir(s), personal account, personal narrative, personal recollections, record, profile, record, résumé, vita

birth *n.* **1.** bearing, beginning, childbearing, childbirth, commencement, creation, debut, dawn, delivery, discovery, emergence, fountainhead, genesis, inception, initiation, invention, onset, opening, origin, origination, production, rise, source, start   **2.** affiliation, ancestry, background, birthright, blood, blood line, derivation, descent, extraction, family, forebears, genealogy, heritage, house, legacy, line, lineage, nativity, origin, parentage, patrimony, pedigree, race, stirps, stock, strain

bit *n.* **1.** atom, binary digit, binary number, cantle, character, bite, chip, dash, division, dot, droplet, excerpt, fraction, fragment, grain, granule, installment, minimum, molecule, morsel, part, particle, piece, point, portion, pulse, sample, scrap, section, segment, shard, share, shaving, shred, slice, sliver, small amount, snippet, specimen, speck, splinter, sprinkling, stub, subdivision, tiny piece, trace, unit, unit of information **2.** instant, little while, minute, moment, second, short time, short while

blacklist *v.* ban, banish, bar from, blackball, boycott, cast aside, cut, discard, disown, exclude, exile, expatriate, expel, isolate, leave out, lock out, outlaw, reject, repudiate, shut out, throw out, vote against

blackmail *n.* bribe, bribery, enforced payment, exacted payment, exaction, extortion, graft, payoff, protection, ransom, tribute

blame *n.* **1.** accountability, answerability, burden, culpability, fault, guilt, incrimination, liability, onus, responsibility **2.** accusation, admonition, allegation, assignment of guilt, attribution, castigation, censure, charge, complaint, condemnation, criticism, denunciation, diatribe, disapprobation, disparagement, implication, imputation, incrimination, inculpation, indictment, objurgation, obloquy, rebuke, recrimination, remonstrance, reprehension, reprimand, reproach, reprobation, reproof, stricture

blame *v.* accuse, admonish, allege, ascribe, assign guilt, attribute, castigate, censure, charge, complain, condemn, criticize, denounce, disapprove, disparage, fault, find fault with, hold accountable, hold responsible, implicate, impute, incriminate, inculpate, indict, involve, objurgate, rebuke, recriminate, remonstrate, reprehend, reprimand, reproach, reprove, sue

blanket *adj.* absolute, across-the-board, all-inclusive, complete, comprehensive, general, overall, sweeping, unconditional, wide-ranging

blend *n.* admixture, alloy, amalgam, amalgamation, assimilation, brew, combination, commingling, commixture, composite, compound, concoction, fusion, half-breed, homogenization, hybrid, hybridization, incorporation, intermixture, intermingling, junction, mingling, mix, mixture, mongrel, mongrelization, synthesis, union

blend *v.* **1.** admix, alloy, amalgamate, coalesce, combine, commingle, commix, compound, fuse, homogenize, hybridize, incorporate, integrate, intermingle, intermix, interweave, intertwine, join, link together, meld, merge, mingle, mix, mongrelize, scramble, stir in, synthesize, unite **2.** arrange, complement, fit, go with, harmonize, integrate, orchestrate, suit, synthesize, unify

blessing *n.* **1.** advocacy, approbation, approval, backing, concurrence, consent, favor, good wishes, patronage, permission, recommendation, regard, respect, sanction, support, valediction **2.** advantage, alms, asset, benediction, benefaction, benefit, bounty, favor, gain, gift, good fortune, good luck, gratuity, luck, offering, profit, relief

blight *n.* affliction, bad luck, bane, calamity, cancer, canker, contamination, curse, decay, disease, fungus, illness, infestation, infliction, mildew, misfortune, mold, pestilence, plague, rot, scourge, sickness, sore, trouble, withering

block *n.* **1.** amount, amount of data, bar, block of data, brick, cake, chunk, clump, cube, group, group of data, loaf, lump, mass, oblong, piece, piece of text, section, section of text, slab, slice, square, unit, unit of text, wedge **2.** bar, barrier, barricade, blockade, blockage, check, constraint, dam, deterrent, drawback, hindrance, hurdle, impasse, impediment, obstacle, obstruction, restraint, roadblock, stoppage, wall

blockade *n.* bar, barricade, barrier, block, blockage, check, closure, deterrent, encirclement, hindrance, hurdle, impediment, jam, obstacle, obstruction, restriction, roadblock, siege, stoppage, wall

blueprint *n.* architectural drawing, architectural plan, design, detailed plan, diagram, drawing, photographic print, plan, plan of action, working drawing

bluff *n.* **1.** boast, bragging, bravado, deceit, deception, delusion, facade, fake, false front, false show, fraud, front, lie, pretense, pretext, ruse, sham, subterfuge, trick **2.** bank, cliff, crag, escarpment, foreland, headland, height, hill, knoll, mountain, palisade, peak, precipice, promontory, ridge, rock, scarp, slope, wall

blunder *n.* error, fault, fiasco, flaw, fumble, gaffe, impropriety, imprudence, inaccuracy, indiscretion, miscalculation, miscarriage, misjudgment, mistake, slip-up

blunt *adj.* **1.** abrupt, bold, brash, brazen, brief, brusque, candid, caustic, curt, direct, discourteous, forthright, frank, impudent, insensitive, insolent, matter-of-fact, open, outspoken, plain-spoken, rude, short, straightforward, tactless, terse, trenchant, unceremonious, uncivil, unpolished **2.** dull, dulled, edgeless, obtuse, pointless, round, rounded, unpointed, unsharpened, thick

board *n.* **1.** advisors, advisory group, cabinet, commission, committee, council, directorate, directors, panel, trustees **2.** daily meals, food, lodging and meals, meals, provisions, room and board **3.** beam, clapboard, flooring, lath, lumber, panel, plank, sheet, siding, slab, slat, stick, strip, timber, wallboard, wood

board *v.* **1.** climb on, come in, embark, enplane, enter, entrain, get on, go aboard, go on, go on board, mount, step aboard **2.** accommodate, bed, care for, eat in, feed, harbor, house, live in, lodge, put up, room in, take meals in

body *n.* **1.** assembly, basis, bed, box, center, central part, chassis, core, frame, fuselage, heart, hub, hull, mass, material, matter, principal part, skeleton, staple, substance, substructure, total, trunk, whole **2.** aggregation, array, band, batch, bunch, bundle, clump, cluster, collection, collectivity, crew, crowd, group, lot, majority, mass, parcel, party, set, society, team, union

boilerplate *n.* preprinted form, standardized form, standardized language, standardized material, syndicated material

bold *adj.* **1.** adventurous, assured, brave, confident, courageous, daring, dauntless, enterprising, fearless, forceful, gallant, hardy, heroic, intrepid, lionhearted, resolute, stalwart, stouthearted, strong, unafraid, unalarmed, undaunted, undismayed, unflinching, valiant, valorous, venturesome **2.** assuming, audacious, brash, brazen, defiant, forward, immodest, impertinent, impudent, insolent, nervy, presumptuous, rash, reckless, rude, shameless, unabashed, unashamed, unreserved **3.** bright, clear, colorful, conspicuous, eye-catching, garish, gaudy, large, lively, loud, obtrusive, obvious, ostentatious, pretentious, prominent, pronounced, showy, spirited, striking, strong, vivid

bolster *v.* boost, brace, buoy, buttress, cradle, cushion, fortify, hold up, lift, pad, pillow, prop, prop up, reinforce, shore up, shoulder, strengthen, support, sustain, uphold

bond *n.* **1.** arrangement, agreement, bargain, cartel, certificate, certificate of debt, collateral, compact, concordat, contract, convention, covenant, deal, debenture, guarantee, guaranty, obligation, pact, performance guarantee, pledge, promise, protection, security, stipulation, surety, transaction, treaty, warrant, warranty, word   **2.** band, belt, binding, braid, chain, connection, cord, cordon, fastener, fetter, handcuffs, harness, ligament, link, manacle, nexus, rein, rope, shackle, strap, thong, tie, trammel, wire, yoke   **3.** affiliation, affinity, allegiance, association, attachment, connection, friendship, interrelationship, liaison, link, loyalty, network, obligation, relationship, union

bond *v.* adhere, attach, bind, cement, coalesce, cohere, congeal, connect, fasten, fuse, glue, gum, hold together, join, paste, set, stick, unite, weld

bonus *n.* additional compensation, award, bestowal, bounty, compensation, endowment, gift, gratuity, handout, honorarium, largess, payment, premium, present, prize, recompense, remuneration, reward, tip

book *n.* best-seller, bible, compendium, dissertation, edition, fiction book, hardcover book, manual, nonfiction book, opus, paperback book, publication, reprint, softcover book, text, title, tome, tract, treatise, volume, work, writing

book *v.* **1.** arrange for, bill, charter, engage beforehand, enroll, enter, hire, line up, log, make reservations for, order, post, procure, program, record, register, reserve, schedule, set up, state   **2.** arrest, bring charges against, charge with, prefer charges against, take into custody

book value *n.* asset value, carrying value, net amount, net asset value, property value, theoretical value

boost *n.* advancement, backing, commendation, encouragement, enlargement, expansion, furtherance, heightening, impetus, improvement, increase, lift, magnification, praise, promotion, raise, stimulus, support

boost *v.* **1.** acclaim, advance, animate, build up, encourage, enliven, extol, facilitate, forward, further, give impetus to, help onward, inspire, laud, praise, promote, publicize, support, uplift   **2.** add to, aggrandize, amplify, augment, bolster, develop, enlarge, expand, extend, heighten, increase, inflate, magnify, multiply, raise, upgrade

border *n.* ambit, border line, boundary, boundary line, bounds, brim, brink, circumference, city limits, compass, confines, dividing line, edge, edging, extremity, frame, fringe, frontier line, hem, horizon, interface, limit(s), line, line of demarcation, margin, outer limits, outline, outpost, outskirts, pale, partition line, perimeter, periphery, rim, skirt, state boundary line, termination, threshold, verge

borderline *adj.*   ambiguous, ambivalent, doubtful, equivocal, halfway, indecisive, indefinite, indeterminate, inexact, intermediate, marginal, problematic, questionable, uncertain, unclassifiable, unclear, undecided, unsettled, unstable, vague

boss *n.*   administrator, chief, controller, director, employer, executive, foreman, head, leader, manager, overseer, owner, person in charge, superintendent, supervisor

bothersome *adj.*   aggravating, annoying, burdensome, difficult, distressing, disturbing, exasperating, inconvenient, irksome, irritating, tiresome, troublesome, troubling, vexing

bottom *n.*   **1.** base, basis, beginning, cause, core, derivation, essence, essentials, foundation, fountainhead, gist, heart, main ingredient, mainspring, origin, pith, principle, quintessence, root, rudiments, soul, source, substance, wellspring **2.** base, basement, basis, bed, bedrock, depths, floor, foot, footing, foundation, ground, groundwork, lowest part, lowest point, nadir, pedestal, pediment, perigee, sole, substratum, substructure, underlayer, underside

bottom line *n.*   last line, main point, net income, net loss, net profit, result

bounds *n.*   See **border**

boundary *n.*   See **border**

bounty *n.*   alms, bonus, benefaction, bestowal, charitableness, charity, concession, contribution, donation, endowment, generosity, gift, grant, gratuity, largess, liberality, munificence, offering, philanthropy, premium, present, prize, reward, subsidy, subvention, tip

bourgeois *adj.*   acquisitive, capitalistic, common, commonplace, conservative, conventional, illiberal, landed, materialistic, middle-class, money-oriented, ordinary, philistine, plebeian, proletarian, propertied, traditional, uncultivated, uncultured, unimaginative, unrefined, working-class

box *n.*   bin, booth, cabinet, caddy, can, canister, carton, casket, chest, coffer, compartment, container, crate, file, pack, package, section, trunk

boycott *v.*   abstain from, avoid, ban, bar, blacklist, cut off, debar, decline, desist from, disallow, embargo, exclude, forbear, forbid, ignore, interdict, keep out, lock out, outlaw, pass over, picket, prevent, prohibit, proscribe, refrain from, refuse, refuse patronage, reject, restrain, shun, shut out, stay away from, stop patronage, strike

brace *n.* arm, band, bar, beam, bearing, block, bolster, bracing, bracket, buttress, cantilever, girder, mainstay, prop, rafter, reinforcement, rib, shore, splice, splint, stanchion, stave, stay, strut, support, truss, underpinning

brain(s) *n.* **1.** aptitude, genius, intellect, intellectual, intellectual power, intelligence, mentality, mind, rationality, reason, smart person, thinker, understanding **2.** cerebellum, cerebrum, encephalon, gray matter, mind, white matter

brainstorm *v.* exchange ideas, have sudden idea, have sudden valuable idea, participate in group session, participate in thinking session

brainwash *v.* alter, catechize, condition, convert, convince, educate, indoctrinate, influence, instill, persuade, reeducate, teach

brake *n.* constraint, control, curb, damper, deterrent, hindrance, impediment, rein, restraint, retarding device

branch *n.* affiliate, annex, arm, auxiliary, bureau, category, chapter, classification, connection, department, dependency, derivative, division, extension, local, local office, member, office, offshoot, outpost, part, portion, post, section, subdivision, subgroup, subsection, subsidiary, tributary, wing

brand *n.* badge, brand name, crest, emblem, ensign, hallmark, identification, imprint, insignia, label, logo, logotype, mark, marker, motto, name, representation, seal, sigil, sign, signet, stamp, symbol, tag, trademark

brave *adj.* chivalrous, confident, courageous, dauntless, determined, fearless, gallant, heroic, intrepid, lionhearted, resolute, stalwart, steadfast, stouthearted, valiant, valorous, venturesome

bravery *n.* boldness, chivalry, confidence, courage, daring, dauntlessness, determination, fearlessness, fortitude, gallantry, heroism, intrepidness, lionheartedness, prowess, resoluteness, self-assurance, stouteartedness, tenacity, valor, valorousness

breach *n.* **1.** contravention, dereliction, disobedience, disregard, infraction, infringement, misdemeanor, misdeed, misfeasance, neglect, noncompliance, nonobservance, offense, transgression, trespass, violation **2.** aperture, break, chasm, cleft, crack, crevice, cut, fissure, fracture, gap, gulf, hole, opening, rent, rift, rupture, slit, split, void

break *n.*   **1.** cessation, coffee break, cutoff, discontinuation, division, downtime, gap, halt, hiatus, interference, interjection, interlude, intermission, interruption, interval, intervention, intrusion, lacuna, lull, machine downtime, omission, pause, recess, refreshment break, respite, rest, space, stoppage, suspension, time off, time out   **2.** breakage, chip, cleft, crack, fissure, flaw, fracture, rent, rift, rupture, splinter, split, tear

breakdown *n.*   **1.** accounting, analysis, arrangement, categorization, classification, diagnosis, dissection, division, itemization, listing, order, organization, outline, resolution, review, sorting out, summary   **2.** collapse, disintegration, disruption, failure, foundering, malfunction, mishap, wearing out

breakthrough *n.*   achievement, advance, development, discovery, find, finding, gain, improvement, increase, leap forward, major achievement, offensive, opening, overcoming, penetration, progress, revolution, step forward, success

breed *n.*   ancestry, clan, class, common ancestry, extraction, family, genus, kind, line, lineage, nature, pedigree, progeny, race, sort, species, stock, strain, type, variety

breeding *n.*   **1.** ancestry, engenderment, extraction, fertilization, lineage, parentage, procreation, propagation, reproduction   **2.** bearing, behavior, civility, comportment, conduct, courtesy, cultivation, gentility, grace, manners, nurture, politeness, rearing, refinement, upbringing   **3.** background, culture, development, education, improvement, rearing, schooling, teaching, training, upbringing

brevity *n.*   briefness, compactness, compendiousness, compression, conciseness, crispness, curtness, ephemerality, impermanence, incisiveness, pithiness, pointedness, shortness, succinctness, terseness, transience

bribe *n.*   allure, bait, blackmail, bribery, corrupt payment, enticement, gift, graft, gratuity, incentive, inducement, kickback, lure, payoff, present, protection money, reward

bridge *n.*   arch, bond, connection, connecting structure, crossing, link, overpass, span, tie, viaduct

brief *n.*   abstract, analysis, argument, case, compendium, conspectus, demonstration, digest, epitome, evidence, extract, ground, outline, précis, proof, prospectus, sketch, summary, syllabus, synopsis

brief *adj.* **1.** abrupt, ephemeral, fast, fleeting, hasty, impermanent, momentary, passing, quick, short, short-lived, short-term, swift, temporary, transient, transitory **2.** abbreviated, abridged, abrupt, brusque, compressed, concise, condensed, contracted, crisp, curt, curtailed, direct, elliptical, hasty, limited, little, pithy, pointed, sententious, short, small, straightforward, succinct, summarized, synoptic, terse

brief *v.* abridge, abstract, acquaint, advise, apprise, communicate, digest, disclose, edify, enlighten, epitomize, explain, impart, inform, instruct, orient, outline, prepare, prime, recapitulate, sketch, summarize, update

briefcase *n.* attache case, bag, baggage, case, document case, folder, portable case, portfolio

briefing *n.* background meeting, conference, directions, discussion, guidance, information, initiation, instruction, introduction, meeting, orientation, outlining, preparation, summary, training session, update

bring *v.* bear, carry, conduct, convey, deliver, escort, gather, get, guide, import, lead, send, take, transfer, transmit, transport, truck, usher

broad *adj.* **1.** all-embracing, all-inclusive, blanket, boundless, catholic, compendious, comprehensive, copious, encyclopedic, exhaustive, expansive, extended, extensive, far-reaching, general, inclusive, nonspecific, sweeping, ubiquitous, universal, unlimited, vague, wide, wide-ranging, widespread, worldwide **2.** ample, capacious, commodious, expansive, extended, extensive, full, generous, immense, large, outspread, outstretched, roomy, spacious, spread out, thick, vast, voluminous, wide, widespread

broadcast *n.* air time, electronic broadcast, newscast, on-line report, program, radio broadcast, radio program, show, simulcast, telecast, television program, transmission

broadcast *v.* **1.** air, beam, cable, fax, put on the air, radio, relay, report on-line, send out, simulcast, telecast, televise, transmit **2.** advertise, announce, circulate, communicate, declare, disperse, disseminate, distribute, herald, make known, make public, proclaim, promulgate, propagate, publish, report, send out, spread, transmit, voice

broadcasting *n.* airing, broadcasting electronically, newscasting, radio broadcasting, radio transmission, reporting on-line, telecasting, television transmission, televising, transmitting

brochure *n.* advertisement, booklet, bulletin, catalog, circular, flier, folder, handout, leaflet, pamphlet, prospectus, tract

broker *n.* agent, dealer, distributor, intermediary, medium, negotiator, stockbroker, wholesaler

browse *v.* check over, examine casually, examine cursorily, glance at, glance through, inspect casually, inspect loosely, leaf through, look over, look through, peruse, read, scan, skim, survey, thumb through

budget *n.* allocation of expenses, allotment of expenses, budget allowance, costs, estimated costs, estimated expenses, financial blueprint, financial plan, financial statement, fiscal estimate, funds, general expenses, operating expenses, overhead, plan, statement of expenses

budget *v.* allocate, allot, allow, apportion, calculate, compute, cost, cost out, estimate, plan, predict, ration, schedule

buffer *n.* barrier, bulwark, bumper, computer holding area, cushion, defense, dividing wall, fender, guard, holding area, intermediary, pad, partition, pillow, rampart, safeguard, screen, shield, shock absorber, wall

bug *n.* **1.** computer defect, computer error, defect, difficulty, electronic listening device, error, machine defect, machine error, mistake, program defect, program error, software defect, software error **2.** bacillus, disease, germ, illness, infection, microbe, microorganism, virus

build *n.* body, configuration, figure, form, frame, physical structure, physique, shape

build *v.* **1.** assemble, block, cast, compose, construct, create, devise, erect, fabricate, fashion, fit together, forge, form, frame, invent, make, manufacture, model, mold, originate, produce, put together, put up, raise, reconstruct, sculpture, set up, shape **2.** base, begin, establish, formulate, found, inaugurate, initiate, institute, originate, start

builder *n.* architect, construction worker, contractor, craftsperson, framer, inventor, maker, manufacturer, mason, producer, supervisor

building *n.* construction, domicile, edifice, erection, factory, framework, house, lodge, offices, plant, structure, superstructure

buildup *n.* accretion, accumulation, advertising, amassing, development, enlargement, escalation, expansion, gain, growth, increase, praise, promotion, publicity, stockpile

built-in *adj.* attached, congenital, deep-seated, essential, implicit, inborn, inbred, included, incorporated, ingrained, inherent, innate, integral, permanent

bulletin *n.* announcement, brochure, circular, communication, dispatch, flier, folder, handout, information, leaflet, message, news, news report, notice, notification, pamphlet, poster, program, release, report, statement

bunch *n.* accumulation, agglomeration, array, assemblage, assortment, batch, bundle, chunk, clump, cluster, collection, concentration, conglomeration, galaxy, gathering, group, host, lot, mass, multitude, pile, quantity, series, set, stack, thicket

bundle *n.* accumulation, agglomeration, array, assemblage, assortment, batch, box, bunch, carton, clump, cluster, collection, crate, group, lot, mass, pack, package, packet, pallet, parcel, pile, quantity, roll, set, stack

burden *n.* affliction, care, charge, difficulty, duty, encumbrance, handicap, hardship, hindrance, impediment, load, millstone, obligation, obstruction, onus, oppression, responsibility, strain, stress, tax, trial, tribulation, trouble, weight, work

burdensome *adj.* bothersome, bulky, crushing, cumbersome, cumbrous, demanding, difficult, distressing, disturbing, irksome, massive, onerous, oppressive, ponderous, taxing, tiresome, troublesome, trying, unwieldy, vexatious, wearing, wearisome, weighty, worrisome

bureau [*organization*]: *n.* agency, board, branch, commission, department, division, office, service, subdivision

bureaucracy *n.* administration, authority, civil service, controlling system, directorate, government, management, ministry, officialdom, regulatory agency, system

burglary *n.* break-in, breaking and entering, crime, felony, forced entry, housebreaking, larceny, looting, robbery, stealing, theft, thieving

burnish *v.* brighten, buff, glaze, gloss, grind, polish, put on finish, rub, shine, smooth, wax

business *n.* **1.** cartel, company, concern, corporation, enterprise, establishment, factory, firm, house, institution, market, mill, monopoly, organization, partnership, shop, store, syndicate, team, trust   **2.** affairs, bargaining, buying and selling, career, commercialism, contracting, craft, dealings, distribution, employment, field, free enterprise, function, industrialism, industry, job, line of work, livelihood, manufacturing, marketing, merchandising, occupation, proceedings, production, profession, promotion, pursuit, selling, specialty, trade, transacting, undertaking, venture, vocation, work

businesslike *adj.* accurate, assiduous, careful, conventional, correct, diligent, direct, disciplined, earnest, effective, effectual, efficient, enterprising, expeditious, functional, hardworking, industrious, matter-of-fact, methodical, orderly, organized, painstaking, practical, pragmatic, precise, professional, purposeful, realistic, regular, routine, sedulous, serious, skillful, systematic, thorough, well-ordered

businessperson *n.* capitalist, dealer, employer, entrepreneur, executive, financier, industrialist, manager, merchandiser, merchant, operator, professional, professional person, storekeeper, tradesperson, working person

busy *adj.* active, assiduous, diligent, employed, engaged, engrossed, industrious, involved, occupied, on assignment, on duty, overloaded, persevering, preoccupied, unavailable, working

buttress *n.* bar, beam, brace, column, cornerstone, mainstay, pillar, post, prop, reinforcement, shore, stanchion, stay, strut, support, underpinning

buy *v.* acquire, contract for, engage, get, hire, invest in, obtain, pay for, procure, purchase, put money in, secure, take on

buyer *n.* client, consumer, customer, end user, patron, purchaser, shopper, user, vendee

bypass *v.* avoid, circumnavigate, circumvent, depart from, detour, deviate from, elude, evade, go around, ignore, miss, neglect, omit, overlook, pass over, sidestep

byte [*computer*]: *n.* consecutive binary digits, 8 bits (personal computer), high byte(s), low byte(s), 1 character storage, memory unit, sequence of bits, storage unit

cabinet *n.* **1.** administration, administrators, advisors, advisory group, assembly, board, bureau, bureaucracy, committee, council, department heads, directors, executives, governing body, government, ministry, panel, trustees **2.** box, case, chest, container, file, locker, safe, storage cabinet

cache *n.* **1.** area of RAM, cache memory, disk cache, RAM cache **2.** accumulation, crypt, fund, hidden supply, hidden treasure, hideout, hiding place, hoard, repository, reserve, savings, stash, stockpile, store, supplies, treasure, vault, wealth

cadence *n.* accent, beat, count, emphasis, inflection, intonation, measure, meter, modulation, pulse, rhythm, speech pattern, tempo

calculate *v.* add, compute, count, divide, enumerate, figure, multiply, subtract, sum up, tally, value, work out

calculation *n.* adding, addition, arithmetic, computation, computing, counting, dividing, division, estimation, estimating, figuring, multiplication, multiplying, subtracting, subtraction, summation, totaling

call *n.* **1.** alarm, appeal, bidding, command, declaration, exclamation, invitation, invocation, phone call, plea, proclamation, request, signal, solicitation, summons, telephone call, visit **2.** demand for payment, early redemption, notice, option, option to buy, order, right to buy, right to redeem

call *v.* announce, appeal to, ask, assemble, bid, call meeting, call together, call to order, charge, command, contact, convene, convoke, declare, decree, invite, muster, order, phone, proclaim, rally, request, summon, telephone, visit

calling *n.* See **career**

calm *adj.* **1.** civil, collected, composed, cool, detached, dispassionate, even-tempered, impassive, imperturbable, level-headed, listless, moderate, neutral, passionless, patient, philosophical, placid, poised, relaxed, sedate, self-controlled, self-possessed, serene, staid, stoical, temperate, unconcerned, undemonstrative, undisturbed, unemotional, unexcitable, unexcited, unflappable, uninterested, unmoved, unperturbed, unruffled, untroubled **2.** hushed, inactive, inanimate, mild, motionless, peaceful, placid, quiescent, quiet, reposeful, reposing, restful, serene, slow, smooth, soothing, stationary, still, stormless, tranquil, unagitated, undisturbed, unruffled, waveless, windless

campaign *n.* attack, battle, battle plan, course of action, crusade, expedition, fight, maneuver, movement, offensive, operation, strategy, tactics, war, warfare

campaign *v.* agitate, contend for, contest, crusade, electioneer, run for, solicit votes, stand for, tour

cancel *v.* abolish, abort, abrogate, annul, avoid, break off, call off, cease, clear, close, countermand, declare invalid, delete, destroy, discharge, eliminate, end, eradicate, erase, expunge, ignore, invalidate, negate, neutralize, nullify, offset, omit, override, recall, remove, render inert, render invalid, render null and void, repeal, repudiate, rescind, retract, revoke, set aside, strike out, stop, suppress, terminate, undo, vacate, veto, void

cancellation *n.* abandoning, abandonment, abolishing, abolishment, abolition, abrogation, annulment, avoidance, canceling, defeasance, deletion, dissolution, dissolving, elimination, ending, erasure, invalidating, invalidation, negation, nullification, overriding, overruling, recall, recalling, recision, repeal, repudiation, retraction, reversal, revocation, suspension, termination, undoing, veto, vitiation, voidance, withdrawal, withdrawing

candid *adj.* aboveboard, blunt, bold, direct, explicit, forthright, frank, free, genuine, honest, ingenuous, open, outspoken, sincere, straightforward, unambiguous, unequivocal, unreserved, unrestrained

candidate *n.* applicant, aspirant, bidder, competitor, contender, contestant, entrant, job hunter, job seeker, nominee, office seeker, petitioner, solicitant

canon *n.* command, commandment, criterion, declaration, decree, dictate, doctrine, dogma, edict, ethic, formula, law, maxim, order, ordinance, precept, principle, regulation, rule, standard, statute, tenet

canvass *v.* analyze, campaign, check, check over, consult, examine, inquire into, inspect, investigate, peruse, petition, poll, request, review, scan, scrutinize, solicit, solicit votes, study, survey

capability *n.* ability, adeptness, adequacy, adroitness, aptitude, aptness, capacity, competence, competency, effectiveness, efficacy, facility, faculty, intelligence, potential, potentiality, power, proficiency, qualification, readiness, skill, talent

capable *adj.* able, accomplished, adapted, adept, adequate, adroit, apt, clever, competent, effective, efficient, experienced, gifted, intelligent, knowledgeable, proficient, proper, qualified, ready, skillful, sufficient, suited, talented

capacity *n.* **1.** amplitude, bulk, dimensions, expanse, extent, holding ability, holding power, limits, magnitude, mass, maximum, measure, number, production ability, proportions, quantity, range, retention, room, scope, size, space, spread, sufficiency, volume **2.** ability, acumen, adequacy, aptitude, aptness, brains, capability, competence, competency, endowment, facility, faculty, genius, gift, intellect, intelligence, mental ability, mind, potential, power, qualification, readiness, sagacity, sense, skill, stature, strength, sufficiency, talent

capital *n.* assets, cash, equity, equity interest, finances, financing, fixed assets, funds, goods, investment, liquid assets, long-term assets, means, money, principal, property, reserve, resources, revenue, savings, shareholder interest, stock, ways and means, wealth, working capital

capitalism *n.* commercialism, free enterprise, free-market system, industrialism, laissez-faire economics, mercantilism, private enterprise, private-ownership system

capitalist *n.* banker, businessperson, entrepreneur, financier, investor, landowner

capitalization *n.* allocation, computation, conversion, determination of value, expense allocation, financing, method of computation, total capital, total long-term capital, total liabilities, use of capital letters

caption *n.* banner, head, heading, headline, inscription, legend, subtitle, title

card *n.* agenda, badge, business card, calendar, calling card, docket, greeting card, ID, identification, mass card, playing card(s), postcard, program, schedule, ticket, timetable, visiting card, voucher

career *n.* area of specialization, business, career, craft, employment, field of activity, life's work, line of work, mission, occupation, office job, profession, pursuit, specialty, trade, vocation, work

careful *adj.* **1.** accurate, assiduous, choosy, conscientious, demanding, correct, critical, deliberate, detailed, exact, exacting, fastidious, finicky, fussy, meticulous, painstaking, particular, precise, protective, rigorous, scrupulous, self-disciplined, strict, thorough   **2.** alert, apprehensive, attentive, aware, cautious, chary, circumspect, concerned, conservative, considerate, discreet, guarded, heedful, judicious, mindful, observant, prudent, regardful, self-disciplined, solicitous, thoughtful, vigilant, wary, watchful

careless *adj.*   **1.** cursory, disorderly, error-prone, imprecise, inaccurate, incorrect, inexact, lax, messy, neglectful, negligent, remiss, slipshod, sloppy, unconcerned, uncritical, undemanding, undisciplined, unorganized, untidy   **2.** absentminded, casual, disregardful, forgetful, hasty, heedless, improvident, imprudent, inadvertent, inattentive, incautious, inconsiderate, indifferent, indiscreet, indolent, injudicious, irresponsible, lackadaisical, mindless, negligent, nonchalant, oblivious, perfunctory, rash, reckless, regardless, remiss, tactless, thoughtless, uncaring, uncircumspect, unconcerned, unguarded, unheeding, unmindful, unobservant, unreflective, unthinking, unwary

caretaker *n.*   concierge, conservator, curator, custodian, guard, guardian, janitor, maintenance person, manager, overseer, steward, superintendent, supervisor, warden

cargo *n.*   baggage, burden, carload, charge, consignment, contents, freight, goods, lading, load, merchandise, shipload, shipment, truckload

carry *v.*   **1.** bear, bring, convey, deliver, dispatch, displace, ferry, haul, import, move, relay, relocate, remove, shift, take, transfer, transmit, transplant, transport   **2.** air, broadcast, broadcast electronically, communicate, conduct, convey, display, disseminate, publish, relay, release, send, transfer, transmit

carte blanche *n.*   authority, freedom, free rein, free license, full power, full rights, license, permission, power of attorney, prerogative, sanction, unconditional right

cartel *n.*   bloc, business group, chain, combination, combine, conglomerate, consortium, group, monopoly, syndicate, trust

carton *n.*   box, case, cardboard box, container, corrugated box, crate, package, packing box

case *n.*   **1.** action, argument, cause, claim, controversy, dispute, evidence, lawsuit, legal case, litigation, petition, proceedings, suit, trial   **2.** case history, circumstance, conditions, context, crisis, dilemma, event, example, exemplification, history, illustration, incident, instance, occasion, occurrence, position, predicament, problem, representative, sample, sampling, situation, specimen, status **3.** bag, baggage, bin, box, cabinet, caddy, can, canister, carton, casket, chest, coffer, container, cover, covering, crate, envelope, folder, holder, jacket, package, receptacle, safe, sheath, shell, suitcase, tray, trunk, wrapper, wrapping

cash *n.* asset account, cash payments, cash receipts, coins, coinage, currency, immediate deposits, legal tender, money, savings, wherewithal

casualty *n.* accident, blow, calamity, catastrophe, chance, contingency, debacle, disaster, fatality, ill fortune, liability, loss, misadventure, misfortune, mishap, unfortunate circumstance, unfortunate person

catalog *n.* bulletin, classification, compilation, directory, enumeration, index, inventory, list, listing, record, register, schedule, slate, table

catalyst *n.* activist, agitator, enzyme, impetus, impulse, incendiary, incentive, incitation, incitement, motivation, motivator, reactant, spur, stimulant, stimulus

catastrophe *n.* accident, adversity, bad luck, blow, calamity, car crash, casualty, cataclysm, collision, debacle, devastation, disaster, hardship, misadventure, misery, misfortune, mishap, tragedy, wreck

catchword *n.* buzzword, byword, catchphrase, cliche, epithet, maxim, motto, refrain, saying, shibboleth, slogan, watchword

categorize *v.* arrange, assort, class, classify, compile, enumerate, group, identify, order, rank, sort

category *n.* class, classification, denomination, department, division, family, genus, grade, group, heading, kind, league, level, list, order, position, rank, section, sort, species, status, tier, variety

catholic *adj.* all-embracing, all-encompassing, all-inclusive, broad, broad-minded, comprehensive, diffuse, ecumenical, even-handed, extensive, fair, general, generic, global, impartial, inclusive, large-scale, liberal, nonsectarian, open-minded, unbiased, universal, unprejudiced, whole, wide, widespread, worldwide

caucus *n.* assemblage, assembly, conclave, conference, convention, council, gathering, meeting, parley, session

cause *n.* **1.** agent, antecedent, author, base, basis, beginning, causation, creator, determinant, explanation, foundation, fountainhead, genesis, ground(s), incentive, incitement, inducement, inspiration, instigation, justification, mainspring, motivation, motive, occasion, origin, originator, producer, purpose, rationale, reason, root, source, stimulation, stimulus **2.** belief, conviction, creed, enterprise, end, faith, goal, ideal, intent, intention, objective, principle, purpose, reason for being, tenet

caution *n.* **1.** admonition, advice, caveat, counsel, forewarning, hint, indication, injunction, monition, notice, omen, premonition, sign **2.** alertness, attention, attentiveness, care, carefulness, circumspection, concern, deliberation, discreetness, discretion, foresight, forethought, guardedness, heed, heedfulness, mindfulness, prudence, regard, thought, vigilance, watchfulness

cautious *adj.* alert, careful, chary, circumspect, considerate, discreet, guarded, heedful, judicious, leery, precautionary, provident, prudent, vigilant, wary, watchful

caveat *n.* admonition, alarm, caution, emphasis, forewarning, monition, warning

cease *v.* check, close, close out, conclude, culminate, desist, discontinue, fail, halt, quell, refrain from, shut down, silence, stop, suppress, terminate

cede *v.* bequeath, convey, deed, donate, give over, give up, grant, part with, release, relinquish, render, renounce, sign over, surrender, tender, transfer, turn over to, yield

celebration *n.* anniversary, ball, birthday, carnival, ceremony, commemoration, consecration, dedication, extravaganza, feast day, festival, festivity, fete, formalities, gala, holiday, holy day, honoring, jubilation, jubilee, memorialization, observance, party, performance, recognition, religious feast day, remembrance, rite, ritualization, sanctification, solemnization

cell *n.* alcove, antechamber, apartment, berth, booth, cage, cavity, chamber, cloister, closet, compartment, coordinate location, cubicle, den, enclosure, hold, hole, keep, lockup, nook, point of intersection, receptacle, recess, retreat, room, smallest unit, stall, storage, vault

censor *v.* abridge, amend, criticize, cut, delete, edit, examine, excise, expurgate, forbid, inspect, purge, repress, restrain, restrict, review, strike out, suppress, withhold

censorship *n.* abridgment, amendment, ban, criticism, deletion, editing, examination, excision, expurgation, forbiddance, forbidding, inspection, purgation, repression, restraint, restriction, review, suppression, withholding

censure *n.* accusation, admonishment, admonition, blame, castigation, condemnation, criticism, denunciation, disapprobation, disapproval, imputation, incrimination, inculpation, objection, objurgation, official reprimand, punishment, rebuke, remonstrance, reprehension, reprimand, reproach, reprobation, reproof, stricture, vituperation

center *adj.* axial, basal, basic, cardinal, centric, chief, dominant, essential, focal, foremost, fundamental, important, inner, innermost, inland, interior, intermediate, internal, inward, key, main, mean, median, mid, middle, middlemost, midland, midmost, midway, most important, outstanding, overriding, paramount, pivotal, predominant, primary, prime, principal, salient, significant, uppermost

centralize *v.* accumulate, aggregate, assemble, collect, come together, compact, concenter, concentrate, condense, congregate, consolidate, converge, focus, gather, incorporate, integrate, organize, streamline, unify, unite

ceremonial *adj.* august, ceremonious, commemorative, formal, imposing, liturgical, lofty, majestic, ritual, ritualistic, sacramental, solemn, stately

ceremony *n.* **1.** ceremonial, commemoration, custom, formality, function, liturgy, observance, parade, rite, ritual, sacrament, service, show, solemnity **2.** conformity, conventionality, decorum, etiquette, form, formal courtesy, formality, politeness, pomp, preciseness, prescription, propriety, protocol, strictness

certificate *n.* acknowledgment, affidavit, affirmation, attestation, authentication, authorization, certification, coupon, credential, declaration, deposition, diploma, document, endorsement, guarantee, license, permit, record, statement, testament, testimonial, testimony, ticket, voucher, warrant, warranty

certify *v.* accept, accredit, affirm, approve, assert, assure, attest to, authenticate, authorize, aver, avow, commission, confirm, corroborate, declare true, depose, document, endorse, evidence, guarantee, insure, license, pledge, promise, prove, ratify, reassure, sanction, show, state under oath, substantiate, support, sustain, swear to, testify to, uphold, validate, verify, vouch for, vow, warrant

chairperson *n.* chair, chairman/woman, director, facilitator, leader, master of ceremonies, moderator, monitor, president, presiding officer

challenge *n.* attack, confrontation, countercharge, dare, defiance, exception, objection, opposition, protest, provocation, remonstrance, test, threat, trial, ultimatum

chamber *n.* **1.** antechamber, berth, cell, compartment, cubicle, lodging, room, salon, sitting room, stall, study **2.** assembly, congress, council, court, diet, divan, judicature, legislature, soviet, synod, tribunal

champion *n.* advocate, ally, backer, campaigner, conqueror, defender, guardian, hero, knight, leader, patron, proponent, protector, subduer, subjugator, supporter, sympathizer, upholder, victor, vindicator

change *v.* adapt, adjust, alter, alternate, bend, convert, disguise, distort, diversify, exchange, fluctuate, inflect, interchange, invert, make over, metamorphose, modify, modulate, mutate, permute, recondition, reconstruct, redo, regenerate, remake, remodel, renovate, reorder, reorganize, replace, restyle, reverse, revolutionize, shift, substitute, swap, switch, trade, transfigure, transform, translate, transmute, transpose, turn, twist, vacillate, vary, warp

channel *n.* approach, aqueduct, artery, avenue, basin, bay, bed, bight, bottom, canal, circuit, conduit, corridor, creek, depths, dike, ditch, duct, estuary, facility, fjord, floor, furrow, groove, gulf, gully, gutter, inlet, lagoon, lane, line, link, narrows, neck, pass, passage, passageway, path, pipe, ravine, road, route, runway, sound, strait, stream, trail, transmission path, trough, tube, watercourse, waterway, way

chaos *n.* anarchy, bedlam, clamor, commotion, confusion, disarray, discord, disorder, disorganization, disquiet, disunion, fray, lawlessness, muddle, pandemonium, tumult, turmoil, unrest, unruliness, upheaval, uproar

chapter *n.* **1.** affiliate, branch, division, member, offshoot, part, portion, section, subdivision, unit **2.** age, era, episode, event, occurrence, period, phase, stage, time

character *n.* **1.** attributes, bent, characteristics, complexion, constitution, disposition, essential qualities, features, genius, idiosyncrasy, individuality, integrity, makeup, nature, notability, personality, reputation, repute, singularity, standing, style, temper, temperament, traits **2.** badge, brand, cipher, code, crest, device, digit, emblem, figure, ensign, formatting symbol, graphics symbol, ideogram, ideograph, insignia, label, letter, mark, marker, name, notation, number, punctuation mark, rune, seal, sigil, sign, signet, stamp, symbol, trademark

characteristic *n.* aspect, attribute, bearing, bent, bias, caliber, cast, character, complexion, component, disposition, distinction, endowment, essence, essential quality, feature, idiosyncrasy, inclination, individuality, mannerism, mark, nature, particularity, peculiarity, personality, property, quality, singularity, specialty, style, symptom, temperament, tendency, trait, turn

charge *v.* **1.** ask price, assess, bill, buy on credit, debit, debit account, fine, fix price at, impose, incur debt, levy, price, put on account, receive credit, sell for, tax **2.** accuse, allege, arraign, assert, assign, attribute, blame, book, censure, cite, criminate, impeach, implicate, impugn, impute, incriminate, inculpate, indict, involve, reprehend, reproach **3.** adjure, ask, bid, command, dictate, direct, instruct, order, request, solicit, tell, warn

charity *n.* **1.** alms, assistance, benefaction, bestowal, contribution, dole, donation, endowment, financial assistance, generosity, gift, gratuity, largesse, offering, philanthropy, present **2.** altruism, beneficence, benevolence, compassion, generosity, goodness, goodwill, humanity, indulgence, kindness, kindheartedness, kindliness, magnanimity, mercy, tenderheartedness, service

chart *n.* blueprint, diagram, flowchart, graph, guide, map, outline, plan, plat, scheme, sketch, table, tabulation, visual representation

charter *n.* agreement, articles of incorporation, authorization, bond, compact, constitution, contract, covenant, document, franchise, grant, license, pact, treaty, written instrument

check *n.* **1.** bank draft, bill, certificate, coupon, draft, receipt, stub, ticket, voucher **2.** analysis, audit, checkup, control, inquiry, investigation, perusal, probe, research, review, scrutiny, study, test, test run, trial, trial run **3.** bar, barrier, block, constraint, control, curb, dampener, damper, deterrent, impediment, inhibition, limitation, rebuff, rejection, repression, restrainer, restraint, restriction, retardant, retardation, stoppage

check *v.* **1.** analyze, audit, compare, confirm, determine, determine accuracy, examine, find out, inspect, investigate, monitor, review, substantiate, verify **2.** abridge, arrest, bar, bridle, constrain, control, counteract, curb, curtail, cut short, decrease, delay, diminish, discourage, end, frustrate, halt, hinder, hold back, impede, inhibit, interrupt, lessen, limit, moderate, neutralize, obstruct, preclude, prevent, quell, rebuff, reduce, repress, repulse, restrain, retard, slow, stall, stay, stop, suppress, terminate, thwart, withhold

chief *n.* boss, commander, head, leader, monarch, principal, ruler, sovereign

chief *adj.* cardinal, central, commanding, controlling, crucial, directing, especial, essential, first, foremost, governing, head, indispensable, key, leading, main, major, master, most important, necessary, outstanding, paramount, predominant, preeminent, premier, primary, prime, principal, reigning, ruling, significant, supreme, uppermost

choice *n.* alternative, choosing, conclusion, decision, determination, discernment, discretion, discrimination, election, favorite, judgment, pick, opinion, option, partiality, predilection, preference, selection, verdict, volition, vote

choice *adj.* best, elite, excellent, exceptional, exclusive, exquisite, extraordinary, fine, first-class, first-rate, paramount, precious, preeminent, preferential, preferred, priceless, prime, rare, select, special, superior, superlative, supreme, uncommon, unusual, valuable

choose *v.* accept, adopt, appoint, commit oneself to, co-opt, cull, decide on, designate, desire, determine, discriminate, distinguish, elect, embrace, espouse, fancy, favor, judge, like, make choice, make decision, name, opt for, pick, prefer, select, separate, set apart, set aside, single out, sort, take, take up, want, wish for

chronicle *n.* account, adventures, almanac, annals, archive, autobiography, biography, chronology, diary, document, epic, history, journal, legend, log, memoirs, memorandum, minutes, narration, narrative, proceedings, recital, record, register, report, saga, story, transactions

chronicle *v.* document, enter, record, recount, register, relate, report, set down, take minutes, tell

chronological *adj.* chronographic, chronologic, chronometric, chronoscopic, consecutive, dated, ordered, progressive, sequent, sequential, serial, temporal, time-measured

cipher *n.* code, cryptograph, digit, figure, integer, naught, nil, nonentity, notation, nothing, nothingness, nullity, number, numeral, sign, symbol, zero

cipher *v.* add, calculate, code, decode, compute, count, decipher, do arithmetic, do math, estimate, figure, number, total

circa *prep.* about, approximately, around, near, roughly

circle *n.* **1.** annulus, aureole, band, belt, circumference, coil, cordon, corona, coronet, crown, disk, hoop, ring, ringlet, round, wheel, wreath **2.** associates, association, cabal, camarilla, clan, clique, club, companions, comrades, coterie, crew, faction, friends, gang, group, insiders, intimates, ring, set, society

circuit *n.* ambit, beat, bounds, circle, circumference, communication link, compass, course, cycle, electrical system, globe, journey, lap, line, loop, orb, orbit, path, pathway, perimeter, periphery, range, revolution, round, route, sphere, tour, track, tract, trajectory, trip, turn, zone

circular *n.* advertisement, announcement, bill, booklet, brochure, bulletin, flier, folder, handout, insert, leaflet, letter, notice, pamphlet, poster, release, statement

circular *adj.* arched, circling, curved, curvilinear, indirect, round, rounded, spheroidic

circulate *v.* advertise, diffuse, disperse, disseminate, distribute, exchange, intersperse, issue, make known, make public, promulgate, propagate, publicize, publish, put forth, send out, spread

circulation *n.* **1.** apportionment, conveyance, diffusion, dispatch, dispersion, dissemination, distribution, interspersion, propagation, scattering, spread, spreading, transmission **2.** circling, circuit, circumrotation, circumvolution, compassing, flow, flowing, gyration, gyre, motion, orbit, passage, pivot, revolution, rolling, rotation, round, rounding, spin, spiral, swivel, turn, volution, whirl, winding

circumference *n.* ambit, border, boundary, boundary line, bounds, circuit, compass, confines, edge, extremity, frame, fringe, girth, limits, lip, margin, outline, perimeter, periphery, rim, verge

circumlocution *n.* convolution, diffuseness, digression, indirectness, periphrasis, pleonasm, profuseness, prolixity, roundabout speech, tautology, verbiage, verbosity, wordiness

circumstance *n.* accident, affair, aspect, case, condition, crisis, detail, element, episode, event, exigency, fact, factor, feature, happening, incidence, incident, instance, item, occasion, occurrence, particular, phenomenon, point, proviso, respect, situation, stipulation

citation *n.* act of quoting, citing a case, excerpt, formal mention, identifiction of authority, identification of source, official summons, quote, reference

cite *v.* call upon, document source, give source, mention formally, name in a citation, provide authority, provide source, quote, refer to, refer to authority, refer to source, state authority, state source, summon officially

citizen *n.* civilian, city dweller, dweller, inhabitant, member of community, native, naturalized resident, resident, rural dweller, taxpayer, townsperson, villager, voter

city *n.* capital, commercial center, large town, metropolis, metropolitan area, municipality, town, urban area

civic *adj.* civil, communal, community, metropolitan, municipal, neighborhood, public, social, town, urban

civil *adj.* **1.** civic, civilian, communal, domestic, governmental, home, interior, internal, local, metropolitan, municipal, national, political, public, urban **2.** accommodating, affable, agreeable, civilized, complaisant, cordial, courteous, courtly, cultivated, deferential, diplomatic, formal, genial, genteel, gracious, mannerly, obliging, pleasant, polished, polite, politic, proper, refined, respectful, tactful, urbane, well-behaved, well-bred, well-mannered

civilian *n.* citizen, laic, layperson, nonmilitary person, private citizen

civilian *adj.* civil, laical, lay, nonmilitary, nonreligious, private, secular

civilization *n.* **1.** community, culture, humanity, humankind, human society, nation, people, society **2.** acculturation, advancement, breeding, civility, cultivation, culture, development, edification, education, elevation, enlightenment, illumination, inculcation, instruction, polish, progress, refinement, schooling, socialization, sophistication, teaching, worldliness

claim *v.* affirm, allege, appeal, assert, assert right, aver, avow, call for, challenge, charge, command, declare, demand, entreat, hold, insist, lay claim to, petition, postulate, proclaim, profess, pronounce, request indemnification, request payment, require, sue

clandestine *adj.* artful, closed, closet, collusive, confidential, conspiratorial, covert, crafty, cunning, furtive, illegitimate, illicit, private, secret, sly, sneaky, stealthy, surreptitious, unauthorized, undercover, underhanded

clarification *n.* annotation, comment, definition, description, disclosure, elucidation, explanation, exposition, footnote, interpretation, resolution, revelation, simplification, specification

clarify *v.* annotate, clear up, decipher, define, delineate, demonstrate, describe, elucidate, exhibit, explain, explicate, footnote, illuminate, illustrate, interpret, make clear, make plain, make understandable, render intelligible, resolve, show, simplify, specify, straighten out

clarity *n.* accuracy, articulateness, brightness, certainty, clearness, comprehensibility, conspicuousness, decipherability, definiteness, directness, distinctness, exactness, explicitness, intelligibility, legibility, lucidity, obviousness, overtness, perceptibility, perspicuity, plainness, preciseness, precision, prominence, purity, salience, simplicity, tangibility, translucence, transparency, visibility

class *n.* **1.** arrangement, branch, brand, cast, category, character, classification, collection, color, composition, denomination, department, description, designation, division, domain, feather, form, genre, genus, grade, grain, group, grouping, hierarchy, kind, make, mold, name, order, origin, property, province, quality, range, rank, realm, school, sect, section, selection, set, sort, source, species, sphere, stripe, style, suit, type, value, variety **2.** ancestry, background, birth, breed, caste, circle, clan, clique, connection, coterie, cultural level, derivation, descent, estate, extraction, family, genealogy, grade, importance, influence, league, level, lineage, nobility, origin, pedigree, place, position, power, prestige, quality, rank, sect, social group, social rank, source, sphere, standing, state, station, status, stock, strain, stratum, tribe, weight

class *v.* See **classify**

classic *n.* archetype, example, exemplar, ideal, masterpiece, model, original, paradigm, paragon, prototype, quintessence, standard, standard work

classic(al) *adj.* archetypal, best, characteristic, consummate, definitive, distinguished, excellent, exemplary, extraordinary, finest, first-class, first-rate, ideal, model, outstanding, paradigmatic, perfect, prime, prototypical, quintessential, remarkable, representative, standard, superior, typical, vintage, well-known

classical *adj.* **1.** balanced, classic, elegant, harmonious, plain, polished, proportional, pure, refined, regular, restrained, simple, symmetrical, tasteful, understated, well-proportioned **2.** Attic, Doric, Grecian, Greek, Homeric, Ionic, Hellenistic

classification *n.* **1.** allocating, allocation, allotting, allotment, apportioning, apportionment, arrangement, arranging, assigning, assignment, cataloguing, categorization, categorizing, codification, codifying, collocating, collocation, denomination, designating, designation, disposing, disposition, distributing, distribution, grading, grouping, methodizing, ordering, organization, organizing, sizing, sorting, systematization, systematizing, taxonomy, typecasting **2.** assortment, branch, category, class, code, collection, directory, division, genre, gradation, grade, group, index, kind, order, range, rank, section, selection, set, sort, system, taxonomy, type, variety

classify *v.* allocate, allot, alphabetize, arrange, assort, brand, catalog, categorize, class, codify, dispose, distinguish, distribute, file, grade, group, index, label, name, number, order, organize, place, range, rank, rate, segregate, size, sort, ticket, type

clause *n.* addendum, addition, appendix, article, codicil, condition, covenant, division, item, limitation, paragraph, passage, point, provision, proviso, qualification, reservation, rider, section, sentence, sentences, sentences and paragraphs, specification, stipulation, supplement, term

clear *adj.* **1.** apparent, apprehensible, articulate, audible, clear-cut, cogent, coherent, comprehensible, conclusive, conspicuous, definite, discernible, distinct, distinguishable, evident, explicit, express, graphic, incontrovertible, intelligible, irrefutable, legible, lucid, manifest, obvious, palpable, patent, perceptible, perspicuous, plain, precise, prominent, pronounced, readable, recognizable, salient, sharp, simple, straightforward, transparent, transpicuous, unambiguous, uncomplicated, undeniable, understandable, undisguised, unequivocal, unmistakable, unquestionable, visible, vivid, well-defined **2.** bright, brilliant, clarion, cloudless, crystal, crystalline, fair, fine, glassy, glowing, halcyon, illuminated, incandescent, light, lighted, lit, lucent, luminescent, luminous, mild, pellucid, pure, radiant, rainless, shining, shiny, sunny, sunshiny, translucent, transparent, unclouded, undarkened, undimmed

clear *v.* **1.** brighten, clarify, clean, cleanse, clear away, clear out, clear up, disencumber, disengage, disentangle, eliminate, elucidate, empty, enlighten, erase, expunge, expurgate, extricate, free, illuminate, lighten, loosen, lose, open, purge, purify, remove, rid, unblock, unburden, unclog, unload, unloose, unravel, untie, vacate, void, wipe **2.** absolve, acquit, discharge, emancipate, exculpate, excuse, exonerate, find innocent, forgive, free, let go, let off, liberate, pardon, release, set free, vindicate

clearance *n.* **1.** approval, authorization, consent, permission, sanction **2.** allowance, gap, headroom, headway, leeway, margin, opening, open space, space

clear-cut *adj.* apparent, comprehensible, definite, definitive, detailed, discernible, distinct, evident, exact, explicit, express, indubitable, intelligible, lucid, obvious, perceptible, perspicuous, plain, precise, specific, straightforward, unambiguous, understandable, undisputed, unequivocal, unmistakable, well-defined

clearly *adv.* apparently, audibly, certainly, conclusively, conspicuously, decidedly, decisively, definitely, discernibly, distinctly, evidently, explicitly, implicitly, incontestably, indubitably, lucidly, manifestly, markedly, noticeably, observably, obviously, overtly, patently, perceptibly, plainly, positively, prominently, recognizably, translucently, transparently, unambiguously, undeniably, undoubtedly, unequivocally, unmistakably, unquestionably, visibly

clerical *adj.* **1.** accounting, bookkeeping, data processing, information processing, office, professional, secretarial, stenographic, typing, white-collar, word processing **2.** apostolic, canonical, churchly, cleric, ecclesiastic, ecclesiastical, holy, ministerial, monastic, papal, pastoral, pontifical, prelatic, priestly, rabbinical, sacerdotal, sacred, theocratic, theocratical

clerk *n.* assistant, cashier, counterperson, court clerk, employee, file clerk, notary, office worker, operator, receptionist, recorder, record keeper, registrar, salesperson, secretary, seller, shopkeeper, stenographer, teller, transcriber, transcriptionist, typist, word processor

cliche *n.* adage, banality, commonplace, hackneyed phrase, motto, overused phrase, platitude, proverb, saying, shibboleth, stale saying, stereotype, triteness, trite phrase, triviality

client *n.* buyer, consumer, customer, patient, patron, protégé, purchaser, shopper, user, vendee, ward

clientele *n.* audience, business, buyers, clients, constituency, customers, following, market, patronage, patrons, public, purchasers, regulars, shoppers, trade

climate *n.* **1.** air, ambience, atmosphere, aura, disposition, environment, ethos, feeling, ideology, milieu, mood, mores, norms, sense, spirit, surroundings, temper, tendency, tone, trend, worldview **2.** atmospheric conditions, characteristic weather, clime, meteorological conditions, meteorologic conditions, prevailing conditions, prevailing weather, weather

climax *n.* acme, cap, crest, crown, crowning point, culmination, extremity, fruition, head, heights, highlight, limit, maturity, maximum, meridian, payoff, peak, pinnacle, pitch, prime, supreme moment, tip, top, utmost, zenith

clinical *adj.* analytical, antiseptic, austere, detached, disinterested, dispassionate, emotionless, impersonal, objective, scientific, unemotional

clip art *n.* art collection, drawings, free art, free illustrations, graphics images, illustrations, line art, printed art, printed illustrations, reproducible art, reproducible illustrations, stored art, stored illustrations, uncopyrighted art, uncopyrighted illustrations, usable art, usable illustrations

clique *n.* band, circle, clan, club, community, crew, crowd, faction, friends, group, group of friends, insiders, sect, set, team, troop

clone *n.* copy, DNA replica, duplicate, exact copy, exact duplicate, exact imitation, genetic duplicate, identical cells, imitation, laboratory copy, machine replica, replica, technological duplication

close *n.* bring to conclusion, closing accounting books, conclusion, consummation of agreement, consummation of sale, end, end of session, final period, final-trade price, last half hour of trading session

closed *adj.* bankrupt, bolted, completed, concluded, decided, ended, finalized, finished, locked, out-of-service, padlocked, resolved, restricted, sealed, secured, settled, terminated

closing *n.* concluding part, consummation of transaction, final procedure, real estate meeting, settlement, transference of title

closure *n.* **1.** cessation, closing, completion, conclusion, culmination, desistance, end, ending, finish, fulfillment, peroration, realization, stoppage, termination **2.** barrier, blockade, bolt, cap, cork, cover, fastener, impediment, latch, lid, obstruction, padlock, plug, seal, stop, stoppage, stopper, stopple, top

club *n.* affiliation, alliance, association, band, circle, clique, coalition, community, consortium, faction, group, guild, league, lodge, organization, set, society, sodality, team, troop, union

clue *n.* cue, evidence, glimmer, hint, implication, indication, inference, inkling, insinuation, intimation, key, lead, mark, note, notion, pointer, proof, sign, suggestion, suspicion, symptom, tip, trace

cluster *n.* accumulation, agglomeration, aggregation, array, assemblage, assembly, assortment, band, batch, bevy, body, bunch, bundle, clump, collection, concentration, congregation, covey, crowd, gathering, group, herd, jumble, lot, mass, medley, number, pack, school, series, set, swarm

clutter *n.* chaos, confusion, disarray, disorder, huddle, jumble, litter, mess, trash, untidiness

coalesce *v.* amalgamate, associate, blend, coincide, combine, come together, commingle, commix, conjoin, connect, consolidate, converge, fuse, incorporate, integrate, intermingle, join, link, merge, mingle, mix, unite

coalition *n.* affiliation, alliance, amalgamation, association, blending, bloc, cartel, combination, confederation, conglomeration, conjugation, consolidation, consortium, entente, federation, fusing, fusion, incorporation, integration, junction, melding, merger, partnership, syndicate, synthesis, trust, unification, union

code *n.* **1.** canon, compilation of laws, criterion, digest, ethic, ethics, guidelines, law, maxim, morality, morals, prescription, principle, principles, regulation, rules, set of laws, set of rules, standard, value system **2.** cipher, cryptogram, cryptograph, cryptography, secret language

codicil *n.* addendum, addition, addition to will, appendix, epilog, postscript, rider, subscript, supplement

codify *v.* abstract, alphabetize, arrange, catalog, classify, code, condense, consolidate, convert, digest, grade, group, index, list, methodize, order, organize, rank, rate, standardize, summarize, synopsize, systematize, tabulate, write

coercion *n.* automatic conversion, browbeating, bullying, compulsion, constraint, conversion, duress, enforcement, force, frightening, inducement, insistence, intimidation, menacing, necessitation, obligation, persuasion, pressure, provocation, requirement, restraint, threat, threatening, violence

cognate *adj.* affiliated, agnate, akin, alike, allied, associated, comparable, comparative, congeneric, connatural, consanguine, correlated, corresponding, generic, kindred, related, relative, similar

coherence *n.* accord, adherence, agreement, attachment, bond, cementation, coalescence, cohesion, comprehensibility, concordance, conformity, congruity, consistency, consolidation, consonance, correspondence, harmony, inseparability, intelligibility, rationality, relation, solidarity, union, unity

coherent *adj.* articulate, comprehensible, consistent, harmonious, intelligible, logical, lucid, meaningful, orderly, organized, rational, reasoned, sound, systematic

coincidence *n.* **1.** accident, accidental happening, chance, fate, fluke, happening, incident, incidental occurrence, unpredictable event **2.** accord, accordance, agreement, coexistence, concert, concomitance, concord, concurrence, conformity, consonance, correspondence, harmony, parallelism, rapport, synchronism, unanimity, uniformity, union, unity

collaborate *v.* act jointly, coact, combine, concur, conspire, cooperate, join forces, join together, participate, team up, unite, work together, work with

collaborator *n.* accessory, confederate, conspirator, contributor, cooperator, helper, participant, partner, teammate

collapse *n.* breakdown, cataclysm, catastrophe, cave-in, crash, demolition, destruction, detonation, devastation, disaster, disintegration, downfall, exhaustion, explosion, failure, prostration, rupture, termination

collate *v.* analogize, assemble, compare, examine, group, juxtapose, merge, order, verify

collateral *n.* asset, assurance, bond, deposit, endorsement, guarantee, insurance, pledge, security, surety, warrant

colleague *n.* accessory, adjunct, adjuvant, aide, ally, assistant, associate, coadjutant, coadjutor, cohort, collaborator, companion, compatriot, comrade, confederate, consociate, cooperator, coworker, friend, partner, peer, teammate

collect *v.* **1.** acquire, earn, raise, request payment, requisition, save, secure, solicit, stockpile, take in **2.** accumulate, agglomerate, aggregate, amass, assemble, bring together, call together, call up, cluster, come together, compile, congregate, convene, convoke, flock together, gather, group, herd, meet, muster, rally, round up, summon, surge, swarm, throng

collection *n.* accumulation, acquisition, agglomeration, aggregation, amassment, analects, anthology, array, assemblage, assembly, assortment, batch, body, clump, cluster, collected works, combination, compilation, concentration, conglomeration, congregation, crowd, cumulation, digest, fund, garland, gathering, group, hoard, holdings, host, lot, mass, medley, miscellany, multitude, muster, number, omnibus, pile, savings, selection, series, set, stock, stockpile, store, supply, throng, treasure, variety

collective *adj.* accumulated, agglomerate, aggregate, collaborative, collected, combined, common, compiled, composite, concerted, concurrent, conglomerate, consonant, cooperative, corporate, cumulative, gathered, massed, mutual, representative, unified, united

colloquy *n.* chat, conference, conversation, debate, dialog, discourse, discussion, interlocution, palaver, parlance, parley, talk, verbal exchange

collusion *n.* complicity, connivance, deceit, plot, secret agreement, secret pact

color *n.* **1.** appearance, deception, disguise, facade, false front, guise, mask, pretense, pretext, semblance, show **2.** blush, cast, coloration, coloring, complexion, dye, hue, paint, pigment, pigmentation, shade, skin color, tinct, tincture, tinge, tint, tone, value, wash

combination *n.* **1.** affiliation, agreement, alliance, association, bloc, cabal, cartel, coalition, company, confederacy, confederation, connection, consolidation, consortium, conspiracy, convention, corporation, federation, group, guild, joint concern, league, merger, monopoly, network, organization, partnership, party, society, syndicate, trust, unification, union **2.** agglomeration, aggregate, aggregation, array, assortment, cluster, collection, combo, composition, conglomeration, consolidation, grouping, medley, mélange, miscellany, mix, mixture, potpourri, series, set, synthesis

combine *v.* admix, affiliate, ally, alloy, amalgamate, associate, attach, band, bind, blend, bond, coalesce, commingle, commix, compound, conjoin, connect, consolidate, couple, fuse, homogenize, incorporate, integrate, interface, intermingle, intermix, join, link, merge, mingle, mix, pool, put together, syndicate, synthesize, tie together, unite, weld

combustible *adj.* combustive, explosive, fiery, flammable, ignitable, incendiary, inflammable, inflammatory, volatile

comfort *n.* abundance, amenity, cheer, cheerfulness, consolation, contentment, convenience, ease, enjoyment, gratification, happiness, luxury, opulence, peacefulness, pleasure, plenty, reassurance, relaxation, relief, repose, rest, restfulness, satisfaction, solace, sufficiency, sympathy, warmth, well-being

comfortable *adj.* **1.** acceptable, adequate, agreeable, appropriate, calm, cheerful, complacent, contented, convenient, delightful, easy, enjoyable, gratified, gratifying, happy, healthy, peaceful, placid, pleasant, pleased, pleasing, protected, quiet, relaxed, relaxing, relieved, rested, restful, satisfactory, satisfying, serene, sheltered, sufficient, tranquil, untroubled, useful, warm, well-off, undisturbed **2.** affluent, ample, luxurious, palatial, prosperous, rich, spacious, substantial, wealthy, well-off, well-to-do

command *n.* absolutism, authority, authorization, computer instruction, control signal, despotism, direction, domination, dominion, government, imperialism, influence, instruction, jurisdiction, leadership, management, oversight, power, regulation, reign, rule, sovereignty, supervision, supremacy, sway, tyranny

commemorate *v.* celebrate, ceremonialize, dedicate, honor, immortalize, keep, memorialize, observe, pay tribute to, perpetuate, recognize, remember, ritualize, salute, sanctify, solemnize

commemoration *n.* acknowledgment, celebration, ceremonial, ceremony, citation, commemorative, commendation, congratulations, dedication, eulogy, exaltation, honorable mention, honoring, laudation, memorial, memorial service, observance, praise, recognition, remembrance, rite, ritual, testimonial, tribute

commendable *adj.* admirable, creditable, deserving, estimable, excellent, exemplary, honorable, laudable, meritorious, praiseworthy, superior, upright, worthy

commendation *n.* acclaim, acclamation, applause, approbation, approval, award, citation, compliment, congratulations, credit, endorsement, honor, laudation, pay, praise, recognition, recommendation, sanction, testimonial, tribute

comment *n.* affirmation, annotation, assertion, clarification, commentary, conclusion, criticism, disclosure, discussion, editorial, elucidation, exegesis, explanation, exposition, footnote, gloss, illumination, illustration, interjection, interpretation, mention, note, observation, opinion, postscript, pronouncement, reflection, remark, response, review, statement, utterance, word

comment *v.* affirm, annotate, assert, clarify, conclude, criticize, disclose, discuss, editorialize, elucidate, exemplify, expand on, explain, expound on, express view, footnote, gloss, illuminate, illustrate, interject, interpret, make note of, make statement, mention, note, observe, point out, pronounce, reflect, remark, respond, review, say something, state, utter

commentary *n.* analysis, annotation, comments, criticism, critique, discourse, discussion, dissertation, editorial, essay, exegesis, explanation, exposé, exposition, footnotes, gloss, lecture, monograph, narration, notes, observation, remarks, review, speech, study, thesis, tract, treatise

commentator *n.* analyst, anchorperson, annotator, announcer, author, correspondent, critic, editorialist, essayist, expositor, expounder, glossarist, interpreter, lecturer, newscaster, reporter, reviewer, speaker, sportscaster, writer

commerce *n.* business, business dealings, buying and selling, commercialism, dealings, exchange, interchange, marketing, mercantilism, merchandising, retailing, trade, traffic, transactions, wholesaling

commercial *adj.* economic, financial, marketable, marketing, mass-produced, materialistic, mercantile, merchandising, monetary, profitable, profit-making, retail, retailing, saleable, sales, trade, trading, wholesale, wholesaling

commission *n.* **1.** agent's fee, agent's percentage, allotment, allowance, bonus, compensation, cut, fee, part, pay, payment, percentage, piece, portion, profit, remuneration, salesperson's fee, salesperson's percentage, share **2.** agency, board, cabinet, chamber, commissioners, committee, congress, consul, council, delegation, embassy, group, legation, legislature, mission, regulatory body **3.** appointment, assignment, authority, berth, business, certificate, charge, consignment, delegation, deputation, diploma, duty, employment, function, instruction, job, legation, license, mandate, mission, obligation, occupation, office, permit, place, position, post, power, power of attorney, proxy, rank, responsibility, sanction, service, station, task, trust, work

commission *v.* accredit, adjure, appoint, assign, authorize, bid, book, charge, charter, command, consign, contract for, decree, delegate, depute, deputize, dictate, employ, empower, enable, endow, engage, enjoin, enlist, entitle, entrust, hire, inaugurate, induct, institute, invest, license, name, nominate, ordain, order, permit, qualify, requisition, retain, select, warrant

commitment *n.* agreement, assurance, certification, committal, covenant, guarantee, liability, obligation, pledge, promise, responsibility, undertaking, vow, warrant, word

committee *n.* advisory group, board, cabinet, chamber, commission, council, deliberative body, detail, group, jury, mission, panel, task force, trustees, working group

commodities *n.* articles, assets, belongings, bulk goods, chattels, goods, items, materials, merchandise, objects, possessions, produce, products, property, resources, staples, stock, things, wares

common sense *n.* discernment, good sense, intelligence, intuition, levelheadedness, native intelligence, practicality, prudence, reasonableness, sense, sound judgment, sound thinking, wisdom

commonsense *adj.* commonsensical, down-to-earth, intelligent, judicious, just, levelheaded, logical, matter-of-fact, practical, prudent, rational, realistic, reasonable, sagacious, sane, sensible, sound, wise

communicate *v.* acquaint, advise, announce, apprise, broadcast, confer, contact, convey, correspond, declare, disclose, disseminate, divulge, enlighten, exchange information, impart, inform, interact, make known, network, notify, pass on, point out, present, proclaim, pronounce, publicize, publish, relate, report, reveal, share, speak, spread, state, suggest, tell, transfer, transmit, voice, write

communication *n.* advice, announcement, articulation, assertion, communion, conversation, correspondence, declaration, disclosure, discourse, discussion, dissemination, elucidation, enunciation, exchange of information, expression, flow, flow of information, information exchange, information flow, information interchange, interchange, interchange of information, intercommunication, mention, notification, pronouncement, publication, revelation, speaking, talk, translation, transmission, writing

communications *n.* advertising, communications system, film, information technology, journalism, magazines, media, news media, the press, publicity, public relations, publishing, radio, telecommunications, television

community *n.* body politic, borough, center, citizenry, commonality, commonwealth, district, general public, hamlet, nation, neighborhood, parish, people, populace, population, public, society, state, town, township, village

commute *v.* **1.** drive, drive back and forth, shuttle, take a bus, take the subway, take a train, travel, travel to work **2.** allay, alleviate, assuage, curtail, decrease, diminish, extenuate, mitigate, modify, mollify, reduce, relieve, remit, shorten, soften

commuter *n.* city worker, daily traveler, driver, regular traveler, suburbanite, traveler

compact *n.* agreement, alliance, arrangement, bargain, bond, concordat, conditions, contract, covenant, deal, engagement, formal agreement, guarantee, indenture, pact, settlement, stipulation, terms, transaction, treaty

compact disk *n.* CD, digital disk, digital recording, disk, laser disk, music disk, optical disk, plastic disk, record, recording, release, text disk

company *n.* **1.** association, business, business organization, concern, conglomerate, corporation, enterprise, establishment, firm, holding company, house, industrial concern, multinational corporation, organization, parent company, partnership, syndicate **2.** boarder, boarders, caller, callers, companionship, diner, diners, fellowship, friendship, guest, guests, invited guest, invited guests, social friend, social friends, visitor, visitors

compartment *n.* alcove, apartment, area, bay, berth, bin, booth, box, cabin, cage, cell, chamber, closet, corner, cubbyhole, cubicle, department, division, drawer, enclosure, hold, locker, niche, nook, part, partition, pew, pigeonhole, place, receptacle, room, roomette, section, slot, stall, subdivision, tray, well

compatibility *n.* affinity, agreeableness, amicability, amity, congeniality, congruity, consonance, cordial relations, harmoniousness, harmony, interworking ability, like-mindedness, rapport, unity

compendium *n.* abbreviation, abridgment, abstract, brief, compilation, condensation, conspectus, digest, discourse, epitome, extract, outline, overview, précis, reduction, résumé, review, sketch, summary, syllabus, symposium, synopsis

compensation *n.* amends, atonement, coverage, damages, expiation, fine, indemnification, indemnity, pay, payment, payoff, recompense, rectification, redress, reimbursement, remuneration, reparation, repayment, reprisal, requital, restitution, retribution, reward, satisfaction, settlement

compete *v.* battle, challenge, clash, collide, combat, contend, contest, encounter, engage, enter, face, fight, go against, meet, oppose, participate in, play, play against, rival, spar, strive, struggle, take part, try, vie

competence *n.* ability, adequacy, adroitness, capability, capableness, competency, effectiveness, efficacy, eligibility, expertise, facility, fitness, knowledgeability, legal fitness, preparedness, proficiency, qualification, readiness, skill, skillfulness, suitability

competent *adj.* adept, adroit, capable, effective, efficient, eligible, expert, fit, knowledgeable, legally fit, prepared, proficient, qualified, ready, skilled, skillful, suitable, trained, wellinformed

competition *n.* athletic event, bout, challenge, clash, conflict, contention, contest, encounter, engagement, fight, game, match, meet, members of the trade, opposition, race, rivalry, struggle, tournament

competitor *n.* aspirant, candidate, challenger, competer, contender, contestant, entrant, fighter, opponent, rival

compilation *n.* accumulation, aggregation, anthology, assemblage, assembly, assortment, collection, collocation, combination, compendium, digest, gathering, thesaurus, translation, treasury

compile *v.* accumulate, amass, anthologize, arrange, assemble, bring together, codify, collate, collect, colligate, collocate, compose, consolidate, draw together, garner, gather, glean, group, group together, marshal, methodize, muster, order, organize, prepare, put together, systematize, unite

complaint *n.* accusation, cavil, charge, condemnation, criticism, demur, denunciation, expostulation, first pleading, grievance, imputation, inculpation, lament, objection, plaintiff's first pleading, preliminary accusation, preliminary charge, protest, protestation, rebuke, remonstrance, remonstration, reprimand, reproach, reprobation

complement *n.* accessory, accompaniment, addition, aggregate, augmentation, balance, companion, completion, correlate, correlative, counterpart, enhancement, filler, final touch, finishing touch, number, remainder, supplement

complete *v.* accomplish, achieve, actualize, bring about, bring to fruition, bring to maturity, carry out, close, complement, conclude, develop, discharge, dispose of, do, effect, effectuate, enact, end, execute, fill, fill in, fill out, finalize, finish, fulfill, furnish, make up, perfect, perform, realize, replenish, round off, round out, settle, supplement, terminate

completion *n.* accomplishing, achieving, bringing about, close, closing, complementing, concluding, conclusion, discharging, doing, effectuating, enacting, end, ending, executing, filling in, filling out, finale, finalization, finalizing, finish, finishing, fulfilling, fulfillment, making up, realization, realizing, replenishment, rounding off, rounding out, settling

complex *n.* **1.** aggregation, association, combination, composite, compound, conglomeration, conglomerate, ensemble, entanglement, network, organization, structure, system, totality **2.** anxiety, delusion, fixation, fixed idea, mania, obsession, preoccupation, psychological problem

compliance *n.* acquiescence, adaptability, agreeableness, amenability, assent, capitulation, complaisance, concession, concurrence, conformity, consent, deference, docility, faithfulness, malleability, obedience, observance, passivity, pliancy, submission, submissiveness, tractability, yielding

complication *n.* complexity, difficult situation, difficulty, dilemma, entanglement, intricacy, obstacle, predicament, problem

compliment *n.* acclaim, acclamation, admiration, adulation, applause, commendation, congratulations, encomium, endorsement, eulogy, exaltation, extolment, flattery, glorification, good word, homage, honor, laudation, ovation, panegyric, praise, respects, tribute, veneration

comply *v.* abide by, accede, accept, accord, acknowledge, acquiesce in, adhere to, agree to, be faithful to, carry out, concur, conform to, consent to, discharge, execute, follow, fulfill, obey, observe, perform, respect, satisfy, submit to, yield

component *n.* allotment, basic part, complement, constituent, detail, division, element, factor, feature, fraction, fragment, fundamental, ingredient, integral part, item, member, module, parcel, part, peripheral, piece, portion, principle, section, segment, share, subdivision, unit

composite *n.* blend, combination, commixture, composition, compound, concoction, conglomerate, conglomeration, consolidation, intermixture, medley, merger, mix, mixture, synthesis, union

composition *n.* **1.** arrangement, arranging, article, book, concerto, creative writing, dissertation, draft, drama, English, essay, exposition, expository writing, grammar, instrumentation, literary technique, literary work, lyricizing, manuscript, melody, music, novel, opus, paper, piece, play, poetry, rhapsody, rhetoric, score, short story, song, songwriting, style, theme, thesis, type selection, typesetting, verse, work, writing **2.** architecture, arrangement, balance, combination, configuration, constitution, content, design, form, formation, framework, layout, makeup, structure, style, symmetry, weave

compound *n.* blend, combination, combo, commixture, composite, composition, concoction, conglomerate, conglomeration, consolidation, intermixture, merger, merging, mix, mixture, synthesis, union

comprehension *n.* apprehension, capacity, grasp, intellect, intelligence, judgment, knowledge, understanding

compromise *n.* accommodation, accord, adjustment, agreement, arrangement, compact, composition, concession, concord, contract, covenant, middle course, middle ground, modification, pact, reconciliation, settlement, tradeoff, treaty, understanding, yielding

compromise *v.* **1.** accommodate, adjust, agree, arbitrate, come to terms, conciliate, make a deal, make concession, meet halfway, modify, negotiate, settle, trade off, yield **2.** discredit, dishonor, embarrass, endanger, expose, hazard, imperil, implicate, jeopardize, prejudice, risk, weaken

compulsory *adj.* binding, compulsive, demanding, enforced, forced, imperative, inescapable, mandatory, necessary, obligatory, prerequisite, required, requisite

computation *n.* adding, addition, arithmetic, calculation, ciphering, computing, counting, enumeration, estimating, estimation, figuring, numeration, summation, summing up, totaling

compute *v.* add, ascertain, calculate, cipher, count, enumerate, estimate, figure, sum, sum up, tally, total

computer *n.* adding machine, analog computer, artificial intelligence, calculating machine, calculator, central processing unit, CPU, data processing machine, data processor, digital computer, mainframe computer, microcomputer, minicomputer, PC, personal computer

concede *v.* abide by, accede, accept, acknowledge, acquiesce, admit, agree, allow, assent, award, be persuaded, capitulate, confess, defer to, give in, give up, grant, hand over, quit, recognize, relinquish, surrender, yield

concentration *n.* **1.** absorption, academic major, application, centralization, close attention, compression, concern, consideration, consolidation, convergence, converging, deliberation, engrossment, focus, focusing, heed, intensification, major field of study, narrowing, strengthening, study **2.** accumulation, agglomeration, aggregation, array, assemblage, assembly, cluster, collection, conglomeration, congregation, convergence, crowd, gathering, group, mass

concept *n.* abstraction, belief, conception, conceptualization, conclusion, conjecture, consideration, conviction, hypothesis, idea, impression, inference, judgment, notion, opinion, perception, postulate, presumption, supposition, theory, thought, view

conception *n.* **1.** abstraction, assumption, belief, comprehension, conceiving, concept, conceptualization, conjecture, conviction, design, draft, explanation, exposition, hypothesis, idea, image, impression, interpretation, mental grasp, notion, opinion, outline, perception, picture, plan, principle, realization, representation, speculation, supposition, thought, understanding, version, view **2.** beginning, birth, commencement, emergence, fertilization, formation, genesis, germination, inauguration, inception, initiation, introduction, origin, origination, outset, source, start

concern *n.* **1.** affair, business, charge, company, corporation, department, difficulty, duty, enterprise, establishment, field, firm, franchise, house, interest, involvement, job, matter, matter of interest, mission, occupation, organization, responsibility, specialty, subject, task **2.** alertness, anxiety, apprehension, attention, care, carefulness, caution, consciousness, consideration, disquietude, distress, heed, heedfulness, interest, mindfulness, prudence, regard, thought, unease, vigilance, wariness, watchfulness, worry

concession *n.* accession, acknowledgment, acquiescence, adjustment, admission, agreement, allowance, assent, authorization, capitulation, compensation, compliance, compromise, conceding, confession, giving in, grant, granting, license, permission, permit, privilege, recognition, right, surrender, tradeoff, warrant, yielding

conclusion *n.* **1.** attainment, cessation, climax, close, closure, completion, culmination, denouement, end, ending, eventuality, finale, finish, fruition, fulfillment, last part, outcome, realization, result, termination **2.** agreement, conviction, corollary, decision, deduction, determination, finding, inference, judgment, opinion, resolution, resolve, sentence, settlement, verdict

concord *n.* **1.** armistice, compact, concordat, contract, convention, covenant, pact, settlement, truce, understanding **2.** accord, affinity, agreement, amity, concert, concordance, concurrence, conformity, congeniality, consensus, consonance, cordial relations, friendship, goodwill, harmony, oneness, peace, rapport, unanimity, understanding, unison, unity

condemnation *n.* accusation, blame, censure, criticism, damnation, denouncement, denunciation, derogation, disapprobation, disapproval, judgment, objurgation, proscription, rebuke, remonstration, reprehension, reprimand, reproach, reprobation, reproof, stricture, vituperation

condensation *n.* **1.** abbreviation, abridgment, abstract, brief, compendium, compression, concentration, consolidation, conspectus, curtailment, digest, epitome, précis, prospectus, reduction, résumé, sketch, summary, syllabus, synopsis **2.** crystallization, dew, distillation, fluidization, liquefaction, precipitation, rainfall

condition *n.* **1.** action, arrangement, article, assumption, clause, codicil, contingency, contingent, demand, essential, exception, hypothesis, limitation, modification, necessity, point, postulate, precondition, premise, prerequisite, provision, proviso, qualification, requirement, requisite, reservation, restriction, rule, stipulation, terms **2.** case, circumstance, class, degree, estate, form, level, mode, order, phase, place, position, posture, predicament, quality, rank, reputation, set of circumstances, shape, situation, stage, standing, state, state of affairs, state of being, station, status

conditional *adj.* contingent, dependent, limited, limiting, modified, provisional, provisionary, provisory, qualified, relative, restricted, restrictive, stipulatory, tentative

conduct *n.* **1.** administration, care, charge, command, control, direction, discharge, engineering, execution, government, guidance, handling, leadership, management, manipulation, operation, orchestration, organization, oversight, performance, regulation, running, superintendence, supervision, treatment **2.** actions, attitude, behavior, comportment, demeanor, deportment, manner, reactions, responses, stance

conference *n.* caucus, colloquium, colloquy, communication, communion, consultation, convention, conversation, council, deliberation, discussion, interchange, meeting, parley, session, talk

confession *n.* acknowledgment, admission, affirmation, allowance, assertion, avowal, concession, declaration, disclosure, divulgence, profession, revelation, statement

confidence *n.* **1.** aplomb, assertiveness, assurance, boldness, brashness, calmness, certainty, coolness, courage, determination, faith in self, fearlessness, fortitude, heart, impudence, nerve, poise, presumption, resoluteness, self-assurance, self-confidence, self-reliance, spirit, stamina, sureness, tenacity **2.** assurance, assuredness, dependence, faith, positiveness, reliance, security, sureness, trust

confidential *adj.* classified, intimate, personal, private, restricted

configure *v.* adjust, arrange, assemble, build, cast, conform, construct, design, figure, form, frame, outline, set up, shape

confirm *v.* acknowledge, affirm, approve, assure, attest, authenticate, aver, back, bear out, certify, corroborate, double-check, endorse, establish, evidence, justify, make sure, prove, ratify, sanction, strengthen, subscribe, substantiate, support, testify, uphold, validate, verify, vouch for, warrant

confirmation *n.* assurance, corroboration, formal memo, providing evidence, ratification, securities transaction details, statement of transaction, transaction details, transaction disclosure

conflict *n.* **1.** animosity, antagonism, antipathy, argument, contention, controversy, difference, disagreement, discord, dispute, dissension, dissent, dissidence, disunity, feud, friction, hostility, ill will, interference, opposition, variance **2.** battle, clash, collision, combat, contest, encounter, engagement, fight, fighting, hostilities, strife, struggle, war, warfare

conform *v.* abide by, accommodate, accord with, acquiesce in, adapt to, adhere to, adjust to, agree to, agree with, assimilate, comply, consent to, correspond, follow, harmonize, integrate, match, obey, observe, reconcile with, submit to, suit, tailor, yield

conformity *n.* **1.** accord, accordance, affinity, agreement, coherence, concord, conformance, congruity, consistency, consonance, correspondence, harmony, likeness, resemblance, similarity, unanimity **2.** acquiescence, allegiance, assent, capitulation, compliance, consent, conventionality, deference, obedience, observance, orthodoxy, resignation, submission, yielding

confront *v.*   accost, affront, assail, assault, attack, brave, challenge, charge, counter, defy, oppose, resist, stand up to, threaten, thwart

confrontation *n.*   assailment, assault, attack, battle, charging, conflict, contest, crisis, counteraction, dispute, encounter, fight, showdown

confusion *n.*   anarchy, bedlam, chaos, clutter, commotion, complexity, complication, disarrangement, disarray, dislocation, disorder, disorganization, disoriented state, disturbance, jumble, mess, pandemonium, riot, trouble, tumult, turbulence, turmoil, untidiness, upheaval, uproar

conglomerate *n.*   agglomerate, agglomeration, aggregate, aggregation, cartel, chain, conglomeration, corporation, group, monopoly, multinational corporation, syndicate, trust

conglomeration *n.*   accumulation, agglomeration, aggregation, amassment, assortment, collection, combination, composite, cumulation, medley, miscellany, potpourri

congratulate *v.*   acclaim, applaud, cheer, compliment, extol, give regards to, laud, praise, rejoice with, toast, wish joy to, wish one well

congratulations *n.*   acknowledgment, best wishes, commendation, compliments, good wishes

congregation *n.*   assemblage, assembly, audience, body, churchgoers, circle, company, crowd, disciples, following, gathering, group, host, meeting, multitude, parishioners, public, throng, troop, troupe

congress *n.*   assemblage, assembly, bloc, caucus, conclave, concourse, conference, convention, convocation, council, delegation, government, house of representatives, legislature, lower house, meeting, parliament, senate, upper house

conjecture *n.*   assumption, conclusion, conviction, guess, hunch, inference, intuition, judgment, notion, opinion, sentiment, speculation, surmise, suspicion, theorizing, thinking, viewpoint

connection *n.*   affiliation, agent, alliance, association, attachment, bond, conjunction, conjuncture, contact, correlation, correspondence, coupling, fastening, hookup, intermediary, interrelation, joining, joint, junction, juncture, link, linkage, network, nexus, relation, relationship, relevance, seam, splice, sponsor, tie, union

connoisseur *n.* aesthete, aficionado, authority, cognoscente, critic, epicure, expert, gourmet, judge, maven, savant, specialist

conscience *n.* ethics, honesty, inner voice, integrity, morals, moral sense, principles, probity, scruples, sense of right and wrong, standards, uprightness

conscientious *adj.* **1.** accurate, attentive, circumspect, correct, critical, dedicated, demanding, detailed, devoted, diligent, discreet, earnest, exact, exacting, faithful, fastidious, fussy, good, hardworking, heedful, judicious, meticulous, mindful, painstaking, particular, precise, proper, prudent, punctual, regardful, rigorous, sincere, strict, thorough, thoughtful, upstanding **2.** conscionable, ethical, honorable, incorruptible, just, moral, pious, principled, righteous, right-minded, scrupulous, upright

consensus *n.* accord, common assent, compliance, concert, concord, concurrence, conformity, consent, consonance, harmony, like-mindedness, oneness, single-mindedness, unanimity, unison, unity

consent *n.* acceptance, accord, acquiescence, agreement, allowance, approbation, approval, assent, authorization, compliance, concession, concurrence, conformity, consensus, endorsement, permission, permit, ratification, sanction

consequence *n.* **1.** aftereffect, aftermath, conclusion, effect, end, event, fallout, follow through, follow-up, implication, issue, outcome, outgrowth, reaction, repercussion, result, reverberation, sequel, sequence, spin-off, upshot, **2.** concern, emphasis, force, gravity, greatness, import, importance, interest, magnitude, merit, momentousness, note, portent, renown, repute, significance, substance, urgency, value, weight

conservation *n.* care, conservancy, conserving, control, custody, guardianship, guarding, keeping, maintenance, management, managing, preservation, preserving, protecting, protection, reservation, safeguarding, safekeeping, saving, supervising, supervision, support, sustentation, upkeep

consider *v.* adjudge, analyze, appraise, bear in mind, contemplate, deem, estimate, gauge, heed, inspect, judge, look at, mull over, note, ponder, rate, reason, regard, respect, scrutinize, speculate, take into account, take into consideration, think over, value, weigh

consideration *n.* **1.** attention, cogitation, consultation, contemplation, deliberation, estimation, examination, forethought, heed, inspection, meditation, mental analysis, notice, observation, premeditation, reflection, regard, review, rumination, scrutiny, speculation, thought   **2.** attentiveness, beneficence, benevolence, compassion, concern, considerateness, esteem, forbearance, friendliness, generosity, high regard, kindheartedness, kindliness, kindness, mercy, mindfulness, patience, respect, solicitude, sympathy, tact, thoughtfulness, tolerance   **3.** commission, compensation, fee, gratuity, inducement, payment, percentage, perquisite, recompense, remuneration, reward, salary, something of value, tip, wage

consign *v.* appoint, assign, authorize, bequeath, commend to, commission, commit to, confide to, convey, delegate, deliver, deposit with, dispatch, entrust, forward, give, hand over, issue, leave to, mail, refer to, relegate, remand, remit, route, send, ship, transfer, transmit, turn over, yield

consignment *n.* assignment, bailment, bequest, commission, delegation, delivery, dispatch, entrusting, handing over, marketing arrangement, relegation, relinquishment, transferral, transmittal

consistent *adj.* **1.** constant, dependable, expected, identical, invariable, regular, same, selfsame, steady, unchanging, undeviating, unfailing, uniform, unvarying   **2.** accordant, agreeable, agreeing, comfortable, compatible, congruous, consonant, harmonious

consolidate *v.* amalgamate, bind, blend, bond, cement, centralize, coalesce, congeal, cohere, combine, concentrate, condense, conjoin, connect, federate, fuse, harden, incorporate, join, league, meld, merge, mix, pool, reinforce, set, solidify, strengthen, syndicate, thicken, tie together, unify, unite

consolidation *n.* amalgamation, association, centralization, coalescence, coalition, coherence, combination, compression, concentration, condensation, confederation, conglomeration, federation, fortification, fusion, incorporation, melding, mergence, merger, merging, reinforcement, solidification, strengthening, syndication, unification, union, unity

constant *adj.* **1.** abiding, consistent, enduring, equable, even, firm, fixed, identical, immutable, invariable, permanent, regular, regularized, same, solid, stable, standardized, steadfast, steady, unalterable, unchanging, uniform, unvarying   **2.** ceaseless, chronic, continual, continuous, endless, enduring, eternal, everlasting, habitual, incessant, interminable, lasting, never-ending, nonstop, perpetual, persistent, persisting, recurrent, relentless, repeated, sustained, unbroken, unceasing, unending, uninterrupted, unrelenting, unremitting **3.** dependable, determined, devoted, faithful, indomitable, loyal, persevering, relentless, reliable, resolute, serious, staunch, steadfast, true, trustworthy, unfailing, unfaltering, unflagging, unshaken, unwavering, unyielding

constituency *n.* body of voters, citizenry, electorate, electors, people, voters, voting public

constitution *n.* body of laws, canon, charter, code, laws, pandect, principles, principles of law, rules, written laws

constraint *n.* captivity, check, confinement, curb, detention, deterrent, hindrance, limitation, obstruction, restraint, restriction

construct *v.* assemble, build, cast, compose, create, design, devise, elevate, erect, establish, fabricate, fashion, forge, form, formulate, frame, invent, make, manufacture, model, mold, produce, put together, put up, raise, sculpture, set up, shape

construction *n.* architecture, arrangement, assembly, building, cast, composition, configuration, constitution, creation, design, edifice, elevation, erecting, erection, fabric, fabricating, fabrication, forging, form, format, formation, forming, formulation, framework, layout, makeup, making, manufacture, molding, production, shaping, structure

consul *n.* agent, attaché, consul general, delegate, emissary, envoy

consulate *n.* consular office, embassy, government office, ministry

consult *v.* ask, ask advice of, call in, compare notes, confer with, consider, deliberate, discuss with, examine, exchange views, hold conference, refer to, regard, respect, seek advice from, seek opinion of, take into account, talk over, talk with, turn to

consultation *n.* asking, communication, conference, consideration, deliberation, discussion, examination, meeting

consumer *n.* buyer, customer, end user, purchaser, shopper, user, vendee

contact *n.* acquaintance, association, communication, connection, meeting, network, reference, referral, touch, union, unity

contact *v.*   approach, be in touch with, call, check with, communicate with, get in touch with, meet, network, notify, reach, relate to, see, seek out, speak to, talk with, telephone, visit, write to

contemplation   *n.*   concentration, consideration, deep thought, deliberation, evaluation, examination, inspection, meditation, observation, planning, pondering, reflection, rumination, scrutiny, speculation, study, surveying, thought, viewing

contemporary *adj.* **1.** current, existent, extant, latest, living, modern, new, present, present-day, recent, state-of-the-art, topical, ultramodern, up-to-date, up-to-the-minute **2.** accompanying, coetaneous, coeval, coexistent, coexisting, coincident, concomitant, concurrent, contemporaneous, parallel, related, simultaneous, synchronal, synchronous

content *n.*   area, bulk, capacity, cargo, compass, density, dimension, freight, load, magnitude, mass, measure, packing, range, shipment, size, space, stuffing, volume

contents *n.*   chapters, components, constituents, details, divisions, episodes, essence, filling, gist, idea, import, ingredients, inside, intent, matter, meaning, movable items, nonattached items, purport, significance, subject, subject matter, subjects, substance, text, theme, topics

contest *n.* **1.** athletic event, challenge, competition, game, match, meet, race, regatta, rivalry, sport, sweepstakes, test, tournament, trial **2.** action, altercation, battle, clash, combat, conflict, controversy, dispute, encounter, engagement, fight, hostilities, skirmish, struggle, war, warfare

context *n.*   background, circumstances, connection, framework, meaning, relation, relationship, situation, subject, substance, text, theme, topic

contingency *n.*   accident, chance, chance happening, chance occurrence, circumstance, crisis, emergency, event, eventuality, exigency, fortuity, happening, incident, juncture, likelihood, occasion, odds, possible occurrence, possibility, predicament, uncertainty

continuation *n.*   addition, appendix, augmentation, continuance, continuity, duration, epilog, extension, furtherance, installment, line, maintenance, perpetuation, persistence, postscript, preservation, production, progression, prolongation, propagation, protraction, sequel, sequence, succession, supplement, sustenance

continue *v.* **1.** abide, advance, be constant, be permanent, be steadfast, carry forward, carry on, endure, extend, follow up, forge ahead, go on, keep at, keep on, keep up, lengthen, linger, live on, maintain, move ahead, outlast, outlive, perpetuate, persevere, persist, preserve, press on, progress, prolong, promote, protract, pursue, remain, rest, retain, run on, stay, stay on, stick to, stick with, survive, sustain, uphold **2.** begin again, begin over, proceed, recapitulate, recommence, reestablish, reinstate, reinstitute, renew, reopen, restart, restore, resume, return to

contract *n.* agreement, alliance, arrangement, bargain, bond, commitment, compact, concordat, convention, covenant, deal, entente, obligation, pact, promise, set of promises, settlement, stipulation, transaction, treaty, understanding

contract *v.* **1.** accept offer, adjust, agree on, agree to, arrange, assume, bargain, circumscribe, come to terms, commit to, consent to, covenant, embark on, engage in, enter into, establish, institute, limit, make a bargain, make offer, make terms, negotiate, pledge, promise, settle, stipulate, take on, undertake, work out **2.** abbreviate, abridge, abstract, compress, concentrate, condense, constrict, curtail, cut, decrease, digest, diminish, edit, epitomize, lessen, make smaller, narrow, reduce, retrench, shorten, subtract, syncopate, synopsize, take in, tighten, trim

contradiction *n.* ambivalence, antithesis, confutation, contrariety, contravention, difference, difference of opinion, disagreement, discrepancy, disparity, incongruity, inconsistency, negation, opposite, opposition, variance

contrast *n.* antithesis, contradiction, contradistinction, contraposition, contrariety, difference, differentiation, disparity, dissimilarity, dissimilitude, distinction, divergence, diversity, incongruousness, inconsistency, inequality, oppositeness, opposition, polarity, polarization, unlikeness, variance, variation

contribute *v.* accommodate, accord, bequeath, bestow, commit, confer, cooperate, dispense, donate, endow, enrich, equip, furnish, give, give away, grant, hand out, help, present, proffer, provide, share, subsidize, supply, tender, will

contribution *n.* alms, benefaction, bestowal, charity, compensation, conferral, donation, endowment, gift, grant, handout, offering, present, presentation, subsidy, supplement

control *n.* **1.** ascendancy, authority, charge, conduct, determination, dictate, dictation, direction, discipline, domination, dominion, force, guidance, influence, jurisdiction, management, manipulation, oversight, power, regimentation, regulation, rule, sovereignty, subjection, subjugation, subordination, superintendence, supervision, supremacy, sway **2.** bar, brake, bridle, check, confinement, constraint, containment, curb, damper, determent, dissuasion, inhibition, interdiction, limitation, prevention, rein, restraint, restriction

control *v.* **1.** administer, administrate, be in charge of, be in control of, boss, command, conduct, dictate, direct, discipline, dominate, exercise control over, govern, guide, handle, have charge of, head, instruct, lead, maintain order, manage, manipulate, order, oversee, preside over, regiment, regulate, reign over, rule over, run, subjugate, superintend, supervise, wield power over **2.** adjust, arrest, block, bridle, check, confine, constrain, contain, curb, dissuade, forbid, harness, hold back, hold in, impede, inhibit, interdict, keep in check, leash, limit, monopolize, prohibit, quell, regulate, rein in, repress, restrain, restrict, stop, subdue, suppress

controversy *n.* altercation, argument, brawl, contention, contestation, debate, difference, difference of opinion, disagreement, disputation, dispute, dissention, embroilment, quarrel, squabble

convention *n.* **1.** assemblage, assembly, caucus, conference, conclave, congregation, congress, convocation, council, gathering, meeting **2.** agreement, arrangement, bargain, compact, concordat, contract, covenant, deal, entente, pact, stipulation, transaction, treaty **3.** accepted procedure, conventionality, custom, etiquette, fashion, form, formality, habit, orthodoxy, practice, propriety, protocol, rule, standard procedure, tradition, understanding, usage

conversation *n.* chat, colloquy, comment, communication, communion, consultation, dialog, discourse, discussion, exchange, expression, interlocution, speech, talk, verbal exchange

conversion *n.* adaptation, alteration, appropriation, change, changeover, exchange, interchange, metamorphosis, modification, mutation, permutation, proselytization, rearrangement, recasting, reconstruction, refashioning, reformation, regeneration, remodeling, reordering, reorganization, reshaping, restyling, substitution, switch, transfer, transference, transfiguration, transformation, translation, transmutation, transposition

convey *v.* **1.** communicate, deliver, disclose, divulge, express, grant, impart, make known, pass on, relate, reveal, send, tell, transmit **2.** bear, bring, carry, channel, conduct, dispatch, ferry, forward, guide, haul, move, pack, send, shift, take, tote, transfer, transmit, transport, truck

conviction *n.* **1.** assurance, certainty, certitude, creed, doctrine, faith, feeling, judgment, persuasion, position, principle, sentiment, tenet, trust, view **2.** adjudication, condemnation, determination of guilt, guilty sentence, judgment, penalty, proof of guilt, punishment, unfavorable verdict

convince *v.* assure, confirm, demonstrate, establish, gain confidence of, induce, overcome, persuade, prove, reassure, refute, satisfy, sway, talk into, win over

cooperate *v.* act in concert, aid, assist, back up, be a party to, befriend, collaborate, combine, comply with, concur, conspire, contribute, go along with, help, join forces, join in, participate, pool resources, share in, take part, unite, uphold, work together

cooperation *n.* accordance, aid, assistance, coaction, collaboration, combined effort, concert, concord, concurrence, coordinated effort, doing business with, harmony, help, helpfulness, interaction, joint action, joint operation, participation, partnership, reciprocity, synergism, synergy, teamwork, unanimity, union, unity

cooperative *adj.* **1.** accommodating, assisting, companionable, helpful, obliging, responsive, supportive **2.** accordant, agreeing, coactive, coadjutant, collaborative, collective, collusive, combined, common, concerted, concurring, coordinated, harmonious, interactive, interdependent, joint, mutual, participating, reciprocal, shared, synergetic, team, unanimous, unified, united

coordinate *v.* adapt, adjust, arrange, balance, classify, correlate, group, harmonize, manage, match, place, rank, regulate, relate, synchronize

coordinates *n.* intersection, location, set of numbers, set of points, set of variables

cope *v.* battle with, carry on, contend with, deal with, dispatch, endure, get along, grapple, handle, live with, manage, struggle, subsist, survive

copy *n.* clone, counterfeit, counterpart, duplication, example, facsimile, forgery, hard copy, image, imitation, impersonation, impression, imprint, likeness, miniature, model, parallel, pattern, photocopy, photograph, photostat, portrait, print, reflection, replica, replication, representation, reprint, reproduction, sample, semblance, simulation, specimen, transcript, Xerox

copy *v.* act like, clone, counterfeit, depict, draw, duplicate, echo, embody, emulate, engrave, engross, epitomize, follow, follow example, forge, illustrate, imitate, impersonate, mimic, mirror, mock, model, parallel, paraphrase, parody, personify, photocopy, photostat, picture, pirate, plagiarize, portray, reflect, repeat, replicate, represent, reproduce, rewrite, simulate, sketch, transcribe, typify

core *n.* center, corpus, crux, essence, essential, focus, germ, gist, heart, importance, kernel, main idea, marrow, middle, midpoint, nub, nucleus, nut, part, pith, quintessence, seed, significance, substance

corollary *n.* conclusion, consequence, culmination, deduction, effect, end, end product, inference, illation, result, upshot

corporation *n.* artificial person, association of shareholders, business, business organization, company, conglomerate, corporate body, enterprise, firm, legal entity, multinational corporation, organization, parent company, syndicate, trust

correct *adj.* **1.** accepted, accurate, appropriate, approved, apt, befitting, established, exact, free-of-error, precise, unerring **2.** acceptable, conforming, conventional, customary, diplomatic, fitting, natural, normal, prescribed, prevailing, proper, routine, seemly, standard, suitable, traditional, usual

correct *v.* adjust, alter, ameliorate, amend, better, change, cure, edit, emend, fix, fix up, improve, make over, make right, meliorate, mend, modify, move down, move up, readjust, reconstruct, rectify, redress, reform, rehabilitate, remedy, remodel, reorganize, repair, restore, revise, set right, set straight, straighten out, touch up

correction *n.* adjustment, alteration, amelioration, amendment, changing, editing, emendation, improvement, indemnification, mending, modification, rectification, redress, remedy, remodeling, repair, reparation, revision, revising, righting

correctness *n.* **1.** accuracy, certainty, definiteness, exactitude, exactness, faultlessness, fidelity, infallibleness, positiveness, preciseness, precision, sureness, unerringness, unfailingness **2.** amenities, appropriateness, aptness, civilities, conventions, customs, decorousness, decorum, etiquette, fitness, graces, order, properness, propriety, seemliness, suitableness, suitability

correlate *v.* agree, associate, bring together, compare, connect, coordinate, correspond, equate, interact, link, parallel, relate mutually

correlation *n.* connection, correspondence, degree of relationship, equating, equivalence, interaction, interconnection, interdependence, interrelation, interrelationship, mutuality, mutual relationship, parallel, reciprocity, relationship

correspond *v.* **1.** answer, exchange letters, reply, respond, send letter, send message, write, write to **2.** agree, balance, coequal, cohere, coincide, compare with, complement, comply, concur, conform, correlate, equal, equate, fit, follow, harmonize, match, parallel, reciprocate, relate, resemble, rival, tally

correspondence *n.* **1.** communication, epistles, exchange, exchange of letters, exchange of messages, letters, mail, memos, messages, missives **2.** accord, agreement, analogy, balance, coequality, coherence, concord, concordance, concurrence, conformity, congruity, consistency, correlation, equilibrium, equivalence, harmony, likeness, mutuality, proportion, reciprocity, resemblance, similarity, symmetry, uniformity

correspondent *n.* communicator, contributor, freelancer, journalist, letter writer, newswriter, reporter

cosmopolitan *adj.* broad-minded, catholic, cultivated, cultured, global, international, liberal, metropolitan, polished, sophisticated, universal, urbane, worldly, worldwide

cost *n.* **1.** amount, asking price, asset, charge, disbursement, expenditure, expense, face value, fare, figure, market price, market value, outlay, payment, price, price paid, price tag, quotation, rate, tariff, toll, valuation, value, worth **2.** damage, detriment, harm, injury, loss, pain, penalty, sacrifice, suffering

cost *v.* **1.** amount to, bring in, come to, command a price, get, require, sell at, sell for, take, yield **2.** damage, do disservice to, exact penalty, harm, hurt, injure, obligate, overburden

council *n.* advisors, advisory board, assembly, board, board of directors, cabinet, caucus, committee, conclave, conference, congregation, congress, convention, convocation, directorate, directors, gathering, governing body, meeting, ministry, study group, synod, task force, trustees

counsel *n.* **1.** advisor, advocate, attorney, barrister, counselor, lawyer, legal advisor, legal representative, solicitor, trial lawyer   **2.** admonition, advice, advisement, caution, consideration, consultation, deliberation, direction, guidance, instruction, opinion, recommendation, suggestion, teaching, warning

counsel *v.*   admonish, advise, advocate, caution, direct, exhort, give advice, guide, inform, instruct, offer opinion, persuade, prescribe, recommend, suggest, teach, urge, warn

counselor *n.*   advisor, advocate, attorney, coach, confidant, counsel, guidance counselor, guide, instructor, lawyer, legal advisor, legal representative, mentor, solicitor, teacher, trial lawyer, tutor

count *n.*   aggregate, calculation, computation, counting, enumeration, lot, number, numbering, numeration, sum, tally, tallying, total, whole

count *v.*   **1.** add, add up, calculate, compute, count off, enumerate, estimate, figure, list, name, number, numerate, score, sum, tally, total   **2.** number among, take into account, take into consideration,   **3.** carry weight, have importance, have worth, matter, rate, weigh

counteract *v.*   act against, check, contradict, contravene, counterbalance, countercheck, countervail, cross, defeat, foil, frustrate, go against, halt, hinder, impede, interfere with, invalidate, negate, neutralize, nullify, obstruct, offset, oppose, repress, resist, restrain, run counter to, thwart, traverse, undo

counterbalance *v.*   balance, compensate, counteract, counterpoise, countervail, equalize, equilibrate, make up for, neutralize, offset, offset an action, undo

countermand *v.*   abolish, abrogate, annul, cancel, discharge, disenact, disestablish, invalidate, nullify, override, overrule, recall, repeal, rescind, retract, reverse, revoke, set aside, take back, void, withdraw

counterpart *n.*   alternate, analog, close copy, close imitation, close match, coequal, complement, copy, correlate, correlative, correspondent part, corresponding part, double, duplication, duplicate, equal, equivalent, identical thing, look-alike, parallel, peer, pendant, supplement, twin, two of a kind

country *n.*   **1.** area, citizenry, citizens, city-state, commonwealth, community, confederation, constituents, district, electors, grass roots, homeland, inhabitants, kingdom, land, nation, nation-state, native land, people, place, political territory, populace, public, realm, region, residents, society, sovereign state, state, terrain, territory, union, voters **2.** back country, backwoods, countryside, farmland, forests, frontier, hinterland, outback, outdoors, province, rural area, wilderness, wilds, woodlands, woods

coup *n.* accomplishment, achievement, action, deed, exploit, feat, overthrow, plot, revolution, stratagem, stunt, successful maneuver

coupon *n.* advertisement, certificate, credit slip, detachable certificate, detachable part, detachable slip, discount, negotiable certificate, order blank, premium certificate, redemption slip, slip, voucher

courage *n.* audaciousness, audacity, backbone, boldness, bravado, braveness, bravery, chivalry, daring, dash, dauntlessness, determination, endurance, fearlessness, firmness, fortitude, gallantry, heroism, intrepidity, intrepidness, lionheartedness, mettle, panache, prowess, resoluteness, resolution, spirit, steadfastness, stoutheartedness, tenacity, valiancy, valor, valorousness, will

courier *n.* bearer, carrier, emissary, envoy, herald, legate, letter carrier, mail carrier, messenger, nuncio, porter, rider, runner

courtesy *n.* affability, amenities, amiability, ceremony, chivalry, civility, cordiality, correctness, courteousness, courtliness, cultivation, decorousness, decorum, deference, diplomacy, friendliness, gallantry, geniality, gentility, gentleness, good behavior, good breeding, good manners, graciousness, kindness, manners, politeness, properness, propriety, protocol, refinement, respect, respectfulness, social graces, social procedures, suavity, tact, thoughtfulness, urbanity

covenant *n.* agreement, alliance, arrangement, bargain, bond, commitment, compact, concordat, contract, convention, deal, deed, entente, guarantee, guaranty, incidental promise, lease, obligation, pact, pledge, promise, settlement, transaction, treaty, understanding, warrant, warranty, word, written agreement

cover *n.* **1.** binding, blanket, canopy, cap, case, ceiling, cloak, coating, covering, curtain, dome, envelope, film, front, hood, jacket, lid, mantle, mask, overhead, overlay, roof, screen, seal, shade, sheath, sheet, shroud, tarp, tent, top, umbrella, veil, wrapper, wrap, wrapping **2.** camouflage, cover-up, disguise, facade, false front, feigning, guise, masquerade, pretense, smoke screen   **3.** asylum, blind, concealment, covert, den, harbor, haven, lair, protection, refuge, retreat, safety, sanctuary, security, shelter

craft *n.*   **1.** ability, adeptness, adroitness, aptitude, art, artistry, career, dexterity, expertise, expertness, facility, flair, handicraft, ingenuity, knack, know-how, occupation, profession, proficiency, pursuit, skill, skillfulness, talent, technique, trade, vocation, work, workmanship   **2.** aircraft, airplane, barge, boat, plane, ship, spacecraft, vehicle, vessel, watercraft

craftsperson *n.*   artisan, artist, handicrafter, machinist, manufacturer, mechanic, skilled worker, specialist, technician

crash *v.*   become inoperable, bump into, collapse, collide with, crash-land, drive into, fail, fall, give way, overturn, plunge, run into, smash into, splash down, topple

create *v.*   actualize, appoint, bring about, bring into being, bring into existence, bring to life, build, coin, compose, conceive, constitute, construct, contrive, define database fields, design, develop, devise, dream up, engender, erect, establish, fabricate, fashion, forge, form, formulate, found, frame, generate, imagine, initiate, innovate, institute, invent, invest, launch, make, make a file, mold, open a file, originate, plan, procreate, produce, set up, shape, start

creation *n.*   **1.** beginning, conception, constitution, construction, development, engendering, establishment, fabrication, formation, formulation, foundation, generation, genesis, inception, innovation, institution, origination, procreation, production, realization, setting up   **2.** achievement, brainchild, concept, concoction, dream, handiwork, invention, plan, production, vision, work

creative *adj.*   accomplished, adept, adroit, artistic, clever, fertile, gifted, imaginative, ingenious, innovative, inspired, inventive, original, prolific, resourceful, skilled, talented, visionary

credentials *n.*   attestation, authorization, certificate, deed, degree, diploma, document, documentation, endorsement, license, passport, permit, record, references, testament, testimonial, title, visa, voucher, warrant

credit *n.*   **1.** ability to borrow, ability to pay, accounting entry, adjustment, balance, credit line, debt, deduction from balance due, deferred payment, extension, financial worthiness, installment buying, installment plan, lien, loan, money receivable, money received, payment terms, purchase on account, surplus cash, tax offset   **2.** acclaim, acknowledgment, approval, commendation, confidence, credence, distinction, merit, notice, praise, recognition, regard, tribute, trust

credit *v.* **1.** enter, post, record **2.** accept, believe, consider, deem, depend on, feel, have faith in, hold, put confidence in, put trust in, rely on, sense, think, trust **3.** accredit, accuse, ascribe to, assign to, attribute to, blame, charge to, charge with, refer to

creed *n.* articles of faith, axiom, belief, canon, catechism, conviction, doctrine, dogma, faith, formula, ideology, maxim, persuasion, principles, rule, teaching, tenet, theorem

crest *n.* **1.** acme, apex, apogee, climax, crown, culmination, head, heights, highest point, meridian, mountain top, peak, pinnacle, ridge, summit, top, vertex, zenith **2.** arms, badge, bearing, charge, device, emblem, insignia

crew *n.* assemblage, company, congregation, corps, crowd, group, party, squad, team, troop, troupe, workers

crisis *n.* calamity, catastrophe, climax, confrontation, conjuncture, critical situation, crossroads, deadlock, difficulty, dilemma, disaster, emergency, entanglement, exigency, extremity, imbroglio, impasse, juncture, mess, pass, plight, point of no return, predicament, quandary, strait, trouble, turning point, zero hour

criterion *n.* archetype, barometer, benchmark, canon, classic example, code, example, exemplar, gauge, guide, guideline, law, lead, maxim, measure, model, norm, original, paradigm, pattern, point of comparison, precedent, prototype, rule, scale, standard, test, touchstone, type, yardstick

critic *n.* **1.** analyst, analyzer, arbiter, authority, caricaturist, censor, commentator, connoisseur, editorialist, essayist, evaluator, expert, expositor, expounder, interpreter, judge, maven, pundit, reviewer, savant, specialist **2.** attacker, belittler, blamer, carper, caviler, censurer, complainer, detractor, faultfinder, maligner, quibbler, scolder, vilifier

criticism *n.* **1.** analysis, appraisal, appreciation, assessment, commentary, critique, elucidation, essay, estimation, evaluation, examination, exposition, interpretation, judgment, observation, opinion, review, study **2.** aspersion, carping, caviling, censoriousness, censure, condemnation, critical remarks, denunciation, derogation, disaccord, disagreement, disapproval, disparagement, faultfinding, objection, quibbling, reproach, reproof, stricture, vitriol

criticize *v.* **1.** adjudge, analyze, appraise, assess, comment on, estimate, evaluate, examine, give opinion on, interpret, judge, pass judgment on, review, scrutinize, study, survey **2.** attack, berate, blame, castigate, censure, chastise, condemn, denounce, disapprove, disparage, frown upon, judge as bad, malign, pan, reprehend, reprimand, reproach, reprobate, reprove, take offense, vilify

critique *n.* analysis, appraisal, article, assessment, commentary, critical notice, criticism, editorial, essay, examination, exegesis, exposition, judgment, notice, report, review, study

cross-examine *v.* ask questions, catechize, check out, cross-question, examine, examine closely, explore thoroughly, grill, interrogate, investigate, probe, pump, question, quiz, scrutinize

crowd *n.* army, assemblage, assembly, audience, body, circle, cluster, company, concentration, concourse, confluence, congregation, coterie, crew, deluge, drove, fans, gathering, group, host, house, jam, mass, mob, multitude, party, people, populace, public, press, set, spectators, swarm, team, throng, troop, troupe, viewers, watchers

crucial *adj.* acute, all-important, central, climactic, compelling, critical, deciding, decisive, demanding, determining, essential, eventful, exigent, high-priority, imperative, important, major, momentous, necessary, pivotal, pressing, profound, serious, severe, urgent, vital

crusade *n.* campaign, cause, drive, expedition, march, movement, push, struggle

crux *n.* body, central point, critical point, core, decisive point, essence, gist, heart, insoluble problem, kernel, nub, pith, purport, puzzling problem, substance, thrust

cue *n.* catchword, clue, hint, implication, indication, innuendo, insinuation, intimation, key, key word, nod, pointer, prompt, prompting, reminder, sign, signal, suggestion, tip, warning

cull *v.* choose, extract, glean, pick out, pick over, pluck, select, separate, sift, single out, sort out, take out, thin out, winnow

culmination *n.* acme, apex, apogee, cap, capstone, climax, closing, completion, consummation, crest, crown, crowning touch, ending, finale, finish, heights, high point, keystone, limit, maximum, meridian, peak, perfection, pinnacle, point, spire, summit, supreme moment, termination, tip, top, zenith, vertex

culpable *adj.* answerable, blamable, blameworthy, censurable, guilty, impeachable, indictable, liable, punishable, reprehensible, reproachable, reprovable, responsible, transgressive, wrong

cultivate *v.* **1.** abet, advance, aid, assist, back, better, cherish, civilize, develop, devote to, discipline, educate, elevate, encourage, enlighten, enrich, finish, foster, further, help, improve, instruct, nourish, nurse, nurture, patronize, perfect, polish, promote, pursue, refine, school, support, take care of, teach, train, uphold **2.** dress, farm, fertilize, harrow, hoe, plant, plow, prepare, rake, spade, tend, till, work, work the land

cultivation *n.* **1.** abetment, advancement, advocacy, aid, assistance, backing, breeding, civility, culture, development, discernment, discretion, discrimination, education, encouragement, enlightenment, following, fostering, furtherance, gentility, good taste, help, improvement, learning, manners, nurture, patronage, polish, progress, promotion, pursuit, refined taste, refinement, schooling, sophistication, study, support, tact, taste **2.** agronomy, aquaculture, aquiculture, farming, gardening, geoponics, horticulture, husbandry, hydroponics, planting, plowing, tillage, tilling, working the land

culture *n.* **1.** civilization, conventions, customs, ethnology, folkways, habits, knowledge, life-style, mores, society, the arts, values, way of life, ways **2.** accomplishment, advancement, art, breeding, civility, civilization, cultivation, delicacy, discernment, discrimination, edification, education, elegance, elevation, enlightenment, erudition, fashion, gentility, good taste, grace, knowledge, learning, manners, nobility, polish, politeness, refinement, sophistication, taste, training, urbanity, worldliness

cumulative *adj.* accruing, accumulative, additive, aggregate, amassed, collective, growing, increasing, multiplying

curb *v.* bridle, contain, control, deny, hamper, hinder, hold back, hold down, impede, inhibit, leash, moderate, refrain, rein in, retard, shackle, subdue, suppress, withhold

curiosity *n.* **1.** inquiring mind, inquisitiveness, interference, intrusiveness, meddlesomeness, meddling, mental acquisitiveness, nosiness, officiousness, prying, questioning, searching, studying, thirst for knowledge **2.** anomaly, conversation piece, curio, knickknack, marvel, novelty, oddity, peculiar object, phenomenon, prodigy, rarity, singular object, spectacle, unusual object, wonder

curious *adj.* **1.** examining, inquiring, inquisitive, interfering, interrogative, intruding, intrusive, investigative, meddlesome, meddling, nosy, obtrusive, officious, peeping, peering, prying, questioning, scrutinizing, searching, studying   **2.** bizarre, erratic, funny, grotesque, mysterious, odd, offbeat, peculiar, puzzling, quizzical, strange, weird

currency *n.*   bank notes, bills, cash, coinage, coins, folding money, legal tender, medium of exchange, money, notes, paper money, specie

current *n.*   air current, alternating current, course, crosscurrent, direct current, downdraft, draft, drift, electricity, flow, flux, jet stream, progression, stream, tidal motion, tide, undercurrent, updraft, wind

current *adj.*   accepted, circulating, coexistent, common, contemporaneous, contemporary, customary, existent, extant, fashionable, immediate, imminent, instant, modern, occurring, ongoing, popular, present, present-day, prevailing, prevalent, ruling, simultaneous, state-of-the-art, synchronous, trendy, up-to-date, widespread

cursory *adj.*   brief, careless, casual, desultory, discursive, ephemeral, fast, fleeting, hasty, hurried, loose, offhand, passing, perfunctory, quick, random, rapid, shallow, short, sketchy, slight, speedy, summary, superficial, swift, transient, uncritical

curt *adj.*   abbreviated, abrupt, blunt, brief, brusque, compendious, concise, crusty, gruff, impolite, laconic, offhand, petulant, pithy, rude, short, succinct, summary, tart, terse, unceremonious, uncivil, ungracious

curve *n.*   arc, arch, bend, bow, camber, circle, circuit, compass, concavity, contour, crescent, curvature, ellipse, half-moon, horseshoe, incurvation, incurvature, loop, meniscus, parabola, turn, vault

curve *v.*   arch, bend, bow, bulge, coil, crook, curl, hook, incurve, inflect, loop, spiral, swerve, turn, wind

custodian *n.*   cleaner, cleaning person, concierge, conservator, curator, defender, director, guard, guardian, janitor, keeper, maintenance person, manager, overseer, preserver, protector, security guard, steward, superintendent, supervisor, warden, watchdog

custody *n.*   care, guarding, inspection, keeping, maintenance, management, preservation, security, watching over

custom *n.* addiction, characteristic, fashion, form, habit, habitude, manner, mode, observance, policy, practice, praxis, procedure, routine, rule, usage, use, way

customary *adj.* accepted, accustomed, common, commonplace, confirmed, conventional, daily, established, everyday, familiar, favorite, fixed, frequent, general, habitual, natural, normal, ordinary, orthodox, popular, prevailing, prevalent, recognized, regular, routine, set, standard, traditional, universal, usual, well-known

customer *n.* buyer, client, clientele, consumer, patron, purchaser, shopper, vendee

customs *n.* canon, ceremonies, conventions, established way, etiquette, formalities, mores, observances, practices, precedents, precepts, rites, rituals, social system, traditions, unwritten laws, unwritten rules, usage, use, way, ways

cut *v.* **1.** abate, abbreviate, abridge, abstract, clip, condense, contract, crop, curtail, cut back, cut down, decrease, delete, diminish, edit out, eliminate, epitomize, excise, lessen, lower, mark down, pare, précis, reduce, shorten, summarize, trim **2.** amputate, bisect, carve, chop, cleave, crop, dice, dismember, dissect, divide, incise, intersect, lacerate, lance, lay open, notch, perforate, pierce, rend, saw, score, sever, shear, slice, slit, split, transect

cutback *n.* curtailment, cut, decrease, lessening, reduction, retrenchment, reversal, shortening

cut back *v.* abate, abbreviate, abridge, clip, condense, contract, curb, curtail, cut, cut down, decrease, diminish, economize, edit, eliminate, lessen, lower, mark down, mark off, reduce, retrench, shorten, summarize, trim

cycle *n.* **1.** course, interval, loop, orbit, periodic sequence, phase, revolution, rotation, round, run, sequence, series, succession, wheel **2.** aeon, age, eon, epoch, era, period

cynical *adj.* contemptuous, critical, derisive, disbelieving, disdainful, disparaging, distrustful, doubtful, doubting, faultfinding, ironic, misanthropic, mocking, negative, nonbelieving, pessimistic, ridiculing, sarcastic, sardonic, satirical, scornful, skeptical, suspicious, unbelieving, wry

D

daily *adj.* circadian, common, commonplace, customary, cyclical, day-by-day, day-to-day, diurnal, everyday, habitual, once-a-day, once-daily, ordinary, per diem, quotidian, regular, routine, usual

damage *n.* **1.** accident, blow, bruise, casualty, catastrophe, destruction, devastation, evil, hardship, harm, hurt, impairment, infliction, injury, loss, mischief, mishap, outrage, ruin, suffering, wound, wreckage, wrong **2.** blemish, blight, breakage, contamination, corrosion, debasement, defacement, defilement, deterioration, dilapidation, disintegration, disrepair, erosion, marring, mutilation, pollution, ravage, scar, scratch, spoilage, vandalism, wear and tear

damage *v.* abuse, blight, break, cause injury, cause loss, contaminate, corrupt, cripple, deal blow to, debase, defile, despoil, harm, hurt, impair, incapacitate, injure, maim, pollute, ruin, spoil, stain, taint, tamper with, tarnish, wound, wreck, wrong

damages *n.* bill, charge, compensation, cost, expense, fine, indemnity, loss, loss of value, monetary compensation, penalty, recompense, recoverable money, reimbursement, reparation, satisfaction

danger *n.* endangerment, hazard, insecurity, instability, jeopardy, liability, menace, peril, pitfall, precariousness, risk, susceptibility, threat, vulnerability

dangerous *adj.* alarming, deadly, exposed, formidable, hazardous, impending, insecure, looming, menacing, ominous, perilous, portentous, precarious, shaky, terrible, threatening, treacherous, unhealthy, unsafe, unsound, unstable, vulnerable

data *n.* abstracts, assumptions, compilations, conclusions, details, documents, dossier, evidence, facts, factual information, figures, graphic representation, grounds, information, input, materials, measurements, memos, notes, papers, premises, proof, reports, results, statistics, textual representation, unprocessed information

databank *n.* See **database**

database *n.* collection of data, computer data, databank, data collection, data library, file, hierarchical database, large file, organized collection, relational database, set of data, set of facts

date *n.* **1.** age, century, day, decade, duration, eon, epoch, era, generation, interval, month, period, quarter, semester, space, span, spell, term, time, year   **2.** appointment, assignation, engagement, interview, meeting, rendezvous, social engagement, visit

date *v.* **1.** affix date to, assign date to, assign time, carbondate, chronicle, come from, determine date of, fix date of, fix period of, originate in, record date, register date   **2.** antiquate, become obsolete, be dated, obsolesce, put out of use, show age

dawn *n.* **1.** advent, alpha, appearance, arrival, awakening, beginning, birth, commencement, emergence, foundation, genesis, inauguration, inception, initiation, nascency, onset, opening, origin, outset, rise, source, start, unfolding   **2.** aurora, beginning of day, break of day, dawning, daybreak, daylight, early light, first light, sunrise, sunup

day *n.* daylight, daytime, full sun, light of day, mean solar day, solar day, sunlight, sunshine, 24 hours, working day **2.** age, ascendancy, cycle, epoch, era, generation, height, period, prime, time, zenith

dead *adj.* **1.** arid, barren, defunct, depleted, dormant, exhausted, extinct, fruitless, impoverished, inactive, inert, infertile, inoperable, inoperative, lost, obsolete, spent, stagnant, stationary, sterile, still, unemployed, unproductive, unprofitable, unyielding, used up, useless, worn-out   **2.** cadaverous, deceased, defunct, departed, erased, expired, extinct, late, perished, spiritless

deadlock *n.* blockage, cessation, checkmate, dead end, dilemma, draw, gridlock, halt, impasse, pause, stalemate, standoff, standstill, stoppage, tie

deal *n.* **1.** accord, agreement, arrangement, bargain, business transaction, compact, compromise, concordat, contract, dealings, negotiation, pact, transaction, understanding, negotiation   **2.** amount, degree, distribution, extent, lot, portion, quantity, share, uncertain amount

deal with *v.* arrange with, bargain with, call on, come to terms with, do business with, exchange with, negotiate with, sell to, swap with, trade with, work out deal with

dealer *n.* banker, business owner, businessperson, marketer, merchandiser, merchant, retailer, trader, tradesperson, vendor, wholesaler

dealings *n.* affairs, business, business relations, buying and selling, commerce, exchange, management, negotiation, practice, proceedings, relations, trade, traffic, transactions

debacle *n.* breakdown, breakup, catastrophe, collapse, devastation, disaster, disintegration, dispersion, disruption, dissolution, downfall, failure, fiasco, havoc, overthrow, ruin, ruination, trouncing, tumult, turmoil, wreck

debase *v.* **1.** admix, adulterate, alloy, contaminate, defile, dilute, mar, mix, pervert, pollute, spoil, taint, thin, weaken **2.** belittle, cheapen, debauch, debilitate, degrade, demean, demoralize, demote, depose, deprecate, depreciate, depress, deteriorate, devaluate, devalue, disable, discredit, disgrace, dishonor, disparage, humble, humiliate, impair, lower, mortify, reduce, shame, undermine, vitiate, weaken

debate *n.* argument, argumentation, careful thought, cogitation, competition, contemplation, contention, contest, controversy, deliberation, difference of opinion, disputation, dispute, dissention, heated argument, meditation, polemic, reflection, variance, verbal controversy

debate *v.* bandy words, compete, consider, contend, deliberate, differ, discuss, dispute, dissent, meditate, reason, reflect, think carefully

debris *n.* detritus, dregs, dross, flotsam, fragments, garbage, jetsam, junk, litter, refuse, remains, rubbish, rubble, ruins, trash, waste, wreckage

debt *n.* account, accountability, amount owed, answerability, arrears, claim, financial commitment, debit, deficit, encumbrance, financial obligation, indebtedness, legal obligation, liability, money owed, note, obligation, promissory note, responsibility, services owed

debug *v.* correct error, detect error, eliminate malfunction, eliminate problem, locate error, remove device, remove error, remove problem

debut *n.* beginning, coming out, entrance, first appearance, first attempt, first step, inauguration, initial performance, initiation, introduction, launching, opener, premiere, trial, undertaking

deceive *v.* be dishonest, cheat, delude, dupe, fool, lead on, misguide, misinform, mislead, take advantage of, trick, victimize

decent *adj.* **1.** appropriate, becoming, befitting, conforming, correct, decorous, dependable, dignified, ethical, fitting, good, honest, honorable, mannerly, moral, polite, presentable, proper, respectable, right, seemly, suitable, tasteful, trustworthy, upright, virtuous, worthy   **2.** acceptable, adequate, average, common, fair, fairly good, mediocre, moderate, moderately good, ordinary, passable, reasonable, satisfactory, sufficient, sufficing, tolerable, unobjectionable

deception *n.* cheating, circumvention, cunning, deceit, deceitfulness, deceptiveness, dishonesty, dissimulation, duplicity, falseness, fraud, fraudulence, guile, hypocrisy, illusion, insincerity, pretense, slyness, trickery, trickiness, untruthfulness, wiliness

decide *v.* adjudge, adjudicate, agree to, arbitrate, arrange terms, arrive at conclusion, award, choose, come to agreement, come to conclusion, come to decision, commit to, conclude, consider, determine, draw conclusion, establish, evaluate, form opinion, judge, make decision, make determination, make up mind, mediate, opt for, order, pick, pronounce judgment, reach conclusion, reach decision, referee, resolve, rule, select, settle, surmise, take stand, umpire, weigh

decipher *v.* break down, cipher, construe, decode, deduce, disentangle, explain, figure out, interpret, make clear, make out, read, render, solve, spell out, translate, understand, unravel, work out

decision *n.* accommodation, accord, adjudication, adjustment, agreement, arbitration, arrangement, choice, compromise, conclusion, determination, finding, judgment, opinion, outcome, resolution, result, ruling, selection, sentence, settlement, understanding, verdict

decisive *adj.* absolute, assured, categorical, certain, conclusive, decided, definite, definitive, determined, emphatic, final, firm, imperative, incisive, positive, resolute, settled, unconditional, unqualified

declaration *n.* **1.** affidavit, announcement, bulletin, constitution, credo, creed, edict, formal notice, formal statement, indictment, manifesto, notification, official proclamation, official statement, proclamation, promulgation, pronouncement, resolution **2.** acknowledgment, admission, affirmation, allegation, assertion, attestation, averment, avowal, deposition, disclosure, enunciation, explanation, exposition, formal pleading, oath, presentation, profession, protestation, publication, revelation, statement, testimony

declare *v.* acknowledge, admit, affirm, announce, annunciate, assert, attest, aver, avow, broadcast, certify, claim, confess, confirm, convey, decree, disclose, divulge, enunciate, impart, indicate, inform, insist, maintain, manifest, notify, proclaim, profess, promulgate, pronounce, propound, publish, reaffirm, reassert, repeat, represent, reveal, show, state, stress, swear, testify, validate, vouch

decline *n.* abatement, comedown, declivity, decrease, degeneracy, degeneration, depression, descent, deterioration, devolution, diminution, dip, downfall, downgrade, downslide, downswing, downtrend, downturn, drop, drop-off, dwindling, ebb, ebbing, failing, failure, fall, falling off, fall-off, incline, lapse, lessening, loss, lowering, plunge, recession, relapse, slide, slope, slump, wane, waning, weakening, worsening

decline *v.* **1.** abstain from, avoid, balk, bypass, demur, deny, desist, dismiss, dissent, do without, forbear, frown on, pass on, protest, rebuff, refrain from, refuse, reject, renounce, repel, repudiate, resist, say no, send regrets, shun, spurn, turn down, veto, withhold consent **2.** abate, approach end, become less, contract, decay, decrease, degenerate, depreciate, deteriorate, die, die out, diminish, disintegrate, droop, dwindle, ebb, fade away, fail, fall, fall off, flag, languish, lapse, lessen, let up, lose value, lower, recede, relapse, return, revert, shrink, sink, slide, subside, taper off, vanish, wane, weaken, wither, worsen **3.** bend down, depress, descend, dip, droop, drop off, fall, go down, incline, lean, lower, sag, set, settle, sink, slant, slope, tilt, turn down

decode *v.* convert, determine meaning, interpret, restore, reverse, translate

decorate *v.* **1.** adorn, beautify, color, dress up, embellish, enhance, enrich, fix up, furbish, garnish, gild, illuminate, ornament, paint, renovate, trim **2.** cite, do honor, give medal, honor, pay honor to, pin medal on

decoration *n.* **1.** adornment, beautification, beautifying, elaboration, embellishment, enhancement, enrichment, flounce, flourish, frill, furbelow, garnish, garnishing, garnishment, illumination, ornament, ornamentation, redecoration, spangle, tinsel, trimming **2.** award, badge, citation, colors, cordon, cross, distinction, emblem, garter, laurels, medal, order, ribbon, sash, star, wreath

decorum *n.* appropriate behavior, appropriateness, best behavior, breeding, civility, conduct, conformity, correctness, decency, demeanor, deportment, dignity, etiquette, form, gentility, good form, good manners, habits, mannerliness, order, orderliness, politeness, properness, propriety, protocol, respectability, sedateness, seemliness, suitability, suitableness, tact

decrease *n.* abatement, abbreviation, abridgment, compression, condensation, constriction, contraction, curtailment, cutback, declension, decline, declining, deescalation, depression, diminishing, diminution, discount, downturn, drop-off, dwindling, ebb, falling off, lessening, loss, narrowing, recession, reduction, retrenchment, shortening, shrinkage, sinking, slowdown, subsidence, waning, wasting away, weakening, wearing away

decrease *v.* abate, abbreviate, abridge, check, clip, compress, condense, constrict, contract, crop, curb, curtail, cut, cut down, cut short, decline, deescalate, depreciate, devaluate, die down, die out, diminish, dock, drop, drop off, dwindle, ease, ebb, evaporate, fade, fall off, grow less, lessen, let up, lighten, lop, lower, make less, narrow down, pare, prune, quell, recede, reduce, restrain, scale down, shorten, shrink, sink, slacken, slack off, slow down, subside, taper off, wane, weaken, wear away, wear down, wind down, wither

dedicate *v.* **1.** address, assign, commit, consign, devote, donate, give, inscribe, name, offer, pledge, preface, surrender **2.** anoint, bless, consecrate, deify, enshrine, hallow, make holy, sanctify, set apart

dedicated *adj.* committed, devoted, programmed, purposeful, reserved, single-hearted, single-minded, single-use, special-purpose, tailored, wholehearted, zealous

dedication *n.* **1.** adherence, allegiance, commitment, devotedness, devotion, faithfulness, fealty, fidelity, loyalty, single-mindedness, wholeheartedness **2.** address, celebration, consecration, enshrinement, glorification, hallowing, inscription, message, ordination, preface, sanctification, speech

deduction *n.* **1.** adjustment, allowance, cut, cutback, decrease, discount, excision, markdown, rebate, refund, removal, rollback, subtraction, withdrawal, write-off **2.** assumption, conclusion, consequence, corollary, derivation, finding, inference, judgment, ratiocination, reasoning, result, understanding

deed *n.* **1.** agreement, certificate, charter, compact, contract, conveyance, covenant, instrument, legal document, legal instrument, legal paper, property record, property transfer, transaction, warranty **2.** act, action, adventure, commission, enterprise, execution, exploit, feat, job, performance, plan, proceeding, project, quest, stunt, task, undertaking, work

deface *v.* blemish, cancel, cross out, damage, deform, delete, destroy, disfigure, efface, eradicate, erase, expunge, harm, impair, injure, mar, mutilate, obliterate, ruin, scratch, spoil, strike out, trash, vandalize, wreck

de facto *adv.* actually, genuinely, practically, really, tangibly, truly, veritably

defamation *n.* abuse, aspersion, calumny, censure, character assassination, denigration, detraction, disparagement, false accusation, falsehood, imputation, injurious statement, injury, innuendo, insinuation, libel, lie, maliciousness, misrepresentation, opprobrium, scandal, slander, slur, smear, vilification, vituperation

defamatory *adj.* abusive, calumnious, contumelious, defiling, denigrating, derogatory, disparaging, false, imputative, injurious, insulting, maliciously false, maligning, misrepresentative, opprobrious, untrue, vilifying, vituperative

defame *v.* abuse, accuse falsely, asperse, belie, blemish, calumniate, cast aspersions on, denigrate, discredit, disgrace, dishonor, disparage, falsify, impute, injure, insinuate, insult, libel, malign, misrepresent, scandalize, slander, smear, stigmatize, traduce, vilify, vituperate

default *n.* **1.** absence, deficiency, delinquency, dereliction, disregard, failure, fault, forfeiture, inadequacy, insufficiency, lack, lapse, neglect, nonfeasance, nonfulfillment, nonpayment, nonperformance, nonremittance, omission, oversight, shortage, shortcoming **2.** automatic setting, computer assumption, computer setting, preassigned option, preassigned parameter, preassigned value, preset choice, preset value, prespecified value

default *v.* be negligent, bilk, cheat, decline to pay, dishonor, dodge payment, evade payment, fail to pay, forfeit, lapse, neglect to pay, refuse bill, refuse charge

defeat *n.* annihilation, beating, breakdown, collapse, conquest, destruction, disappointment, discomfiture, downfall, failure, fall, frustration, loss, overthrow, rebuff, reversal, ruin, setback, subjugation, thwarting, upset, vanquishment

defeat *v.* annihilate, arrest, bar, beat, block, check, conquer, control, crush, demolish, discomfit, entrap, foil, halt, hinder, impede, obliterate, obstruct, oppress, outmaneuver, outsmart, overcome, overpower, overthrow, overwhelm, prevail over, prevent, quell, repel, repress, repulse, rout, smash, stop, subdue, subjugate, suppress, surmount, thwart, triumph over, vanquish

defect *n.* birthmark, blemish, blot, blotch, computer bug, crack, deficiency, deformity, discoloration, drawback, error, failing, failure, fault, flaw, foible, frailty, imperfection, inadequacy, infirmity, insufficiency, irregularity, kink, lack, liability, mark, mistake, omission, rough spot, scar, scratch, shortage, shortcoming, snag, spot, stain, tear, unsoundness, vice, want, weakness, weak point

defend *v.* **1.** advocate, apologize for, argue for, back, back up, befriend, bolster, champion, come to defense of, endorse, espouse, exonerate, explain, give a reason for, guarantee, justify, maintain, make a case for, make excuses for, plead, prove a case, rationalize, recommend, represent, speak up for, stand behind, stand up for, support, sustain, uphold, vindicate, warrant **2.** arm, battle, beat off, care for, fend off, fight for, fortify, garrison, guard, guard against, hold, hold at bay, insure, keep safe, look after, maintain, parry, preserve, protect, provide sanctuary, repel danger, safeguard, save, screen, secure, shelter, shield, stave off, sustain, take in, uphold, ward off, watch over

defense *n.* **1.** answer, apologia, apology, argument, excuse, explanation, extenuation, justification, palliation, plea, rationalization, reply, response, retort, vindication **2.** aegis, armament, armor, arms, cover, deterrence, immunity, protection, resistance, screen, shelter, shield, warfare, weaponry, weapons

defer *v.* **1.** adjourn, break, break off, delay, discontinue, extend, hold off, intermit, interrupt, lengthen, pause, postpone, prolong, put off, recess, set aside, shelve, suspend, table, waive **2.** accede, accommodate, acquiesce, adapt, adjust, agree, assent, bow to, capitulate, comply, concede, submit, yield

deferred *adj.* adjourned, charged, delayed, discontinued, held up, postponed, prolonged, put off, stalled, suspended, tabled, waived

deficiency *n.* absence, dearth, default, defect, deficit, destitution, failing, failure, fault, flaw, frailty, imperfection, inadequacy, incompleteness, insufficiency, lack, loss, meagerness, paucity, scantiness, scarcity, shortage, shortcoming, shortfall, short supply, tax liability, want, weakness

deficit *n.* arrears, debit balance, indebtedness, insufficiency, lack, loss, monetary deficiency, monetary insufficiency, shortage, shortfall, want

define *v.* **1.** characterize, construe, delineate, denote, describe, designate, detail, elucidate, exemplify, explain, expound, give description, give explanation, illustrate, interpret, specify, spell out, translate **2.** bound, circumscribe, confine, delimit, delineate, demarcate, encircle, enclose, encompass, envelop, establish, fix, gird, limit, mark, outline, set bounds to, set out, stake out, surround, wall in

definitely *adv.* absolutely, categorically, certainly, clearly, conclusively, decidedly, doubtlessly, explicitly, expressly, finally, indisputably, indubitably, obviously, plainly, positively, specifically, surely, undeniably, unequivocally, unmistakably, unquestionably

definition *n.* characterization, clarification, commentary, delimitation, delineation, demarcation, denotation, description, determination, diagnosis, elucidation, exemplification, explanation, explication, exposition, expounding, gloss, illustration, interpretation, rationale, rendition, representation, statement of meaning, translation

defraud *v.* bilk, cheat, con, deceive, deprive, mislead, swindle, victimize

defunct *adj.* dead, deceased, discontinued, expired, extinct, inoperative, lapsed, nonexistent, obsolete, outmoded

degree *n.* **1.** amount, breadth, broadness, bulk, caliber, capacity, compass, content, depth, dimension, extent, fullness, gauge, gradation, grade, height, intensity, length, limit, magnitude, mark, measure, notch, plane, point, proportion, quantity, range, reach, rung, scale, scope, shade, size, span, spread, stage, standard, step, strength, volume, wideness, width **2.** caste, class, condition, credentials, distinction, eminence, estate, grade, honor, lot, merit, position, qualification, quality, rank, situation, standard, standing, station, status, value, worth

de jure *adv.* lawfully, legitimately, rightfully

delay *n.* adjournment, deferment, deferral, detention, dilatoriness, discontinuation, filibuster, hesitation, holding, interruption, interval, lag, lingering, moratorium, postponement, procrastination, prolongation, prorogation, protraction, recess, reprieve, retardation, setback, stall, stay, stop, stoppage, suspension, tardiness, tarrying, tie-up, wait, waiting period

delay *v.* adjourn, break off, defer, detain, discontinue, hold, hold over, impede, inhibit, interrupt, lag, linger, loiter, pause, postpone, recess, remand, retard, shelve, stall, stop, suspend, table, withhold

delegate *n.* agent, alternate, appointee, commissary, commissioner, consul, deputy, diplomat, emissary, envoy, functionary, intermediary, legate, member, messenger, minister, plenipotentiary, proxy, regent, representative, spokesperson, substitute, surrogate, vice regent, viceroy

delegate *v.* appoint, assign, authorize, charge, commission, commit, consign, deputize, designate, devolve, elect, empower, enable, entrust, induct, install, invest, name, nominate, ordain, place in office, relegate, select, vote in

delegation *n.* **1.** appointment, assignment, authorization, charge, charging, commissioning, consigning, consignment, deputation, deputization, deputizing, designation, devolution, empowering, entrusting, induction, installation, nomination, ordination **2.** commission, committee, contingent, delegates, deputies, embassy, envoys, legation, mission, representatives, subcommittee

delete *v.* blot out, cancel, cross out, cut out, destroy, edit out, efface, eliminate, eradicate, erase, exclude, expunge, mark out, obliterate, omit, remove, rub out, scratch out, strike out, take out, wipe out

deliberation *n.* cogitation, conference, consideration, consultation, contemplation, debate, discussion, examination, inspection, meditation, mulling over, musing, pondering, reasoning, reflection, rumination, review, scrutinization, serious thought, speculation, study, thinking about, weighing

delinquent *n.* culprit, criminal, juvenile, lawbreaker, malefactor, offender, wrongdoer

delinquent *adj.* behind, blameworthy, careless, culpable, defaulting, derelict, guilty, irresponsible, late, neglectful, negligent, outstanding, overdue, past-due, remiss, reprehensible, slack, tardy, unpaid, unsettled

deliver *v.* **1.** bequeath, cede, concede, convey, dispense, distribute, forward, give out, give up, grant, hand out, hand-carry, hand over, pass over, present, provide, relinquish, remit, supply, surrender, transfer, transport, truck, turn over, yield **2.** address, announce, communicate, declare, enunciate, express, impart, present, proclaim, promulgate, pronounce, publish, recite, speak, state, tell, utter, voice

delivery *n.* **1.** allotment, consignment, conveyance, dispatch, dispensation, distribution, giving over, giving up, handing over, entrusting, mailing, relinquishment, rendition, shipment, surrender, transfer, transferal, transmission, transmittal, voluntary transfer **2.** accent, articulation, diction, elocution, emphasis, enunciation, execution, expression, inflection, intonation, manner, modulation, performance, presentation, pronunciation, speech, style, utterance

deluxe *adj.* choice, elegant, exclusive, expensive, exquisite, first-class, grand, luxuriant, luxurious, opulent, palatial, plush, rare, rich, select, special, splendid, sumptuous, super, superior

demand *n.* application, behest, bidding, call, charge, claim, command, counterclaim, decree, direction, draft, exaction, imposition, injunction, insistence, mandate, necessity, need, order, petition, precept, question, request, requirement, requisition, stipulation, suit, ultimatum, want

demand *v.* **1.** appeal for, apply for, ask, badger, bid, challenge, charge, claim, clamor for, coerce, command, compel, direct, dun, entreat, force, implore, importune, impose, inquire after, insist on, invoke, order, petition, press, request, requisition, solicit, stipulate, sue for, summon, urge **2.** be in need of, call for, crave, cry out for, lack, necessitate, need, require, want

demarcation *n.* border, bound, boundary, definition, delimitation, differentiation, distinction, division, frontier, limit, line, margin, pale, separation

demeanor *n.* actions, air, appearance, attitude, bearing, behavior, carriage, comportment, conduct, deportment, disposition, expression, manner, manners, poise, port, posture, presence, stance, style

democracy *n.* commonwealth, constitutional government, democratic government, government by the people, liberal government, popular government, representative government, republic, self-government

democratic *adj.* constitutional, popular, populist, proletarian, representative, republican, self-governing

demonstrate *v.* **1.** authenticate, confirm, describe, display, establish, evidence, exhibit, explain, explicate, expound, express, give an idea of, illustrate, indicate, make clear, make evident, manifest, proclaim, prove, set forth, show, show how, substantiate, teach, test, validate **2.** march, march on, parade, picket, protest, rally, sit in, stage walkout, strike, take public action, walk out

demonstration *n.* **1.** affirmation, authentication, clarification, confirmation, description, elucidation, evidence, exhibition, explanation, exposition, expression, illustration, induction, manifestation, presentation, proof, substantiation, test, testimony, trial, validation, verification **2.** march, lobby, parade, peace march, picket, picket line, protest, rally, strike, walkout

demote *v.* break, declass, degrade, demerit, disrate, downgrade, lower, lower in rank, reduce, reduce in rank, set back, strip of rank

demur *v.* be unwilling, contest, disagree, disapprove, dispute, dissent, doubt, hesitate, object, oppose, pause, protest, refuse, remonstrate, resist, shy away from, take exception to, waver

denomination *n.* **1.** body, category, class, classification, grade, group, kind, monetary unit, size, sort, type, unit **2.** church, communion, creed, cult, faith, persuasion, religion, religious belief, religious connection, religious group, school, sect

denounce *v.* accuse, admonish, arraign, assail, attack, belittle, castigate, censure, charge, charge with, condemn, criticize, declaim against, decry, deprecate, disapprove, disparage, impeach, incriminate, indict, inveigh against, proscribe, rebuke, remonstrate, reprehend, reprimand, reproach, reprobate, reprove, scold, upbraid, vituperate

denunciation *n.* accusation, aspersion, blame, castigation, censure, charge, condemnation, criticism, denouncement, derogation, disapproval, fulmination, imputation, incrimination, inculpation, indictment, objection, obloquy, rebuke, reprehension, reprimand, reproach, reprobation, reproof, scolding, upbraiding, vituperation

deny *v.* ban, contradict, contravene, controvert, decline, demur, disaffirm, disagree, disallow, disavow, disbelieve, disclaim, discredit, disprove, dispute, exclude, forbid, forsake, negate, nullify, oppose, prohibit, protest, rebuff, rebut, recant, refuse, refute, reject, renounce, repudiate, revoke, say no to, spurn, take exception to, turn down, veto, withhold

depart *v.* **1.** abandon, abdicate, decamp, desert, embark, emigrate, escape, evacuate, exit, get away, go, go away, go forth, leave, make an exit, march out, migrate, move on, move out, pull out, retire, retreat, secede, set forth, start out, vacate **2.** branch out, deviate, differ, digress, diverge, fork, move away, ramble, stray, swerve, turn aside, vary, veer, wander

department *n.* **1.** agency, area, board, branch, bureau, canton, circuit, class, commission, compartment, diocese, division, group, head, office, parish, precinct, province, quarter, region, section, segment, state, station, subdivision, territory, unit, ward   **2.** activity, area of expertise, area of interest, arena, assignment, authority, berth, business activity, capacity, circle, control, domain, dominion, duty, field, function, jurisdiction, line, occupation, office, realm, responsibility, specialty, sphere, sphere of influence, station, sway

departure *n.*   **1.** abandonment, departing, desertion, embarkation, emigration, escape, evacuation, exit, exodus, flight, going away, leave, leave-taking, leaving, migration, parting, running away, sailing, secession, separation, setting out, starting out, takeoff, taking leave, vacation, walkout   **2.** aberration, branching off, branching out, change, deviation, difference, digression, divergence, diversion, innovation, moving away, rambling, straying, swerving, turning aside, variance, variation, veering, wandering

dependable *adj.*   conscientious, faithful, honest, honorable, loyal, principled, reliable, reputable, responsible, secure, stable, steadfast, steady, sure, true, trustworthy, unfailing

dependence *n.*   addiction, attachment, contingency, defenselessness, deference, helplessness, need, servility, servitude, subjection, subjugation, submission, subordination, subservience, vulnerability, weakness, yoke

dependency *n.*   See **dependence**

deplete *v.*   bankrupt, consume, decrease, diminish, drain, empty, evacuate, exhaust, expend, finish, impoverish, lessen, reduce, run out of, spend, squander, undermine, unload, use up, wash up, waste, weaken

depleted *adj.*   bare, consumed, decreased, deprived of, drained, emptied, evacuated, exhausted, lessened, sold-out, spent, used, used-up, vacant, washed-out, wasted, weakened, worn-out

deploy *v.*   arrange, base, bring into action, display, distribute, position, put in action, put in use, redistribute, set out, set up, spread out, station

deport *v.*   banish, cast out, eject, evict, exile, expatriate, expel, extradite, oust, proscribe, ship out, throw out

deportment *n.*   actions, air, appearance, aspect, bearing, behavior, carriage, comportment, conduct, demeanor, etiquette, manner, manners, posture, stance

deposit *n.* **1.** down payment, earnest money, installment, money, partial payment, pledge, retainer, security **2.** alluvium, deposition, dregs, lees, loess, moraine, precipitation, sediment, silt

deposit *v.* bank, deliver, drop, entrust, give in trust, hoard, invest, lay, lay away, locate, place, precipitate, put, put away, save, settle, store, stow

deposition *n.* affidavit, attestation, recorded statement, sworn statement, testimony, written statement

depository *n.* archive, bank, depot, magazine, museum, repertory, repository, reservoir, safe, safe-deposit box, storage place, storehouse, storeroom, treasury, vault, warehouse

depot *n.* base, bus station, cache, depository, magazine, railroad station, repository, station, station house, stopping place, storage place, storehouse, terminal, terminus, train station, warehouse, yard

depreciate *v.* cheapen, cut, decline, decrease, deflate, depress, devaluate, devalue, diminish, downgrade, drop, erode, fall, fall off, go down, lessen, lose value, lower, mark down, reduce, sink, slash, slide, slip, slump, spread costs, subtract from

depredation *n.* burglary, crime, desecration, despoiling, destruction, devastation, larceny, pillage, plunder, robbery, stealing, theft

depression *n.* **1.** downturn, economic decline, economic failure, economic paralysis, inactivity, recession, slowdown, slump, stagflation, stagnation, standstill, unemployment **2.** basin, bowl, cavity, concavity, crater, dent, dimple, dip, excavation, hole, hollow, indention, pit, recess, sink, sink hole, valley **3.** cheerlessness, crestfallenness, dejection, desolation, despair, despondency, dispiritedness, doldrums, dolefulness, downheartedness, gloominess, hopelessness, low spirits, melancholy, sadness, sorrowfulness, unhappiness

depth *n.* **1.** base, bottom, declination, deepness, distance across, distance down, drop, expanse, extent, lower register, pit, pitch **2.** acuity, acumen, astuteness, awareness, discernment, insight, intellect, intelligence, intuition, perception, profoundness, profundity, sagacity, shrewdness, understanding

deputy *n.* agent, alternate, ambassador, appointee, assistant, commissary, commissioner, delegate, diplomat, emissary, envoy, intermediary, legate, messenger, minister, proxy, regent, representative, spokesperson, substitute, surrogate

derivation *n.* **1.** by-product, consequence, derivation, descendant, offshoot, outgrowth, product, spin-off **2.** ancestry, basis, beginning, commencement, descent, etymology, foundation, fountainhead, genealogy, inception, origin, origination, root, source, spring, wellspring

derive *v.* acquire, arrive at, bring forth, collect, conclude, deduce, deduct, determine, develop, educe, elicit, evolve, extract, follow, formulate, gain, gather, get, glean, guess, infer, obtain, presume, procure, reach, reason, receive, secure, suppose, surmise, trace, track, work out

derogatory *adj.* belittling, censorious, contumelious, critical, defamatory, degrading, demeaning, deprecatory, depreciative, detracting, disapproving, disdainful, dishonoring, disparaging, fault-finding, impeaching, injurious, libelous, malicious, maligning, offensive, opprobrious, reproachful, scornful, slanderous, uncomplimentary, unfavorable, unflattering, vilifying

describe *v.* annotate, characterize, chronicle, connote, convey, define, delineate, denote, depict, detail, distinguish, draw, elucidate, epitomize, exemplify, explain, explicate, expound, express, footnote, give account of, illuminate, illustrate, impart, indicate, label, make clear, narrate, paint, picture, portray, pronounce, recite, recount, relate, report, represent, set out, signify, specify, state, tell

description *n.* **1.** characterization, definition, delineation, depiction, elaboration, explanation, explication, picture, portraiture, portrayal, representation, sketch, specification, summary **2.** brand, breed, brood, cast, category, character, class, classification, color, composition, constitution, denomination, designation, feather, form, genre, genus, grain, hue, kind, make, makeup, mold, order, sort, species, stamp, stripe, suit, tone, type, variety

deserve *v.* be entitled to, be qualified for, be worthy of, earn, have a claim to, have a right to, merit

design *n.* arrangement, blueprint, chart, composition, conception, configuration, constitution, construction, delineation, depiction, diagram, draft, drawing, dummy, formation, idea, illustration, layout, makeup, map, model, motif, outline, paste-up, pattern, perspective, plan, planning process, preliminary sketch, proposal, rough draft, scheme, sketch, structure, study, style, system, treatment

design *v.* arrange, block out, blueprint, build, chart, compose, conceive, construct, contrive, create, define, delineate, depict, detail, develop, devise, diagram, draft, draw, draw plans, effect, erect, fabricate, fashion, figure, forge, form, frame, innovate, invent, lay out, make up, mold, originate, outline, plan, plot, portray, produce, represent, scheme, set out, shape, sketch, think up, trace, work out

designate *v.* **1.** allocate, allot, appoint, assign, baptize, call, charge, choose, christen, commission, consign, delegate, denominate, deputize, dub, entitle, induct, label, name, nickname, nominate, ordain, select, style, term, title **2.** address, apportion, authorize, characterize, connote, constitute, define, delineate, denote, depict, describe, dictate, evidence, express, favor, formulate, identify, illustrate, indicate, individualize, make known, mark, mention, note, outline, pin down, pinpoint, point out, prefer, represent, set apart, set aside, show, signal, signify, specify, state, stipulate

designation *n.* allotment, appellation, assignment, byword, choice, class, classification, consignment, delegation, denomination, description, election, epithet, identification, induction, key word, label, name, naming, nickname, nomination, ordination, relegation, selection, style, title

desirable *adj.* admirable, advantageous, agreeable, alluring, attractive, beneficial, captivating, charming, eligible, enticing, enviable, excellent, expedient, fascinating, fetching, fine, helpful, inviting, pleasing, preferable, prime, popular, profitable, seductive, superb, superior, useful, valuable, welcome, winning, worthwhile, worthy

destination *n.* **1.** journey's end, landing place, last stop, place of debarkation, port of call, station, stop, stopping place, target, terminus **2.** aim, ambition, design, end, goal, intention, motive, object, objective, purpose, reason, target **3.** data address, data file, file copy location, receiving device, receiving file

destined *adj.* appointed, assigned, booked, chosen, consigned, delegated, designated, determined, directed, prepared, scheduled, specified

destroy *v.* abolish, annihilate, annul, blot out, consume, crush, delete, demolish, desolate, devastate, dismantle, end, eradicate, erase, expunge, exterminate, extinguish, extirpate, finish, kill, lay waste, liquidate, nullify, obliterate, overthrow, overturn, pulverize, quell, ruin, slaughter, slay, stamp out, strike out, suppress, terminate, vitiate, wipe out, wreck

detach *v.* abstract, cut off, disassemble, disassociate, disconnect, disengage, disentangle, disjoin, dissociate, disunite, free, isolate, loosen, remove, segregate, separate, sever, uncouple, unfasten, unhitch, withdraw

detachment *n.* **1.** disconnection, disengagement, disjoining, dissolution, disunion, division, loosening, segregation, separation, severing   **2.** absentmindedness, aloofness, broadmindedness, coldness, coolness, disinterestedness, impartiality, inattention, indifference, neutrality, objectivity, preoccupation, remoteness, unconcern

detail *n.* accessory, aspect, attribute, circumstance, component, element, fact, factor, feature, fine point, member, minor point, part, particular, point, respect, specific, technicality, unit

detail *v.* **1.** catalog, cite, codify, delineate, depict, describe, designate, differentiate, elaborate, enumerate, indicate, itemize, list, make clear, mention, narrate, particularize, point out, portray, quote, recite, recount, relate, report, set forth, show, specify, spell out, stipulate, tabulate, tell   **2.** appoint, assign, charge, commission, delegate, elect, nominate, select

detect *v.* apprehend, ascertain, bring out, catch, descry, determine, discern, discover, distinguish, encounter, espy, establish, expose, find, note, notice, observe, perceive, recognize, reveal, see, spot, track down, turn up, uncover, unearth, unmask, unveil

deter *v.* arrest, avert, bar, block, check, chill, cool, dampen, daunt, discourage, dishearten, disincline, dismay, dispirit, dissuade, divert, foil, forestall, frighten, frustrate, inhibit, intimidate, obstruct, preclude, prevent, prohibit, scare, stop, thwart, turn away, turn off, warn

deterioration *n.* atrophy, corrosion, debasement, decadence, decay, declension, declination, decline, decomposition, degeneration, descent, dilapidation, disintegration, disrepair, downturn, drop, fall, lapse, perversion, retrogression, slump, subversion, vitiation

determination *n.* **1.** conclusion, decision, end, judgment, opinion, outcome, perception, result, settlement, solution, verdict   **2.** ardor, boldness, constancy, conviction, courage, dauntlessness, dedication, drive, energy, firmness, fortitude, grit, indomitability, mettle, nerve, obstinacy, perseverance, persistence, purpose, purposefulness, push, resoluteness, resolution, resolve, self-confidence, single-mindedness, spirit, stability, stamina, steadfastness, steadiness, stubbornness, tenacity, will, willpower, zeal

determine *v.* **1.** adjudge, arbitrate, choose, conclude, decide, dispose, elect, fix, fix upon, impel, incline, induce, influence, judge, lead, ordain, predetermine, prompt, regulate, resolve, select, settle, sway, turn, will **2.** add up to, ascertain, catch on, certify, check, demonstrate, detect, discover, divine, establish, figure, figure out, find out, hear, learn, make out, opine, see, size up, tell, tumble, unearth, verify, work out

deterrent *n.* bar, barricade, barrier, block, blockage, bridle, catch, curb, drawback, hindrance, impediment, liability, obstacle, obstruction, preventive, rein, restraint, snag

devalue *v.* cheapen, cut rates, debase, decrease, depreciate, devaluate, lessen, lower, mark down, reduce rates, revalue, take down, underrate, undervalue

develop *v.* **1.** actualize, add to, advance, amplify, augment, broaden, build up, cultivate, deepen, dilate, elaborate, enlarge, enrich, expand, extend, heighten, improve, intensify, lengthen, magnify, promote, reinforce, spread, strengthen, stretch, supplement, widen **2.** advance, bloom, blossom, cultivate, enlarge, evolve, expand, exploit, flourish, flower, foster, increase, maturate, mellow, progress, promote, prosper, ripen, thrive **3.** arise, begin, break out, breed, bring up, build, coin, commence, compose, constitute, cultivate, erect, establish, fashion, form, generate, hatch, institute, invent, occur, organize, originate, propagate, rear, start, transpire **4.** appear, become evident, become manifest, be disclosed, become, dawn, disclose, elaborate, evolve, explain, explicate, lay open, make known, materialize, recount, reveal, state, uncover, unfold, unravel

development *n.* **1.** circumstance, conclusion, event, happening, incident, issue, item, materialization, occurrence, outcome, phenomenon, result, situation **2.** adding to, addition, advance, advancement, aggrandizement, amplification, augmentation, blooming, blossoming, buildup, elaboration, enlargement, evolution, expansion, flowering, furtherance, growing, growth, improvement, increase, maturation, maturity, opening, progress, promotion, reinforcement, ripeness, ripening, spread, strengthening, unfolding

deviation *n.* aberration, abnormality, anomaly, bend, bending, change, curve, curving, declension, declination, departure, difference, discrepancy, disparity, divergence, inconsistency, irregularity, shift, shifting, turn, turning, variable, variance, variation, veer, veering

device *n.* **1.** accessory, apparatus, appliance, computer peripheral, contrivance, equipment, gadget, hardware component, hardware unit, instrument, invention, machine, mechanism **2.** artifice, blind, clever move, conspiracy, deception, design, dodge, evasion, feint, gimmick, machination, maneuver, plan, plot, ploy, project, ruse, scheme, shift, stratagem, strategy, subterfuge, trap, trick, wile

devise *v.* **1.** bequeath, bestow, confer, convey, hand down, transfer, will **2.** arrange, compose, conceive, concoct, construct, contrive, create, design, draft, dream up, frame, forge, invent, originate, plan, prepare, project, scheme, shape, think up, work out, work up

devoted *adj.* admiring, affectionate, ardent, caring, committed, concerned, consecrated, constant, dedicated, devout, dutiful, faithful, loyal, pledged, staunch, steadfast, thoughtful, true, zealous

diagnose *v.* analyze, determine, distinguish, identify, interpret, investigate, make a diagnosis, pinpoint, pronounce, recognize

diagnosis *n.* analysis, conclusion, description, detection, determination, distinguishing, examination, identification, interpretation, investigation, isolation, opinion, pronouncement, scrutiny, summary

diagram *n.* blueprint, chart, delineation, draft, drawing, figure, graph, illustration, line drawing, outline, picture, profile, representation, schematic representation, scheme, skeleton, sketch, view

dial *v.* buzz, call, phone, rotate, telephone, tune, turn

dialect *n.* accent, colloquialism, idiom, language, localism, local speech, nonstandard version, pronunciation, provincialism, regionalism, speech, speech pattern, tongue, vernacular, vocabulary

dialog *n.* communication, conversation, converse, debate, discourse, discussion, duologue, exchange of ideas, interlocution, lines, question and answer session, remarks, script, talk, verbal exchange

diameter *n.* breadth, broadness, length, thickness, width

diary *n.* annals, appointment book, chronicle, computer utility, daily record, daybook, engagement book, history, journal, log, logbook, record, utility

dictate *v.* **1.** compose, deliver, draft correspondence, emit, formulate, prepare draft, record, say, speak, talk, transmit, verbalize **2.** bid, charge, command, constrain, decree, direct, enjoin, give instructions, impose, instruct, lay down, lay down the law, necessitate, oblige, ordain, order, prescribe, pronounce, rule, set

diction *n.* accent, articulation, command of language, delivery, elocution, eloquence, enunciation, expression, fluency, inflection, intonation, language, oratory, phrase, phraseology, phrasing, pronunciation, rhetoric, stress, style of speech, usage, verbalism, vocabulary, word choice, wording, word sense

dictionary *n.* book of word meanings, cyclopedia, encyclopedia, glossary, lexicon, reference book, terminology book, vocabulary, wordbook

dictum *n.* **1.** adage, aphorism, apothegm, axiom, gnome, maxim, moral, precept, proverb, saying **2.** behest, bidding, caveat, charge, command, declaration, decree, dictate, edict, mandate, order, pronouncement

difference *n.* **1.** aberration, anomaly, antithesis, contrariness, contrast, departure, deviation, differentiation, digression, discrepancy, disparity, dissimilarity, distinction, distinctness, divergence, diversity, eccentricity, exception, idiosyncrasy, incongruity, inconsistency, individuality, inequality, irregularity, nonconformity, opposition, particularity, peculiarity, singularity, unlikeness, variance, variation, variety **2.** argument, brawl, clash, conflict, contention, controversy, debate, disaccord, disagreement, discord, dispute, dissension, dissent, misunderstanding, opposing views, quarrel

different *adj.* **1.** altered, changed, contradistinctive, contrary, contrasting, deviant, discrepant, disparate, dissimilar, distinct, distinctive, divergent, diverse, incomparable, incongruous, inconsistent, individual, mismatched, modified, other, peculiar, singular, unequal, unlike, unsimilar, variant **2.** another, atypical, bizarre, distinct, distinctive, diverse, especial, exceptional, extraordinary, individual, new, noteworthy, novel, original, other, particular, peculiar, rare, remarkable, separate, several, singular, special, specialized, startling, strange, uncommon, unconventional, unfamiliar, unique, unusual **3.** abundant, assorted, collected, divergent, divers, diverse, diversified, heterogeneous, manifold, many, miscellaneous, mixed, multifarious, multiform, numerous, several, some, sundry, varicolored, varied, variegated, various

differentiate *v.* **1.** characterize, contrast, discriminate, distinguish, individualize, individuate, make a distinction, mark off, separate, set apart, tell apart **2.** adapt, adjust, alter, change, convert, diversify, make different, modify, transform, vary

difficult *adj.* **1.** abstract, abstruse, baffling, bewildering, complex, complicated, confounding, confusing, esoteric, formidable, hard, hard-to-comprehend, hard-to-explain, hard-to-manage, hard-to-solve, hard-to-understand, inexplicable, intricate, involved, knotty, mysterious, mystifying, obscure, obstinate, perplexing, profound, puzzling, recondite, thorny, ticklish, troublesome, unclear, uncompromising, unfathomable, unintelligible, unmanageable, unyielding, vexing **2.** arduous, challenging, exacting, hard, hard-to-do, intricate, labored, laborious, rough, severe, strenuous, unyielding

difficulty *n.* **1.** arduousness, crisis, dilemma, emergency, exigency, frustration, hardship, hazard, hindrance, impasse, labor, laboriousness, mess, misfortune, muddle, obstacle, obstruction, ordeal, pain, painfulness, paradox, plight, predicament, quagmire, quandary, strain, straits, strenuousness, struggle, tribulation, trouble, urgency **2.** aggravation, annoyance, anxiety, bafflement, bother, complication, crisis, depression, discouragement, distress, embarrassment, emergency, exigency, frustration, grievance, harassment, inconvenience, irritation, misery, oppression, perplexity, predicament, pressure, puzzle, quandary, responsibility, setback, strain, strait, stress, strife, struggle, trouble, vicissitude, weight, worry

diffusion *n.* circulation, circumfusion, dispensation, dispersal, dispersion, dissemination, dissipation, propagation, scattering, spreading, wide dispersion, wide distribution

digest *v.* **1.** abbreviate, abridge, abstract, compress, condense, cut, cut down, decrease, edit, epitomize, make shorter, outline, reduce, shorten, sketch, summarize, synopsize, trim **2.** absorb, assimilate, come to understand, comprehend, consider, contemplate, grasp, master, meditate on, mull over, ponder, reflect, take in, think over, understand, weigh

digit *n.* Arabic number, cipher, figure, integer, number, numeral, symbol, whole number

dilemma *n.* complicated problem, crisis, difficult choice, difficulty, fix, impasse, perplexity, plight, predicament, problem, puzzle, quandary, trouble, uncertainty

diligence *n.* application, assiduity, assiduousness, attentiveness, constancy, earnestness, exertion, heedfulness, industriousness, industry, intensity, intentness, labor, perseverance, persistence, pertinacity, sedulousness

dimensions *n.* bigness, capacity, dimensionality, extent, field, gravity, greatness, import, importance, largeness, magnitude, measure, measurement, proportions, range, reach, scope, seriousness, significance, size, span, spread, sweep, urgency, volume, weight

diminish *v.* **1.** abate, abbreviate, abridge, become less, become smaller, compress, condense, constrict, contract, crop, curtail, cut, decrease, die out, drain, dwindle, ebb, lessen, lower, narrow, recede, reduce, shorten, subside, taper off, wane, weaken **2.** cheapen, debase, degrade, demean, depreciate, derogate, detract from, devalue, discredit, disparage, downgrade, humiliate, vitiate

dinner *n.* banquet, collation, evening meal, feast, main meal, principal meal, refection, repast, supper

diploma *n.* academic recognition, award, certificate, charter, confirmation, credentials, degree, graduation certificate, parchment

diplomacy *n.* artfulness, delicacy, discretion, finesse, judiciousness, politics, prudence, skill, statecraft, statesmanship, subtlety, tactfulness

diplomat *n.* agent, ambassador, arbitrator, attaché, chargé d'affaires, consul, emissary, envoy, intermediary, legate, mediator, minister, negotiator, peacemaker, plenipotentiary, politician, representative

diplomatic *adj.* artful, capable, conciliatory, courteous, deft, delicate, discreet, gracious, judicious, polite, politic, prudent, sensitive, subtle, tactful

direct *adj.* **1.** continuous, nearest, nonstop, shortest, straight, straightaway, through, unbroken, undeviating, uninterrupted, unswerving **2.** aboveboard, absolute, blunt, candid, clear, explicit, forthright, frank, honest, matter-of-fact, open, outspoken, plain, plainspoken, simple, sincere, straightforward, unambiguous, unconditional, undisguised, unequivocal, unmistakable, unqualified

direct *v.* **1.** administer, boss, carry out, conduct, control, dominate, drive, engineer, govern, guide, handle, lead, manage, operate, orchestrate, oversee, preside over, regulate, rule, run, steer, superintend, supervise   **2.** adjure, address, advise, bid, brief, charge, command, counsel, decree, dictate, enjoin, give directions, give instructions, give orders, inform, instruct, lecture, ordain, order, prescribe, recommend, specify, teach, tell   **3.** aim at, escort, focus, guide, head toward, indicate, move toward, pilot, point, point the way, point toward, route, shepherd, show, sight on, steer toward, target

direction *n.* **1.** administration, care, charge, conduct, control, domination, government, guidance, handling, leadership, management, ministry, navigation, operation, orchestration, oversight, regulation, rule, statecraft, superintendence, supervision   **2.** address, advice, advisement, briefing, command, dictate, directive, guidance, guideline, instruction, order, plan, prescription, recipe, recommendation, specification   **3.** aim, angle, aspect, bearing, bent, bias, compass point, course, drift, heading, inclination, line, movement, objective, orientation, path, range, road, route, set, slant, spot, tendency, track, trajectory, trend, vector, way

directive *n.* charge, command, decree, dictate, edict, injunction, instruction, mandate, notice, order, ordinance, regulation, ruling

directly *adv.* **1.** exactly, forthrightly, precisely, straightly, undeviatingly, unswervingly   **2.** immediately, instantaneously, instantly, momentarily, presently, promptly, quickly, shortly, speedily   **3.** candidly, honestly, literally, openly, personally, plainly, straightforwardly, truthfully, unequivocally

director *n.* administrator, boss, bureaucrat, chief, commander, controller, executive officer, head, manager, marshal, official, overseer, president, presiding officer, principal, superintendent, supervisor

directory *n.* address book, book, catalog, classified listing, files, hard-disk section, index, index file, listing, record, reference book, register, roster, telephone book

disable *v.* deprive, impair, incapacitate, inhibit, make ineffective, prevent operations, remove, weaken

disagree *v.* **1.** altercate, argue, battle, be at odds, bicker, bring action, clash, contend, contest, debate, disaccord, discord, dispute, dissent, feud, fight, object, oppose, quarrel, quibble, spar, sue, take issue with   **2.** be different, be dissimilar, be unlike, conflict, contradict, contrast, contravene, counter, depart from, deviate from, differ, dissent, diverge, oppose, run counter to, vary

disagreement *n.* **1.** conflict, contradiction, contrast, contravention, departure, deviation, difference, discrepancy, disparity, dissent, dissension, dissimilarity, dissimilitude, divergence, divergency, diversity, incompatibility, incongruity, incongruousness, inconsistency, unlikeness, variance **2.** altercation, argument, battle, bickering, clash, clashing, conflict, contention, contest, controversy, debate, discord, dispute, dissension, dissent, disunion, disunity, division, divisiveness, feud, fight, friction, hostility, misunderstanding, objection, opposition, quarrel, quarreling, rupture, split, squabble, strife, vendetta

disallow *v.* abjure, avoid, ban, bar, debar, deny, disaffirm, disavow, disclaim, disown, disregard, except, exclude, forbid, ignore, prohibit, proscribe, rebuff, refuse, reject, repel, repudiate, repulse, restrain, restrict, say no to, set aside, shut out, veto, withhold

disappointed *adj.* crestfallen, depressed, disconcerted, discontented, discouraged, disenchanted, disgruntled, disillusioned, dissatisfied, distressed, downcast, foiled, frustrated, let down, saddened, thwarted, unsatisfied

disappointment *n.* **1.** chagrin, depression, discontent, discouragement, disenchantment, disgruntlement, disillusionment, displeasure, dissatisfaction, distress, frustration, letdown, regret, unfulfillment **2.** blow, calamity, defeat, disaster, failure, fiasco, impasse, inefficacy, letdown, miscalculation, miscarriage, misfortune, mishap, mistake, nonsuccess, obstacle, saddening situation, setback, washout

disapproval *n.* berating, castigation, censure, condemnation, criticism, denunciation, deprecation, disapprobation, discountenance, disfavor, dislike, disparagement, displeasure, dissatisfaction, objection, objurgation, ostracism, rejection, reproach, reproof

disarray *n.* chaos, clutter, confusion, disarrangement, discomposure, disharmony, dishevelment, dislocation, disorder, disorganization, displacement, jumble, muddle, snarl, tangle, unruliness, unsettledness, untidiness

disavow *v.* abjure, contradict, deny, disaffirm, disallow, disclaim, disinherit, disown, forswear, gainsay, impugn, recall, recant, refuse, reject, renege, repudiate, retract, take back

disburse *v.* dispense, disperse, distribute, divide, dole out, expend, give, issue, lay out, measure out, mete out, parcel out, pay out, portion out, spend, spend money

disbursement *n.* discharge, dispensation, dispersion, disposal, distribution, expenditure, expense, issuance, outlay, paying out, payment, spending

discharge *n.* **1.** demobilization, dismissal, displacement, ejection, excusing, expulsion, firing, freeing, giving notice, layoff, letting go, liberation, ouster, relieving, removal, replacement, supplanting, termination   **2.** abidance, accomplishment, achievement, carrying out, execution, fulfillment, observance, performance   **3.** disbursement, liquidation, payment, satisfaction, settlement   **4.** absolution, acquittal, clearance, dismissal, exculpation, excusing, exemption, exoneration, freeing, liberation, pardon, parole, release, reprieve, setting free   **5.** ejection, elimination, emission, emptying, eruption, excretion, expulsion, flow, flowing, pouring forth, projection, secretion, seepage, vent, voidance, voiding   **6.** abolishment, abolition, abrogation, annulment, banishment, cancellation, destruction, dissolution, invalidation, nullification, voidance

discharge *v.* **1.** demobilize, dismiss, displace, eject, excuse, expel, fire, give notice, lay off, let go, oust, relieve, remove, replace, supplant, terminate   **2.** abide by, accomplish, achieve, do, carry out, execute, fulfill, meet, observe, perform   **3.** disburse, honor, liquidate, meet, pay, satisfy, settle   **4.** absolve, acquit, allow to go, clear, dismiss, exculpate, exempt, exonerate, free, liberate, pardon, parole, release, relieve, reprieve, set free   **5.** eject, eliminate, emit, empty, erupt, excrete, expel, exude, flow, gush, leak, pour forth, project, release, secrete, send forth, send out, void   **6.** abolish, abrogate, annul, banish, cancel, dissolve, invalidate, nullify, render void, void

disciple *n.* adherent, advocate, apostle, apprentice, believer, convert, defender, devotee, enthusiast, follower, learner, partisan, proponent, proselyte, pupil, satellite, student, supporter, votary

discipline *n.* **1.** area of study, branch of knowledge, course, course of study, curriculum, field of study, major, specialty, subject   **2.** coaching, conduct, control, development, drill, drilling, exercise, inculcation, indoctrination, instruction, method, orderliness, practice, preparation, regimen, regulation, restraint, schooling, self-command, self-control, self-restraint, strictness, systematization, willpower   **3.** castigation, chastisement, correction, penalty, punishment, rebuke, reprimand, reproof

disclaim *v.* abjure, contradict, decline, deny, disaffirm, disallow, disavow, disinherit, disown, forswear, gainsay, ignore, negate, recall, recant, refuse, reject, renounce, repudiate, retract, revoke, say no to, take back, turn down

disclaimer *n.* denial, disavowal, refusal, relinquishment, repudiation

disclosure *n.* acknowledgment, admission, announcement, avowal, broadcast, confession, divulgence, elaboration, enlightenment, explanation, exposé, exposition, exposure, publication, revelation, revealing, report, uncovering, unveiling

disconnected *adj.* detached, discontinuous, disengaged, disentangled, disjoined, interrupted, loose, segregated, separated, uncoordinated, uncoupled, undone, unfastened, unhinged, unhooked

discontinue *v.* abandon, abstain from, break off, cease, desist from, drop, end, finish, give up, halt, intermit, interrupt, leave off, pause, put end to, put stop to, quit, refrain from, stop, suspend, terminate

discord *n.* animosity, argument, clashing, conflict, contention, disagreement, disharmony, dispute, dissension, dissidence, dissonance, disunity, diversity, division, friction, hostility, incompatibility, incongruity, opposition, rupture, split, strife, variance, warfare, wrangling

discount *n.* allowance, concession, cut, cutback, cut rate, decrease, deduction, exemption, markdown, rebate, reduction, rollback, subtraction

discount *v.* **1.** deduct, sell at discount, subtract, take off **2.** disregard, forget, gloss over, ignore, minimize, neglect, omit, overlook, pass over, reject

discourage *v.* **1.** admonish, advise against, curb, deprecate, deter, discountenance, dissuade, divert, frighten, hinder, hold back, impede, inhibit, interfere, keep back, prevent, put off, remonstrate, repress, scare, squelch, suppress, talk out of, turn aside, warn, withhold **2.** dampen spirits, daunt, deject, demoralize, depress, disenchant, dishearten, dismay, dispirit, frighten, intimidate, overawe, scare, trouble, unnerve

discourse *n.* address, chat, communication, conversation, declamation, descant, dialog, discussion, dissertation, essay, lecture, monograph, oration, paper, sermon, speech, study, talk, thesis, treatise, verbal exchange, verbalization

discover *v.* ascertain, behold, come across, come upon, conceive, contrive, design, detect, determine, devise, discern, distinguish, espy, find, find out, happen upon, hear of, identify, invent, learn of, locate, look up, notice, observe, originate, patent, perceive, pioneer, realize, recognize, see, spot, think of, uncover, unearth

discovery *n.* **1.** ascertaining, detection, determination, discernment, distinguishing, encounter, exploration, finding, identification, introduction, locating, location, origination, perception, realization, recognition, revelation, sighting, uncovering, unearthing **2.** breakthrough, conclusion, contrivance, find, finding, innovation, invention, result, secret, treasure

discrepancy *n.* contrariety, deviation, difference, disagreement, discordance, disparity, dissimilarity, divergence, error, incongruity, inconsistency, miscalculation, variance, variation

discrete *adj.* detached, disconnected, discontinuous, disjunct, disjunctive, distinct, separate, unattached

discrimination *n.* **1.** bias, bigotry, favoritism, injustice, intolerance, narrow-mindedness, partiality, prejudice, racism, sexism, unfairness **2.** acumen, acuteness, astuteness, carefulness, caution, differentiation, discernment, discretion, distinction, insight, judgment, particularity, penetration, perception, perspicacity, prudence, refinement, sagacity, sharpness, shrewdness, taste, wisdom

discuss *v.* compare notes, confer, consider, consult with, converse, debate, deliberate, examine, exchange views, explain, get together, go over, reason about, review, talk about, talk over, weigh

discussion *n.* conference, consideration, consultation, conversation, debate, deliberation, dialog, discourse, examination, exchange of ideas, meeting, review, talk

disembark *v.* alight, climb down from, debark, deplane, detrain, dismount, get off, go ashore, land, leave, put ashore, step out of, unload

disengage *v.* break the connection, cut loose, detach, disconnect, disjoin, disunite, divide, extricate, free, liberate, loose, loosen, release, separate, set free, unattach, unbind, uncouple, undo, unfasten, unhook, unlatch, unloosen

disguise *n.* blind, camouflage, charade, cloak, concealment, costume, cover, covering, deception, facade, false front, front, guise, mask, masquerade, pretense, ruse, screen, subterfuge, trickery, veil, veneer

disguise *v.* alter, camouflage, change, change appearance of, cloak, conceal, cover, cover over, cover up, deceive, dissemble, dissimulate, dress up, fake, falsify, garble, give false picture of, gloss over, hide, mask, masquerade as, misrepresent, muffle, obscure, put on act, put on false front, screen, shroud, simulate, veil

dishonest *adj.* cheating, corrupt, criminal, deceitful, deceptive, dishonorable, disingenuous, false, felonious, fraudulent, hypocritical, illegal, immoral, insincere, lying, mendacious, misleading, phony, swindling, traitorous, treacherous, tricky, underhanded, unfair, unjust, unlawful, unprincipled, unscrupulous, untrustworthy, untruthful, wrongful

dishonesty *n.* cheating, corruption, deceit, deviousness, disingenuousness, duplicity, faithlessness, falsity, fraud, graft, hypocrisy, immorality, improbity, infidelity, insincerity, larceny, lying, malfeasance, mendacity, misconduct, robbery, stealing, thievery, treachery, unfairness, unscrupulousness, untruthfulness, wrongdoing

disinherit *v.* cut off, deprive, disown, dispossess, divest, evict, exclude, oust, renounce, repudiate, turn out

disintegrate *v.* break apart, break down, break up, crumble, decay, decompose, disband, disperse, dissolve, erode, fall apart, reduce, wash away, wash out

disinterested *adj.* aloof, candid, detached, dispassionate, equitable, even-handed, fair, impartial, impersonal, indifferent, just, neutral, open-minded, unbiased, unconcerned, uninvolved, unprejudiced

disk *n.* circle, compact disk, computer device, diskette, flan, floppy disk, hard disk, magnetic disk, optical disk, phonograph record, plate, record, recording, storage medium

diskette *n.* See **disk**

dislocate *v.* disarticulate, disconnect, disengage, disjoint, disorder, disorganize, displace, disturb, disunite, misplace, mix up, put out of place, unhinge, upset

dislocation *n.* disarray, disarticulation, disconnection, disengagement, disorder, disorganization, displacement, disruption, disturbance, jumble, misplacement, unhinging

dismantle *v.* break down, break up, demolish, deprive of, destroy, disassemble, disencumber, dismember, fell, knock down, level, pull down, raze, remove from, ruin, strike, strip, take apart, take down, tear down, undo

dismiss *v.* **1.** cancel contract, depose, deselect, discharge, disemploy, drop, fire, furlough, give notice to, impeach, lay off, oust, release, remove, retire, suspend, terminate, turn away, unseat **2.** abolish, adjourn, banish, decline, disband, discard, dispel, dispense with, disperse, dispose of, disregard, dissolve, drive out, drop, eject, expel, free, lay aside, let go, push aside, put away, put out of mind, reject, release, relinquish, remove, repel, repudiate, repulse, send away, send off, set aside, turn away, turn out

dismissal *n.* adjournment, banishment, deportation, deposal, discharge, dissolution, end, eviction, exile, expulsion, freedom to leave, firing, layoff, liberation, ouster, permission to go, release, removal, suspension

disobedience *n.* defiance, delinquency, dereliction, disregard, indiscipline, infraction, infringement, insubordination, insurgence, insurrection, intractableness, misbehavior, mutiny, neglect, noncompliance, nonobservance, obstinacy, perverseness, rebellion, recalcitrance, revolt, revolution, strike, stubbornness, transgression, treason, unruliness, uprising, violation, waywardness

disorder *n.* **1.** chaos, clutter, confusion, disarray, dishevelment, disorderliness, disorganization, displacement, jumble, mess, muddle, snarl, tangle, untidiness **2.** agitation, anarchy, bedlam, chaos, commotion, confusion, discomposure, discord, disquiet, disruption, disturbance, ferment, fray, insurrection, lawlessness, mayhem, melee, rebellion, revolution, riot, strike, tumult, turbulence, turmoil, unrest, unruliness, uproar, upset

disorderly *adj.* **1.** chaotic, cluttered, confused, disarranged, disheveled, disorganized, indiscriminate, irregular, jumbled, messy, muddled, scrambled, tangled, unkempt, unmethodical, unorganized, unsystematic, untidy **2.** boisterous, disobedient, disruptive, intractable, lawless, misbehaving, mutinous, noisy, obstreperous, rebellious, riotous, rough, rowdy, tumultuous, turbulent, uncontrollable, undisciplined, ungovernable, unmanageable, unrestrained, unruly, violent, wild

disorganization *n.* anarchy, chaos, confusion, derangement, disarrangement, disarray, dishevelment, disjointedness, disorder, disorderliness, disruption, disunion, incoherence, lawlessness, turmoil, unconnectedness, unruliness

disorganized *adj.* chaotic, confused, disjointed, disordered, disorderly, haphazard, incoherent, jumbled, muddled, unconnected, unmethodical, unsystematic

disparity *n.* contrariety, contrast, difference, discrepancy, disproportion, dissimilarity, dissimilitude, distinction, divergency, imparity, incongruity, inequality, unevenness, unlikeness, variation

dispatch *n.* **1.** bulletin, communication, instruction, letter, message, missive, note, rejoinder, reply, report **2.** celerity, expedition, expeditiousness, haste, hurry, precipitance, promptness, quickness, rapidity, speed, speediness, swiftness

dispensable *adj.* disposable, expendable, gratuitous, needless, nonessential, removable, replaceable, superfluous, unimportant, unnecessary, unrequired, useless

dispensation *n.* **1.** allocation, allotment, apportionment, assignation, assignment, award, bestowal, conferment, consignment, disbursement, distribution, endowment, supplying **2.** administration, arrangement, charge, command, conduct, control, direction, discharge, disposal, disposition, implementation, management, ministration, operation, order, organization, oversight, regulation, stewardship, supervision, system

dispense *v.* **1.** allocate, allot, apportion, assign, award, bestow, deal out, disburse, distribute, divide, dole out, furnish, give out, grant, hand out, measure, mete out, parcel out, portion, prorate, share, supply **2.** administer, apply, carry out, command, direct, discharge, execute, implement, manage, minister, operate, prescribe, prosecute, regulate, wield **3.** absolve, acquit, clear, discharge, except, excuse, exempt, exonerate, free, let off, pardon, release, reprieve

dispense with *v.* abolish, abrogate, abstain from, annul, cancel, dispose of, disregard, do away with, do without, forgo, give up, ignore, nullify, omit, refrain from, reject, relinquish, renounce, repeal, rescind, revoke, waive, yield

disperse *v.* banish, break up, broadcast, circulate, clear out, diffuse, disappear, disband, dismiss, dispel, disseminate, dissipate, dissolve, distribute, dole out, drive away, eject, measure out, scatter, separate, sow, spread, sprinkle, vanish

display *n.* **1.** act, advertisement, arrangement, array, demonstration, example, exhibit, exhibition, exposition, layout, panorama, presentation, sample, scheme, show, spread **2.** computer screen, indicators, lights, monitor, screen

display *v.* advertise, arrange, demonstrate, disclose, evince, exhibit, expose, extend, feature, flaunt, illustrate, lay out, manifest, model, open out, place, post, present, publicize, set forth, set out, show, spread out, stretch out, uncover, unfold, unfurl, unveil

disposal *n.* allocation, arrangement, array, assignment, assortment, bestowal, classification, consignment, conveyance, dispensation, disposition, distribution, division, grouping, order, ordering, organization, placing, provision, transfer

dispose *v.* actuate, align, arrange, array, assort, bend, bias, class, classify, coordinate, deal with, decide, determine, direct, distribute, end, finish, group, incline, induce, influence, lead, line up, marshal, motivate, move, order, organize, place, predispose, prepare, prime, prompt, range, rank, ready, regulate, settle, set up, systematize, tempt

disposition *n.* **1.** arrangement, conclusion, control, decision, direction, disposal, grouping, management, order, organization, outcome, placement, regulation, resolution, result, settlement **2.** bent, bias, character, constitution, frame of mind, humor, inclination, leaning, make-up, mood, nature, outlook, penchant, personality, predilection, predisposition, proclivity, propensity, readiness, spirit, temper, temperament, tendency, tenor, vein

disproportionate *adj.* asymmetrical, disparate, disproportional, excessive, incommensurate, incongruous, inconsistent, inconsonant, inordinate, irregular, lopsided, nonsymmetrical, out-of-balance, out-of-proportion, top-heavy, unbalanced, unequal, uneven, unreasonable, unsymmetrical

disprove *v.* belie, confute, contradict, controvert, defeat, deny, discredit, expose, invalidate, negate, overthrow, overturn, prove false, puncture, rebut, refute

dispute *n.* altercation, argument, bickering, conflict, contention, contest, controversy, debate, difference, disagreement, discord, discussion, dissension, disturbance, feud, friction, misunderstanding, quarrel, squabble

disregard *v.* discount, dismiss, disobey, forget, gloss over, ignore, let alone, let be, minimize, neglect, omit, overlook, pass by, pass over, pay no attention to, rebuff, reject, set aside, slight, take no notice of, waive

disrupt *v.* **1.** disarrange, disarray, dislocate, disorder, disorganize, displace, jumble, mix up, scramble, shuffle **2.** arrest, block, break, break into, break up, discontinue, halt, interfere with, intermit, interrupt, obstruct, stop, suspend

dissatisfaction *n.* annoyance, chagrin, dejection, disappointment, disapproval, discontent, dislike, dismay, displeasure, disquiet, distaste, distress, exasperation, frustration, irritation, uneasiness, unhappiness

dissatisfied *adj.* annoyed, chagrined, dejected, disappointed, disapproving, discontented, dismayed, displeased, disturbed, exasperated, frustrated, irked, irritated, offended, resentful, uneasy, unfulfilled, ungratified, unhappy, unsatisfied

disseminate *v.* broadcast, circulate, diffuse, dispense, disperse, dissipate, distribute, give out, promulgate, propagate, publicize, publish, scatter, spread

dissemination *n.* broadcasting, circulation, diffusion, dispensation, dispersal, dissipation, giving out, promulgation, propagation, publication, publishing, scattering, spread, spreading

dissent *n.* denial, difference, disagreement, disapproval, disavowal, discord, heterodoxy, nonagreement, noncompliance, nonconcurrence, nonconformity, objection, opposition, protest, refusal, rejection, repudiation, resistance, variance

dissent *v.* abandon, argue, challenge, contest, contradict, disagree, dispute, disavow, object, protest, reject, repudiate, resist

dissertation *n.* address, commentary, critique, discourse, disquisition, essay, exposition, lecture, oration, sermon, speech, thesis, treatise

disservice *n.* bad turn, damage, detriment, disfavor, harm, injury, injustice, unkindness, wrong

dissolution *n.* adjournment, break-up, decomposition, detachment, disassociation, disbandment, disconnection, discontinuation, disengagement, disintegration, disjunction, dismissal, dispersal, disunion, division, end, evaporation, extinction, finish, parting, partition, resolution, separation, severance, split-up, suspension, termination

dissuade *v.* advise against, caution against, counsel against, deprecate, deter, discourage, disincline, divert, expostulate, persuade not to, prevent, remonstrate, stop, talk out of, thwart, urge against, warn

distance *n.* area, breadth, circumference, compass, expanse, extension, extent, field, gap, horizon, interspace, interval, lapse, length, radius, range, reach, remoteness, remove, scope, space, span, spread, stretch, sweep, width

distinct *adj.* **1.** different, discrete, disparate, dissimilar, distinctive, divergent, diverse, individual, particular, peculiar, separate, special, unassociated, unattached, unconnected, unique, unlike, various **2.** apparent, certain, clear, clear-cut, decided, definite, evident, explicit, express, graphic, lucid, manifest, obvious, palpable, patent, plain, pointed, recognizable, self-evident, sharp, specific, tangible, unambiguous, unequivocal, unmistakable, vivid, well-defined

distinction *n.* **1.** clearness, contradistinction, contrast, difference, differential, differentiation, discernment, discreteness, discretion, discrimination, disparity, dissimilarity, distinctiveness, divergence, divergency, diversity, feature, individuality, nicety, nuance, otherness, particularity, peculiarity, penetration, perception, quality, separation, unattachment, unlikeness **2.** account, achievement, award, celebrity, consequence, credit, decoration, eminence, excellence, fame, glory, greatness, illustriousness, importance, laurels, mark, merit, note, preeminence, prestige, prominence, rank, renown, reputation, repute, significance

distinguish *v.* **1.** ascertain, categorize, characterize, circumscribe, classify, decide, define, delimit, demarcate, denote, designate, detail, detect, determine, differentiate, discern, discriminate, grade, group, identify, indicate, individualize, judge, label, mark, mark off, name, note, particularize, pick out, pinpoint, place, point out, segregate, select, separate, set apart, signalize, single out, size, sort out, specify, tag, tell, tell apart, tell between, tell the difference **2.** acclaim, acknowledge, applaud, bestow honor on, celebrate, commend, commemorate, dignify, ennoble, extol, glorify, honor, immortalize, make famous, memorialize, pay tribute to, praise, salute

distinguished *adj.* acclaimed, aristocratic, celebrated, dignified, distinct, eminent, esteemed, exalted, extraordinary, famed, great, illustrious, imperial, marked, noble, notable, noted, outstanding, pointed, preeminent, prominent, remarkable, renowned, salient, signal, special, stately, striking, unforgettable, well-known

distraction *n.* aberration, abstraction, agitation, amusement, bewilderment, commotion, confusion, discord, disorder, disturbance, diversion, divertissement, entertainment, friction, game, interference, interruption, pastime, perplexity, preoccupation, recreation, refreshment, relaxation

distribute *v.* **1.** administer, allocate, allot, apportion, assign, award, bestow, broadcast, circulate, convey, deal out, deliver, diffuse, dispense, disperse, disseminate, divide, dole out, endow, give out, hand out, issue, measure out, mete out, parcel out, partition, pass out, prorate, spread, sprinkle, transmit **2.** arrange, assort, categorize, catalog, class, classify, codify, divide, file, group, order, separate, systematize, tabulate

distribution *n.* **1.** allocation, allotment, apportionment, assignment, broadcast, circulation, delivery, diffusion, dispensation, dispersal, dispersion, disposal, dissemination, division, issuance, marketing, partition, propagation, proration, rationing, scattering, shipment, spreading, trading, transport, transportation **2.** arrangement, assortment, cataloging, classification, codification, collation, formulating, gradation, grouping, order, ordering, organization, sequence, tabulation

district *n.* area, commune, community, department, division, domain, geographical area, locale, locality, neighborhood, precinct, province, quarter, realm, region, section, sector, sphere, territory, ward, zone

disturbance *n.* agitation, annoyance, brawl, commotion, derangement, disarrangement, disarray, disorder, disruption, distraction, eruption, fray, insurrection, interruption, noise, perturbation, racket, rampage, rebellion, revolt, riot, tumult, turbulence, turmoil, unrest, upheaval, uprising, uproar, upset

diverse *adj.* assorted, contrasted, different, differing, disparate, dissimilar, distinct, divergent, diversified, diversiform, manifold, multiform, miscellaneous, separate, sundry, unlike, variant, varied, variegated, various, varying

diversify *v.* alter, assort, change, expand, mix, modify, transform, variegate, vary

diversity *n.* antithesis, assortment, contrast, deviation, difference, disparity, dissent, dissimilarity, diversification, heterogeneity, inequality, irregularity, noncomformity, unlikeness, variance, variation, variety

divest *v.* bare, denude, deprive, despoil, disencumber, disinherit, dismantle, dispose of, dispossess, expose, free from, get rid of, oust, purge, put off, relieve of, remove, rid of, strip, take from, take off, uncover, unload

divide *v.* **1.** allocate, allot, apportion, assign, deal out, dispense, disperse, distribute, dole out, hand out, measure out,

parcel out, portion out, prorate, ration, share, slice, split up
2. arrange, assort, catalog, categorize, classify, grade, group, label, put in order, rate, segregate, separate, sort **3.** bisect, branch, break, cleave, cut, cut up, demarcate, detach, disconnect, disengage, disentangle, disjoin, dissect, dissever, disunite, diverge, fork, halve, intersect, isolate, open, part, partition, quarter, rend, section, segregate, separate, sever, split, subdivide, unbind, undo

dividend *n.*   allotment, allowance, bonus, dispensation, distributed earnings, distribution, earnings distribution, extra, fringe benefit, interest, pay, portion, premium, proceeds, profit, return, share

division *n.* **1.** apportionment, bisection, breach, break, carving, cutting up, demarcation, departmentalizing, detaching, detachment, disconnection, disjunction, dismemberment, dissolution, distribution, disunion, dividing, parceling, parting, partitioning, reduction, rupture, segmentation, separation, severance **2.** affiliate, border, boundary, branch, category, chunk, class, compartment, component, demarcation, department, fraction, fragment, member, offshoot, parcel, part, partition, piece, portion, room, section, sector, segment, share, slice, subdivision

docket *n.*   agenda, calendar, card, program, schedule, ticket, timetable

doctrine *n.*   article of faith, axiom, belief, canon, concept, convention, conviction, creed, declaration, dictum, dogma, gospel, law, maxim, opinion, postulate, precept, principle, pronouncement, proposition, rule, teaching, tenet, theory, thesis

document *n.*   certificate, charter, chronicle, credentials, deed, form, instrument, official paper, paper, record, report, testament, testimony, voucher, writ, written communication, written work

documentation   *n.*   background information, comments, description, document preparation, guidelines, help system, information, instruction book, instruction manual, instructions, on-line information, on-line instructions, printed information, reference material, remarks, software instructions, tutorial, user information, user instructions, user reference

dogma *n.*   article of faith, axiom, belief, canon, code, conviction, creed, doctrine, firm belief, fixed opinion, maxim, opinion, precept, principle, rule, teachings, tenet, theory

dollar *n.* bank note, bill, currency, denomination, exchange medium, legal tender, money, note, paper dollar, paper money, silver dollar

domain *n.* area, area of knowledge, arena, department, district, dominion, empire, estate, field, jurisdiction, land, problem area, quarter, realm, region, section, set of data values, set of values, sphere, territory, zone

domicile *n.* accommodations, dwelling place, habitation, home, house, housing, legal residence, living quarters, residence, residency

dominate *v.* **1.** boss, command, control, dictate, direct, domineer, govern, head, intimidate, lead, manage, monopolize, oppress, order, overpower, overrun, overshadow, predominate, prevail over, reign over, rule over, run, subdue, subject, subjugate, subordinate, suppress, sway, tyrannize, wield power over **2.** bestride, crown, eclipse, hang over, loom over, overlook, project, stand over, survey, tower above

dominion *n.* **1.** authority, command, commission, control, dominance, domination, government, grasp, hegemony, hold, jurisdiction, leadership, management, power, preeminence, regimentation, reign, rule, sovereignty, supremacy, sway **2.** See **domain**

donate *v.* allot, allow, award, bequeath, bestow, confer, contribute, extend, give, grant, hand out, impart, issue, make a gift of, offer, pledge, present, provide, subscribe, tender, will, yield

donation *n.* allotment, allowance, assistance, benefaction, bequest, bestowal, charity, conferral, contribution, endowment, gift, grant, gratuity, handout, offering, present, presentation, subsidy

donor *n.* backer, benefactor, bestower, conferrer, contributor, donator, giver, grantor, patron, philanthropist, supporter

dormant *adj.* asleep, closed, comatose, fallow, hibernating, immobile, inactive, inert, inoperative, latent, lethargic, lifeless, motionless, passive, sleeping, sluggish, stagnant, torpid, undeveloped, unmoving

double *n.* clone, copy, counterpart, duplicate, facsimile, image, impersonator, match, replica, stand-in, substitute, twin, understudy

double *adj.* bifold, binary, coupled, doubled, dual, duplex, duplicate, duplicated, identical, paired, repeated, replicated, twin, twofold

double *v.* amplify, augment, copy, duplicate, enlarge, geminate, increase, magnify, match, multiply, repeat, replicate, supplement

double entendre *n.* ambiguity, anagram, double meaning, equivocation, hidden meaning, innuendo, paradox, play on words, pun, word play

doubt *n.* agnosticism, ambiguity, confusion, diffidence, dilemma, disbelief, distrust, dubiousness, faithlessness, fear, hesitancy, hesitation, incertitude, incredulity, indecision, irresolution, lack of certainty, lack of confidence, lack of faith, misgiving, mistrust, perplexity, quandary, question, reluctance, skepticism, suspicion, uncertainty, undecidedness, vacillation, wavering

doubt *v.* be apprehensive, be dubious, be in a quandary, be uncertain, be undetermined, challenge, disbelieve, dispute, distrust, fear, have qualms, hesitate, lack confidence in, mistrust, query, question, suspect, vacillate, waver

down [*equipment*]: *adj.* inoperative, malfunctioning, nonavailable, nonfunctioning, nonoperative, out of order, unavailable

downgrade *v.* belittle, criticize, declass, decrease, degrade, demerit, demote, denigrate, depreciate, detract from, devalue, disparage, mark down, minimize, reduce, run down, set back, understate, undervalue

download [*computer*]: *v.* accept, move, receive, store, transfer, transmit, unload

downsize *v.* cut back, decrease, diminish, lessen, lower, make less, make smaller, reduce

downturn *n.* decline, decrease, downward shift, downward turn

draft *n.* **1.** blueprint, design, outline, plan, preliminary form, rough composition, rough version **2.** bank draft, bill of exchange, check, clean draft, debenture, documentary draft, order, sight draft, time draft, written order

draft *v.* compose, design, devise, draw, draw up, fashion, formulate, frame, plan, prepare, shape

drain *v.* deplete, diminish, discharge, dissipate, divert, draw off, dry up, empty, evacuate, extract, filter off, filtrate, flow out, get rid of, lessen, milk, percolate, pump out, reduce, remove, run off, seep out, siphon off, take away, tap, use up, withdraw

drama *n.* **1.** crisis, emotion, excitement, spectacle, tension, theatrics, turmoil **2.** acting, dramatic art, dramatization, dramaturgy, histrionic art, play, production, show, stagecraft, stage show, theater, theatrical, theatrical work, thespian art

dramatic *adj.* effective, electrifying, emotional, exciting, expressive, forceful, graphic, histrionic, impressive, moving, potent, powerful, sensational, startling, striking, suspenseful, theatrical, thespian, thrilling, tragic, vivid

drawback *n.* bar, barrier, defect, deficiency, deterrent, detriment, difficulty, disadvantage, encumbrance, estoppel, failing, fault, flaw, handicap, hindrance, hurdle, impediment, imperfection, inconvenience, liability, minus, nuisance, obstacle, obstruction, problem, shortcoming, weakness

drawing *n.* caricature, cartoon, commercial art, composition, copy, delineation, depiction, design, diagram, etching, figure, illustration, outline, picture, portrait, portrayal, representation, sketch, tracing

drill *n.* **1.** coaching, conditioning, discipline, drilling, exercise, gymnastics, indoctrination, initiation, instruction, maneuvers, marching, physical training, practice, repetition, teaching, training, warm-up, workout **2.** auger, bit, borer, boring tool, cutting instrument, countersink, implement, jackhammer, rotary tool

drill *v.* **1.** coach, condition, discipline, exercise, indoctrinate, initiate, instruct, practice, rehearse, school, teach, train, tutor, warm up, work out **2.** bore, bore hole, pass through, penetrate, perforate, pierce, puncture

drink *n.* alcohol, alcoholic beverage, beverage, cold drink, draft, liquid, liquor, nonalcoholic beverage, refreshment, soft drink

drive *n.* **1.** appeal, campaign, crusade, fund raiser, fund raising, solicitation **2.** CD drive, computer drive, disk drive, electromechanical device, hard drive **3.** aggressiveness, ambition, ambitiousness, energy, enterprise, impetus, industry, initiative, momentum, motivation, pep, verve, vigor, vitality, will

drive *v.* actuate, advance, animate, arouse, coerce, compel, demand, direct, encourage, force, goad, guide, herd, hurry, impel, induce, inspire, make, manage, motivate, move, oblige, operate, press, pressure, prod, prompt, propel, provoke, push, require, rouse, rush, set in motion, shepherd, shove, spur, steer, stimulate, thrust, urge

drop *n.* cut, cutback, decline, decrease, depreciation, descent, deterioration, devaluation, dip, downfall, downgrade, downslide, downswing, downtrend, downturn, drop-off, fall, fall-off, lessening, lowering, reduction, slide, slump, upset

drop *v.* abandon, abort, break with, call off, cancel, cast off, cease, collapse, decline, descend, desert, desist from, discard, discontinue, dismiss, dispense with, dive, end, fall, forfeit, forget about, forgo, forsake, give up, interrupt, leave, leave behind, let go, lower, part with, plunge, quit, reject, release, relinquish, renounce, repudiate, resign, retire from, sink, stop, terminate, throw away, throw over, unload, waive, withdraw from

dry *adj.* **1.** apathetic, boring, commonplace, dreary, dull, impassive, indifferent, insipid, matter-of-fact, monotonous, plain, tedious, tiresome, trite, unadorned, unemotional, uninteresting, wearisome **2.** anhydrous, arid, bare, barren, dehydrated, desert, desiccated, dried-out, dried-up, dusty, evaporated, juiceless, moistureless, parched, rainless, sapless, seared, thirsty, undampened, unmoistened, unwatered, waterless

dual *adj.* bifold, biform, binary, coupled, double, dualistic, duplex, duplicate, matched, paired, twin, twofold

dub *v.* add, add sound, baptize, bestow, call, christen, confer, copy, denominate, designate, inaugurate, induct, instate, invest, knight, label, name, nickname, nominate, style, tag, term, title, transfer

duct *n.* aqueduct, canal, channel, chimney, conduit, culvert, drain, flue, funnel, passage, pipe, tube, vessel, watercourse

due *n.* birthright, claim, compensation, entitlement, natural right, payment, prerogative, privilege, recompense, repayment, retribution, reward, right, rights, satisfaction

due *adj.* **1.** collectible, expected, immediately payable, in arrears, mature, outstanding, overdue, owed, payable, payable immediately, receivable, unpaid **2.** appropriate, apt, commensurate, correct, deserved, earned, equitable, fair, fitting, just, lawful, merited, proper, rightful, satisfactory, suitable, warranted, well-earned

dues *n.* assessment, charge, charges, fee, fees, membership fee, membership payment, rates

dull *adj.* **1.** boring, colorless, dismal, dreary, familiar, hackneyed, lifeless, monotonous, ordinary, placid, plain, routine,

stale, tedious, tired, tiresome, trite, unexciting, unimaginative, uninspiring, uninteresting, usual, wearisome, worn-out
2. backward, dull-witted, dumb, ignorant, obtuse, simple,
simple-minded, slow, slow-witted, stolid, stupid, unintellectu-
al, unintelligent, vacuous, witless   **3.** blunt, blunted, edgeless, flat, obtuse, pointless, round, square, unpointed,
unsharpened

duly *adv.*   accordingly, appropriately, befittingly, correctly,
decorously, properly, rightfully, rightly, suitably

duplicate *n.*   clone, copy, counterfeit, counterpart, double,
duplication, facsimile, image, imitation, likeness, lookalike,
match, mate, parallel, photocopy, photostat, repetition, replica, replication, reproduction, second, transcript, twin

duplicate *adj.*   alike, bifold, corresponding, double, duplex,
equal, equivalent, identical, indistinguishable, matched,
matching, same, twin, twofold

duplicate *v.*   clone, copy, counterfeit, do again, double, echo,
imitate, make copy, make replica, make twofold, mirror, perform again, photocopy, photostat, repeat, replicate, reproduce, run off

duplicity *n.*   betrayal, breach of trust, chicanery, deceit, deception, dishonesty, disloyalty, faithlessness, falsehood, fraud,
hypocrisy, improbity, infidelity, insincerity, mendacity, per-
fidy, treacherousness, treachery

durability *n.*   constancy, dependability, durableness,
endurance, immutability, imperishability, lastingness, longevi-
ty, permanence, persistence, reliability, stability, stamina,
sturdiness

durable *adj.*   abiding, changeless, constant, continuing,
dependable, endless, enduring, firm, fixed, immutable, imperishable, lasting, long-lasting, long-standing, perdurable, permanent, persisting, reliable, resistant, stable, steadfast,
steady, stout, strong, substantial, tough, unchangeable

duration *n.*   age, continuance, continuation, continuum,
course, endurance, existence, extension, extent, length, life,
lifetime, period, perpetuation, run, space, span, spell, stage,
stretch, term, time

duty *n.*   **1.** assessment, charge, customs, excise tax, fee,
impost, levy, rate, tariff, tax, toll   **2.** assignment, burden,
business, calling, care, charge, chore, commission, commitment, contract, devoir, engagement, function, job, mission,

ligation, occupation, office, onus, requirement, responsibility, role, routine, service, task, trust, undertaking, weight, work **3.** accountability, allegiance, answerability, deference, faithfulness, fealty, fidelity, homage, honesty, integrity, loyalty, obedience, obligation, pledge, respect, reverence

dwindle *v.* abate, become less, become smaller, compact, condense, contract, curtail, decay, decline, decrease, deteriorate, die away, die down, die out, diminish, drop, ebb, fade, fall, grow less, lessen, reduce, shorten, shrink, shrivel, sink, subside, taper off, wane, waste away, wither

dynamic *adj.* active, aggressive, alive, brisk, charismatic, compelling, driving, eager, effective, effectual, electric, emphatic, energetic, energizing, enterprising, forceful, forcible, high-powered, impelling, intense, lively, magnetic, potent, powerful, spirited, strenuous, strong, vigorous, vital, vitalizing, zealous

E

eager *adj.* ambitious, anxious, ardent, avid, craving, desiring, desirous, earnest, enthusiastic, fervid, hopeful, impatient, impulsive, intent, longing, resolute, restless, vehement, voracious, wholehearted, wishful, yearning, zealous

early *adj.* **1.** advanced, expeditious, fast, immediate, preceding, premature, previous, prompt, punctual, quick, rapid, speedy, timely, undelayed **2.** aboriginal, ancient, antiquated, archaic, earliest, initial, original, prehistoric, premier, primal, primeval, primitive, primordial, pristine, virgin

early *adv.* beforehand, directly, immediately, instantaneously, instantly, newly, prematurely, presently, primitively, promptly, recently, seasonably, shortly, summarily, timely, unexpectedly

earmark *n.* attribute, badge, band, character, characteristic, feature, hallmark, idiosyncrasy, label, marking, peculiarity, property, quality, sign, signature, stamp, style, tag, token, trademark, trait

earmark *v.* band, brand, designate, fold, hold, identify, label, mark, name, put away, reserve, set aside, stamp, tag

earn *v.* acquire, attain, bring in, collect, gain, get, make, merit, obtain, procure, profit, realize, reap, receive, secure, yield

earnest money *n.* advance, binder, deposit, down payment, earnest, installment, payment, pledge, promise, retainer, security, surety

earnings *n.* benefits, gain, money, net income, profits, receipts, recompense, remuneration, revenues, reward, salary, wages

easily *adv.* **1.** adroitly, comfortably, dexterously, efficiently, effortlessly, facilely, freely, handily, readily, simply, skillfully, smoothly, surely **2.** absolutely, assuredly, certainly, clearly, decidedly, definitely, doubtlessly, indisputably, indubitably, obviously, positively, surely, truly, undeniably, undoubtedly, unquestionably

easy *adj.* **1.** effortless, elementary, light, manageable, mere, obvious, painless, plain, simple, smooth, straightforward, uncomplicated, undemanding **2.** calm, comfortable, composed, contented, easygoing, effortless, gentle, mild, moderate, peaceful, pleasant, quiet, relaxed, relieved, satisfied, secure, serene, tranquil, undemanding, undisturbed, untroubled, unworried   **3.** accommodating, amenable, charitable, compassionate, forgiving, indulgent, kindly, lax, lenient, liberal, merciful, moderate, pampering, pardoning, permissive, spoiling, sympathetic, temperate, tolerant, trusting

easygoing *adj.*   accepting, amenable, calm, carefree, casual, cheerful, complacent, composed, flexible, imperturbable, indulgent, lenient, liberal, mild-tempered, moderate, nonchalant, patient, permissive, placid, relaxed, serene, tolerant, tranquil, unconcerned, uncritical, undemanding, understanding, unexcitable, unruffled, unworried

economic *adj.*   budgetary, commercial, financial, financially rewarding, fiscal, material, monetary, pecuniary, productive, profit-making, remunerative

economical *adj.*   **1.** careful, chary, closefisted, conservative, cost-effective, economizing, efficient, frugal, miserly, money-saving, provident, prudent, saving, scrimping, skimping, sparing, stingy, thrifty, tight   **2.** cheap, cut-rate, inexpensive, low-priced, marked-down, reasonable, reduced

economize *v.*   be economical, be frugal, be prudent, be sparing, conserve, curb, curtail, cut, cut back, cut down, limit, put aside, reduce, restrict, retrench, save, save for, scrimp, skimp

economy *n.*   **1.** care, carefulness, caution, conservation, control, curtailment, cutback, decrease, economizing, frugality, prudence, reduction, restraint, restriction, retrenchment, saving, scrimping, skimping, sparingness, stinginess, thrift, thrift management, thriftiness   **2.** earnings, GNP, gross, income, national earnings, national income, national product, net national product

ecumenical *adj.*   all-inclusive, comprehensive, general, global, unifying, universal, worldwide

edict *n.*   act, canon, command, commandment, declaration, decree, dictum, directive, enactment, fiat, injunction, law, mandate, manifesto, order, ordinance, policy statement, prescript, proclamation, pronouncement, public notice, regulation, rule, ruling, statute, writ

edifice *n.*   building, construction, high-rise, pile, skyscraper, tower

edit *v.*   adapt, alter, amend, annotate, compile, compose, copyedit, correct, delete, emend, excise, modify, polish, prepare, put together, rectify, refine, rephrase, revise, rewrite, style

edition *n.* impression, issue, number, press run, printing, version, volume

educate *v.* brief, coach, cultivate, develop, direct, discipline, drill, edify, enlighten, exercise, explain, foster, guide, indoctrinate, inform, initiate, instruct, nourish, nurture, practice, prepare, school, teach, train, tutor

educated *adj.* accomplished, coached, erudite, experienced, expert, formed, informed, instructed, knowledgeable, learned, lettered, literary, literate, prepared, professional, scholarly, schooled, shaped, skilled, trained, tutored, versed in, well-informed, well-read, well-taught, well-versed

education *n.* accomplishment, apprenticeship, coaching, development, direction, discipline, erudition, guidance, indoctrination, information, initiation, instruction, knowledge, learning, literacy, preparation, scholarship, schooling, skill, study, teaching, training, tutelage

effect *n.* **1.** accomplishment, achievement, aftereffect, aftermath, backlash, conclusion, consequence, corollary, development, end, event, fallout, issue, outcome, outgrowth, ramification, reaction, realization, repercussion, response, result, sequel, side effect   **2.** bearing, effectiveness, efficiency, essence, gist, impact, implication, import, impression, imprint, influence, intent, intention, meaning, objective, purport, purpose, sense, significance, tenor

effect *v.* accomplish, achieve, act out, begin, bring about, bring to pass, carry out, carry through, cause, complete, conclude, consummate, do, effectuate, enact, ensure, execute, fulfill, generate, implement, induce, initiate, invoke, make, make certain, make happen, perform, produce, reach, realize, secure

effective *adj.* adequate, arousing, capable, cogent, competent, effectual, efficacious, efficient, fit, forceful, forcible, functioning, impressive, moving, operative, persuasive, pointed, potent, powerful, practical, productive, remarkable, serviceable, striking, sufficient, telling, useful, valid

efficiency *n.* adeptness, adroitness, competence, competency, deftness, effectiveness, effectualness, efficacy, expertise, expertness, facility, faculty, input cost, know-how, mastery, potency, productiveness, productivity, proficiency, skill, skillfulness

efficient *adj.* adapted, adept, adequate, adroit, apt, businesslike, competent, deft, economical, effective, effectual, efficacious, expert, potent, productive, proficient, skilled, skillful

effort *n.* **1.** application, discipline, drill, energy, exercise, exertion, force, impulse, industry, labor, practice, production, push, strain, stress, strife, striving, struggle, training, work **2.** aim, attempt, endeavor, purpose, trial, try, undertaking, venture **3.** accomplishment, achievement, act, attainment, deed, exploit, feat

egregious *adj.* atrocious, blatant, bold, conspicuous, deplorable, extreme, flagrant, glaring, grievous, heinous, infamous, insufferable, intolerable, notorious, obtrusive, outrageous, outright, overt, preposterous, prominent, scandalous, shocking

egress *n.* departure, door, egression, emergence, escape, exit, issue, outlet, vent

eject *v.* banish, cast out, deport, discharge, dislodge, dismiss, displace, dispossess, drive away, eliminate, erupt, evict, exclude, exile, expel, fire, force out, get rid of, impel, jettison, oust, project, propel, reject, remove, throw out, thrust out, turn out

elaborate *adj.* busy, complete, complex, complicated, comprehensive, decorated, detailed, elegant, embellished, exhaustive, extensive, extravagant, fussy, garnished, imposing, intricate, involved, labored, luxurious, minute, ornamented, ornate, ostentatious, painstaking, precise, refined, showy, skillful, sophisticated, studied, thorough

elaborate *v.* add detail, add to, amplify, beautify, clarify, comment, cultivate, decorate, develop, devise, discuss, embellish, enhance, enlarge, expand, explain, expound, flesh out, garnish, improve, increase, make detailed, ornament, perfect, polish, prepare, produce, refine, work up

elect *v.* appoint, assign, cast ballot, choose, cull, decide on, designate, determine, draw, judge, name, pick, pick out, select, settle on, single out, vote, vote for

election *n.* appointment, ballot, balloting, choice, choosing, decision, designation, determination, direct vote, electing, judgment, naming, picking out, plebiscite, poll, polls, popular vote, primary, public vote, referendum, selection, vote, voting

elective *adj.* appointive, choosing, discretionary, electing, electoral, nonobligatory, optional, selecting, selective, voluntary

elegant *adj.*   aesthetic, artistic, beautiful, chic, choice, classic, courtly, cultivated, cultured, delicate, exquisite, fashionable, fine, graceful, grand, handsome, luxurious, majestic, opulent, ornamental, ornate, polished, refined, rich, select, sophisticated, stately, stylish, sumptuous, superior, tasteful

element *n.* **1.** aspect, complement, component, constituent, detail, essential, facet, factor, feature, fundamental, ingredient, item, member, module, parcel, part, particular, piece, potion, section, segment, unit **2.** circle, domain, environment, field, habitat, medium, milieu, native state, quarter, realm, sphere, zone

elementary *adj.* basal, basic, beginning, easy, elemental, essential, facile, fundamental, introductory, original, plain, prefatory, preliminary, primary, primitive, root, rudimentary, simple, uncomplex, uncomplicated, underlying, understandable

elevate *v.* **1.** erect, heighten, hoist, levitate, lift, lift up, move up, raise, rear, thrust up, uplift **2.** advance, aggrandize, augment, boost, build up, crown, dignify, ennoble, exalt, extol, further, glorify, heighten, honor, increase, intensify, magnify, prefer, promote **3.** animate, brighten, buoy, cheer, cheer up, elate, enliven, excite, exhilarate, gladden, hearten, inspire, lift, raise, revive, uplift, vitalize

eligible *adj.* acceptable, appropriate, desirable, employable, fit, proper, qualified, satisfactory, suitable, suited, trained, worthwhile, worthy

eliminate *v.* abolish, cancel, cast aside, cast away, cut out, discard, discharge, dismiss, dispense with, dispose of, disregard, drop, edit out, eradicate, erase, expunge, exterminate, extinguish, extirpate, fire, get rid of, leave out, obliterate, omit, phase out, reject, remove, rule out, take out

elite *n.* aristocracy, celebrities, high society, meritocracy, nobility, privileged class, prize, quality, ruling class, select, upper class

elite *adj.* aristocratic, best, choice, elect, exclusive, selected, top, upper-class

elucidate *v.* annotate, clarify, clear up, comment on, define, delineate, demonstrate, enlighten, exemplify, explain, explicate, expound, gloss, illuminate, illustrate, interpret, make clear, make plain, prove, show, simplify, spell out

embargo *n.* ban, bar, barrier, blockage, check, hindrance, impediment, interdiction, prohibition, proscription, restraint, restriction, stoppage

embarrassment *n.* abashment, awkwardness, bashfulness, bind, chagrin, clumsiness, difficulty, dilemma, discomfiture, discomfort, discomposure, distress, humiliation, indiscretion, mortification, plight, predicament, quandary, scrape, self-consciousness, shame, timidity, unease, uneasiness

embassy *n.* commission, consular office, consulate, delegation, diplomatic office, legation, ministry, mission

embellish *v.* adorn, beautify, brighten, color, decorate, embroider, enhance, enrich, exaggerate, furbish, garnish, gloss over, make beautiful, ornament, paint, trim

embellishment *n.* adornment, beautification, brightening, coloration, coloring, decorating, decoration, elaboration, embroidering, embroidery, enhancement, enrichment, exaggeration, flounce, flourish, frill, garnish, gilding, glossing over, ornament, ornamentation, ostentation, trimming

emblem *n.* attribute, badge, banner, brand, character, coat of arms, design, ensign, figure, flag, identification, image, insignia, logo, mark, marker, medal, memento, monogram, motto, pennant, regalia, reminder, representation, seal, sign, standard, symbol, token, trademark, type

emend *v.* alter, amend, correct, edit, improve, polish, redact, revise, rewrite, touch up

emergency *n.* accident, bind, conjuncture, contingency, crisis, danger, difficulty, exigency, extremity, fix, juncture, pass, plight, predicament, quandary, serious situation, straits, urgency

emigrant *n.* alien, colonist, defector, displaced person, émigré, evacuee, expatriate, fugitive, migrant, migrator, refugee

emigrate *v.* depart, leave, migrate, move, move abroad, move to another country, quit, remove

eminent *adj.* celebrated, distinguished, esteemed, exalted, famed, famous, foremost, high-ranking, illustrious, notable, noted, noteworthy, outstanding, preeminent, prestigious, prominent, renowned

emissary *n.* agent, ambassador, attaché, courier, delegate, deputy, diplomat, envoy, intermediary, internuncio, legate, messenger, nuncio, plenipotentiary, representative, vicar

emission *n.* discharge, effusion, ejection, emanation, eruption, evacuation, excretion, extrusion, exudation, transmission, venting

emotional *adj.* affective, ardent, demonstrative, dramatic, emotive, excitable, expressive, feeling, fervent, fiery, high-strung, hysterical, impetuous, impulsive, melodramatic, moving, nervous, overwrought, passionate, poignant, roused, sensitive, sensuous, sentient, sentimental, susceptible, sympathetic, temperamental, tender, volatile, warm, zealous

empathy *n.* affinity, appreciation, attribution, compassion, comprehension, concord, insight, rapport, recognition, responsiveness, sympathy, understanding, warmth

emphasis *n.* accent, accentuation, attention, force, import, importance, intensity, italics, mark, moment, note, preeminence, priority, prominence, significance, stress, underlining, underscoring, weight

emphasize *v.* accent, accentuate, belabor, call attention to, charge, dramatize, dwell on, enunciate, feature, give emphasis to, give priority to, headline, highlight, intensify, italicize, make clear, make emphatic, mark, press home, punctuate, spotlight, stress, underline, underscore, weight

employ *v.* **1.** apprentice, commission, contract for, engage, enlist, enroll, hire, retain, take on **2.** apply, devote, exercise, handle, manipulate, occupy, operate, spend, use, wield, work

employed *adj.* active, engaged, hired, laboring, occupied, operating, selected, working

employee *n.* apprentice, assistant, attendant, hand, helper, hireling, jobholder, laborer, staff member, wage-earner, worker, working person

employer *n.* boss, businessperson, capitalist, chief, company, corporation, director, entrepreneur, executive, firm, head, headquarters, management, manager, organization, overseer, owner, president, proprietor

employment *n.* **1.** appointment, assignment, business, calling, charge, commission, craft, duty, employ, engagement, enrollment, field, function, job, mission, occupation, position, post, profession, pursuit, service, situation, task, trade, undertaking, vocation **2.** application, disposition, exercise, handling, operation, usage, use

empower *v.* accredit, allow, approve, authorize, capacitate, certify, charge, commission, confirm, consent to, countenance, delegate, enable, endow, entitle, entrust, equip, grant, invest, license, pass, permit, qualify, ratify, sanction, validate, vest, vote for, warrant

enact *v.* approve, authorize, constitute, decree, dictate, establish, establish as law, execute, formulate, institute, legislate, make into law, make laws, ordain, order, pass, pass into law, proclaim, pronounce, put in force, ratify, sanction, transact

enclose *v.* blockade, box up, circle, close in, cover, encircle, enfold, fence in, hem in, insert, pen in, put inside, shut in, wrap

encounter *v.* **1.** chance upon, come across, come upon, confront, face, happen upon, meet, meet with, run across, run into, turn up **2.** attack, battle, clash with, conflict with, confront, contend, engage, face, fight, join, meet, skirmish, struggle

encourage *v.* **1.** animate, applaud, arouse, assure, boost, brighten, buoy, buoy up, cheer, cheer up, comfort, console, embolden, energize, enliven, excite, exhilarate, fortify, galvanize, gladden, goad, hearten, impel, incite, induce, inflame, inspire, inspirit, instigate, persuade, praise, prevail on, push, rally, reassure, refresh, restore, revitalize, revivify, rouse, spur, steel, stimulate, stir, stir up, strengthen, sway, urge, urge on **2.** abet, advance, advocate, aid, approve, assist, back, bolster, comfort, console, countenance, endorse, favor, fortify, foster, further, get behind, give support, help, lobby, maintain, patronize, promote, push, recommend, reinforce, relieve, sanction, second, subscribe to, subsidize, support, sustain, underwrite, uphold

encouragement *n.* advocacy, aid, animation, assistance, assurance, backing, boost, buoyancy, cheer, cheering, comfort, confidence, consolation, help, helpfulness, hope, incentive, incitement, inducement, inspiration, invigoration, motivation, optimism, persuasion, promotion, reassurance, reassuring, stimulation, support, urging

encumbrance *n.* burden, claim, disadvantage, duty, handicap, hindrance, impediment, obligation, responsibility, tax

encyclopedic *adj.* all-embracing, all-encompassing, all-inclusive, broad, complete, comprehensive, diversified, exhaustive, extensive, thorough, universal, vast, wide-ranging, widespread

end *n.* **1.** accomplishment, achievement, adjournment, attainment, cessation, close, closing, closure, completion, conclusion, consequence, consummation, culmination, denouement, discontinuance, ending, epilog, expiration, finale, finish, fulfillment, issue, outcome, period, realization, resolution, result, retirement, stop, stoppage, termination, windup **2.** aim, aspiration, design, destination, goal, intent, intention, motivation, motive, object, objective, purpose, reason **3.** border, borderline, bound, boundary, confine, edge, extreme, extremity, head, limit, limitation, margin, nib, point, pole, tail end, terminal, termination, terminus, tip, top, ultimate, utmost

end *v.* abort, accomplish, achieve, break off, bring to an end, cease, close, close out, complete, conclude, consummate, culminate, cut, cut short, die out, discontinue, dissolve, drop, expire, finish, halt, quit, relinquish, settle, stop, terminate

ending *n.* catastrophe, cessation, close, closing, closure, completion, conclusion, consummation, culmination, denouement, end, epilog, expiration, finale, finish, outcome, period, realization, resolution, result, stop, stoppage, termination, windup

endorse *v.* **1.** advocate, affirm, approve, attest to, back up, champion, commend, confirm, corroborate, favor, give testimonial, pass, praise, ratify, recommend, sanction, seal, stand behind, subscribe to, substantiate, testify to, uphold, vote for, vouch for, warrant **2.** authenticate, autograph, cosign, countersign, notarize, put signature on, sign, sign for, underwrite

endorsement *n.* **1.** acceptance, advocacy, affirmation, approbation, approval, attestation, backing, championing, commendation, confirmation, corroboration, praise, ratification, recommendation, sanction, seal, stamp, subscription, substantiation, support, testament, testimonial, vote, warrant **2.** agreement, attachment, authentication, autograph, cosignature, countersignature, notarization, signature, underwriting

endowment *n.* aid, allotment, allowance, award, benefaction, bequest, bestowal, conferment, conferral, contribution, dispensation, donation, endowing, funding, gift, gifting, grant, granting, inheritance, permanent fund, presentation, stipend, subsidizing, subsidy, trust

endowments *n.* abilities, aptitudes, attributes, capabilities, capacities, characteristics, faculties, features, gifts, powers, properties, qualifications, qualities, strengths, talents

energy *n.* **1.** ambition, drive, efficacy, enterprise, force, forcefulness, initiative, intensity, potency, potentiality, power **2.** alertness, animation, ardor, cheer, enthusiasm, exuberance, flair, liveliness, spirit, verve, vigor, vitality, vivacity, zeal, zest

enforce *v.* administer, apply, apply pressure, back up, carry out, carry through, cause, coerce, compel, complete, conduct, control, demand, direct, discharge, drive, exact, execute, force, fulfill, impel, implement, impose, impress, insist on, invoke, make, manage, necessitate, oblige, perform, press, pressure, prosecute, put in force, put into effect, realize, reinforce, require, supervise, urge

enforcement *n.* administration, application, applying pressure, carrying out, carrying through, coercion, compulsion, compulsory law, constraint, control, demand, direction, discharge, domination, drive, duress, enforcing, exaction, execution, force, fulfilling, fulfillment, implementation, imposition, impulsion, insistence, management, necessitation, obligation, prescription, pressure, prosecution, putting in force, realization, reinforcement, requirement, spur, spurring, supervision, urging, whip, whipping

engage *v.* **1.** appoint, book, charter, commission, contract for, delegate, employ, enlist, enroll, hire, put on payroll, put to work, reserve, retain, secure, sign up, take on, use **2.** activate, attach, begin operation, energize, fasten, interact, interconnect, interlace, interlock, intermesh, start operation, switch on **3.** become involved, be occupied, embark on, employ, engross, enter into, immerse, involve, join, occupy oneself, partake, participate, set about, take part, take up, undertake

engagement *n.* appointment, arrangement, assignment, commitment, conference, date, interview, rendezvous, visit

engineer *v.* arrange, bring about, cause, control, devise, direct, effect, manage, negotiate, plan, plot, set up, wangle

enjoy *v.* **1.** appreciate, be fond of, be pleased with, delight in, derive pleasure from, fancy, feast on, have a good time, have fun, indulge in, like, love, luxuriate in, rejoice in, relish, revel in, savor, take joy in, take pleasure in, take satisfaction in **2.** avail oneself of, benefit from, have, have benefit of, have use of, make use of, possess, profit from, put to use, use, use to advantage

enjoyment *n.* **1.** appreciation, cheer, contentment, delectation, delight, ecstasy, enjoying, exhilaration, fun, gladness, gratification, happiness, indulgence, joy, luxury, pleasure, rejoicing, relish, revelry, satisfaction, self-indulgence, zest **2.** benefit, ownership, possession, profit, use, using

enlargement *n.* amplification, augmentation, blowup, increase, large copy, magnification, multiplication, supplementation

enroll *v.*   accept, admit, affix, book, catalog, chronicle, employ, engage, enlist, enter, join, join up, list, matriculate, muster, recruit, record, register, serve, sign up, subscribe, take course

enrollment *n.*   acceptance, admission, attendance, engagement, enlistment, entrance, entry, induction, joining, listing, matriculation, membership list, record, recruitment, register, registration, roster, student body, students, subscription

ensemble *n.*   act, band, cast, chamber orchestra, choir, chorus, company, entirety, group, number, performance, piece, quartet, routine, show, sum, total, totality, trio, troupe, whole, whole thing

ensure *v.*   assure, bring about, certify, cinch, clinch, confirm, effect, guarantee, insure, make certain, make secure, make sure, secure, set up, warrant

enter *v.*   **1.** calendar, catalog, chronicle, document, file, index, inscribe, insert, inventory, list, log, note, post, put in, record, register, set down, tabulate, take down, tally   **2.** access, arrive, break in, burst in, come, come in, crack, crawl, creep, drive in, drop in, embark, fall into, flow into, gain entry, get in, go in, immigrate, insert, insinuate, introduce, intrude, jump in, make an entrance, make way, move into, pass into, pile in, probe, rush in, set foot in, slip, sneak, trespass, work in, wriggle   **3.** admit, be accepted, be admitted, become member, begin, commence, commit oneself to, enlist in, enroll, inaugurate, join, launch, lead off, matriculate, obtain entrance, open, participate in, register, set about, set out on, sign up, start, subscribe to, take part in, take up, undertake

enterprise *n.*   **1.** activity, adventure, attempt, business, company, concern, effort, endeavor, essay, establishment, firm, operation, outfit, plan, program, pursuit, scheme, undertaking, venture, work   **2.** ambition, boldness, courage, drive, eagerness, enthusiasm, force, industry, initiative, intensity, inventiveness, power, push, readiness, resourcefulness, venturesomeness, vitality, zeal, zest

enterprising *adj.*   active, adventurous, aggressive, alert, ambitious, ardent, aspiring, assertive, assiduous, avid, bold, constructive, determined, diligent, driving, eager, earnest, energetic, enthusiastic, fervent, forceful, goal-oriented, hardworking, imaginative, industrious, intent, productive, progressive, pushing, resolute, resolved, resourceful, self-reliant, self-starting, smart, spirited, striving, venturesome, venturous, vigorous, zealous

entertain *v.* **1.** accommodate visitors, be host, give party, have company, have guests, have visitors, host, lodge, receive, show hospitality, take to dinner, take to lunch, treat, welcome **2.** consider, contemplate, deliberate, heed, keep in mind, muse over, ponder, take into consideration, think over, think seriously about, weigh **3.** absorb, amuse, captivate, charm, cheer, delight, divert, elate, engage, engross, enliven, enthrall, gladden, gratify, humor, indulge, interest, occupy, please

entertainment *n.* amusement, celebration, cheer, delight, distraction, diversion, divertissement, enjoyment, festivities, fete, fun, gaiety, gala, gratification, hospitality, joviality, leisure activity, merriment, merrymaking, pastime, play, pleasantry, pleasure, recreation, relaxation, sport

enthusiasm *n.* ardor, buoyancy, devotedness, devotion, eagerness, earnestness, emotion, excitement, exhilaration, exuberance, fanaticism, fervor, fire, glow, intensity, intentness, joyfulness, keen interest, keenness, life, liveliness, passion, spirit, verve, vitality, vivacity, warmth, zeal, zealousness, zest

entice *v.* allure, coax, inveigle, lure, persuade, pique, prevail on, seduce, tantalize, tempt

enticement *n.* allure, attraction, bait, blandishment, cajolery, coaxing, decoy, inducement, inveiglement, invitation, lure, persuasion, seduction, snare, tantalization, temptation, trap

entire *adj.* aggregate, all, all-inclusive, complete, comprehensive, full, intact, integral, total, unabridged, undivided, unified, whole

entirely *adv.* absolutely, aggregately, completely, comprehensively, exclusively, fully, inclusively, purely, solely, totally, undividedly, uniquely, universally, utterly, wholly

entity *n.* **1.** article, being, body, company, creature, existence, firm, individual, item, life form, object, organism, organization, person, real thing **2.** essence, essential nature, existence, inner being, nature, quintessence, reality, subsistence

entourage *n.* attendants, company, convoy, cortege, court, escort, followers, following, retinue, staff, suite, train

entrance *n.* **1.** access, approach, archway, corridor, door, doorway, driveway, entry, entryway, gate, gateway, hall, hallway, ingress, inlet, lobby, opening, passage, passageway, path, pathway, porch, port, portico, ramp, threshold, vestibule, walk, walkway **2.** access, accession, admission, admittance, approach, arrival at, beginning, commencement, debut, enrollment, entree, entry, inception, initiation, introduction, passage, penetration, start

entrée *n.* access, admission, admittance, approach, connection, door, doorway, entrance, entry, entryway, ingress, inlet, introduction, main course, principal dish

entrepreneur *n.* backer, businessperson, contractor, director, employer, enterpriser, executive, founder, manager, organizer, producer, promoter

entry *n.* **1.** account, inscription, insertion, item, listing, memo, note, record, recording **2.** See **entrance 1**. **3.** See **entrance 2**. **4.** candidate, competitor, contestant, entrant, opponent, participant, player, rival

enumerate *v.* add up, calculate, catalog, check off, cite, compute, count, detail, estimate, itemize, list, name, number, numerate, reckon, recount, specify, sum, take account of, tally, total

envelope *n.* capsule, case, casing, container, cover, covering, holder, jacket, receptacle, sheath, skin, wrapper, wrapping

environment *n.* ambiance, atmosphere, aura, backdrop, background, circumstances, climate, conditions, element, entourage, habitat, locale, medium, neighborhood, scene, setting, surroundings, terrain, territory

envoy *n.* agent, ambassador, attaché, chargé d'affaires, consul, courier, delegate, deputy, diplomat, emissary, intermediary, internuncio, legate, messenger, minister, nuncio, plenipotentiary, representative

epilog *n.* afterword, conclusion, ending, finale, follow-up, peroration, postlude, postscript, summation

epistle *n.* communication, correspondence, encyclical, letter, memo, message, missive, note

epithet *n.* **1.** appellation, description, label, nickname, pet name **2.** curse, expletive, oath, obscenity

equal *n.* associate, coequal, colleague, compeer, copy, counterpart, double, duplicate, equivalent, likeness, parallel, partner, peer, rival

equal *adj.* **1.** alike, analogous, coequal, commensurate, comparable, correspondent, double, duplicate, equivalent, identical, indistinguishable, interchangeable, like, matched, matching, parallel, proportionate, same, selfsame, synonymous, tantamount, unvarying   **2.** balanced, constant, dispassionate, egalitarian, even, even-handed, fair, impartial, just, level, nondiscriminatory, nonpartisan, objective, regular, steady, unbiased, unprejudiced

equality *n.*   agreement, balance, coequality, commensurability, comparability, correspondence, egalitarianism, equilibrium, equivalence, evenness, identity, likeness, par, parallelism, parity, proportion, sameness, symmetry, uniformity

equalize *v.*   balance, emulate, equate, even, even up, level, make the same, match, parallel, regularize, smooth, square, standardize

equate *v.*   ally, assimilate, balance, be commensurate, compare, equalize, even up, level, liken, make correspond, make equal, match, parallel, relate, square

equilibrium *n.*   balance, calm, calmness, composure, cool, coolness, equality, equalization, equanimity, equipoise, equivalence, evenness, imperturbability, levelheadedness, par, parity, poise, self-control, stability, steadiness, symmetry, uniformity

equip *v.*   adorn, arm, array, attire, deck, decorate, dress, furnish, make ready, provide, set up, supply

equipment *n.*   apparatus, appliances, articles, contrivances, devices, fittings, fixtures, furnishings, furniture, gadgets, implements, machinery, machines, materials, outfit, paraphernalia, supplies, tools, utensils

equitable *adj.*   broad-minded, disinterested, ethical, even, even-handed, fair, fair-minded, honest, impartial, impersonal, just, neutral, nondiscriminatory, objective, open-minded, reasonable, right, rightful, tolerant, unbiased, unprejudiced

equity *n.*   **1.** assets minus liabilities, capital, investment, money, outlay, ownership, ownership interest, property ownership, residual ownership   **2.** broad-mindedness, disinterestedness, equitableness, even-handedness, evenness, fair-mindedness, fairness, fair play, honesty, impartiality, justice, neutrality, nondiscrimination, objectivity, open-mindedness, reasonableness, tolerance

equivalent *n.*   correspondent, counterpart, double, equal, equivalence, match, parallel, same, substitute

equivalent *adj.*   alike, analogous, coequal, commensurate, comparable, correspondent, corresponding, duplicate, equal, identical, indistinguishable, interchangeable, like, parallel, reciprocal, same, similar, substitute, synonymous

era *n.* age, cycle, date, day, days, eon, epoch, generation, period, span, stage, time

erase *v.* cancel, cut out, delete, eliminate, eradicate, expunge, extirpate, obliterate, remove, rub out, take out, wipe out, withdraw

erect *v.* assemble, build, construct, create, elevate, establish, fabricate, fit together, form, found, hoist, institute, lift, make, mount, organize, pitch, produce, put together, put up, raise, set up, stand up

erosion *n.* abrasion, attrition, consumption, corrosion, despoliation, deterioration, disintegration, eroding, washing away, wear, wearing away, wearing down

errand *n.* assignment, charge, chore, commission, duty, job, mission, task

erroneous *adj.* amiss, faulty, flawed, illogical, imprecise, inaccurate, incorrect, inexact, mistaken, unsound, wrong

error *n.* blunder, delusion, erroneousness, fallacy, falsity, fault, flaw, inaccuracy, incorrectness, misapprehension, miscalculation, misconception, misconduct, miscue, misdeed, misestimation, misidentification, misinterpretation, misjudgment, misstep, mistake, misunderstanding, omission, oversight, slip, slipup, untruth, wrong

escalate *v.* amplify, broaden, enlarge, expand, heighten, increase, intensify, magnify, raise, step up, widen

especially *adv.* chiefly, conspicuously, exceptionally, exclusively, expressly, mainly, markedly, mostly, notably, noticeably, particularly, predominantly, primarily, principally, signally, specially, specifically, strikingly

essay *n.* **1.** article, commentary, composition, discourse, disquisition, dissertation, editorial, manuscript, paper, piece, study, theme, thesis, tract, treatise, written composition **2.** attempt, effort, endeavor, enterprise, exertion, experiment, struggle, test, trial, try, undertaking, venture

essence *n.* **1.** actuality, basis, being, chief constituent, core, crux, essentiality, essentialness, essential part, gist, heart, import, kernel, life, lifeblood, main idea, marrow, nucleus, pith, principle, quintessence, reality, root, sense, significance, soul, spirit, substance **2.** abstraction, concentrate, concentration, distillate, distillation, elixir, extract, potion, tincture

essential *n.* basic, condition, element, essence, fundamental, heart, must, necessity, precondition, prerequisite, principle, quintessence, requirement, requisite, rudiment, stuff, substance, vital part

essential *adj.* basic, capital, cardinal, characteristic, chief, constitutional, crucial, elemental, foremost, fundamental, imperative, important, indispensable, inherent, intrinsic, key, leading, main, material, necessary, primary, prime, principal, quintessential, required, requisite, underlying, vital

establish *v.* **1.** bring into being, build, coin, compose, constitute, construct, create, erect, fabricate, fashion, form, found, give rise to, ground, install, institute, lodge, make, make up, organize, originate, place, plant, put, root, seat, secure, settle, set up, start, station, stick **2.** adjudge, appoint, authenticate, authorize, certify, confirm, corroborate, decree, enact, legalize, legislate, license, prescribe, prove, ratify, sanction, show, substantiate, validate, verify

establishment *n.* **1.** association, building, business, cartel, combine, company, concern, corporation, enterprise, factory, firm, foundation, institute, institution, organization, plant, shop, structure, syndicate, trust **2.** authority, bureaucracy, established order, officialdom, power elite, power structure **3.** creation, enactment, formation, formulation, foundation, founding, inauguration, installation, institution, organization

estate *n.* assets, belongings, chattel, chose, effects, fortune, grounds, holdings, land, personal assets, personal property, personalty, possessions, properties, property, real estate, real property, residence, resources, wealth, worth

estimate *n.* approximation, conjecture, educated guess, estimation, guess, judgment, opinion, projection, surmise

estimate *v.* approximate, calculate approximately, calculate roughly, compute roughly, conjecture, figure, gauge, guess, make estimate, measure, predict, rank, rate, surmise, value, weigh

estimation *n.* approximation, assessment, belief, conjecture, deduction, estimate, guess, inference, judgment, opinion, prediction, rough valuation, surmise

ethical *adj.* conscientious, correct, decent, equitable, fair, faithful, high-principled, honest, honorable, just, moral, principled, proper, right, righteous, right-minded, upright, upstanding, virtuous

ethics *n.* conscience, conscientiousness, decency, goodness, honesty, honor, integrity, justness, moral code, moral philosophy, morality, principles, propriety, righteousness, rules of conduct, standards, uprightness, values, virtue

ethnic *adj.* cultural, national, racial, religious, tribal

etiquette *n.* accepted forms, code, conventions, customs, decorum, form, formalities, good behavior, manners, politeness, proper behavior, propriety, protocol, rules, seemliness

evaluate *v.* appraise, ascertain, calculate, check out, compute, determine, estimate, figure, figure out, gauge, judge, measure, rank, rate, survey, test, weigh

evaluation *n.* appraisal, appraisement, calculation, computation, determination, estimate, estimation, figuring, gauging, judgment, measure, ranking, rating, survey, surveying, test, weighing

event *n.* **1.** affair, function, happening, incident, occasion, occurrence, proceeding, situation **2.** aftereffect, aftermath, conclusion, consequence, effect, eventuality, issue, outcome, result, sequel, subsequence, upshot

everyday *adj.* accustomed, average, common, commonplace, conventional, customary, daily, diurnal, familiar, habitual, informal, mainstream, matter-of-fact, mundane, normal, ordinary, plain, prosaic, regular, routine, simple, stock, usual, vernacular

evidence *n.* attestation, authentication, body of facts, certification, confirmation, corroboration, demonstration, deposition, exemplification, grounds, indication, sign, substantiation, support, sworn statement, testament, testimonial, testimony, validation, verification, warrant, witness

evidently *adv.* apparently, clearly, doubtlessly, incontestably, incontrovertibly, indisputably, indubitably, manifestly, obviously, ostensibly, patently, plainly, seemingly, undeniably, undoubtedly, unmistakably, unquestionably, visibly

evoke *v.* adjure, arouse, awaken, bring about, call, call forth, cause, conjure up, educe, elicit, excite, induce, invite, invoke, kindle, provoke, reawake, recall, rekindle, remind, rouse, suggest, stimulate, stir, summon

evolution *n.* development, elaboration, evolvement, flowering, fruition, growth, maturation, production, progress, progression, ripening, succession, transformation, unfolding, unrolling

evolve *v.*   advance, become, develop, emerge, expand, grow, increase, mature, open, progress, result, ripen, turn into, unfold, unroll

exact *adj.*   **1.** accurate, conforming, correct, definite, explicit, faithful, precise, unequivocal, unerring, verbatim   **2.** careful, conscientious, demanding, detailed, exacting, fastidious, finicky, fussy, methodical, meticulous, painstaking, particular, rigorous, scrupulous, severe, strict, thorough, unyielding

exaggerate *v.*   build up, color, embroider, hyperbolize, inflate, overdo, overemphasize, oversell, overstate, overstress, stretch

exaggeration *n.*   building up, coloring, embellishment, embroidering, embroidery, hyperbole, inflation, magnification, overdoing, overemphasis, overselling, overstatement, overstressing, stretching

examination *n.*   analysis, appraisal, assessment, audit, canvass, catechism, checking, checkup, close observation, cross-examination, dissection, exploration, grilling, inquiry, inquisition, inspection, interrogation, investigation, probe, questionnaire, quiz, research, review, scrutiny, search, set of questions, study, survey, test

examine *v.*   analyze, appraise, assess, audit, canvass, catechize, check, check into, check out, consider, cross-examine, dissect, explore, go over, grill, inquire, inquire into, inspect, interrogate, investigate, look into, probe, question closely, quiz, research, review, scrutinize, search, study, survey, test, weigh

example *n.*   benchmark, case, citation, exemplar, exemplification, ideal, illustration, instance, model, paradigm, paragon, parallel case, pattern, piece, prototype, representation, sample, sampling, specimen, standard, typical situation

execute *v.*   carry out, create, do, make valid, perform, put into effect

excel *v.*   beat, be good at, be proficient at, be skillful at, be superior at, better, come first, eclipse, exceed, outdistance, outdo, outshine, outstrip, surpass, take precedence over, top, transcend

excellence *n.*   distinction, eminence, greatness, high quality, merit, perfection, preeminence, quality, superbness, superiority, supremacy, transcendence, value, virtue, worth

excellent *adj.*   admirable, capital, choice, distinctive, distinguished, estimable, exceptional, exemplary, exquisite, extraordinary, first-class, first-rate, magnificent, notable, noteworthy, outstanding, peerless, priceless, prime, remarkable, select, superb, superior, superlative, supreme, transcendent

exception *n.*   **1.** barring, debarment, excepting, exclusion, leaving out, noninclusion, omission, rejection   **2.** anomaly, departure, deviation, difference, freak, inconsistency, irregularity, nonconformity, oddity, peculiarity, quirk, uncommon case, unusual case

excerpt *n.*   citation, extract, fragment, passage, portion, quotation, quote, section, selection

excerpt *v.*   abridge, cite, cull, extract, pick out, quote, select

excess *n.*   **1.** balance, by-product, leftover, overdose, overflow, overload, overrun, oversupply, plethora, profusion, redundancy, remainder, residue, rest, superabundance, superfluity, surfeit, surplus   **2.** dissipation, dissoluteness, exorbitance, extravagance, immoderation, inordinateness, intemperance, overdoing, overindulgence, prodigality, unrestraint

exchange *n.*   **1.** barter, buying and selling, change, commerce, commutation, interchange, reciprocation, reciprocity, replacement, return, substitution, swap, switch, trade, trade-off, transaction, transfer, transposing, transposition   **2.** the Big Board, central office, stock exchange, stock market, switching point, Wall Street

exchange *v.*   barter, buy and sell, change, commute, interchange, reciprocate, replace, return, substitute, swap, switch, trade, trade off, transact, transfer, transpose

excise *n.*   customs, duty, levy, surcharge, tariff, tax, toll

excitement *n.*   action, agitation, animation, confusion, disturbance, enthusiasm, excitation, exhilaration, ferment, fever, hysteria, incitement, instigation, intoxication, invigoration, motivation, perturbation, provocation, stimulation, tension, trepidation

exclude *v.*   ban, banish, bar, blacklist, boycott, count out, debar, deny, deport, disallow, drive out, eject, eliminate, embargo, except, exile, expel, forbid, force out, get rid of, keep out, leave out, lock out, omit, ostracize, oust, pass over, preclude, prevent, prohibit, put out, refuse, refuse admittance, reject, remove, repudiate, rule out, set apart, shut out, skip, spurn, throw out, turn out

exclusion *n.*   ban, banishment, bar, blacklist, boycott, counting out, debarment, denial, denial of coverage, deportation, disallowance, driving out, ejection, elimination, embargo, eviction, exception, exile, expulsion, forbiddance, forcing out, item not covered, keeping out, leaving out, lockout, omission, ostracism, ouster, passing over, preclusion, prevention, prohibition, putting out, refusal, rejection, removal, repudiation, ruling out, setting apart, shutout, shutting out, skipping, spurning, throwing out, turning out

excursion *n.*   cruise, digression, drive, expedition, hike, jaunt, journey, outing, pilgrimage, ride, tour, trek, trip, voyage, walk

excuse *n.*   alibi, apology, argument, assertion, defense, explanation, extenuation, grounds, justification, plea, rationalization, reason, story

excuse *v.*   absolve, acquit, allow, apologize for, clear, condone, defend, discharge, dismiss, dispense with, disregard, exculpate, exempt, exonerate, extenuate, forgive, free, ignore, justify, liberate, make allowances for, pardon, permit, rationalize, release, relieve, remit, spare, vindicate, waive

execute *v.*   accomplish, achieve, administer, bring about, bring to fruition, carry out, cause, complete, consummate, discharge, do, effect, enact, finish, follow instruction, fulfill, give validity to, implement, make happen, manage, perform, put into effect, transact, work out

execution *n.*   accomplishment, achievement, administration, bringing about, bringing to fruition, carrying out, completion, consummation, discharge, doing, effect, enactment, finishing, fulfilling, fulfillment, implementation, making happen, management, performance, putting into effect, working out

executive *n.*   administrator, boss, businessperson, chief, commander, director, entrepreneur, leader, manager, officer, official, overseer, president, principal, supervisor

executive *adj.*   administrative, authoritative, directorial, governing, managerial, official, regulatory, supervisory

exemplar *n.*   archetype, benchmark, epitome, example, exemplification, form, ideal, illustration, measure, model, mold, original, paradigm, paragon, pattern, pilot, prototype, representative, sample, specimen, standard

exempt *v.*   absolve, dispense with, except, exclude from, excuse from, free from, let off, release from, relieve of, spare from

exemption *n.*   absolution, dispensation, excusing, exempting, freedom, immunity, impunity, indemnity, privilege, release

exercise *n.* act, acting on, action, activity, calisthenics, discipline, drill, effort, exercising, exertion, gymnastics, making use of, movement, practice, training, warm-up, work, workout

exhibit *n.* demonstration, display, exhibition, exposition, performance, presentation, production, show, showing, staging, unveiling, viewing

exhibit *v.* air, array, brandish, demonstrate, display, expose, parade, present, put on display, set forth, set up, show, show off, unveil

exhibition *n.* See **exhibit**

exhortation *n.* admonition, advice, caution, counsel, encouragement, enjoiner, entreaty, incentive, incitement, inducement, instigation, lecture, persuasion, prescription, provocation, recommendation, stimulation, stimulus, urging, warning

exit *n.* **1.** door, gate, opening, outlet, passage out, way out **2.** departure, discharge, egress, evacuation, exodus, going out, leaving, retirement, retreat, taking off, withdrawal

exit *v.* bid farewell, depart, discharge, evacuate, get away, get off, go, go away, go out, issue, move, move out, quit, retire, retreat, take off, vacate, withdraw

exorbitant *adj.* costly, disproportionate, enormous, excessive, expensive, extravagant, extreme, high, high-priced, immoderate, inordinate, outrageous, overpriced, preposterous, prohibitive, unconscionable, undue, unnecessary, unreasonable, unwarranted, usurious

expand *v.* **1.** add to, amass, amplify, augment, branch out, broaden, build up, deepen, dilate, distend, enlarge, fill out, heighten, increase, inflate, lengthen, magnify, make greater, make larger, multiply, open out, prolong, protract, spread, spread out, supplement, thicken, widen **2.** amplify, develop, detail, elaborate, embellish, enlarge, expound, extend, spell out, supplement

expansion *n.* **1.** aggrandizement, amplification, augmentation, breadth, deepening, diffusion, dilation, distance, distension, enlargement, evolution, expanse, filling out, increase, inflation, lengthening, magnification, maturation, multiplication, opening out, prolongation, protraction, space, spreading out, stretch, swelling, unfolding, unfurling **2.** amplification, detailing, development, elaboration, embellishment, enlargement, expanding, extension, spelling out, supplementation

expect *v.* **1.** anticipate, await, bargain on, believe strongly, conjecture, count on, envisage, feel, imagine, look for, predict, presume, rely on, suppose, surmise, suspect, think, trust **2.** demand, hope for, insist on, need, require, want, wish

expectation *n.* anticipation, apprehension, assurance, belief, calculation, chance, confidence, contemplation, contingency, dependence, expectancy, expecting, hope, liability, likelihood, looking forward to, outlook, possibility, prediction, presumption, probability, prospect, reliance, suspense, trust

expedite *v.* accelerate, accomplish promptly, advance, facilitate, finish quickly, forward, further, hasten, hurry, move faster, precipitate, press forward, promote, push, quicken, rush, speed up, step up, urge on

expendable *adj.* consumable, dispensable, disposable, nonessential, replaceable, superfluous, unimportant, unnecessary

expenditure *n.* charge, cost, disbursement, expense, fee, investment, outgo, outlay, payment, price, rate, valuation, value

expense *n.* amount, business cost, charge, cost, debt, deductible cost, disbursement, expenditure, investment, liability, obligation, outlay, payment, price, rate, value

expensive *adj.* costly, dear, excessive, exorbitant, extravagant, high, high-priced, lavish, overpriced, rich, uneconomical, unreasonable, valuable

experience *n.* **1.** background, empiricism, existence, exposure, familiarity, intimacy, involvement, knowledge, lifework, practice, skill, sophistication, training, understanding, wisdom **2.** adventure, affair, encounter, episode, event, happening, incident, occurrence, ordeal, transaction

experienced *adj.* able, accomplished, adept, capable, competent, expert, familiar, fit, instructed, knowing, knowledgeable, masterful, mature, practiced, prepared, primed, qualified, ready, seasoned, skillful, tested, trained, versed, well-versed

experiment *n.* analysis, assay, authentication, demonstration, examination, exercise, experimentation, inquiry, investigation, proof, questioning, research, speculation, study, test, test procedure, trial, tryout, venture, verification

expert *n.* authority, connoisseur, critic, maven, proficient, scholar, specialist

expert *adj.* accomplished, adept, adroit, competent, deft, dexterous, experienced, facile, knowledgeable, learned, practiced, proficient, qualified, skilled, skillful, trained, well-informed, well-versed

expertise *n.* adeptness, adroitness, competence, deftness, dexterity, experience, expert advice, expertness, facility, knowledge, practice, proficiency, skill, skillfulness, training

expire *v.* be extinguished, cease, close, come due, come to a close, come to an end, complete, conclude, decease, depart, die out, discontinue, elapse, end, fade away, fail, finish, go away, lapse, pass away, perish, run out, stop, stop working, terminate

explain *v.* account for, clarify, clear up, comment on, decipher, define, delineate, demonstrate, describe, disclose, elucidate, explicate, expose, expound, give reason for, go into detail, illustrate, interpret, justify, make clear, make plain, point out, put across, render intelligible, resolve, reveal, show, solve, tell, unfold, unravel, untangle

explanation *n.* account, answer, clarification, commentary, deduction, definition, description, elucidation, excuse, explication, exposition, gloss, illustration, interpretation, meaning, note, reason, statement

explanatory *adj.* declarative, demonstrative, descriptive, elucidatory, enlightening, exegetic, explicative, expositional, expository, illustrative, informative, instructive, justifying

exploration *n.* analysis, canvass, checking into, examination, inquiry, inquisition, inspection, investigation, probe, reconnaissance, research, review, scrutiny, search, study, survey, traveling over, traverse

exponent *n.* **1.** example, exemplar, exemplification, illustration, index, indication, instance, model, paradigm, representation, sample, specimen, symbol, token, type **2.** advocate, backer, champion, defender, expositor, expounder, interpreter, promoter, proponent, spokesperson, supporter, upholder

export *v.* market abroad, market in another country, market overseas, sell abroad, sell in another country, sell overseas, send abroad, send overseas, send to another country, ship abroad, ship overseas, ship to another country, trade abroad, trade overseas, trade with another country, transport abroad, transport overseas, transport to another country

exposition *n.* **1.** account, annotation, commentary, composition, criticism, critique, description, discourse, discussion, dissertation, essay, exegesis, explanation, explication, illustration, interpretation, monograph, paper, presentation, report, study, thesis, treatise, written description **2.** bazaar, display, exhibit, exhibition, fair, market, mart, presentation, production, review, retrospective, show, showing, unveiling

express *adj.* accelerated, direct, expeditious, fast, high-speed, immediate, prompt, quick, rapid, speedy, swift

expression *n.* **1.** announcement, assertion, comment, commentary, communication, criticism, declaration, definition, description, diction, discourse, discussion, enunciation, explanation, explication, exposition, idiom, informing, interpretation, language, locution, mention, phrase, phraseology, proclamation, pronouncement, remark, saying, statement, style, telling, term, utterance, verbalization, word **2.** air, appearance, aspect, carriage, cast, countenance, look

expressway *n.* divided highway, freeway, interstate, major highway, superhighway, thruway

extant *adj.* alive, existent, existing, living, present, subsistent, subsisting, surviving

extend *v.* **1.** advance, award, bestow, confer, donate, give, grant, hold out, impart, offer, present, proffer, put forth, put forward, reach out, submit, tender, yield **2.** add time, add to, amass, amplify, augment, branch out, broaden, continue, develop, dilate, distend, draw out, elongate, enhance, enlarge, expand, expand on, fill out, go on, heighten, increase, inflate, keep up, lengthen, magnify, maintain, make greater, make larger, make longer, multiply, open, perpetuate, prolong, protract, spread, spread out, stretch out, supplement, sustain, thicken, unfold, unfurl, widen

exterior *n.* appearance, aspect, coating, cover, covering, external part, facade, face, finish, outside, rind, shell, skin, surface

extract *n.* **1.** abstract, citation, clipping, elicitation, excerpt, note, passage, quotation, quote, selection **2.** concentrate, concentration, decoction, distillate, distillation, essence, solution

extract *v.* **1.** abstract, choose, cite, cull, excerpt, glean, quote, select quotation **2.** bring forth, derive, distill, draw out, elicit, eradicate, evoke, exact, extirpate, extort, extricate, get out, obtain, pluck out, press out, pry out, pull out, remove, separate, siphon, squeeze out, take out, tear out, uproot, withdraw, wrench from, wrest, wring from

facade *n.* **1.** exterior, face, forefront, front, front elevation, frontage, main face **2.** affectation, appearance, disguise, false impression, guise, look, mask, masquerade, pretense

face *n.* **1.** exterior, facade, finish, first page, front, frontage, frontispiece, surface, top **2.** air, appearance, aspect, countenance, demeanor, disguise, expression, features, guise, lineaments, look, mask, physiognomy, pretense, visage

face *v.* brave, challenge, confront, contend with, cope with, dare, deal with, defy, encounter, endure, experience, grapple with, meet, oppose, resist, withstand

face value *n.* face amount, maturity value, nominal amount, nominal value, par value, stated value, undiscounted value, value

facilitate *v.* advance, aid, assist, clear, encourage, expedite, forward, foster, further, help, make easy, promote, simplify, smooth, speed up, uncomplicate

facility *n.* **1.** building, complex, edifice, network, plant, structure, system, unit, work area **2.** ability, adroitness, aptitude, aptness, capability, competence, dexterity, ease, efficiency, expertness, finesse, fluency, knack, poise, proficiency, readiness, skill, skillfulness, smoothness, suaveness, talent

facsimile *n.* clone, copy, double, duplicate, fax, fax machine, image, imitation, likeness, photocopy, print, replica, representation, reproduction, simulation, transcript

fact *n.* **1.** actuality, authenticity, certainty, certitude, evidence, reality, truism, truth, verity **2.** act, affair, circumstance, component, data, deed, detail, element, episode, event, experience, factor, feature, happening, incident, information, item, occurrence, particular, phenomenon, point, specifics

factor *n.* **1.** aspect, component, consideration, constituent, detail, determinant, element, facet, ingredient, item, part, point, portion, thing **2.** agency, agent, consignee, functionary, intermediary, instrument, merchant, representative, sponsor, supporter

factory *n.* assembly plant, foundry, machine shop, manufactory, manufacturing plant, metalworks, mill, plant, shop, works, workshop

facts *n.* data, details, information, inside information, story

faculty *n.* **1.** ability, adroitness, aptitude, aptness, bent, capability, capacity, deftness, dexterity, facility, flair, force, genius, inclination, knack, potency, potentiality, power, proclivity, proficiency, propensity, property, talent, turn   **2.** academicians, academics, advisors, instructors, lecturers, professoriat, professors, staff, tutors

fail *v.* abort, become insolvent, be defeated, be defective, be demoted, be lacking, be ruined, break down, close down, default, fall, fall short, flop, flounder, founder, go bankrupt, go wrong, lose, lose money, miscarry, miss, slip, stop short

failure *n.* abortion, bankruptcy, breakdown, closing down, collapse, decline, defeat, deficiency, deterioration, failing, fiasco, financial collapse, financial ruin, frustration, going out of business, lack of success, loss, misadventure, miscarriage, nonfulfillment, nonsuccess, overthrow

fair *n.* bazaar, display, exchange, exhibit, exhibition, market, marketplace, mart, show

fairly *adv.* candidly, dispassionately, equitably, honestly, impartially, justly, legitimately, objectively, properly, reasonably, rightly

fairness *n.* equitableness, equity, fair-mindedness, good faith, honesty, impartiality, integrity, justness, open-mindedness, probity, reasonableness, rectitude, rightness, uprightness, veracity

faith *n.* **1.** belief, conviction, creed, denomination, doctrine, dogma, persuasion, principle, religion, religious belief, sect, teaching, tenet, theology   **2.** acceptance, allegiance, assent, assurance, belief, certainty, certitude, commitment, confidence, conviction, credence, dependence, faithfulness, fidelity, hope, loyalty, reliance, sureness, trust

faithful *adj.* **1.** allegiant, conscientious, dedicated, dependable, devoted, dutiful, honest, incorruptible, loyal, obedient, patriotic, reliable, scrupulous, sincere, staunch, steadfast, supportive, true, trustworthy, truthful, unchanging, unswerving, unwavering, upright, veracious   **2.** accurate, actual, authentic, close, correct, errorless, exact, factual, faultless, just, literal, perfect, precise, right, true, undistorted, unerring, valid, veracious

fallacy *n.* casuistry, delusion, erroneousness, error, fallaciousness, falsehood, false notion, heresy, illusion, misapprehension, miscalculation, misconception, misinterpretation, misjudgment, mistake, mistakenness, solecism, sophism, sophistry, wrongness

fallible *adj.* errant, error-prone, imperfect, mistake-prone

false *adj.* **1.** amiss, concocted, distorted, erroneous, fabricated, fictitious, imaginary, improper, incorrect, invalid, lying, mendacious, mistaken, perjured, unfounded, unreal, untrue, untruthful, wrong **2.** corrupt, deceitful, deceptive, devious, dishonest, dishonorable, disingenuous, disloyal, duplicitous, faithless, fallacious, false-hearted, hypocritical, insincere, malevolent, malicious, misleading, misrepresentative, perfidious, recreant, traitorous, treacherous, treasonable, underhanded, unfaithful, unscrupulous, untrustworthy **3.** artificial, bogus, contrived, copied, counterfeit, disguised, factitious, fake, feigned, forged, fraudulent, imitation, mock, phony, pretended, sham, simulated, spurious, substitute, synthetic, unreal

falsify *v.* adulterate, alter, change, color, counterfeit, deceive, distort, exaggerate, fake, lie, misquote, misrepresent, misstate, pervert, tamper with

fame *n.* acclaim, acclamation, celebrity, distinction, eminence, esteem, estimation, glory, greatness, high regard, honor, illustriousness, importance, laurels, notability, note, notoriety, popularity, preeminence, prestige, prominence, public esteem, public regard, rank, recognition, regard, renown, reputation, repute, standing, stardom, superiority, supremacy

familiar *adj.* **1.** accustomed, casual, common, commonplace, conventional, customary, everyday, frequent, habitual, hackneyed, informal, known, mundane, natural, ordinary, plain, proverbial, repeated, simple, stock, traditional, trite, unceremonious, usual, well-known **2.** bold, close, confidential, forward, impudent, informal, intimate, intrusive, presuming, presumptuous, relaxed, unconstrained, unreserved

famous *adj.* august, celebrated, distinguished, eminent, esteemed, famed, foremost, important, influential, notable, noted, preeminent, prominent, renowned, respected, venerable, well-known

fare *n.* charge, cost, fee, passage, payment, price, toll

fashion *n.* convention, craze, current form, custom, fad, general tendency, latest style, latest thing, look, mode, practice, prevailing taste, style, trend, vogue

fashion *v.* accommodate, adapt, adjust, build, carve, compose, conform to, construct, contrive, create, design, devise, erect, fabricate, fit, forge, form, hew, invent, make, make up, manufacture, mold, originate, pattern, plan, sculpt, shape, structure, suit, tailor

fashionable *adj.* accepted, chic, conventional, customary, elegant, popular, prevailing, smart, stylish, trendsetting, up-to-date

fasten *v.* affix, anchor, attach, band, bar, bind, bolt, brace, bracket, buckle, button, catch, chain, clamp, clasp, clinch, clip, close, connect, couple, fix, glue, hasp, hitch, hook, latch, leash, link, lock, make firm, nail, pin, rivet, rope, screw, secure, tack, tether, tie, unite, weld

fatality *n.* accident, casualty, death, disaster, fatal accident, violent death

fatigue *n.* exhaustion, heaviness, languor, listlessness, tiredness, weariness

fault *n.* accountability, answerability, blame, blunder, culpability, error, guilt, impropriety, inaccuracy, indiscretion, lapse, misbehavior, misconduct, misdeed, misdemeanor, mistake, negligence, offense, omission, oversight, responsibility, slipup, transgression, vice, wrong, wrongdoing

faulty *adj.* blamable, damaged, defective, deficient, erroneous, fallacious, fallible, flawed, impaired, imperfect, imprecise, inaccurate, inadequate, incomplete, incorrect, inexact, insufficient, invalid, lacking, malfunctioning, unreliable, unsound, wrong

faux pas *n.* blunder, breach, error, gaffe, impropriety, indiscretion, misconduct, misdeed, mishap, misstep, mistake, offense, slipup, transgression, wrong move

favor *n.* approbation, blessing, boon, consideration, courtesy, friendliness, generosity, gift, good deed, grace, kind act, kind deed, kindness, present, token

favorable *adj.* **1.** advantageous, auspicious, benign, encouraging, fair, fortunate, gratifying, kindly, lucky, opportune, pleasing, profitable, promising, propitious, providential, reassuring, valuable **2.** affirmative, approbative, approving, complimentary, encouraging, enthusiastic, positive, reassuring, supportive, welcoming

favoritism *n.* bias, discrimination, inclination, inequity, leaning, nepotism, one-sidedness, partiality, partisanship, preference, preferential treatment, prejudice, proclivity, unfairness, unjustness

fax *n.* See **facsimile**

fear *n.* alarm, angst, anxiety, apprehension, apprehensiveness, concern, consternation, cowardice, dismay, disquietude, distress, distrust, dread, faintheartedness, fearfulness, foreboding, fright, hesitation, horror, misgiving, mistrust, panic, perturbation, qualm, suspicion, terror, timidity, trepidation, uncertainty, uneasiness, worry

feasible *adj.* achievable, advantageous, appropriate, attainable, conceivable, expedient, fitting, obtainable, practicable, practical, reachable, realistic, realizable, reasonable, suitable, viable, workable, worthwhile

feature *n.* **1.** angle, aspect, attribute, character, characteristic, component, constituent, detail, element, facet, factor, hallmark, idiosyncrasy, ingredient, item, mannerism, mark, particularity, peculiarity, point, property, quality, trademark, trait **2.** highlight, lead item, main item, prominent part, special, special attraction, specialty **3.** article, column, item, piece, report, story

feature *v.* accent, accentuate, advertise, call attention to, characterize, depict, distinguish, emphasize, give prominence to, highlight, italicize, make conspicuous, mark, portray, present, profile, promote, represent, spotlight, star, stress, symbolize, underline, underscore

federation *n.* alliance, amalgamation, association, coalition, combination, combine, confederacy, confederation, league, organization, society, syndicate, union

fee *n.* allowance, bill, charge, commission, compensation, cost, cost of services, deposit, estate, expense, fare, fee simple, gratuity, honorarium, ownership, pay, payment, price, recompense, remuneration, salary, stipend, tip, toll, wage

feedback *n.* comment, information, opinion, output, reaction, response, return, returned information, returned output, review

feel *v.* **1.** assume, believe, conclude, conjecture, guess, intuit, judge, presume, suppose, surmise, suspect, think **2.** appear, be aware of, be excited about, be impressed by, comprehend, discern, endure, enjoy, experience, have, know, note, notice, observe, perceive, savor, see, seem, sense, suffer, undergo, understand **3.** brush, clasp, clutch, finger, grapple, grasp, graze, grip, handle, manipulate, palpate, ply, press, squeeze, stroke, touch

feeling *n.* **1.** awareness, belief, consciousness, conviction, idea, impression, inclination, inkling, instinct, intuition, mind, notion, opinion, outlook, point of view, reaction, suspicion, thought, view, viewpoint **2.** affect, affection, ardor, compassion, discrimination, emotion, empathy, fervor, heat, pity, reaction, sensation, sense, sensibility, sensitivity, sentiment, sympathy, tactility, tenderness, touch, vehemence, warmth

fellowship *n.* affability, affiliation, alliance, amity, association, camaraderie, communion, community, companionship, comradeship, consocation, friendliness, friendship, interchange, intimacy, organization, sociability, society, sodality, togetherness

fertile *adj.* abundant, bountiful, creative, fecund, fruitful, generative, ingenious, inventive, lush, luxurious, plenteous, productive, profuse, proliferous, prolific, rank, resourceful, rich, teeming

festival *n.* anniversary, carnival, celebration, fair, feast, festivities, field day, fiesta, gala, holiday, jubilee, merriment, regalement, revelry, social gathering, special event, special occasion

festivity *n.* See **festival**

feud *n.* altercation, argument, bickering, clash, conflict, contention, contest, controversy, difference of opinion, disagreement, discord, dispute, dissension, estrangement, fight, hostility, quarrel, rivalry, squabble, strife, variance, vendetta

feud *v.* argue, bicker, clash, conflict, contend, contest, differ, disagree, dispute, dissent, fight, quarrel, squabble

fiasco *n.* breakdown, catastrophe, disaster, failure, frustration, miscarriage, nonsuccess

fiat *n.* act, authorization, command, commandment, decree, dictate, dictum, edict, injunction, law, mandate, manifesto, ordinance, precept, rule, sanction, warrant

fiction *n.* anecdote, concoction, creative writing, fabrication, falsehood, fancy, improvisation, invention, misrepresentation, novel, prevarication, romance, story, tale, written work

fictitious *adj.* artificial, assumed, concocted, counterfeit, created, fabricated, fake, faked, false, feigned, fictional, fictive, imaginary, improvised, invented, made-up, make-believe, manufactured, mythical, phony, pretended, sham, simulated, spurious, suppositious, supposititious, synthetic, ungenuine, unreal, untrue

fidelity *n.* **1.** allegiance, conscientiousness, consecration, constancy, dedication, dependability, devotedness, devotion, faithfulness, fealty, incorruptibility, loyalty, patriotism, reliability, resoluteness, responsibleness, sincerity, staunchness, steadfastness, true-heartedness, trustworthiness, unswervingness **2.** accordance, accuracy, adherence, agreement, closeness, conformity, constancy, correspondence, exactitude, exactness, faithfulness, preciseness, precision, similarity, strictness

fiduciary *n.* administrator, executor, property administrator, property holder, trustee

field *n.* **1.** adjacent characters, data positions, group of adjacent characters, group of data, region, section, set of data **2.** area, bailiwick, bounds, confines, department, discipline, domain, environment, expertise, forte, jurisdiction, limits, province, purview, range, reach, scope, specialization, specialty, sphere, territory

field *v.* activate, answer, answer questions, begin, catch, cover, deal with, handle, play, respond to, resume, retrieve

fight *n.* altercation, argument, battle, bout, brawl, clash, combat, conflict, confrontation, contention, controversy, difference of opinion, disagreement, engagement, feud, fighting, hostilities, misunderstanding, quarrel, skirmish, strife, struggle

fight *v.* argue, attack, battle with, brawl, clash with, combat, conflict with, confront, contend, differ with, disagree with, feud, quarrel with, skirmish with, struggle with

figurative *adj.* allegorical, descriptive, emblematic, emblematical, illustrative, metaphoric, metaphorical, parabolic, pictorial, representative, symbolic

figure *n.* **1.** aggregate, amount, cipher, cost, digit, integer, number, numeral, numeric value, price, sum, symbol, total **2.** bust, cast, composition, design, device, diagram, drawing, effigy, emblem, icon, illustration, image, model, mold, pattern, picture, portrait, representation, sculpture, sign, sketch, statue, symbol, type **3.** anatomy, appearance, body, build, cast, configuration, conformation, constitution, delineation, development, form, frame, outline, physique, pose, posture, shape, structure, torso

figure *v.* add, add up, appraise, assess, calculate, cipher, compute, count, enumerate, estimate, number, numerate, sum, sum up, tally, total, work out

file *n.* archives, arrangement, array, assortment, book, box, cabinet, case, collection, collection of information, compartment, container, data, database, data collection, data set, directory, disk, documents, dossier, drawer, envelope, folder, holder, information, information block, input file, organizer, output file, pigeonhole, receptacle, record, register, repository, tape

file *v.* **1.** alphabetize, arrange, catalog, categorize, classify, enter, insert, organize, put in order, record, register, save, set up, systematize **2.** burnish, grate, grind, polish, refine, rub, scrape, sharpen, smooth

fill *v.* **1.** cram, crowd, fill up, inflate, infuse, load, pack, permeate, pervade, pump up, replenish, satisfy, saturate, stock, stuff, supply **2.** act, carry out, discharge, do, execute, fulfill, function, execute, meet, occupy, perform, provide, satisfy, serve, supply, take up

film *n.* **1.** blanket, blur, cloud, coat, coating, cover, covering, dusting, gauze, haze, integument, layer, mask, membrane, mist, pellicle, screen, sheet, skin, steam, veil, web **2.** cinema, feature, motion picture, movie, picture, short, short subject, show

final *adj.* **1.** closing, concluding, end, ending, eventual, finishing, last, terminal, terminating, ultimate **2.** absolute, certain, conclusive, decided, decisive, definite, definitive, determinate, finished, incontrovertible, indisputable, irrefutable, irrevocable, settled, unappealable

finale *n.* close, conclusion, end, ending, epilog, finish, termination

finalize *v.* See **finish 1**

finance *n.* accounting, banking, business, commerce, economic affairs, economics, financial affairs, fiscal matters, investment, money management

finance *v.* capitalize, endow, fund, furnish credit, loan money, pay for, provide funds, put up money, set up, sponsor, subsidize, support, underwrite

finances *n.* assets, bank accounts, capital, cash, holdings, money, net worth, property, resources, revenue, stock, treasury, wealth, worth

financial *adj.* business, commercial, economic, fiscal, monetary, moneyed, monied, pecuniary

financial planning *n.* budgeting, financial analysis, financial assessment, financial projection, financial review

financial statement *n.* balance sheet, financial report, income statement, statement of cash flows, supplementary financial statement, written financial record

financier *n.* backer, banker, broker, capitalist, financial advisor, investor, large-scale investor, moneylender, speculator, treasurer

financing *n.* backing, borrowing, capitalizing, endowing, furnishing credit, offering money, paying for, providing funds, putting up money, raising capital, setting up in business, sponsoring, subsidizing, supplying funds, supporting, underwriting, use of leverage

finding *n.* award, conclusion, court decision, decision, decree, determination, discovery, find, judgment, order, pronouncement, results, sentence, verdict

fine *n.* charge, cost, damages, fee, forfeiture, penalty, settlement

fine *v.* charge, confiscate, impose fine on, levy, make someone pay, penalize

finish *v.* **1.** accomplish, achieve, attain, bring to a close, bring to a conclusion, carry out, carry through, cease, clinch, close, complete, conclude, culminate, end, finalize, follow through with, fulfill, halt, perfect, realize, resolve, settle, shut down, stop, terminate, wrap, wrap up **2.** consume, deplete, devour, dispose of, drain, empty, exhaust, expend, spend, use, use up **3.** conquer, defeat, destroy, kill, liquidate, overcome, overpower, overwhelm, put an end to

finite *adj.* bounded, circumscribed, definable, delimited, demarcated, determinate, exact, fixed, limited, precise, terminable

firm *n.* association, business, company, concern, conglomerate, corporation, enterprise, establishment, house, institution, multinational corporation, organization, outfit, partnership, proprietorship, syndicate, trust

firm offer *n.* binding offer, enforceable offer, established offer, irreversible offer, irrevocable offer, secure offer, serious offer, set offer, unchangeable offer, written offer

first-class *adj.* best, choice, excellent, finest, first-rate, grade A, noteworthy, outstanding, superb, superior, superlative, supreme, top, unparalleled, unsurpassed, very good

first-rate *adj.* See **first-class**

fiscal *adj.* budgetary, capital, commercial, economic, financial, monetary, moneyed, monied, pecuniary

fit *v.* **1.** become, befit, belong, coincide, concur, conform, connect, correspond to, equal, go together, go with, harmonize, interlock, join, match, meet, parallel, suit, synchronize **2.** accommodate, adapt, adjust, arm, calibrate, change, equip, fashion, fix, furnish, make up, modify, outfit, position, prepare, provide, ready, regulate, shape, tailor

fix *v.* **1.** adjust, amend, correct, debug, fix up, mend, overhaul, patch, rebuild, recondition, reconstruct, rectify, remedy, renew, renovate, repair, restore, revamp, revise, touch up, tune up **2.** affix, anchor, attach, bar, bind, bolt, brace, buckle, cement, clamp, clasp, clinch, congeal, connect, couple, establish, fasten, fuse, gird, glue, graft, harden, hasp, implant, install, link, lock, make fast, nail, pin, plant, position, prop, rivet, screw, secure, set, settle, solder, solidify, stay, stick, stiffen, tether, tie, weld **3.** agree on, appoint, arrange, conclude, decide, define, determine, establish, found, institute, limit, organize, resolve, seal, set, settle, solve, specify, work out

fixed *adj.* **1.** anchored, attached, bound, cemented, clasped, connected, coupled, established, fastened, firm, immobile, immovable, linked, made fast, permanent, rigid, rooted, secured, set, settled, situated, solid, stable, stationary, steady, tied, unwavering **2.** certain, changeless, confirmed, decided, definite, enduring, established, firm, limited, narrow, precise, resolute, resolved, restricted, set, unbending, unchangeable, undeviating, unfaltering, unflinching, unwavering **3.** adjusted, amended, corrected, debugged, mended, overhauled, patched, rebuilt, reconditioned, reconstructed, rectified, refitted, renewed, repaired, restored, revamped, revised, tuned-up

fixed costs *n.* constant costs, nonvariable costs, regular costs, stable costs, undeviating costs

fixtures *n.* appliances, attached personal property, attachments, attachments to real property, equipment, fixed assets, instruments, physical assets, real property

flair *n.* ability, adroitness, aptitude, aptness, bent, capability, capacity, deftness, dexterity, disposition, facility, faculty, finesse, forte, genius, gift, knack, panache, presence, proclivity, propensity, skill, style, talent, tendency, turn

flatter *v.* adulate, blandish, cajole, compliment, exalt, extol, glorify, laud, praise, salute, stroke

flaunt *v.* air, brandish, display, draw attention to, emphasize, exhibit, flash, flourish, parade, showcase, show off, spotlight, wave around

flaw *n.* blemish, blot, blotch, bug, defect, disfigurement, failing, fault, imperfection, mark, scar, scratch, smudge, speck, spot, stain, taint, vice, weakness

flawless *adj.* defectless, faultless, immaculate, impeccable, intact, perfect, sound, spotless, stainless, taintless, unblemished, unbroken, undamaged, unflawed, unimpaired, unmarred, unspoiled, unsullied, whole

flexibility *n.* adaptability, adjustability, bendability, compliance, elasticity, flexibleness, give, limberness, litheness, pliability, pliancy, resilience, springiness, stretchability, suppleness, tractability

flexible *adj.* **1.** acquiescent, adaptable, adjustable, affable, agreeable, amenable, complaisant, compliant, conformable, cooperative, docile, manageable, obedient, open, predisposed, receptive, responsive, submissive, willing **2.** bendable, ductile, elastic, extensible, flexible, limber, lithe, malleable, plastic, pliable, pliant, resilient, spongy, springy, stretchable, supple, tensile, tractable, tractile, yielding

flight *n.* arrival, aviation, cruising, departure, flying, gliding, journey, sailing, scheduled air transportation, shuttle, soaring, transport, trip, voyage

floppy disk *n.* See **disk**

flowchart *n.* chart, connected symbols, diagram, flow diagram, graph, pathways, representation, schematic, steps

fluctuate *v.* alternate, be uncertain, be undecided, change, hesitate, oscillate, shift, swing, undulate, vacillate, vary, veer, wave

flux *n.* alteration, change, fluctuation, instability, motion, mutation, oscillation, shifting, transition, unrest, vacillation, wavering

fly-by-night *adj.* brief, ephemeral, fleeting, impermanent, irresponsible, momentary, shady, shifty, short-lived, transient, undependable, unreliable, unstable, unsteady, transitory, untrustworthy

focus *n.*   center, center of attention, central point, core, crux, focal point, heart, hub, kernel, locus, marrow, middle, nucleus, point of concentration, point of convergence, pole, target

focus *v.*   adjust, aim attention at, bring into focus, center, centralize, clear up, concenter, concentrate, converge, direct, line up

fold *v.* **1.** become insolvent, be ruined, close, collapse, fail, go bankrupt, go out of business, lose everything, shut down **2.** bend, crease, crimp, double, double over, gather, overlap, pleat, tuck, turn under

folder *n.*   case, cover, envelope, file, file folder, holder, pocket, portfolio, wrapper

follow *v.* **1.** come after, come next, go after, go next, postdate, replace, succeed, supersede, supplant, take the place of **2.** abide by, accept as authority, act in accordance with, adhere to, adopt, attend, be consistent with, be devoted to, be guided by, comply with, conform to, copy, do like, emulate, give allegiance to, heed, imitate, live up to, mimic, mind, model after, note, obey, observe, pattern oneself on, reflect, regard, simulate, support, understand, use as example, yield to

follower *n.*   adherent, admirer, advocate, apostle, apprentice, believer, convert, copyist, defender, devotee, disciple, emulator, fan, fancier, imitator, participant, partisan, promoter, proponent, proselyte, protégé, pupil, representative, sectarian, student, supporter, worshiper, zealot

follow through *v.*   bring to completion, bring to conclusion, bring to fruition, carry out, complete, conclude, consummate, finish, follow up, see through

follow up *v.*   act further, check out, check status, communicate again, find out about, follow through, inquire again, inquire further, investigate, look into, pursue, remind, send reminder, take additional action

foolish *adj.*   absurd, ill-advised, ill-considered, imprudent, indiscreet, irrational, irresponsible, nonsensical, preposterous, senseless, short-sighted, silly, unreasonable, unwise

foolishly *adv.*   absurdly, idiotically, ill-advisedly, imprudently, indiscreetly, ludicrously, preposterously, ridiculously, short-sightedly, stupidly, unwisely

footnote *n.* annotation, comment, explanation, explanatory data, note, reference note, source note

forbid *v.* ban, block, censor, check, debar, declare illegal, deny, deter, disallow, eliminate, embargo, exclude, halt, hinder, hold back, impede, interdict, lock out, outlaw, preclude, prevent, prohibit, proscribe, refuse, reject, rule out, stop, turn down, veto

forbidding *adj.* daunting, evil, foreboding, frightening, grim, hostile, menacing, odious, ominous, repellent, sinister, threatening, tough, ugly, unfriendly

force *n.* **1.** ability, agency, authority, capability, coercion, determination, dominance, drive, effectiveness, efficacy, emphasis, forcefulness, influence, intensity, persistence, persuasiveness, pressure, push, significance, stress, validity, vehemence, vigor, weight, willpower **2.** coercion, compulsion, constraint, duress, effort, energy, enforcement, impact, impetus, impulse, might, momentum, physical power, potency, potential, pressure, punch, speed, stimulus, strain, strength, stress, tension, velocity, vigor, violence, vitality

forceful *adj.* cogent, commanding, compelling, convincing, definite, dominant, dynamic, effective, emphatic, energetic, forcible, intensive, mighty, persuasive, positive, potent, powerful, robust, strong, vehement, vigorous, weighty

forecast *n.* augury, calculation, conjecture, divination, estimate, estimation, foreboding, forecasting, foresight, foretelling, forewarning, guess, outlook, prefigurement, prognosis, prognostication, projection, prophecy, speculation

forecast *v.* forewarn, calculate, conjecture, divine, estimate, foresee, foretell, guess, predict, prefigure, prognosticate, project, prophesy, speculate

foregoing *adj.* above, aforementioned, aforesaid, aforestated, antecedent, anterior, earlier, former, precedent, preceding, preliminary, previous, prior

foreign *adj.* **1.** alien, curious, different, distant, exotic, external, faraway, far-off, imported, nonresident, odd, offshore, outlandish, outlying, overseas, peculiar, remote, strange, unfamiliar, unknown **2.** adventitious, extraneous, extrinsic, immaterial, impertinent, inappropriate, incompatible, incongruous, inconsistent, irrelevant, outside, removed, uncharacteristic, unconnected, unrelated

foreigner *n.* alien, emigrant, immigrant, newcomer, nonnative, nonresident, outlander, outsider, stranger

foreman/woman *n.* boss, chief, director, head, line manager, overseer, superintendent, supervisor

foreword *n.* exordium, introduction, preamble, preface, preliminary, prelude, proem, prolegomenon, prologue

forfeit *v.* abandon, default, drop, escheat, give over, give up, hand over, relinquish, sacrifice

forfeiture *n.* divestiture, giving up, losing, loss, penalty, permanent loss, relinquishment, surrender

form *n.* **1.** application blank, attachment, data sheet, entry blank, fill-in document, paper, questionnaire **2.** behavior, ceremony, conduct, convention, custom, decorum, deportment, etiquette, fashion, formality, manner, manners, method, mode, motions, ordinance, practice, procedure, propriety, protocol, rite, ritual, rule, style, usage **3.** anatomy, appearance, arrangement, cast, configuration, conformation, construction, contour, design, exterior, fashion, figure, formation, frame, framework, guide, matrix, model, mold, outline, pattern, profile, shape, silhouette, skeleton, structure, style

form *v.* **1.** arrange, assemble, build, cast, coin, compose, conceive, construct, contrive, create, delineate, design, develop, devise, draw, elevate, engender, erect, establish, fabricate, fashion, forge, formulate, found, frame, generate, inaugurate, initiate, institute, invent, manufacture, model, mold, organize, originate, outline, pattern, plan, plot, project, put together, put up, raise, set up, shape, sketch, start, trace, turn out **2.** appear, arise, become a reality, become visible, come into being, come into existence, develop, eventuate, grow into, materialize, mature, rise, show up, take shape **3.** act as, be a part of, compose, comprise, constitute, make up, serve as

formal *adj.* affected, aloof, ceremonial, ceremonious, conventional, correct, customary, decorous, elaborate, established, fixed, formalistic, observant, official, orderly, polite, precise, pretentious, proper, regular, reserved, rigid, ritual, ritualistic, set, solemn, standard, stiff, strict

formality *n.* ceremoniousness, ceremony, convention, correctness, custom, decorum, etiquette, form, gesture, liturgy, practice, procedure, propriety, protocol, rite, ritual, service, tradition, usage

format *n.* appearance, arrangement, aspect, blueprint, contour, design, dimensions, form, framework, layout, look, makeup, measurements, setup, shape, specifications, structure

format *v.* arrange, convert, design, determine, form, initialize, lay out, make up, organize, prepare, shape, specify, style

formation *n.* arrangement, building, compilation, composition, configuration, construction, creation, design, development, establishment, evolution, fabrication, forming, founding, framing, generation, genesis, institution, invention, makeup, manufacture, organization, origination, production, synthesis

former *adj.* above, aforementioned, aforesaid, ancient, antecedent, anterior, bygone, departed, earlier, erstwhile, foregoing, late, one-time, past, preceding, preliminary, previous, prior

formula *n.* blueprint, canon, code, credo, creed, directions, doctrine, equation, formulary, method, password, prescription, principle, procedure, recipe, ritual, rubric, rule, set order, set procedure, specifications

formulate *v.* articulate, compose, conceive, concoct, create, define, design, designate, detail, develop, devise, draft, express, frame, invent, make up, map out, originate, particularize, plan, prepare, specify, state clearly, systematize, work out

forte *n.* ability, aptitude, competence, effectiveness, faculty, speciality, specialty, strength, talent

forthcoming *adj.* approaching, available, awaited, coming, destined, expected, imminent, impending, inevitable, nearing, oncoming, pending, predestined, prospective, resulting, upcoming

fortify *v.* assure, augment, back, brace, build up, buoy, cheer, defend, embolden, empower, encourage, energize, enhance, hearten, increase, intensify, invigorate, magnify, protect, reassure, reinforce, renew, restore, safeguard, strengthen, supplement, sustain

fortunate *adj.* advantageous, auspicious, blessed, booming, bright, convenient, encouraging, favorable, favored, felicitous, flourishing, fortuitous, happy, lucky, opportune, promising, propitious, prosperous, providential, rosy, succeeding, successful, thriving, timely, victorious, well-off, well-timed, well-to-do

fortune *n.* **1.** affluence, assets, capital, estate, income, inheritance, means, money, opulence, portion, possessions, property, prosperity, resources, revenue, riches, substance, treasure,

wealth, worth   **2.** accident, chance, circumstances, coincidence, contingency, destiny, expectation, fate, fortuity, life, lot,
luck, portion, promise, providence, success, vicissitudes

foster *v.*   accommodate, advance, advocate, aid, approve,
assist, back, boost, champion, contribute to, cultivate, encourage, favor, foment, forward, further, help, minister to, nourish, nurture, patronize, promote, push, raise, sanction,
stimulate, support, sustain

foundation *n.* **1.** association, charity, company, corporation,
establishment, institute, nonprofit organization, organization,
society, trusteeship   **2.** authority, basics, basis, cause, fundamental, grounds, groundwork, justification, motive, principle, purpose, rationale, reason, root, rudiment, source   **3.**
base, basement, bed, bedrock, bottom, cellar, foot, footing,
ground, infrastructure, prop, stand, substratum, substructure, support, underpinning, understructure

founder *n.*   architect, author, builder, creator, designer, dis-
coverer, establisher, framer, generator, initiator, institutor,
inventor, maker, organizer, originator, planner, prime mover,
producer

founder *v.*   break down, collapse, fail, fall, fall through, falter,
flounder, go down, go under, miscarry, sink, sprawl, stagger,
stumble, submerge, submerse, trip, topple

fraction *n.*   bit, chunk, division, fragment, part, particle, piece,
portion, quotient, ratio, section, segment, share, slice, subdivision

fractional *adj.*   apportioned, compartmental, divided, fragmentary, incomplete, insignificant, minor, partial, sectional,
segmented, small

fragment *n.*   bit, chip, chunk, corner, crumb, fraction, iota,
morsel, particle, piece, portion, remainder, remnant, scrap,
section, segment, shred, sliver, snippet, whit

frame *n.*   body, build, casing, chassis, composition, configuration, construction, fabric, form, foundation, framework,
groundwork, hull, outline, physique, plan, scaffolding, shell,
skeleton, structure, substructure, support

framework *n.* See **frame**

franchise *n.*   authority, authorization, ballot, charter, consent,
enfranchisement, grant, license, permission, prerogative,
privilege, right, suffrage, vote, warrant, warranty

fraud *n.* **1.** artifice, concealment, deceit, deception, dishonest act, duplicity, fake, falsification, fraudulence, hoax, intentional deception, intentional misrepresentation, intentional omission, misrepresentation, omission, ruse, sham, spuriousness, subterfuge, treachery, trick, trickery **2.** bluffer, charlatan, cheat, cheater, deceiver, fake, impostor, masquerader, phony, pretender, quack, swindler

fraudulent *adj.* bogus, counterfeit, criminal, crooked, deceitful, deceptive, devious, dishonest, dishonorable, fake, false, guileful, phony, spurious, swindling, treacherous, ungenuine

freight *n.* burden, cargo, charge, consignment, contents, conveyance, freightage, goods, haul, lading, load, merchandise, shipment, shipping, transportation, weight

frequency *n.* commonness, constancy, frequentness, iteration, number, periodicity, persistence, prevalence, recurrence, regularity, reiteration, repetition, repetitiveness

frequent *adj.* common, constant, continual, customary, daily, everyday, habitual, iterative, many, normal, numerous, ordinary, periodic, persistent, profuse, recurrent, regular, reiterative, repeated, several, standard, successive, usual

frequently *adv.* commonly, constantly, continually, customarily, generally, habitually, intermittently, often, oftentimes, ordinarily, periodically, persistently, recurrently, regularly, repeatedly, successively, usually

freshness *n.* brightness, cleanness, clearness, inexperience, innovativeness, inventiveness, modernism, modernness, newness, novelty, originality, recentness

friction *n.* **1.** animosity, antagonism, bickering, clash, conflict, contention, contrariety, controversy, difference of opinion, disagreement, discontent, discord, disharmony, dispute, dissension, dissent, hostility, opposition, quarrel, resistance, rivalry, strife **2.** abrasion, attrition, chafing, erosion, filing, grating, grinding, massage, rasping, resistance, rubbing, scraping, wearing against

friend *n.* acquaintance, advocate, ally, associate, backer, benefactor, colleague, companion, compatriot, comrade, confidant, coworker, supporter, teammate

friendly *adj.* affable, agreeable, amiable, attentive, benevolent, benign, communicative, companionable, comradely, conciliatory, cordial, easygoing, favorable, generous, genial, helpful, intimate, kind, kindly, loyal, propitious, receptive, sociable, sympathetic, understanding, unreserved

fringe benefit *n.*   additional benefit, benefit, compensation, employee benefit, employment benefit, perquisite

frontier *n.*   backcountry, backwoods, border, borderland, borderline, bound, boundary, confines, edge, far reaches, hinterland, limit, march, outback, perimeter, unexplored territory

frugality *n.*   careful management, carefulness, conservation, economizing, economy, frugalness, miserliness, moderation, parsimoniousness, parsimony, penuriousness, prudence, saving, scrimping, self-control, sparingness, stinginess, temperance, thrift, thriftiness

fruition *n.*   achievement, attainment, completion, consummation, enjoyment, fulfillment, gratification, maturation, perfection, pleasure, realization, ripeness, satisfaction, success

fuel *n.*   combustible, encouragement, food, incitement, nourishment, propellant, provocation

fuel *v.*   charge, fan, feed, fill up, fire, gas, give energy to, give impetus to, incite, inflame, nourish, service, supply, sustain

fulfill *v.*   abide by, accomplish, achieve, adhere to, answer, be faithful to, bring about, bring to completion, carry out, complete, comply with, conclude, deliver, discharge, do, effect, execute, fill, finish, follow, implement, meet, obey, observe, perfect, perform, realize, respect, satisfy

fulfillment *n.*   abiding by, accomplishment, achievement, adherence, answering, being faithful to, bringing about, bringing to completion, carrying out, completion, complying with, conclusion, contentedness, contentment, crowning, delivering, discharge, discharging, doing, effecting, end, executing, filling, finishing, following, gratification, implementation, meeting, obeying, observance, perfection, performance, realization, respect, satisfaction

full-scale *adj.*   across-the-board, all-encompassing, all-out, complete, comprehensive, entire, exhaustive, extensive, in-depth, major, radical, sweeping, thorough, total, wide-ranging, widespread

fully *adv.*   absolutely, abundantly, adequately, amply, comprehensively, entirely, generally, perfectly, plentifully, positively, sufficiently, thoroughly, totally, utterly, wholly

function *n.* **1.** activity, affair, assignment, business, capacity, charge, chore, concern, duty, employment, instructions, interest, job, mission, occupation, office, operation, position, post, province, purpose, responsibility, role, set of instructions, situation, station, task, use, work **2.** affair, business activity, celebration, ceremony, fete, gala, observance, party, reception, ritual, social event, social occasion

function *v.* act, be in action, be in commission, be in operation, be running, do, go, officiate, operate, perform, run, serve, work

functional *adj.* operational, operative, practical, serviceable, useful, utilitarian, working

fund *n.* assets, available money, capital, collection, endowment, foundation, grant, investment, pool, portfolio, repository, reserve, reservoir, stock, store, storehouse, supply, treasury, trust

fund *v.* back, capitalize, endow, finance, grant, invest in, pay for, provide funds for, provide money for, put money into, refinance, subsidize, support

fundamental *n.* basis, core, cornerstone, essence, essential component, essential factor, essential part, foundation, gist, groundwork, heart, nucleus, pith, principle, rule, theorem

fundamental *adj.* basal, basic, cardinal, central, constitutional, critical, crucial, elemental, elementary, essential, first, foundational, important, indispensable, inherent, initial, integral, intrinsic, organic, original, primary, prime, principal, structural, supporting, underlying

funds *n.* available cash, available money, cash reserve, ready cash, ready money

furbish *v.* brighten up, clean up, fix up, polish, redecorate, redo, refurbish, renew, renovate, repaint, shine

furnish *v.* **1.** adorn, arm, array, decorate, endow, equip, fit, gear, outfit, provide, purvey, render, rig, supply, turn out **2.** afford, bestow, communicate, contribute, deliver, dispense, give, hand over, impart, offer, present, provide, render, reveal, send, supply, transfer, turn over

furniture *n.* appointments, articles, effects, fixtures, furnishings, goods, material, movables, personal property, possessions, supplies

fusion *n.* amalgamation, blending, coadunation, coalescence, combination, commixture, consolidation, convergence, dissolving, interfusion, intermixture, liquefaction, melding, melting, merging, mixture, smelting, unification, union

futile *adj.* abortive, barren, empty, fruitless, gainless, hollow, hopeless, idle, impractical, inane, inconsequential, ineffective, ineffectual, insignificant, pointless, profitless, sterile, trifling, trivial, unproductive, unprofitable, unsuccessful, useless, vain, valueless, worthless

future *n.* anticipation, eventuality, expectation, futurity, hereafter, life to come, millennium, offing, outlook, posterity, prospect, time to come, tomorrow

future *adj.* anticipated, approaching, coming, eventual, expected, forthcoming, impending, inevitable, later, likely, next, pending, probable, prospective

G

gadget *n.*   apparatus, appliance, artifice, contraption, contrivance, device, implement, invention, mechanism, novelty, object, tool, utensil

gaffe *n.*   blunder, error, impropriety, indecorum, indiscretion, misjudgment, mistake, social error

gain *n.*   achievement, acquisition, advance, advantage, attainment, avail, benefit, dividend, earnings, efficacy, excess, good, growth, harvest, improvement, income, increase, increment, net, proceeds, procurement, produce, profit, progress, realization, receipts, return, share, usefulness, winnings, yield

gain *v.*   achieve, acquire, advance, arrive at, attain, benefit, bring in, build up, capture, clear, collect, earn, garner, gather, get, glean, harvest, improve, increase, make, merit, net, obtain, overtake, persuade, pick up, prevail, procure, produce, profit, progress, reach, realize, reap, secure, win, win over, yield

gainful *adj.*   advantageous, beneficial, desirable, fruitful, lucrative, moneymaking, paying, productive, profitable, remunerative, rewarding, rich, substantial, useful, valuable, well-paying, worthwhile

gains *n.*   See **gain (n)**

gallery *n.*   **1.** arcade, balcony, bleachers, covered walkway, grandstand, loggia, mezzanine, porch, portico, upper gallery, veranda   **2.** assembly, audience, congregation, house, listeners, observers, onlookers, public, spectators   **3.** art gallery, exhibition hall, exhibition room, hall, museum, salon, showroom, studio, theater balcony

galvanize *v.*   animate, arouse, charge, electrify, energize, enliven, excite, exhilarate, inspire, invigorate, jar, jolt, motivate, prod, rouse, shock, spur, stagger, stimulate, stir, thrill, vitalize

gamble *n.*   bet, chance, gambling, hazard, risk, speculation, uncertainty, venture, wager

gamble *v.*   bet, chance, dare, hazard, make a bet, play, plunge, risk, speculate, take a chance, take the risk, venture, wager

gauge *n.*   benchmark, capacity, criterion, degree, depth, extent, guide, guideline, height, indicator, measure, magnitude, meter, norm, rule, scale, scope, size, standard, test, touchstone, width, yardstick

gauge *v.* adjudge, appraise, ascertain, assess, balance, calibrate, check, compute, consider, determine, estimate, evaluate, figure, judge, measure, rate, reckon, value, weigh

general *adj.* **1.** accepted, accustomed, common, commonplace, conventional, customary, everyday, familiar, generic, habitual, household, ordinary, popular, prevailing, prevalent, public, regular, typical, usual, wonted **2.** abstract, approximate, ill-defined, impersonal, imprecise, inaccurate, indefinite, inexact, undetailed, unspecific, vague **3.** blanket, broad, catholic, collective, composite, comprehensive, ecumenical, encyclopedic, extended, extensive, generic, inclusive, limitless, miscellaneous, overall, panoramic, sweeping, total, universal, unlimited, widespread, worldwide

generality *n.* abstraction, abstract principle, generalization, general law, general observation, general principle, general rule, general statement, loose statement, sweeping statement, universality, vague statement

generalize *v.* draw general conclusion, hypothesize, induce, make general assumption, make general inference, make sweeping assumption, observe generally, philosophize, postulate, speculate, theorize

generally *adv.* altogether, approximately, broadly, chiefly, commonly, conventionally, customarily, habitually, largely, mainly, mostly, normally, ordinarily, popularly, predominantly, primarily, principally, regularly, roughly, typically, usually

generate *v.* breed, bring about, bring into existence, bring to pass, coin, create, design, develop, effectuate, engender, establish, fabricate, form, found, give birth to, give rise to, inaugurate, initiate, innovate, institute, invent, make, occasion, originate, procreate, produce, propagate, reproduce, set up, start

generation *n.* **1.** breeding, bringing about, bringing to pass, coining, creation, design, developing, fabrication, formation, founding, genesis, giving birth to, giving rise to, inauguration, initiation, innovation, institution, invention, making, origination, procreation, propagation, reproduction **2.** age, age group, day, days, epoch, era, life span, lifetime, span, time, times

generic *adj.* all-encompassing, all-inclusive, blanket, collective, common, comprehensive, extensive, general, nonexclusive, sweeping, unlabeled

generosity *n.* altruism, beneficence, benevolence, bounteousness, bounty, charitableness, charity, giving, goodness, goodwill, high-mindedness, hospitality, humanitarianism, kindness, liberality, magnanimity, munificence, nobleness, openhandedness, philanthropy, unselfishness

generous *adj.* **1.** altruistic, beneficent, benevolent, bighearted, bounteous, bountiful, charitable, giving, high-minded, hospitable, humanitarian, kind, kind-hearted, kindly, liberal, magnanimous, munificent, noble, open-handed, philanthropic, ungrudging, unselfish **2.** abundant, affluent, ample, bountiful, copious, full, large, lavish, liberal, luxuriant, overflowing, plenteous, plentiful, rich, wealthy

genesis *n.* alpha, beginning, birth, commencement, creation, dawn, formation, generation, inception, nascence, origin, rise, root, source, start

genius *n.* ability, acuity, acumen, aptness, astuteness, bent, brains, brilliance, capability, capacity, cleverness, cognition, facility, faculty, flair, forte, high intellect, imagination, ingenuity, intellectual, intelligence, inventiveness, knack, muse, percipience, perspicacity, prodigy, sagacity, smartness, talent, turn, understanding, virtuoso, wisdom

genre *n.* brand, category, class, classification, fashion, genus, group, kind, school, sort, species, style, type, variety

genuine *adj.* **1.** actual, attested, authentic, authenticated, certified, confirmed, exact, guaranteed, legitimate, official, precise, real, rightful, true, unquestionable, valid, verified, veritable, warranted **2.** artless, earnest, frank, guileless, heartfelt, honest, innocent, natural, open, pure, sincere, straightforward, trustworthy, unaffected, unfeigned, unpretended

germ *n.* alpha, bud, commencement, egg, embryo, fount, fountainhead, inception, origin, root, seed, source, sprout, start

germane *adj.* applicable, appropriate, apt, fitting, material, pertinent, related, relevant, suited

get ahead *v.* achieve, advance, be successful, do well, excel, flourish, make good, progress, prosper, rise up, succeed, thrive

get by *v.* cope, exist, fare, get along, subsist

gift *n.* **1.** allowance, alms, award, benefaction, benefit, bequest, bestowal, bonus, bounty, charity, contribution, donation, endowment, favor, giveaway, grant, gratuity, handout, honorarium, largesse, legacy, offering, offertory, premium, present, presentation, prize, stipend   **2.** ability, adroitness, aptitude, aptness, bent, capability, capacity, dexterity, endowment, facility, faculty, flair, forte, genius, ingenuity, intelligence, knack, power, skill, turn

gifted *adj.*   adroit, apt, astute, brilliant, clever, dexterous, expert, ingenious, intelligent, skilled, smart, talented, well-endowed

gimmick *n.*   apparatus, artifice, catch, contrivance, deceit, deception, device, drawback, feint, gadget, maneuver, plan, ploy, ruse, scheme, shift, stratagem, strategy, subterfuge, trap, trick, wile

give *v.*   **1.** accord, allocate, allow, apportion, assign, award, bestow, confer, consign, contribute, convey, deliver, dispense, distribute, dole out, donate, endow, entrust, furnish, give up, grant, hand out, hand over, leave, lend, mete out, parcel out, pass out, pay, present, proffer, provide, relinquish, subsidize, supply, transfer, transmit, turn over, will   **2.** announce, communicate, concede, deliver, demonstrate, display, express, extend, furnish, impart, indicate, issue, notify, offer, present, pronounce, provide, render, set forth, state, supply, transfer, transmit

glean *v.*   ascertain, collect, cull, deduce, discover, extract, find out, gather, harvest, learn, pick out, pick up, pull in, reap, sift, take in

glitch *n.*   computer error, erroneous response, error, short-term voltage transient, software error

global *adj.*   all-encompassing, all-inclusive, broad, complete, comprehensive, cosmic, earthly, encyclopedic, exhaustive, extensive, far-reaching, globelike, globular, international, overall, planetary, spherical, sweeping, thorough, unbounded, universal, unlimited, vast, wide-ranging, world, worldwide

globe *n.*   celestial globe, earth, map, planet, sphere, spheroid, terrestrial globe, universe, world

glory *n.*   **1.** celebrity, dignity, distinction, eminence, exaltation, fame, greatness, illustriousness, importance, majesty, name, nobility, notability, note, popularity, praise, prestige, renown, reputation, stateliness, triumph, vogue   **2.** brightness, brilliance, effulgence, fanfare, grandeur, illumination, luster, magnificence, pageantry, pomp, radiance, resplendence, richness, splendor, sumptuousness

gloss *n.* **1.** annotation, comment, commentary, critique, definition, elucidation, exegesis, explanation, explication, footnote, interpretation, reading, translation, understanding **2.** alteration, apology, camouflage, coloration, concealment, concoction, contrivance, cover-up, disguise, excuse, explanation, fabrication, falsification, mask, misleading interpretation, misrepresentation, rationalization, veil

gloss *v.* **1.** analyze, annotate, comment on, construe, critique, define, elucidate, explain, explicate, footnote, interpret, read, read into, translate **2.** alter, apologize for, camouflage, color, conceal truth, cover up, disguise, downplay, excuse, explain away, extenuate, falsify, hide, make plausible, mask, misrepresent, palliate, play down, rationalize, smooth over, veil

glossary *n.* annotation, computer storage utility, definitions, listing, list of definitions, nomenclature, storage utility

go-ahead *n.* approval, authorization, consent, leave, permission, sanction

go ahead *v.* advance, begin, continue, go forward, go on, move, move ahead, move on, pass on, proceed, progress, push on

goal *n.* aim, ambition, aspiration, destination, end, endpoint, ideal, intent, intention, mark, mission, object, objective, purpose, target, terminus

go-between *n.* agent, arbiter, arbitrator, broker, connection, consumer advocate, contact, dealer, disinterested party, distributor, factor, interagency, intermediary, internuncio, jobber, judge, liaison, link, mediator, medium, moderator, negotiator, ombudsman/woman, peacemaker, procurer, referee, tie, umpire, wholesaler

good *adj.* **1.** able, acceptable, accomplished, adept, adroit, appropriate, capable, competent, dependable, efficient, expert, loyal, proficient, qualified, reliable, satisfactory, serviceable, skilled, skillful, suitable, talented, useful **2.** admirable, beneficial, benevolent, charitable, choice, commendable, considerate, desirable, ethical, excellent, exemplary, favorable, honest, honorable, humane, kindhearted, moral, nice, pleasing, respectable, respectful, righteous, satisfactory, superb, thoughtful, trustworthy, upright, valuable, wonderful

goods *n.* accessories, belongings, cargo, chattel, commodities, effects, encumbrances, equipment, freight, furnishings, furniture, holdings, material, materials, merchandise, paraphernalia, personal effects, personal possessions, personal property, stock, wares

goodwill *n.* altruism, beneficence, benevolence, charity, concern, cordiality, friendliness, friendship, goodness, graciousness, helpfulness, intangible asset, kindliness, kindness, monetary value, reputation, salable asset, sympathy, unselfishness, value

gospel *n.* authenticity, authority, belief, certainty, Christian doctrine, credo, creed, doctrine, ethic, fact, principle, scripture, tenet, truth, verity

govern *v.* administer, assume command, be in charge, conduct, control, decide, determine, dictate, direct, discipline, exercise authority, exercise control over, guide, hold office, hold sway over, lead, maintain order, manage, order, oversee, preside over, regulate, reign, restrain, run, superintend, supervise, take control, wield power

government *n.* administration, authority, bureaucracy, charge, command, control, direction, dominion, governance, guidance, jurisdiction, law, leadership, management, ministry, overseeing, oversight, power, presidency, regime, regulation, reign, rule, sovereignty, state, statecraft, superintendence, supervision, union

gradation *n.* calibration, consecutiveness, continuation, course, degree, difference, grade, gradual advance, level, mark, measurement, pitch, plane, point, progression, rank, scale, sequence, series, slope, stage, step, succession

grade *n.* **1.** caliber, category, class, classification, degree, division, gradation, group, level, mark, order, place, position, quality, rank, size, stage, standard, station, step **2.** ascent, bank, degree, descent, elevation, embankment, gradient, height, inclination, incline, level, pitch, plane, rise, slant, slope, tilt

grade *v.* arrange, assort, brand, categorize, class, classify, evaluate, group, label, name, order, organize, place, range, rank, rate, size, sort, tag, type, value

gradient *n.* See **gradation**; **grade** (n) **2**

gradually *adv.* constantly, continually, continuously, gently, imperceptibly, moderately, progressively, regularly, steadily, slowly, successively

graduate *n.* alumna, alumnus, baccalaureate, certificate holder, degree holder, diplomate, former student, graduating student, licentiate

graduate *v.* **1.** be commissioned, complete education, confer degree, earn degree, finish, finish education, get a degree, get a diploma, receive degree, receive diploma **2.** arrange, calibrate, classify, divide, grade, group, mark off, measure off, order, range, rank, rate, sort

grammar *n.* accidence, grammatical rules, language rules, language structure, language system, linguistics, morphology, principles of language, syntax, system of language

grant *n.* allotment, allowance, alms, assistantship, award, benefaction, benefit, bequest, bestowal, bounty, contribution, dole, donation, endowment, fee, gratuity, gift, handout, honorarium, largess, pension, present, scholarship, share, stipend, subsidy, tribute

grant *v.* **1.** accord, allot, award, bestow, confer, contribute, convey, dispense, donate, endow, furnish, give, impart, offer, present, provide, supply, surrender, transfer **2.** accede to, acquiesce in, adhere to, admit, agree to, allow, assent to, cede, comply with, concede, conform to, consent to, let, permit, submit to, yield

graph *n.* blueprint, chart, diagram, drawing, grid, map, pictorial representation, picture, representation scheme, schematic, sketch

graphic *adj.* **1.** delineated, depicted, diagrammatic, drawn, engraved, etched, illustrated, illustrative, pictorial, representational, sketched, visual **2.** clear, clear-cut, cogent, concrete, definite, descriptive, detailed, distinct, explicit, expressive, incisive, lively, picturesque, realistic, striking, telling, vivid, well-defined

graphics *n.* computer-generated images, displayed drawings, displayed images, drawings, drawn images, engravings, handling of pictorial material, images, manipulation of pictorial material, pictorial representation, visual art

grasp *n.* awareness, cognition, comprehension, grip, knowledge, perception, realization, scope, sense

gratis *adj.* chargeless, complimentary, cost-free, costless, expense-free, expenseless, free, gratuitous, no-cost

gratitude *n.* acknowledgment, appreciation, appreciativeness, gratefulness, recognition, sense of obligation, thankfulness, thanks, thanksgiving

gratuitous *adj.* **1.** See **gratis** **2.** baseless, groundless, needless, superfluous, uncalled-for, unfounded, ungrounded, unjustified, unnecessary, unreasonable, unwarranted

gratuity *n.* bonus, contribution, extra, fee, fringe benefit, gift, honorarium, offering, perquisite, present, reward, tip, token

gravity *n.* enormity, force, importance, magnitude, momentousness, ponderousness, pressure, seriousness, severity, significance, solemnity, urgency, weight, weightiness

green *adj.* amateurish, awkward, callow, credulous, developing, fresh, growing, gullible, ignorant, immature, inexperienced, inexpert, ingenuous, innocent, maturing, naive, new, pliant, raw, recent, unconversant, undeveloped, unfinished, unpolished, unpracticed, unseasoned, unskillful, unsophisticated, untrained, unversed, young, youthful

greenhorn *n.* amateur, apprentice, beginner, inexperienced person, learner, neophyte, newcomer, novice, novitiate, recruit, rookie

greet *v.* address, bow to, embrace, exchange greetings, extend a hand, hail, meet, nod to, pay respects to, receive, salute, say hello to, shake hands, speak to, wave, welcome

greeting *n.* address, attention, bow, embrace, extending hand, hail, hailing, handshake, meeting, nod, nodding to, ovation, paying respects to, receiving, reception, salutation, salute, saluting, saying hello, shaking hands, speaking to, wave, waving, welcome

grid *n.* chart, horizontal and vertical lines, layout, line intersections, lines, network, organizational system, parallel bars, parallel lines, pattern, rows and columns, set of lines, squares

grievance *n.* accusation, allegation, charge, complaint, damage, disservice, imputation, injury, injustice, objection, outrage, unfairness, unjust act, wrong

gross *n.* aggregate, entirety, highest amount, intake, profits, receipts, sum total, total, total earnings, total income, totality, 12 dozen, whole

gross *adj.* aggregate, before-tax, complete, entire, total, whole

groundless *adj.* baseless, conjectural, false, imaginary, speculative, unfounded, ungrounded, unjustified, unprovoked, unreasonable, unsubstantiated, unsupported, unwarranted

grounds *n.* **1.** argument, base, basis, cause, demonstration, evidence, excuse, foundation, justification, premise, proof, proposition, rationale, reason, testimony **2.** acreage, campus, common, domain, estate, field, gardens, land, lawn, lot, park, property, surroundings, tract, yard **3.** deposit, dregs, grouts, lees, precipitate, residue, sediment, settlings

groundwork *n.* base, basis, bottom, footing, foundation, fundamentals, ground, infrastructure, substratum, underpinning, understructure

group *n.* accumulation, array, assemblage, assembly, assortment, body, branch, bunch, class, clump, cluster, collection, company, conglomeration, congregation, faction, family, gathering, genus, organization, pack, party, phylum, section, series, set, species, subdivision, variety

growth *n.* advancement, aggrandizement, augmentation, buildup, development, enlargement, evolution, expansion, extension, germination, increase, maturation, movement forward, multiplication, opening, progress, proliferation, prosperity, rise, sprouting, success, unfolding

guarantee *n.* agreement, assurance, bail, bargain, bond, certainty, certificate, certification, collateral, covenant, deposit, earnest, earnest money, gage, guaranty, oath, pawn, pledge, promise, security, surety, sworn statement, taking responsibility, warrant, warranty, word, word of honor

guarantee *v.* affirm, answer for, assure, aver, back up, bind, countersign, cover, ensure, give word, indemnify, insure, make certain, mortgage, pledge, promise, protect, sponsor, stand behind, state under oath, swear to, underwrite, witness

guaranteed *adj.* assured, bonded, certified, endorsed, insured, pledged, secured, warranted

guaranty *n.* See **guarantee (n)**

guard *v.* conduct, conserve, convoy, cover, defend, escort, keep under surveillance, keep watch, maintain surveillance, oversee, patrol, police, preserve, protect, safeguard, save, screen, secure, shelter, shield, stand guard over, supervise, take care of, watch, watch over

guardian *n.* caretaker, curator, custodian, fiduciary, foster parent, manager, protector, steward, trustee, warden

guest *n.* boarder, caller, company, lodger, roomer, tenant, vacationer, visitor

guidance *n.* advice, control, counsel, direction, help, instruction, leadership, management, recommendation, regulation, supervision, teaching

guide *n.*   **1.** catalog, compendium, directory, guidebook, handbook, information, instructions, itinerary, landmark, manual, map, model, reference, sign, travel book   **2.** advisor, attendant, captain, coach, conductor, convoy, counselor, director, educator, escort, guidance counselor, instructor, leader, manager, mentor, model, pilot, scout, supervisor, teacher, therapist, trainer, tutor, usher

guide *v.* accompany, advise, attend, conduct, control, convoy, counsel, direct, educate, escort, govern, instruct, lead, manage, navigate, oversee, pilot, preside, recommend, regulate, rule, show, show the way, steer, suggest, supervise, teach, tell about, train, tutor, usher

guidebook *n.*   See **guide (n) 1**

habit *n.* addiction, bent, character, convention, custom, dependence, disposition, fashion, fixed attitude, form, habitude, inclination, leaning, manner, mind-set, mode, nature, observance, pattern, penchant, policy, practice, praxis, predisposition, prescription, procedure, proclivity, proneness, propensity, routine, rule, style, temperament, tendency, tradition, usage, way

hackneyed *adj.* banal, commonplace, dull, familiar, insipid, outdated, outmoded, out-of-date, overdone, overworked, played-out, quotidian, stale, stereotyped, stock, tedious, trite, unimaginative, uninspired, unoriginal, worn-out

handbook *n.* basic text, directory, guide, guidebook, instruction book, instruction manual, manual, pocket manual, primer, text, textbook

handicap *n.* **1.** barrier, block, burden, check, constraint, curb, difficulty, disability, disadvantage, drawback, encumbrance, hindrance, impairment, impediment, inconvenience, limitation, obstacle, obstruction, restraint, restriction, shortcoming **2.** advantage, favor, head start, odds

handicraft *n.* artifact, artisanship, artwork, craft, craftsmanship, handiwork, industrial art, manual art, skill

handle *v.* **1.** administer, command, control, cope with, deal with, direct, employ, execute, exercise, govern, guide, head, manage, maneuver, manipulate, operate, oversee, ply, regulate, run, superintend, supervise, take care of, take charge of, transact, use, utilize, wield **2.** buy and sell, carry, deal in, market, offer, sell, stock, trade, traffic, truck

hall *n.* **1.** amphitheater, assembly hall, assembly room, auditorium, ballroom, classroom, convention hall, large room, lecture room, lyceum, meetinghouse, meeting place, schoolroom, theater **2.** breezeway, corridor, entrance, entry, foyer, gallery, hallway, lobby, passage, passageway, threshold, vestibule

hallmark *n.* authentication, badge, brand, device, earmark, emblem, indicator, mark, plate mark, seal, sign, stamp, symbol, trademark

harass *v.* afflict, annoy, bait, beleaguer, beset, bother, disturb, harry, intimidate, oppress, persecute, pester, plague, provoke, terrorize, trouble, victimize, worry

harassment *n.* affliction, annoyance, badgering, bother, disturbance, intimidation, oppression, persecution, pestering, plaguing, provocation, terrorizing, trouble, victimization, worry

hard *adj.* arduous, bleak, brutal, burdensome, cruel, demanding, difficult, distressing, exacting, exhausting, fatiguing, formidable, grievous, harsh, intolerable, laborious, oppressive, painful, rigorous, rough, ruthless, severe, strenuous, strict, tiresome, tiring, torturous, tough, troublesome, wearisome

hardship *n.* accident, adversity, affliction, austerity, calamity, catastrophe, deprivation, destitution, difficulty, disaster, distress, injury, mischance, misery, misfortune, mishap, need, oppression, ordeal, personal burden, plight, privation, rigor, setback, severity, suffering, torment, tragedy, travail, trial, tribulation, trouble, want

hardware *n.* appliances, computer equipment, durables, equipment, fixtures, furnishings, gear, implements, ironware, machinery, metalware, tools, utensils

harmful *adj.* adverse, bad, baneful, corroding, corrosive, corrupting, damaging, dangerous, deleterious, destructive, detrimental, disadvantageous, disastrous, evil, hurtful, inimical, injurious, menacing, noxious, pernicious, poisonous, ruinous, seditious, sinister, subversive, toxic, treasonous, undermining, unhealthy, unsafe, unwholesome, virulent

harmless *adj.* gentle, innocent, innocuous, inoffensive, manageable, mild, nonirritating, nontoxic, painless, powerless, safe, unobjectionable, unoffending

harmonious *adj.* agreeable, amiable, amicable, balanced, compatible, congenial, congruous, consonant, coordinated, cordial, correspondent, corresponding, euphonious, fraternal, friendly, harmonizing, matching, peaceful, sociable, suitable, sympathetic, synchronized, unified

harmony *n.* accord, accordance, affinity, amicability, amity, balance, compatibility, comradeship, concord, concurrence, conformity, congeniality, consensus, consistency, cooperation, correspondence, friendship, goodwill, like-mindedness, peace, rapport, social agreement, sympathy, synthesis, tranquility, unanimity, understanding, union, unity

haul *v.* bring, carry, convey, convoy, drag, draw, ferry, lug, move, ship, take, tow, transport, truck

havoc *n.* calamity, cataclysm, catastrophe, chaos, confusion, damage, destruction, devastation, disaster, disorder, disruption, mayhem, plunder, ravages, ruination, vandalism, waste, wreckage

hazard *n.* accident, endangerment, imperilment, jeopardy, misfortune, mishap, peril, risk, threat

hazardous *adj.* dangerous, difficult, perilous, precarious, risky, uncertain, unhealthy, unpredictable, unsafe, unsound

head *n.* **1.** administrator, boss, captain, chairperson, chief, commander, controller, director, manager, president, principal, senior, superintendent, supervisor **2.** acme, apex, apogee, cap, crest, crown, peak, pinnacle, pitch, point, promontory, summit, tip, top, vertex, zenith

head *adj.* capital, cardinal, chief, first, foremost, leading, main, most important, paramount, preeminent, premier, prime, principal, supreme

head *v.* administer, captain, command, control, direct, govern, guide, lead, manage, oversee, pilot, pioneer, precede, preside, regulate, rule, run, superintend, supervise

healthful *adj.* See **healthy 2**

healthy *adj.* **1.** able-bodied, active, athletic, fit, hale, healthful, hearty, physically fit, robust, sound, strong, sturdy, vigorous, virile **2.** beneficial, bracing, desirable, healing, health-giving, helpful, hygienic, invigorating, nourishing, nutritious, refreshing, restorative, stimulating, useful, wholesome

hectic *adj.* boisterous, chaotic, confused, disordered, excited, fervid, fevered, feverish, frantic, frenetic, frenzied, furious, riotous, tumultuous, turbulent, unruly, unsettled, wild

hedge *v.* **1.** avoid, avoid commitment, be indefinite, be noncommittal, be vague, dodge, duck, elude, equivocate, escape, evade, hesitate, make qualifications, prevaricate, quibble, shift, shuffle, stall **2.** compensate for, counterbalance, defend against, guard against, leave a way out, make allowances for, protect against, shield against

heir *n.* beneficiary, descendant, devisee, future generation, heir apparent, heiress, heritor, inheritor, legatee, offspring, progeny, posterity, receiver, recipient, scion, successor

help *n.* **1.** accommodation, advice, advocacy, aid, assist, assistance, avail, backing, benefit, benevolence, boost, collaboration, contribute, cooperation, facilitation, guidance, lift, maintenance, patronage, philanthropy, relief, service, sponsorship, subsidy, subvention, support, use, utility **2.** adjutant, adjuvant, aide, ally, assistant, attendant, coadjutant, coadjutor, collaborator, colleague, domestic, employee, helper, servant, subsidiary, supporter, worker

help *v.* **1.** accommodate, advocate, aid, assist, back, befriend, bolster, boost, cheer, collaborate, contribute, cooperate, do a favor for, endorse, further, lift, maintain, oblige, patronize, save, second, support, sustain, uphold, work for **2.** allay, alleviate, ameliorate, better, cure, ease, facilitate, heal, improve, meliorate, mend, mitigate, nourish, recondition, rehabilitate, rejuvenate, relieve, remedy, restore, revive

helper *n.* See **help (n) 2**

helpful *adj.* accommodating, advantageous, beneficial, beneficient, benevolent, caring, conducive, considerate, constructive, contributory, convenient, cooperative, friendly, handy, healthful, instrumental, invaluable, kind, obliging, practical, pragmatic, productive, profitable, propitious, serviceable, significant, supportive, sympathetic, timely, usable, useful, utilitarian, valuable

hereafter *adv.* afterward, eventually, henceforth, hereupon, subsequently, ultimately

heritage *n.* ancestry, background, bequest, birthright, bloodline, culture, custom, descent, extraction, family, history, inheritance, legacy, lineage, lot, past, portion, share, tradition

hesitate *v.* balk, be reluctant, be uncertain, be unwilling, delay, demur, equivocate, falter, fluctuate, hedge, hold back, hold off, oscillate, pause, pull back, refrain from, scruple, shrink, shy away, swerve, vacillate, wait, waver

hesitation *n.* delay, delaying, demurral, equivocation, faltering, fluctuation, hedging, hesitancy, holding back, holding off, indecision, indecisiveness, oscillation, pause, pulling back, reluctance, scruple, shrinking, shying away, swerving, uncertainty, unwillingness, vacillation, waiting, wavering

heterogeneous *adj.* assorted, composite, different, discrepant, disparate, dissimilar, divergent, diverse, diversified, incompatible, incongruous, inharmonious, miscellaneous, mixed, multiform, nonuniform, sundry, unlike, unrelated, variant, varied, variegated, various

hiatus *n.* blank, break, cessation, deferment, disruption, gap, halt, interim, intermission, interruption, interval, lacuna, lapse, lull, opening, pause, postponement, recess, rest, space, standstill, stop, vacancy, vacuum, void

high *adj.* **1.** costly, excessive, exorbitant, expensive, extraordinary, extravagant, extreme, grand, high-priced, lavish, luxurious, rich **2.** capital, chief, critical, crucial, distinguished, eminent, essential, exalted, grave, high-ranking, important, influential, leading, major, noble, notable, powerful, preeminent, prime, prominent, serious, significant, superior, vital **3.** high-pitched, loud, piercing, sharp, shrill

highlight *n.* best part, center of attraction, distinctive feature, essence, feature, focal point, focus, key, main feature, main point, memorable part, outstanding feature, salient point, spotlight

highway *n.* expressway, freeway, interstate, main road, parkway, public road, roadway, state road, street, superhighway, thoroughfare, toll road, turnpike

hinder *v.* arrest, bar, block, check, contravene, counteract, curb, delay, deter, encumber, frustrate, hamper, handicap, hold back, impede, inhibit, interfere, interrupt, obstruct, oppose, preclude, prevent, prohibit, restrain, set back, slow down, stop, thwart

hire *v.* appoint, book, bring in, charter, commission, contract with, employ, engage, enlist, fill a position, find help, lease, let, offer work, provide work, put to work, rent, retain, secure, sign on, sublease, sublet, take on, use

historic *adj.* celebrated, consequential, distinguished, extraordinary, famous, illustrious, important, memorable, momentous, notable, noted, noteworthy, outstanding, prominent, rare, remarkable, significant, special, unforgettable, well-known

historical *adj.* actual, ancient, archival, authentic, chronicled, commemorated, confirmed, documented, factual, important, memorable, real, true, verifiable

history *n.* **1.** account, annals, autobiography, biography, chronicle, chronology, journal, life story, memoirs, narration, narrative, public record, record, register, report, review, saga, tale **2.** ancient times, bygone eras, former times, past events, the past, yesterday

hold *v.* **1.** administer, assemble, bring together, carry on, celebrate, conduct, conduct meeting, convene, direct, engage in, gather, have, officiate at, preside over, run, run meeting

2. accommodate, be equipped for, carry, comprise, contain, cradle, embrace, enclose, include, occupy, possess, retain, seat, sustain, take, wield **3.** acknowledge, advocate, allow, assume, believe, consider, deem, espouse, esteem, feel, judge, maintain, presume, propound, reckon, regard, swear by, think, view **4.** adhere to, apply, be in force, be the case, be true, be valid, continue, endure, follow, go on, hold good, hold true, last, persist, remain, remain in effect, remain true, remain valid, stand up, stay

holiday *n.* celebration, day off, feast day, festival, fete, furlough, gala, holy day, leave, leave of absence, recess, respite, sabbatical, saint's day, time off, vacation

homogeneous *adj.* akin, alike, analogous, cognate, comparable, consistent, consonant, corresponding, identical, like, regular, similar, uniform, unvaried, unvarying

honest *adj.* aboveboard, authentic, candid, decent, dependable, direct, equitable, ethical, forthright, frank, genuine, honorable, ingenuous, open, principled, reliable, reputable, sincere, straightforward, trustworthy, truthful, upright, veracious, virtuous

honesty *n.* candidness, candor, dependability, equity, evenhandedness, fairness, forthrightness, frankness, genuineness, honor, incorruptibility, ingenuousness, integrity, justness, probity, rectitude, reliability, reputability, sincerity, straightforwardness, trustworthiness, truthfulness, uprightness, veracity, virtue

honor *n.* adoration, consideration, conscientiousness, credit, decency, deference, dignity, distinction, eminence, esteem, exaltation, fame, forthrightness, glorification, glory, good name, goodness, homage, honesty, integrity, morality, notability, note, notice, praise, prestige, principles, probity, recognition, rectitude, regard, renown, reputation, repute, respect, reverence, righteousness, scrupulousness, tribute, trustworthiness, truthfulness, uprightness, veneration

honor *v.* acclaim, admire, adore, aggrandize, applaud, celebrate, commemorate, commend, compliment, decorate, defer to, dignify, distinguish, ennoble, esteem, exalt, extol, glorify, hail, idolize, laud, lionize, magnify, pay homage to, pay tribute to, praise, prize, recognize, respect, revere, salute, toast, value, venerate, worship

hope *v.* anticipate, assume, be hopeful, cherish, contemplate, count on, deem likely, depend on, desire, dream about, expect, foresee, have confidence, have faith, hold, long for, look forward to, promise oneself, suppose, surmise, suspect, trust, watch for, wish for

hopeful *adj.* assured, bright, confident, encouraged, encouraging, expectant, favorable, heartened, heartening, inspirited, opportune, optimistic, promising, propitious, reassured, reassuring, trustful, upbeat

hopeless *adj.* dejected, despairing, desperate, despondent, disconsolate, downhearted, forlorn, futile, helpless, impossible, inadequate, incurable, irreparable, irreversible, irrevocable, lost, pointless, sad, unachievable, unavailable, unavailing, unfeasible, unobtainable, unusable, useless, vain

hospitable *adj.* accommodating, agreeable, amenable, amicable, charitable, congenial, convivial, cordial, courteous, friendly, generous, genial, gracious, helpful, kind, neighborly, obliging, open, polite, receptive, sociable, warm, welcoming

hospitality *n.* amicability, congeniality, conviviality, cordiality, courteousness, entertainment, friendliness, generosity, geniality, graciousness, hospitableness, kindheartedness, neighborliness, receptiveness, sociability, warmheartedness, warmth, welcome

hostile *adj.* adverse, aggressive, alien, antagonistic, averse, belligerent, combative, contentious, contrary, discordant, inhospitable, malevolent, malicious, militant, opposed, unfriendly, unkind, unsociable, unsympathetic, vitriolic, warlike

hostility *n.* aggression, animosity, animus, antagonism, antipathy, aversion, belligerence, bitterness, disaffection, dislike, enmity, hatred, ill will, inhospitableness, malevolence, malice, maliciousness, opposition, rancor, spite, unfriendliness

housing *n.* **1.** accommodations, dwelling, habitation, lodging, quarters, residence, shelter **2.** box, capsule, case, cask, container, encasement, enclosure, envelope, jacket, sheath, shield, wrapper

however *adv.* albeit, although, anyhow, anyway, but, despite, nevertheless, nonetheless, notwithstanding, regardless, though, yet

humane *adj.* accommodating, amiable, beneficent, benevolent, benign, charitable, clement, compassionate, considerate, forbearing, forgiving, generous, gentle, good, good-natured, gracious, helpful, human, humanitarian, kind, kindhearted, kindly, lenient, magnanimous, merciful, obliging, pitying, sympathetic, tender, tenderhearted, unselfish, warmhearted

humanitarian *n.* altruist, benefactor, caring person, concerned person, helper, humane person, patron, philanthropist

humiliate *v.* belittle, demean, denigrate, deprecate, derogate, discomfit, disparage, embarrass, humble, impute, make ashamed, mortify, rebuff, rebuke, scorn, slur, snub

humiliation *n.* abasement, affront, belittlement, debasement, degradation, deprecation, derogation, discomfiture, discredit, disfavor, disgrace, dishonor, disparagement, embarrassment, humbleness, humbling, indignity, mortification, self-abasement, shame, vitiation

humility *n.* demureness, diffidence, humbleness, inferiority, meekness, mildness, modesty, obedience, obsequiousness, passiveness, reserve, restraint, self-abasement, servility, subjection, submissiveness, subservience, timidity, timorousness, unobtrusiveness, unpretentiousness, unpresumptuousness

humor *n.* **1.** banter, caricature, comedy, drollery, facetiousness, funniness, gaiety, irony, jest, joking, levity, lightness, parody, repartee, satire, wit **2.** bent, caprice, character, disposition, fancy, frame of mind, makeup, mood, nature, propensity, quirk, spirit, temper, temperament, vagary, vein, whim, whimsy

humorous *adj.* amusing, comical, droll, facetious, farcical, funny, hilarious, jovial, laughable, ludicrous, playful, ridiculous, witty

hurdle *n.* bar, barricade, barrier, block, blockade, check, handicap, hindrance, impediment, interference, obstacle, obstruction, setback, snag, stoppage, stumbling block, wall

hurried *adj.* abrupt, cursory, driven, fast, hasty, hectic, pressing, quick, rash, reckless, rushed, speedy, superficial, swift

hurry *n.* bustle, commotion, dispatch, drive, flurry, haste, motion, precipitateness, precipitation, push, quickness, rush, speed, speediness, swiftness, urgency

hurry *v.* accelerate, act quickly, advance, be quick, bustle, dash, drive on, expedite, facilitate, flee, fly, hasten, hurry up, hustle, jog, make haste, move, move quickly, move speedily, press on, push forward, push on, quicken, race, run, rush, scurry, speed, speed up, sprint

hybrid *n.* combination, composite, compound, conglomerate, crossbreed, half-blood, half-breed, mix, mixed breed, mixture, mongrel

hygienic *adj.* aseptic, clean, disinfected, germ-free, salubrious, sanitary, sterile, uncontaminated

hyperbole *n.* distortion, embellishment, enhancement, enlargement, exaggeration, expansion, inflation, magnification, maximization, overstatement

hypocrisy *n.* affectation, cant, deceit, deceitfulness, deception, deceptiveness, dishonesty, dissimulation, duplicity, faking, false front, false goodness, falseness, false profession, fraud, insincerity, phoniness, pietism, pretense, pretext, quackery, sanctimoniousness, sanctimony, sophistry, speciousness

hypocritical *adj.* canting, deceitful, deceptive, disingenuous, dissembling, faithless, false, feigning, fraudulent, hollow, insincere, lying, phony, pietistic, pretending, sanctimonious, self-righteous, specious, unnatural, untruthful

hypothesis *n.* antecedent, assumption, axiom, basis, conjecture, foundation, ground, inference, postulate, premise, presumption, presupposition, principle, proposition, speculation, starting point, supposition, surmise, theorem, theory, thesis

hypothetical *adj.* academic, assumed, conjectural, debatable, doubtful, guessed, imagined, inferred, postulated, presumed, presumptive, presupposed, problematic, putative, questionable, reputed, speculative, supposed, suppositional, surmised, theoretical, uncertain, undetermined

idea *n.* abstraction, aim, assumption, belief, concept, conception, conceptualization, conclusion, conviction, design, end, fancy, feeling, guess, hypothesis, impression, inference, inkling, intention, judgment, notion, object, objective, observation, opinion, perception, persuasion, plan, position, postulate, scheme, sentiment, suggestion, suspicion, theory, thought, understanding, view, viewpoint, vision

ideal *n.* archetype, epitome, example, exemplar, model, paradigm, paragon, pattern, prototype, standard, type

ideal *adj.* **1.** absolute, archetypal, classical, complete, consummate, excellent, exemplary, faultless, flawless, model, paradigmatic, perfect, prototypical, quintessential, representative, supreme **2.** abstract, chimerical, conceptual, fanciful, fictitious, hypothetical, idealistic, illusory, imaginary, imaginative, intellectual, mental, metaphysical, preposterous, psychological, theoretical, unattainable, unreal, visionary

idealist *n.* dreamer, ideologist, optimist, perfectionist, romanticist, spiritualist, transcendentalist, visionary

identical *adj.* alike, coequal, congruent, corresponding, double, duplicate, equivalent, exact, indistinguishable, interchangeable, matching, same, selfsame, synonymous, tantamount, twin

identification *n.* badge, cataloging, classification, classifying, credentials, description, designation, detection, distinguishing mark, hallmark, ID, identity card, labeling, mark, naming, recognition, selection

identify *v.* ascertain, classify, confirm, corroborate, describe, determine, diagnose, discern, distinguish, establish, label, pick out, pinpoint, recognize, select, verify

identity *n.* **1.** agreement, congruence, congruency, correspondence, equality, equivalence, exactness, identicalness, interchangeability, likeness, oneness, sameness, selfsameness, uniformity, unity **2.** differentness, distinctiveness, identification, individuality, name, oneness, particularity, personality, self, singularity, uniqueness

ideology *n.* axioms, beliefs, canons, credo, creed, doctrine, dogma, outlook, philosophy, postulates, principles, teachings, tenets, theory, thesis

idiom *n.* argot, colloquialism, dialect, expression, jargon, language, localism, locution, phrase, phrasing, provincialism, regionalism, set phrase, speech, style of speech, tongue, vernacular, wording

idiosyncrasy *n.* affectation, characteristic, eccentricity, feature, habit, mannerism, oddity, peculiarity, quality, quirk, singularity, speciality, trait, twist

idle *adj.* abandoned, deserted, dormant, empty, fallow, inactive, inert, inoperative, jobless, laid-off, motionless, out-of-operation, out-of-work, passive, quiet, stationary, unemployed, unoccupied, untouched, unused, vacant

ignorance *n.* bewilderment, blindness, darkness, dumbness, illiteracy, illiterateness, innocence, mental incapacity, obtuseness, simplicity, stupidity, unawareness, unconsciousness, unenlightenment

ignorant *adj.* illiterate, inexperienced, shallow, unaware, unconscious, unconversant, uncultivated, uneducated, unenlightened, uninformed, uninitiated, unknowing, unlearned, unlettered, unread, unschooled, untaught, untrained, unwitting

ignore *v.* avoid, be oblivious to, disregard, do not consider, evade, leave out, neglect, omit, overlook, pass over, pay no attention to, reject, skip, slight

ill-advised *adj.* brash, careless, foolhardy, foolish, hasty, hazardous, ill-considered, ill-judged, ill-suited, impetuous, impolitic, imprudent, impulsive, inadvisable, inappropriate, incautious, indiscreet, inexpedient, injudicious, irresponsible, misguided, rash, reckless, short-sighted, unadvisable, unseemly, unsuitable, wrong, wrong-headed

illegal *adj.* illegitimate, illicit, prohibited, unacceptable, unauthorized, unlawful, unlicensed, unsanctioned, wrongful

illegible *adj.* hieroglyphic, indecipherable, indistinct, obscure, scrawled, unclear, unintelligible, unreadable

illicit *adj.* forbidden, furtive, illegal, illegitimate, improper, prohibited, secret, unauthorized, unlawful, unlicensed, unsanctioned, wrong, wrongful

illiterate *adj.* ignorant, uneducated, unenlightened, uninformed, uninstructed, unlearned, unread, unschooled, untaught

illogical *adj.* absurd, contradictory, faulty, implausible, incongruous, inconsistent, invalid, irrational, preposterous, unproved, unreasonable, unsound, untenable

illumination *n.* **1.** awareness, edification, education, enlightenment, information, insight, knowledge, learning, understanding, wisdom **2.** beaming, gleaming, lighting, luminescence, luminosity, radiance, radiation, shining

illustrate *v.* **1.** cite, clarify, clear up, demonstrate, describe, elucidate, emphasize, exemplify, exhibit, explain, explicate, expound, highlight, illuminate, interpret, make clear, make understandable, present, render intelligible, reveal, show, symbolize, tell **2.** adorn, decorate, delineate, depict, diagram, draw, embellish, garnish, ornament, paint, picture, portray, represent, sketch, trim

illustration *n.* **1.** anecdote, case, case in point, clarification, commentary, definition, demonstration, elucidation, epitome, example, exegesis, exemplar, exemplification, explanation, explication, exponent, exposition, illumination, instance, interpretation, sample, specimen, typical case, typical instance **2.** adornment, artwork, cartoon, decoration, depiction, design, diagram, drawing, engraving, etching, figure, halftone, image, line drawing, painting, photograph, portrait, portrayal, representation, sketch, vignette

illustrative *adj.* clarifying, delineative, descriptive, diagrammatic, elucidative, exegetic, exemplary, exemplifying, explanatory, explicative, expository, graphic, illuminative, interpretive, model, pictorial, representative, sample, typical

image *n.* **1.** appearance, clone, copy, double, drawing, duplicate, effigy, facsimile, figure, form, graphics output, icon, idol, illustration, likeness, match, model, painting, photocopy, photograph, picture, portrait, portrayal, reflection, replica, representation, reproduction, resemblance, sculpture, statue **2.** apprehension, concept, conception, fancy, idea, impression, mental picture, notion, perception, picture, thought, vision

imagination *n.* concept, conception, conceptualization, creative power, creative thought, creativity, fancy, fantasy, idea, illusion, imagery, imaginativeness, impression, ingenuity, inspiration, invention, inventiveness, mental agility, mental image, notion, originality, perception, resourcefulness, thought, vision, visualization

imagine *v.* **1.** conceive, conceptualize, conjure up, dream, dream up, envisage, envision, fancy, fantasize, feature, idealize, image, invent, make up, perceive, picture, project, think of, think up, visualize **2.** apprehend, assume, believe, conclude, conjecture, deduce, expect, guess, infer, presume, reckon, suppose, surmise, suspect, think, understand

imitate *v.* act like, be like, clone, copy, counterfeit, do like, duplicate, emulate, follow, forge, impersonate, match, mimic, mirror, model after, parallel, pattern after, pretend, reflect, repeat, replicate, reproduce, resemble

imitation *n.* adaptation, caricature, clone, copy, counterfeit, duplicate, duplication, facsimile, fake, forgery, imitating, impersonation, impression, mimicking, mimicry, mocking, paraphrase, parody, plagiarism, repetition, replica, representation, reproduction, semblance, simulation, substitution, transcription

immeasurable *adj.* boundless, countless, endless, extensive, fathomless, great, illimitable, immense, incalculable, indefinite, indeterminate, inestimable, inexhaustible, infinite, innumerable, limitless, measureless, neverending, unbounded, uncircumscribed, unfathomable, unlimited, unmeasurable, vast

immediate *adj.* **1.** abrupt, instant, instantaneous, hasty, pressing, prompt, simultaneous, speedy, sudden, swift, urgent **2.** actual, current, existent, existing, extant, latest, present, running **3.** abutting, adjacent, adjoining, approximate, close, closest, contiguous, near, nearest, neighboring, next, proximate

immediately *adv.* abruptly, directly, instantaneously, instantly, presently, rapidly, shortly, suddenly, summarily, unhesitatingly, urgently

immigrant *n.* alien, arrival, entrant, foreigner, naturalized citizen, newcomer, nonnative, outsider

immigrate *v.* arrive, come in, enter country, migrate, move, settle

imminent *adj.* approaching, close, coming, drawing near, forthcoming, immediate, impending, looming, momentary, near, nearing, threatening

immobile *adj.* anchored, constant, fast, fixed, frozen, grounded, immobilized, immotile, immovable, inflexible, motionless, permanent, resolute, rigid, riveted, rooted, secure, set, solid, stable, static, stationary, steadfast, stiff, unalterable, unchangeable, unmovable, unmoving, unwavering, unyielding

immovable *n.* See **immobile**

immune *adj.* clear, excused, exempt, free, inoculated, insusceptible, invulnerable, protected, resistant, safe, unaffected, unsusceptible

immunity *n.* absolution, amnesty, exemption, exoneration, freedom, impunity, indemnity, inoculation, liberty, license, permission, prerogative, protection, release, safety, special treatment

impact *n.* **1.** bearing, burden, consequence, effect, impression, imprint, influence, mark, repercussion, result, significance **2.** bang, blow, brunt, bump, clash, collision, contact, crash, crush, encounter, force, impetus, jolt, knock, momentum, percussion, pressure, punch, shock, slam, slap, strike, stroke, thump

impair *v.* attenuate, blemish, damage, debase, debilitate, destroy, disable, enervate, enfeeble, harm, hinder, hurt, lessen, mark, spoil, undermine, vitiate, weaken

impartial *adj.* detached, disinterested, dispassionate, equitable, even, evenhanded, fair, fair-minded, just, neutral, nondiscriminatory, objective, unbiased, uncolored, uninfluenced, unprejudiced

impasse *n.* blockage, cessation, check, deadlock, dilemma, fix, halt, predicament, stalemate, stop, stoppage, standstill

impatience *n.* agitation, annoyance, anxiety, disquiet, edginess, excitability, fretfulness, irritability, nervousness, restlessness, shortness

impatient *adj.* abrupt, anxious, avid, brusque, eager, fretful, hasty, indignant, intolerant, irascible, irritable, keen, nervous, precipitate, querulous, restive, restless, testy, uneasy

impediment *n.* bar, barricade, barrier, block, blockade, burden, clog, curb, damper, delay, determent, deterrent, difficulty, disadvantage, drawback, embargo, encumbrance, hindrance, hurdle, inhibition, interference, load, obstacle, obstruction, restraint, restriction, setback, snag, stoppage, stricture, wall

impending *adj.* approaching, brewing, close, coming, forthcoming, gathering, hovering, imminent, looming, lurking, near, nearing, portending, threatening, upcoming, waiting

imperative *adj.* **1.** binding, compelling, compulsory, essential, indispensable, inescapable, mandatory, necessary, needed, obligatory, pressing, required, requisite, unavoidable, urgent, vital **2.** authoritarian, authoritative, commanding, dictatorial, dogmatic, domineering, imperious, instructive, mandating, prescriptive, tyrannical

imperfection *n.* blemish, catch, defect, deformity, disfigurement, fault, flaw, malformation, shortcoming, stain, taint, weak point

impersonal *adj.* businesslike, cold, detached, disinterested, dispassionate, emotionless, equitable, fair, formal, impartial, indifferent, neutral, objective, remote, unbiased, unfriendly, unprejudiced

impervious *adj.* **1.** airtight, closed, hermetic, impassable, impenetrable, impermeable, inaccessible, locked, resistant, sealed, tight, waterproof, watertight **2.** callous, coldhearted, indurate, insensitive, obdurate, unreceptive, unresponsive, unsympathetic, unyielding

impetuous *adj.* abrupt, ardent, capricious, careless, eager, energetic, fervid, forceful, hasty, headlong, impulsive, overzealous, passionate, precipitate, quick, rash, spontaneous, swift, thoughtless, unbridled, uncontrolled, unreflective, unrestrained, violent, wild

impetus *n.* catalyst, drive, encouragement, energy, force, impulsion, incentive, incitement, inducement, influence, inspiration, instigation, momentum, motivation, pressure, propulsion, push, stimulant, stimulus, thrust, urging

implausible *adj.* doubtful, dubious, improbable, inconceivable, incredible, questionable, unbelievable, unconvincing, unfounded, unimaginable, unlikely, unreasonable

implement *n.* agent, apparatus, appliance, contrivance, device, engine, equipment, gadget, gear, instrument, invention, machine, mechanism, medium, motor, tool, utensil

implement *v.* accomplish, achieve, bring about, carry out, complete, effect, execute, fulfill, perform, put into effect, realize, start

implication *n.* allusion, assumption, connection, connotation, entanglement, hint, incrimination, inference, innuendo, insinuation, intimation, involvement, presumption, reference, significance, suggestion

implicit *adj.* absolute, assured, certain, complete, entire, explicit, fixed, implied, inferential, inferred, inherent, positive, tacit, total, unconditional, understood, unequivocal, unexpressed, unqualified, unquestioned, unreserved, unspoken

implied *adj.* connoted, deduced, denoted, implicit, indicated, inferential, inferred, insinuated, intimated, signified, suggested, tacit, undeclared, understood, unexpressed, unspoken

imply *v.* assume, connote, denote, designate, entail, express, include, indicate, insinuate, intimate, involve, mean, point to, presume, presuppose, signify, suggest

import *n.* foreign commodity, foreign-made commodity, foreign-made product, foreign product, imported article, international commodity, nondomestic commodity

import *v.* bring, bring from, bring into, carry, carry from, carry into, connote, convey, denote, introduce, portend, purport, suggest

importance *n.* **1.** concern, consequence, effect, emphasis, import, matter, momentousness, relevance, significance, tenor, urgency, usefulness, value, weight **2.** distinction, eminence, esteem, fame, greatness, influence, mark, notability, note, power, prestige, prominence, rank, reputation, standing, status, superiority, sway

important *adj.* **1.** chief, consequential, critical, crucial, decisive, essential, exigent, foremost, grave, heavy, imperative, importunate, material, meaningful, momentous, necessary, paramount, ponderous, portentous, pressing, primary, principal, relevant, salient, serious, signal, significant, urgent, valuable, vital, weighty **2.** commanding, distinctive, distinguished, eminent, esteemed, famous, high-level, high-ranking, illustrious, imposing, impressive, influential, leading, notable, powerful, preeminent, prestigious, prominent, respected, superior, top-level, well-connected

imported *adj.* alien, exotic, foreign, foreign-made, international, nondomestic, outside, rare

impose *v.* appoint, assess, bid, charge, command, compel, decree, demand, dictate, direct, encumber, enjoin, establish, exact, inflict, institute, introduce, intrude, lay on, levy, oblige, obtrude, order, place, prescribe, presume upon, put on, set, tax

impossible *adj.* **1.** absurd, hopeless, illogical, impracticable, impractical, inconceivable, incredible, infeasible, inoperable, insoluble, insurmountable, preposterous, ridiculous, unachievable, unattainable, unbelievable, unimaginable, unobtainable, unthinkable, unworkable, useless   **2.** inadmissible, intolerable, objectionable, offensive, outrageous, unacceptable, undesirable, unreasonable, unsuitable, untenable

impress *v.*   bend, compel, convince, emphasize, establish, impel, induce, influence, inspire, instill, move, oblige, persuade, prevail on, provoke, stimulate, stress, sway, urge, win over

impression *n.*   awareness, belief, conception, conviction, effect, fancy, feeling, hunch, idea, image, influence, inkling, intuition, notion, opinion, perception, reaction, recollection, response, sensation, sense, sensibility, sentiment, suspicion, sway, thought, vague feeling

impressive *adj.*   affecting, arresting, august, awe-inspiring, effective, emotive, exciting, extraordinary, grand, imposing, influential, inspirational, inspiring, lavish, majestic, massive, mighty, momentous, monumental, moving, powerful, profound, remarkable, splendid, stately, stirring, striking, superb, telling, thrilling, touching, towering

imprint *n.*   depression, design, effect, impression, influence, mark, name, pattern, print, seal, stamp, symbol

impromptu *adj.*   ad-lib, extemporaneous, extemporary, extempore, impulsive, spontaneous, unpremeditated, unprepared, unprompted, unrehearsed, unscripted

impropriety *n.*   bad taste, blunder, immodesty, impudence, inappropriateness, incongruity, incorrectness, indecorum, misstep, mistake, nonconformance, unseemliness, unsuitability

improve *v.*   advance, ameliorate, amend, civilize, correct, cultivate, elevate, emend, enhance, fix up, help, make better, meliorate, polish, promote, purify, recover, rectify, redo, refine, reform, refurbish, regenerate, rehabilitate, remodel, repair, restore, revamp, revise, set right, upgrade

improvement *n.*   advance, advancement, amelioration, betterment, capitalized expenditure, civilization, correction, cultivation, development, enhancement, enrichment, furtherance, healing, melioration, progress, progression, recovery, rectification, reformation, refurbishment, regeneration, rehabilitation, remodeling, renovation, repair, reparation, restoration, revision, upgrading

improvise *v.*   ad-lib, coin, concoct, create, devise, dream up, extemporize, invent

impulsive *adj.* careless, extemporaneous, hasty, impetuous, instinctive, offhand, precipitate, quick, rash, spontaneous, sudden, unplanned, unpredictable

impute *v.* accredit, accuse, allege, ascribe, assert, assign, attribute, charge, cite, connect with, credit, implicate, insinuate, intimate, refer

inability *n.* disability, frailty, handicap, impotence, inadequacy, inaptitude, incapability, incapacitation, incapacity, incompetence, ineffectiveness, inefficacy, inefficiency, ineligibility, ineptitude, powerlessness, unfitness, weakness

inaccuracy *n.* blunder, error, erroneousness, faultiness, imprecision, incorrectness, inexactness, miscalculation, misestimation, misjudgment, mistake, slip-up, wrongness

inaccurate *adj.* erroneous, imprecise, incorrect, inexact, mistaken, wrong

inactive *adj.* dormant, dull, idle, immovable, inanimate, indolent, inert, inoperative, languid, latent, lazy, lethargic, lifeless, motionless, nonfunctioning, nonperforming, passive, quiescent, quiet, sedentary, sleepy, slothful, sluggish, somnolent, stagnant, stationary, still, torpid, unemployed, unmoving

inadequacy *n.* dearth, defect, defectiveness, deficiency, deficit, failing, fault, flaw, inability, inadequateness, inaptness, incapability, incapacity, incompetence, incompleteness, ineffectiveness, inefficacy, inefficiency, ineptitude, inferiority, insufficiency, lack, meagerness, mediocrity, paucity, poverty, scantiness, scarcity, shortage, shortcoming, skimpiness, unacceptableness, unfitness, unsuitability, weakness

inadequate *adj.* defective, deficient, faulty, flawed, incapable, incommensurate, incompetent, incomplete, inept, inferior, insufficient, lacking, maladroit, meager, mediocre, scanty, scarce, sparse, unfit, unqualified, unsatisfactory, unsuitable, wanting, weak

inadmissible *adj.* immaterial, improper, inapplicable, inappropriate, irrelevant, objectionable, preclusive, prohibitive, unacceptable, unallowable, undesirable, unqualified, unsatisfactory, unsuitable

inadvisable *adj.* disadvantageous, foolhardy, foolish, ill-advised, impractical, improper, imprudent, inappropriate, inconvenient, indiscreet, inexpedient, injudicious, inopportune, undesirable, unreasonable, unrecommended, unsuitable, unwise

inappropriate *adj.* ill-suited, impolite, impractical, improper, inadvisable, incompatible, incongruous, inconsistent, incorrect, indecorous, indiscreet, inexpedient, tactless, tasteless, unbecoming, unbefitting, unfit, unfitting, unseemly, unsuitable, unsuited, unwarranted

inaugurate *v.* begin, commence, induct, initiate, install, instate, launch, ordain, start

inauguration *n.* beginning, commencement, establishment, induction, initiation, introduction, ordination, outset, start

incapable *adj.* feeble, helpless, impotent, inadequate, incompetent, ineffective, ineligible, inexperienced, insufficient, powerless, unable, unequipped, unfit, unqualified, unskilled, unskillful, unsuitable, weak

incapacitate *v.* damage, deactivate, disable, disarm, disqualify, immobilize, impair, inactivate, indispose, invalidate, neutralize, paralyze, weaken

incentive *n.* bait, catalyst, encouragement, enticement, excuse, exhortation, goad, grounds, impetus, impulse, incitement, inducement, inspiration, instigation, lure, motivation, motive, persuasion, provocation, purpose, reason, spur, stimulant, stimulation, stimulus, temptation

inception *n.* alpha, beginning, birth, commencement, conception, dawn, debut, derivation, first, inauguration, initiation, installation, onset, opening, origin, outset, provenance, root, source, start, starting point, wellspring

incident *n.* adventure, affair, circumstance, encounter, episode, event, experience, fact, happening, matter, occasion, occurrence, phenomenon, proceeding, scene

incidental *adj.* accessory, accidental, casual, chance, circumstantial, coincidental, contingent, fortuitous, inconsequential, insignificant, minor, negligible, nonessential, occasional, odd, parenthetical, random, related, secondary, subordinate, subsidiary, unessential, unimportant

incite *v.* activate, actuate, agitate, animate, arouse, awaken, drive, encourage, enliven, excite, exhort, fire up, foment, force, goad, impel, induce, inflame, influence, inspire, instigate, motivate, move, persuade, press, prevail on, provoke, push, rouse, stimulate, stir up, urge, whip up

inclination *n.* **1.** affection, affinity, aptness, ardor, attraction, bent, bias, desire, disposition, fancy, fondness, leaning, liking, longing, mindset, partiality, penchant, predilection, predisposition, preference, prejudice, proclivity, proneness, propensity, susceptibility, sympathy, taste, tendency, turn, weakness, zeal **2.** acclivity, angle, ascent, bank, bevel, cant, declination, declivity, descent, diagonal, direction, downgrade, grade, gradient, hill, incline, pitch, plane, ramp, rise, slant, slope, tilt

include *v.* add, admit, allow for, append, combine, comprehend, comprise, count, cover, embody, embrace, enclose, hold, incorporate, involve, make allowance for, number, refer to, subjoin, subsume, take in, take into account

inclusion *n.* addition, admittance, allowance for, appending, counting, covering, embodiment, embrace, enclosure, formation, holding, incorporation, insertion, involvement, involving, making allowance for, numbering, reference to, subjoining, subsuming, taking in, taking into account

inclusive *adj.* all-embracing, all-encompassing, broad, compendious, comprehensive, encyclopedic, extensive, full, overall, sweeping, whole, wide

income *n.* earnings, gains, gross, pay, profits, receipts, recompense, returns, revenue, salary, wages, yield

incompetent *adj.* awkward, bungling, clumsy, deficient, floundering, inadequate, incapable, ineffective, ineffectual, inefficient, inept, insufficient, unfit, unqualified, unsuitable, useless

incomplete *adj.* abridged, broken, crude, defective, deficient, fragmentary, garbled, immature, imperfect, insufficient, lacking, partial, rough, rudimentary, short, sketchy, unaccomplished, undeveloped, unexecuted, unfinished, wanting

inconceivable *adj.* absurd, incomprehensible, implausible, impossible, improbable, incredible, ludicrous, outlandish, preposterous, rare, ridiculous, unbelievable, unimaginable, unlikely, unthinkable

inconvenience *n.* annoyance, awkwardness, bother, bothersomeness, cumbersomeness, disturbance, nuisance, trouble, troublesomeness, unfitness, unhandiness, untimeliness

incorporate *v.* affiliate, amalgamate, associate, blend, coalesce, combine, comprise, conjoin, consolidate, embody, embrace, federate, file incorporation papers, form, fuse, include, integrate, join, link, merge, organize, start, unify, unite

incorrect *adj.* defective, erroneous, false, faulty, flawed, imperfect, imprecise, improper, inaccurate, inappropriate, inexact, unfactual, unseemly, unsuitable, untrue, wrong

increase *n.* acceleration, accession, accrual, accumulation, addition, aggrandizement, augmentation, boost, cumulation, development, enhancement, enlargement, escalation, expansion, extension, gain, growth, increment, inflation, intensification, magnification, maximization, multiplication, raise, rise, spread, supplementation, swelling, upgrade, upsurge, upswing, upturn

increase *v.* accumulate, add to, advance, aggrandize, amplify, augment, boost, build up, develop, elevate, enhance, enlarge, escalate, expand, extend, grow, inflate, magnify, make greater, make larger, mature, mount, multiply, proliferate, raise, reinforce, spread out, strengthen, supplement, swell, upgrade

increment *n.* accession, accretion, accrual, addition, amount, augmentation, change, contribution, degree, enlargement, expansion, extension, gain, increase, profit, supplement

incur *v.* acquire, bargain for, be liable, be subject to, bring on, contract, enter into, expose to, invite, lay open to, provoke, run up

indebted *adj.* accountable, answerable, appreciative, beholden, bound, chargeable, grateful, liable, obligated, obliged, owing, responsible, thankful

indecisive *adj.* ambivalent, changeable, diffident, doubtful, faltering, fluctuating, hesitant, inconclusive, indefinite, indeterminate, irresolute, open, uncertain, unclear, undecided, undetermined, unresolved, unsettled, vacillating, wavering

indefinite *adj.* abstract, ambiguous, boundless, confused, doubtful, equivocal, fluctuating, ill-defined, immeasurable, imprecise, incalculable, inconclusive, indeterminable, indeterminate, indistinct, indistinguishable, inexact, inexplicit, infinite, intangible, limitless, obscure, uncertain, unclear, undecided, undefined, undetermined, unfixed, unknown, unlimited, unspecific, unspecified, vague

indemnity *n.* assurance, certification, compensation, endorsement, expiation, guarantee, insurance, protection, redress, reimbursement, remuneration, reparation, restitution, underwriting, warrant

independent *adj.* autonomous, free, individualistic, liberated, neutral, nonaligned, nonpartisan, self-contained, self-determining, self-directing, self-governing, self-legislating, self-ruling, self-sufficient, self-supporting, separate, sovereign, unallied, unattached, unconnected, unconstrained, unrestrained, unrestricted

index *n.* basis, character, clue, device, directory, expression, formula, guide, indication, indicator, key, label, list, mark, number, pointer, ratio, sign, statistical compilation, statistical composite, symbol, table of reference, token

index *v.* adjust, alphabetize, arrange, furnish index, indicate, list, order, provide index, regulate, signal

indicate *v.* add up to, connote, demonstrate, denote, designate, disclose, display, evidence, evince, exhibit, express, illustrate, imply, make known, manifest, mark, mean, point out, point to, present, register, reveal, show, signal, signify, specify, state, suggest, tell

indication *n.* allusion, augury, clue, connotation, denotation, evidence, explanation, expression, foreshadowing, forewarning, hint, implication, intimation, manifestation, mark, mention, omen, portent, showing, sign, signal, suggestion, symptom, token, trace, vestige

indictment *n.* accusation, arraignment, blame, censure, charge, criticism, denunciation, implication, incrimination, rebuke, reprehension, summons

indigenous *adj.* aboriginal, congenital, connate, endemic, fixed, hereditary, inborn, inbred, inherent, inherited, native, native-born, natural, original, permanent

indirect *adj.* ambiguous, circuitous, circumstantial, collateral, contingent, deviant, devious, discursive, erratic, implicit, implied, incidental, meandering, oblique, obscure, rambling, roundabout, secondary, tortuous, wandering, winding

indiscriminate *adj.* aimless, broad, casual, chaotic, desultory, disordered, diverse, diversified, erratic, extensive, haphazard, incoherent, jumbled, miscellaneous, mixed, purposeless, random, scrambled, sweeping, uncritical, undiscriminating, unmethodical, unorganized, unselective, unsystematic, wide

indispensable *adj.* basic, binding, certain, compelling, compulsory, essential, fundamental, high-priority, imperative, important, inescapable, inevitable, mandatory, necessary, obligatory, pressing, required, requisite, substantive, unavoidable, urgent, vital

indistinguishable *adj.* alike, coinciding, comparable, corresponding, duplicate, equal, equivalent, identical, indiscernible, same, selfsame, synonymous

individual *n.* being, character, creature, entity, human, human being, mortal, nonconformist, party, person, personage, somebody, someone, something, soul

individual *adj.* characteristic, detached, different, distinct, distinctive, especial, exclusive, express, isolated, lone, odd, original, particular, peculiar, personal, private, select, separate, single, singular, sole, solitary, special, specific, unconventional, unique, unusual

induce *v.* actuate, arouse, bring about, bring on, cajole, cause, coax, convince, create, drive, effect, encourage, engender, entice, generate, impel, incite, influence, inspire, instigate, make, motivate, move, persuade, prevail on, produce, prompt, propel, stimulate, sway, talk into, urge

inducement *n.* actuating, convincing, encouragement, impetus, incentive, incitement, influence, inspiration, instigating, motive, persuasion, reason, stimulus, urge, urging

industrial *adj.* automated, business, factory-made, heavy-duty, highly developed, industrialized, machine-made, manufactured, manufacturing, mechanized, modern, nonagricultural, streamlined, technical

industrious *adj.* active, assiduous, busy, diligent, dynamic, earnest, energetic, enterprising, hardworking, intent, laborious, persevering, persistent, productive, sedulous, tireless, vigorous, zealous

industry *n.* **1.** business, commerce, construction, establishment, fabrication, industrial enterprise, manufacture, manufacturing, production, trade **2.** activity, determination, diligence, effort, enterprise, hard work, industriousness, intentness, labor, perseverance, persistence, tirelessness, undertaking, vigor, work, zeal

ineffective *adj.* abortive, barren, fruitless, futile, impotent, inadequate, incapable, incompetent, ineffectual, inefficacious, inefficient, inept, inoperative, lame, powerless, profitless, unavailing, unoperative, unproductive, unprofitable, unsuccessful, useless, weak, worthless

ineffectual *adj.* See **ineffective**

inefficient *adj.* careless, deficient, disorganized, haphazard, incapable, incompetent, ineffective, ineffectual, inefficacious, inept, inexpert, lax, slipshod, sloppy, unfit, unprepared, unqualified, unskilled, untrained, wasteful

ineligible *adj.* inappropriate, unacceptable, undesirable, unfit, unqualified, unsuitable

inequality *n.* bias, contrast, difference, discrimination, disparity, disproportion, dissimilarity, dissimilitude, imbalance, imparity, incongruity, injustice, irregularity, nonconformity, partiality, prejudice, roughness, unevenness, unfairness, unjustness, unlikeness, variation

inexpensive *adj.* bargain-basement, budget, cheap, cut-rate, discounted, economical, half-price, low-cost, lowered, low-priced, marked-down, moderately priced, reasonable, reduced, sale-priced

inexperienced *adj.* amateur, fresh, ignorant, immature, innocent, naive, new, unaccustomed, unacquainted, unfamiliar, uninformed, uninitiated, unschooled, unseasoned, unskilled, unsophisticated, untrained, young

infectious *adj.* catching, communicable, contagious, contaminating, endemic, epidemic, infective, miasmic, noxious, pandemic, pestilent, poisonous, spreading, toxic, transferable, transmissible, transmittable, virulent

infer *v.* assume, believe, calculate, conclude, conjecture, construe, deduce, derive answer, draw conclusion, estimate, judge, presume, reach conclusion, reason, surmise, think, understand

inferior *adj.* average, bad, below-standard, common, entry-level, fair, imperfect, junior, lower, lower-level, lower-rank, ordinary, poor, poor-quality, second-rate, secondary, subordinate, subsidiary, subscript, substandard, unacceptable

infinite *adj.* bottomless, boundless, ceaseless, continual, countless, endless, enduring, eternal, everlasting, immeasurable, immense, incalculable, incessant, inestimable, inexhaustible, innumerable, interminable, limitless, measureless, neverending, numberless, perpetual, unbounded, uncountable, unending, unfathomable, unlimited, vast

infinitesimal *adj.* atomic, imperceptible, inappreciable, inconsiderable, insignificant, microscopic, miniature, minuscule, minute, negligible, tiny, trifling, very small

infinity *n.* boundlessness, endlessness, fathomlessness, immeasurability, immensity, infiniteness, infinitude, limitlessness, perpetuity, vastness

inflation *n.* **1.** escalating prices, false prosperity, high prices, increasing prices, oversupply of money **2.** accretion, addition, aggrandizement, augmentation, buildup, development, enhancement, enlargement, exaggeration, extension, increase, intensification, rise, swelling

inflection *n.* accent, articulation, delivery, dialect, diction, elocution, emphasis, enunciation, intonation, modulation, pitch, pronunciation, speech pattern, stress, timbre, tonality, tone, tone quality

inflexible *adj.* **1.** adamant, determined, firm, immovable, intractable, obdurate, obstinate, relentless, resolute, rigid, single-minded, steadfast, strict, stubborn, tenacious, unaccommodating, unadaptable, unbending, unchangeable, uncompliant, uncompromising, unrelenting, unswayable, unvarying, unyielding **2.** firm, hard, hardened, inelastic, nonflexible, rigid, set, stiff, taut, unbendable, unmalleable, unyielding

influence *n.* ascendancy, authority, clout, command, connections, control, direction, domination, dominion, effect, force, guidance, hold, impact, leadership, leverage, magnetism, monopoly, power, predominance, pressure, rule, supremacy, sway

influence *v.* act on, affect, alter, arouse, bias, change, command, compel, control, determine, direct, dominate, effect, guide, impact on, impel, impress, incite, incline, induce, instigate, lead, manage, manipulate, modify, mold, motivate, move, persuade, prompt, regulate, rouse, rule, subject, sway, transform, urge, wield, work on

inform *v.* acquaint, advise, apprise, brief, educate, familiarize, fill in, let know, notify, relate, tell, update

informal *adj.* casual, colloquial, easygoing, everyday, familiar, irregular, natural, ordinary, simple, unassuming, unceremonious, unconventional, unofficial, unpretentious .

information *n.* advice, background, briefing, communication, counsel, dossier, enlightenment, facts, instruction, knowledge, material, message, news, notification, readout, reception, report, wisdom

informative *adj.* advisory, communicative, descriptive, educational, enlightening, explanatory, factual, illuminating, informational, instructional, instructive, newsy

informed *adj.* acquainted, apprised, briefed, cognizant, conversant, enlightened, instructed, knowledgeable, learned, notified, well-read

infrastructure *n.* basic framework, basic system, permanent installation, public works system, resources, underlying foundation

ingenious *adj.* able, adept, adroit, apt, astute, brilliant, clever, creative, dexterous, expert, gifted, imaginative, innovative, intelligent, inventive, original, proficient, resourceful, sagacious, shrewd, skillful, smart, talented, witty

ingenuous *adj.* aboveboard, artless, candid, childlike, direct, genuine, guileless, honest, innocent, naive, open, plain, simple, sincere, straightforward, trustful, trusting, trustworthy, unsophisticated, upright

ingredient *n.* additive, agent, component, constituent, element, factor, feature, fundamental, item, member, part, piece, unit

inhabitant *n.* addressee, boarder, citizen, dweller, lessee, lodger, native, occupant, occupier, permanent resident, renter, resident, resider, roomer, tenant

inherit *v.* **1.** acquire, be bequeathed, become heir to, be willed, come into, get, obtain, receive **2.** accede to, accept, assume, be elevated to, be promoted to, succeed to, take over

inheritance *n.* **1.** bequest, birthright, endowment, estate, inherited possessions, legacy, patrimony, possessions, property **2.** acceptance, accession, assumption, attainment, promotion, succession, taking over

inhospitable *adj.* aloof, antisocial, cold, cool, disagreeable, discourteous, hostile, impolite, intolerant, rude, uncivil, uncongenial, unfriendly, ungracious, unkind, unneighborly, unpleasant, unreceptive, unsociable, unwelcoming

initial *adj.* beginning, commencing, earliest, elementary, first, foremost, fundamental, inaugural, inchoate, incipient, infant, initiating, introductory, nascent, opening, original, primary, prime

initiate *v.* **1.** begin, commence, establish, found, inaugurate, instigate, institute, introduce, launch, open, organize, originate, pioneer, set up, start, take initiative, trigger, usher in **2.** brief, coach, drill, edify, enlighten, exercise, familiarize with, inculcate, indoctrinate, inform, instruct, introduce, practice, prepare, ready, teach, train, tutor

initiation *n.* acceptance, admission, admittance, baptism, beginning, commencement, debut, enrollment, inauguration, inculcation, indoctrination, induction, installation, instruction, introduction, investiture, reception

initiative *n.* ambition, beginning, commencement, drive, eagerness, energy, enterprise, enthusiasm, first move, first step, leadership, resourcefulness, vigor

injunction *n.* admonition, behest, charge, command, decree, demand, dictate, direction, directive, exhortation, instruction, mandate, order, precept, preventive measure, requirement, restraint, restriction, ruling

injurious *adj.* abusive, adverse, baneful, corrupting, damaging, defamatory, deleterious, destructive, detrimental, disadvantageous, harmful, hurtful, libelous, pernicious, prejudicial, ruinous, scandalous, slanderous, unfavorable, unhealthy, unjust, wrongful

injustice *n.* abuse, bias, crime, discrimination, encroachment, favoritism, grievance, inequality, inequity, infringement, injury, maltreatment, offense, oppression, partiality, prejudice, transgression, unfairness, unfair treatment, unjustness, unjust treatment, wrong, wrongdoing

innovation *n.* alteration, change, modernization, new device, new idea, new method, newness, novelty

innovative *adj.* contemporary, creative, ingenious, innovational, inventive, modern, new, original

innuendo *n.* allusion, aspersion, criticism, hint, implication, imputation, insinuation, intimation, suggestion

innumerable *adj.* countless, incalculable, infinite, many, myriad, numberless, numerous, untold

input *n.* advice, amount, channel, comment, data, device, information, opinion, process, production component, production process, putting in, set of devices, transferring to

inquest *n.* delving, examination, finding, inquiry, inquisition, investigation, judicial inquiry, jury, official inquiry, probe, research, trial

inquire *v.* analyze, ask, delve into, examine, explore, grill, inspect, interrogate, investigate, look into, probe, query, question, request information, research, scrutinize, seek information

inquiry *n.* analysis, asking, audit, cross-examination, examination, exploration, inquest, inquisition, inspection, interrogation, investigation, probe, pursuit, query, quest, question, questioning, request, research, scrutiny, search, study, survey

inscribe *v.* autograph, endorse, engrave, imprint, record, register, sign, stamp, write

insensitive *adj.* anesthetized, callous, deadened, hardened, heartless, immune, imperceptive, impervious, indifferent, nonreactive, numb, tactless, tough, uncaring, uncompassionate, unconcerned, unfeeling, unkind, unresponsive, unsympathetic

insert *v.* add, edit in, enter, fill in, implant, include, infuse, inject, inlay, interject, interpolate, interpose, introduce, place in, press in, push in, put in, set in, write in

insight *n.* apperception, awareness, discernment, divination, foresight, intuition, intuitiveness, perception, perspicacity, sagaciousness, sagacity, sensitivity, shrewdness, understanding, vision, wisdom

insignia *n.* badge, decoration, emblem, mark, sign, symbol

insignificant *adj.* immaterial, inconsequential, inconsiderable, infinitesimal, irrelevant, meaningless, minor, negligible, nonessential, paltry, petty, small, trifling, trivial, unimportant, unsubstantial

insist *v.* assert, aver, be emphatic, be firm, be resolute, claim, command, contend, demand, emphasize, exhort, hold, maintain, order, persist, press, require, stress, swear, underscore, urge, vow

insoluble *adj.* baffling, incomprehensible, indecipherable, inexplicable, inextricable, mysterious, mystifying, perplexing, puzzling, unaccountable, unexplainable, unfathomable, unresolvable, unsolvable

insolvent *adj.* bankrupt, financially ruined, impoverished, indebted, penniless, poverty-stricken

inspect *v.* appraise, assess, audit, check, check out, evaluate, examine, go over, investigate, observe, peruse, probe, review, scan, scrutinize, study, survey, view, watch

inspection *n.* appraisal, assessment, audit, check, checkup, evaluation, examination, investigation, observation, perusal, probe, reading, research, review, scan, scrutiny, surveillance, survey, viewing, watching

inspiration *n.* arousal, awakening, creativity, encouragement, enlightenment, enthusiasm, idea, illumination, incentive, incitement, influence, insight, motivation, muse, revelation, stimulation, stimulus, thought, vision

inspire *v.* animate, arouse, awaken, encourage, energize, enliven, enthuse, excite, exhilarate, galvanize, give impetus to, hearten, impress, inflame, influence, infuse, invigorate, kindle, motivate, reassure, rejuvenate, rouse, stimulate, stir, touch, uplift

instability *n.* capriciousness, changeability, disequilibrium, fluctuation, frailty, impermanence, inconsistency, inconstancy, irresolution, lack of balance, pliancy, precariousness, shakiness, uncertainty, undependability, unpredictability, unreliability, unsoundness, unsteadiness, vacillation, volatility, vulnerability, weakness

install *v.* build in, establish, fix, inaugurate, induct, insert, instate, introduce, invest, locate, lodge, place, plant, position, put in, set, set up, situate, station, usher in

installation *n.* **1.** building in, coronation, establishment, furnishing, inauguration, induction, inserting, instatement, introduction, investiture, location, lodging, placement, placing, positioning, putting in, setting up, situating, stationing, ushering in **2.** accommodations, base, camp, equipment, establishment, fortification, lodging, plant, quarters, settlement, station, system

installment *n.* act, advance payment, chapter, deposit, division, earnest money, episode, part, partial payment, payment, periodic payment, portion, regular payment, scene, section, segment

instance *n.* case, case in point, citation, example, exemplification, illustration, occasion, precedent, quotation, representative case, sample, situation, specific situation, specimen, typical situation

instigate *v.* abet, actuate, agitate, arouse, bring about, encourage, excite, foment, generate, goad, impel, incite, induce, inflame, influence, initiate, inspire, kindle, motivate, persuade, prompt, provoke, rouse, spur, start, stimulate, stir up, urge

institute *v.* begin, bring about, bring into being, commence, conceive, create, develop, enact, establish, found, inaugurate, initiate, introduce, launch, lay foundation, lead the way, open, organize, originate, pioneer, put into operation, set up, start, take initiative, usher in

institution *n.* **1.** association, business, company, concern, corporation, establishment, firm, foundation, institute, organization, society, syndicate, trust **2.** bylaw, canon, code, convention, custom, decree, doctrine, edict, fundamental, law, order, ordinance, practice, precept, prescript, principle, regulation, rite, rule, statute, tenet, tradition, usage

instruct *v.* **1.** advise, coach, counsel, drill, educate, enlighten, give lessons, guide, inform, lecture, teach, train, tutor   **2.** bid, charge, command, decree, dictate, direct, enjoin, mandate, order, prescribe, require, tell

instruction *n.* **1.** apprenticeship, coaching, direction, discipline, drilling, education, enlightenment, grounding, guidance, preparation, schooling, teaching, training, tutelage   **2.** advice, briefing, code, command, counsel, demand, direction, directive, guideline, injunction, keyword, mandate, order, precept, writ

instructor *n.* advisor, coach, counselor, educator, guide, lecturer, mentor, professor, schoolteacher, teacher, trainer, tutor

instrument *n.* **1.** apparatus, appliance, contrivance, device, gadget, implement, machine, mechanism, robot, tool, utensil   **2.** agency, agent, catalyst, cause, force, instrumentality, means, mechanism, medium, moving force, organ, power, principle, vehicle, way, wherewithal   **3.** charter, contract, deed, grant, legal document, title, warrant, written agreement

instrumental *adj.* assisting, conducive, contributory, effectual, essential, helpful, important, influential, primary, serviceable, useful, valuable

insubordinate *adj.* contrary, contumacious, defiant, disobedient, disorderly, incorrigible, insurgent, insurrectional, mutinous, rebellious, recalcitrant, refractory, riotous, seditious, uncooperative, undisciplined, ungovernable, unruly

insufficient *adj.* bereft, deficient, faulty, imperfect, inadequate, incapable, incommensurate, incompetent, incomplete, lacking, meager, scant, scarce, short, unqualified, unsatisfactory, wanting

insurance *n.* assurance, bond, coverage, guarantee, indemnification, indemnity, protection, safeguard, security, surety, warrant, warranty

insure *v.* assure, bond, cinch, cover, ensure, guarantee, guard, indemnify, make certain, make secure, safeguard, secure, underwrite, warrant

intangible *adj.* abstract, abstruse, esoteric, ethereal, evanescent, hypothetical, impalpable, imperceptible, imponderable, incorporeal, indefinite, invisible, obscured, shadowy, unapparent, unobservable, untouchable, vague

integral *adj.* **1.** basic, constituent, elemental, essential, fundamental, indispensable, innate, intrinsic, necessary, requisite
2. aggregate, complete, comprehensive, entire, indivisible,
intact, integrated, total, unbroken, undivided, unified, whole

integrate *v.* amalgamate, assimilate, blend, bring together,
coalesce, combine, come together, commingle, consolidate,
desegregate, fuse, harmonize, homogenize, intermix, join,
link, meld with, merge with, mix, put together, unify, unite

intellect *n.* cognition, comprehension, genius, intellectual,
intellectuality, intelligence, mental ability, mental capability,
mentality, mind, reason, sense, understanding

intellectual *n.* academician, genius, intellect, philosopher,
sage, scholar, thinker

intellectual *adj.* cerebral, cognitive, educated, intelligent,
learned, mental, scholarly, smart, very smart

intelligence *n.* acuity, acumen, adroitness, aptitude, astuteness, brilliance, cleverness, cognition, comprehension, discernment, ingenuity, insight, intellect, judgment, mental
capacity, mentality, mind, penetration, perception, perspicacity, reason, sagacity, sense, understanding, wisdom, wit

intelligent *adj.* adroit, apt, astute, brilliant, clever, creative,
discerning, educated, enlightened, ingenious, insightful,
intellectual, inventive, knowledgeable, learned, penetrating,
perceptive, perspicacious, sagacious, sage, smart, well-
informed, wise

intend *v.* aim at, aspire to, contemplate, design, expect, have
in mind, hope to, look forward to, mean, plan, propose,
resolve to, scheme, think of

intent *n.* See **intention**

intention *n.* aim, ambition, aspiration, design, desire, end,
goal, hope, idea, inclination, object, objective, plan, purpose,
resolve, scheme, target, will

intercede *v.* act for, arbitrate, intermediate, interpose, intervene, make peace, mediate, negotiate, reconcile, step in

interchange *n.* barter, change, commerce, exchange, junction, network, reciprocation, switch, trade, transferal, transposition

interchangeable *adj.* changeable, commutable, compatible, convertible, correspondent, equivalent, exchangeable, identical,
mutual, reciprocal, substitutable, synonymous, transposable

interest *n.* **1.** bonus, charge, claim, discount, dividend, earnings, excess, gain, increase, increment, investment, part, percentage, piece, portion, profit, return, share, title **2.** absorption, attention, attentiveness, attraction, care, concern, consequence, curiosity, engagement, engrossment, enthusiasm, excitement, importance, leisure activity, notice, passion, pastime, preoccupation, pursuit, recreation, regard, relaxation, significance **3.** advantage, benefit, good, profit, value, well-being, worth

interest *v.* absorb, appeal to, arouse, attract, captivate, concern, engage, engross, enlist, entertain, excite, fascinate, hold attention of, intrigue, involve, lure, move, please, stimulate, tantalize, tempt

interested *adj.* absorbed, aroused, attracted, biased, captivated, concerned, curious, engaged, engrossed, enticed, excited, fascinated, impressed, inspired, involved, lured, moved, partial, partisan, prejudiced, preoccupied, stimulated, tantalized, tempted

interesting *adj.* absorbing, alluring, amusing, appealing, attractive, captivating, compelling, curious, diverting, enchanting, engaging, engrossing, entertaining, entrancing, exciting, fascinating, gripping, impressive, intriguing, inviting, pleasing, provocative, provoking, riveting, stimulating, tantalizing, tempting, thought-provoking

interface *n.* boundary, commands, common boundary, communication point, devices, graphics, interaction, link, meeting point, point of interaction, prompts, shared boundary

interference *n.* bar, block, check, difficulty, encumbrance, hampering, handicap, hindrance, impediment, interruption, intervention, intrusion, meddlesomeness, meddling, obstacle, obstruction, opposition, resistance, setback, tampering

interim *n.* breach, break, breather, breathing spell, coffee break, cutoff, gap, hiatus, interlude, interruption, interval, intervening time, lacuna, layoff, letup, meantime, meanwhile, pause, recess, respite, time-out

interim *adj.* improvised, intervening, makeshift, pro tem, provisional, stopgap, substitute, temporary

interlocution *n.* colloquy, communication, conference, conversation, dialog, discourse, discussion, parley, talk

intermediary *n.* agent, arbiter, arbitrator, broker, connection, dealer, delegate, disinterested party, distributor, emissary, interceder, intercessor, intermediate, mediator, medium, moderator, negotiator, referee, spokesperson, wholesaler

intermission *n.* abeyance, break, cessation, dormancy, halt, interim, interlude, interruption, interval, latency, lull, pause, quiescence, recess, respite, rest, stop, suspension, time-out

international *adj.* cosmopolitan, ecumenical, foreign, general, global, intercontinental, nonsectarian, universal, world, worldwide

interpolate *v.* add, admit, alter, enter, fill in, include, inject, insert, interject, interline, interpose, introduce, make insertions, put in, work in

interpret *v.* annotate, clarify, comment, construe, decipher, decode, define, describe, elucidate, enact, explain, explicate, expound, figure out, gloss, illuminate, illustrate, make clear, paraphrase, play, read, render, simplify, spell out, transcribe, translate, understand, work out

interruption *n.* abeyance, break, cessation, cutoff, delay, disconnection, discontinuance, disruption, dissolution, disuniting, division, gap, halt, hiatus, interference, interim, interlude, intermission, interval, intrusion, lull, pause, recess, rupture, separation, severance, stop, stoppage, suspension

interval *n.* break, delay, distance, downtime, gap, hiatus, interim, interlude, intermission, interphase, interruption, interstice, lacuna, lull, meantime, meanwhile, opening, pause, rest, space, spell, time-out

interview *n.* audience, colloquy, conference, consultation, dialog, discourse, discussion, evaluation, examination, exchange, hearing, investigation, meeting, parley, question-and-answer session, session, talk

interview *v.* confer with, consult, evaluate, examine, inquire, interrogate, investigate, question, quiz, talk to

introduce *v.* **1.** acquaint, advance, announce, bring in, bring out, bring together, make introductions, make known, present, present formally, promote, propose, put forward, recommend, submit, suggest, usher in   **2.** begin, bring into being, coin, commence, establish, found, inaugurate, initiate, install, institute, launch, open, organize, originate, pioneer, plan, preface, present, set in motion, set up, start, unveil   **3.** add, enter, fill in, implant, import, include, incorporate, inject, insert, instill, interject, interpolate, interpose, put in, work in

introduction *n.* **1.** acquaintance, advancement, announcement, bringing out, bringing together, formal presentation, making introduction, making known, offer, offering, opening remarks, presenting formally, promotion, proposal, recommendation, submission, suggestion, ushering in **2.** beginning, bringing into being, coining, commencement, foreword, founding, inauguration, initiation, installation, institution, launch, lead, opening, organization, originating, pioneering, preamble, preface, planning, preliminaries, prelude, presentation, prologue, setting in motion, setting up, start, unveiling **3.** addition, entry, filling in, implanting, importing, inclusion, incorporation, injection, insertion, instilling, interpolation, interposing, putting in, working in

introductory *adj.* beginning, first, inaugural, initial, initiatory, leading, opening, original, precursory, prefatory, preliminary, preparatory, primary, starting

invalid *adj.* baseless, fallacious, false, illogical, indefensible, inoperative, irrational, nonviable, null, null and void, powerless, unenforceable, unfounded, unjustifiable, unproven, unreasonable, unreasoned, unscientific, unsound, unsupportable, untrue, unwarrantable, void, worthless, wrong

invalidate *v.* abolish, abrogate, annul, cancel, confute, counteract, countermand, disannul, discontinue, discredit, disprove, disqualify, negate, neutralize, nullify, overrule, overthrow, overturn, refute, repeal, rescind, reverse, revoke, stop, undermine, veto, void, weaken

invaluable *adj.* costly, dear, expensive, high-priced, indispensable, inestimable, precious, priceless, rare, valuable

invent *v.* bring into being, coin, compose, conceive, concoct, conjure up, contrive, create, design, devise, discover, dream up, envision, fabricate, fashion, forge, form, formulate, imagine, inaugurate, make, make up, originate, plan, produce, think up, turn out

invention *n.* apparatus, coinage, composition, concoction, construction, contrivance, creation, creativeness, creativity, design, device, discovery, fabrication, gadget, gimmick, imagination, ingenuity, innovation, inspiration, instrument, inventiveness, mechanism, originality, origination, production, resourcefulness

inventory *n.* account, backlog, checklist, contents, enumeration, goods, index, itemization, items, list, listing, list of assets, list of stock, merchandise, merchandise on hand, numeration, price list, produce, provisions, record, register, reserve, roll, roster, schedule, securities, stockpile, store, supplies on hand, supply, table, tabulation, tally, value of goods, wares

invest *v.* **1.** advance, back, buy into, buy stock, endow, expend, finance, fund, lay out, lend, loan, pay out, provide money, put money into, risk, spend, subsidize, venture **2.** authorize, charge, empower, establish, inaugurate, induct, initiate, install, license, ordain, sanction

investigate *v.* analyze, audit, check into, delve into, examine, explore, inquire into, inspect, interrogate, look into, make inquiry into, probe, question, research, scrutinize, search for, study

investigation *n.* analysis, audit, canvass, checking into, delving into, examination, exploration, fact finding, hearing, inquiry into, inquisition, inspection, interrogation, looking into, making inquiry into, observing, probe, probing, quest, questioning, research, review, scrutiny, search for, study

investment *n.* advance, backing, buying into, buying stock, endowment, expenditure, financing, investing, laying out, lending, loan, putting up money, risk, speculation, spending, venture

invitation *n.* allure, appeal, attraction, bait, bidding, call, challenge, dare, enticement, inducement, lure, motion, offer, overture, petition, proffer, proposal, proposition, request, solicitation, suggestion, suit, summons, supplication, tantalization, temptation

invite *v.* allure, appeal to, ask, ask for, attract, beg, bid, call for, call on, court, draw, encourage, entice, entreat, give invitation, implore, include, issue invitation, lure, persuade, petition, plead, pray, prevail on, propose, request, send invitation, solicit, summon, supplicate, tantalize, tempt

invoice *n.* account itemization, amount owed, bill, charge, charges, check, debt, enumeration, itemized account, list, obligation, request for payment, statement, statement of account, statement of indebtedness, tabulation, tally

invoice *v.* bill, charge, enumerate, itemize, list, prepare account, present check, send statement, tabulate, tally

involuntary *adj.* automatic, blind, compulsory, conditioned, disinclined, forced, grudging, impulsive, instinctive, obligatory, reflex, reflexive, reluctant, spontaneous, unconscious, uncontrolled, unintended, unintentional, unmeditated, unpremeditated, unthinking, unwilling, unwitting

involve *v.* absorb, admit, affect, allude to, associate, comprehend, comprise, concern, connect, connote, contain, count in, denote, designate, draw in, embody, embrace, enclose, encompass, engage, enmesh, entail, entangle, epitomize, hold, implicate, include, incorporate, indicate, mean, necessitate, number among, point to, pressure, presuppose, refer to, relate, represent, require, signify, suggest, symbolize, take in, typify

irreconcilable *adj.* clashing, conflicting, contrary, diametrically opposed, discordant, hostile, implacable, incompatible, incongruent, incongruous, inconsistent, inexorable, inflexible, intransigent, irreparable, opposing, uncompromising, unresolvable, unsolvable

irregular *adj.* **1.** asymmetrical, bending, broken, craggy, crooked, disproportionate, elliptical, hilly, jagged, lopsided, lumpy, meandering, off-balance, off-center, out-of-proportion, pitted, rough, rugged, unaligned, unbalanced, unequal, uneven, unlevel, unsymmetrical **2.** aimless, capricious, changeable, desultory, disarranged, disconnected, discontinuous, disordered, eccentric, erratic, fluctuating, haphazard, inconstant, indiscriminate, intermittent, nonuniform, occasional, orderless, random, spasmodic, sporadic, uncertain, uneven, unmethodical, unsettled, unsteady, unsystematic, variable **3.** aberrant, abnormal, anomalous, atypical, bizarre, curious, deviant, different, eccentric, exceptional, extraordinary, odd, peculiar, queer, strange, uncommon, unconventional, unique, unnatural, unorthodox, unusual

irrelevant *adj.* extraneous, immaterial, impertinent, inapplicable, inappropriate, inconsequent, inconsequential, insignificant, nonessential, nongermane, pointless, trivial, unconnected, unimportant, unnecessary, unrelated, unwarranted

isolate *v.* abstract, banish, confine, cut off, detach, disconnect, dissociate, divide, exclude, exile, insulate, keep apart, lock up, quarantine, remove, seclude, segregate, separate, sequester, set apart, sever

issue *n.* **1.** copy, edition, installment, issuance, number, printing, publication, version **2.** argument, concern, contention, controversy, crux, matter, point, point in question, problem, question, subject, topic **3.** aftereffect, aftermath, conclusion, consequence, culmination, effect, end, eventuality, finale, outcome, outgrowth, result, termination, upshot, windup

issue *v.* air, announce, bring out, broadcast, circulate, declare, deliver, dispense, disperse, disseminate, distribute, emit, get out, give out, print, proclaim, promulgate, publish, put in circulation, put out, release, send, send out, transmit

italicize *v.* accentuate, call attention to, emphasize, feature, give emphasis to, highlight, stress, underline, underscore

item *n.* article, aspect, blurb, bulletin, component, consideration, detail, element, entry, feature, filler, incidental, information, ingredient, matter, memo, minor point, note, notice, particular, piece, point, specific

itemize *v.* arrange, catalog, detail, document, enumerate, inventory, list, list particulars, number, record, specify, tabulate

itinerary *n.* agenda, arrangements, calendar, circuit, course, flight plan, path, preparations, program, route, schedule, timetable, travel plan, way

J

jeopardize *v.* endanger, expose, hazard, imperil, menace, put in jeopardy, risk, subject to danger, threaten

job *n.* **1.** appointment, business, calling, capacity, career, commission, craft, employment, engagement, handicraft, line of work, livelihood, occupation, office, position, post, profession, pursuit, situation, trade, venture, vocation, work **2.** accomplishment, act, action, activity, activities, affair, assignment, batch of information, charge, chore, collection of tasks, concern, contribution, deal, deed, duty, effort, errand, exercise, function, group of actions, group of tasks, mission, obligation, operation, project, responsibility, role, set of tasks, task, transaction, undertaking, unit of work, venture, work

jobber *n.* agent, broker, consignor, dealer, market maker, supplier, wholesaler, wholesale merchant

join *v.* **1.** affiliate with, align with, ally with, associate with, band together, centralize, collaborate with, contribute to, cooperate with, enlist, enroll, enter, go along with, mingle with, partake in, participate in, side with, take part in, team up with **2.** affix, append, associate, attach, bind, blend, bridge, cement, clamp, coalesce, combine, commingle, conjoin, connect, couple, entwine, fasten, fuse, incorporate, intermix, link, lock, merge, mix, put together, span, splice, tie, unify, unite, weld, yoke **3.** abut, adjoin, be adjacent to, be contiguous to, border, border on, butt, coincide, conjoin, juxtapose, lean against, lie beside, meet, touch, verge on

journal *n.* account, accounting record, album, almanac, annals, calendar, chronicle, chronological record, chronology, daily, daybook, diary, dossier, history, house organ, log, magazine, memoir, minutes, monthly, narrative, notebook, notes, periodical, publication, quarterly, record, record book, register, reminiscence, review, scrapbook, weekly

journalism *n.* broadcasting, composition, editing, factual writing, feature writing, news collection, news coverage, news editing, news reporting, objective writing, print media, public press, the press

journey *n.* adventure, campaign, course, cruise, drive, excursion, expedition, exploration, march, migration, odyssey, outing, passage, pilgrimage, progress, quest, ride, route, safari, tour, transit, transmigration, travel, traveling, trek, trip, venture, voyage

judge *v.* adjudge, adjudicate, appraise, arbitrate, ascertain, assess, conclude, consider, criticize, decide, decree, deduce, determine, estimate, evaluate, examine, find, form opinion, gauge, give verdict, hear arguments, hear evidence, hold hearing, make judgment, measure, mediate, pass sentence, pronounce sentence, referee, resolve, review, rule, sentence, settle, test, try, umpire, weigh

judgment *n.* **1.** adjudication, appraisal, assessment, award, conclusion, conviction, court order, decision, decree, determination, estimation, evaluation, finding, inference, judicial decision, official opinion, opinion, resolution, result, ruling, sentence, verdict, view **2.** doom, fate, punishment, retribution, sentence **3.** acumen, astuteness, common sense, comprehension, discernment, discrimination, good sense, grasp, intelligence, judiciousness, knowledge, levelheadedness, penetration, perception, perspicacity, prudence, rationality, reasoning ability, sagacity, sense, sharpness, shrewdness, soundness, understanding, wisdom

judicious *adj.* acute, astute, calculating, careful, cautious, circumspect, diplomatic, discerning, discreet, discriminating, enlightened, expedient, far-sighted, heedful, intelligent, judicial, logical, mindful, perceptive, perspicacious, politic, practiced, provident, prudent, rational, reasonable, sagacious, sage, sapient, sensible, sharp, shrewd, thoughtful, wary, well-advised, wise

jurisdiction *n.* administration, area, area of authority, area of supervision, authority, control, district, domain, domination, dominion, extent of authority, geographical entity, hegemony, influence, judicature, legal authority, legal power, legal right, limits, political entity, power, prerogative, province, purview, range, reign, right, rule, scope, sovereignty, sphere, sway, territory

just *adj.* conscionable, correct, decent, deserved, disinterested, dispassionate, due, equitable, ethical, evenhanded, fair, fair-minded, good, honest, honorable, impartial, justified, neutral, nondiscriminatory, objective, open-minded, principled, proper, reasonable, right, righteous, true, trustworthy, truthful, unbiased, unprejudiced, upright, veracious, well-deserved, well-founded

justifiable *adj.* acceptable, defensible, excusable, fair, forgivable, just, lawful, legitimate, pardonable, proper, reasonable, right, rightful, understandable, valid, warrantable, well-founded, well-grounded

justification *n.* account, answer, apology, argument, basis, defense, excuse, exculpation, exoneration, explanation, extenuation, grounds, just cause, legitimation, plea, proof, rationale, rationalization, reason, reply, response, substantiation, support, validation, warrant

justify *v.* **1.** acquit, advocate, answer for, apologize for, argue for, assert, clear, condone, defend, explain, exculpate, excuse, explain, give grounds for, give reason for, give sufficient grounds for, legalize, legitimate, legitimize, maintain, make allowances, make excuses, pardon, plead for, rationalize, remove guilt, show cause, show just cause for, stand up for, substantiate, support, sustain, uphold, vindicate, warrant **2.** adjust, align, arrange, place flush at margin, set flush, shift

juxtapose *v.* pair, place near, place parallel, place side by side, put alongside, put side by side

K

key *n.* annotation, answer, answer book, blueprint, catalog, clarification, code, code book, data item, description, directory, explanation, explication, gloss, group of characters, guide, index, interpretation, legend, manual, note, password, solution, table, translation

key *adj.* basic, cardinal, chief, crucial, essential, fundamental, important, leading, main, major, primary, principal

keynote *n.* basic idea, center, core, essence, gist, heart, leading point, main idea, marrow, note, nucleus, pith, salient point, substance, theme, topic

keyword *n.* access word, code, code word, identification, identifying word, index, key, locator, password, significant word

kill *v.* cancel, cease, defeat, delete, discontinue, eradicate, erase, excise, expunge, extinguish, forbid, halt, neutralize, nullify, obliterate, prohibit, quash, refuse, reject, remove, revoke, shut off, stop, suppress, terminate, turn down, turn off, veto, vote down, withdraw

kind *n.* brand, breed, category, character, class, classification, family, genre, genus, group, order, phylum, race, set, sort, species, strain, type, variety

know *v.* **1.** apprehend, be aware of, be cognizant of, be educated in, be experienced in, be informed about, comprehend, discern, fathom, grasp, have information about, have knowledge of, perceive, realize, recognize, see, sense, understand **2.** associate with, be acquainted with, be familiar with, be friends with, have dealings with, socialize with

know-how *n.* ability, adeptness, adroitness, aptitude, capability, competence, dexterity, experience, expertise, expertness, facility, faculty, gift, ingenuity, knowledge, proficiency, skill, skillfulness, talent

knowledge *n.* acquaintance, awareness, beliefs, comprehension, consciousness, education, enlightenment, erudition, expertise, facts, familiarity, information, insight, instruction, intelligence, judgment, know-how, learning, rules, scholarship, schooling, understanding, wisdom

knowledgeable *adj.* academic, acquainted, discerning, educated, enlightened, erudite, experienced, expert, familiar, informed, insightful, intelligent, learned, perceptive, proficient, sagacious, sage, scholarly, understanding, versed, well-educated, well-informed, well-read, wise

L

label *n.* badge, brand, characterization, classification, code name, epithet, hallmark, heading, identification, identifier, logo, mark, marker, name, price tag, set of symbols, stamp, statement, sticker, symbol, tag, ticket, trademark

label *v.* categorize, characterize, class, classify, describe, designate, identify, imprint, mark, name, put label on, put sticker on, stamp, tag, ticket, title

labor *n.* **1.** activity, chore, diligence, drudgery, effort, employment, endeavor, exercise, exertion, industriousness, job, operation, physical work, strain, struggle, task, toil, travail **2.** blue-collar workers, employees, help, laborers, manual laborers, proletariat, unskilled laborers, white-collar workers, workers, work force, working class, working people

labor *v.* be employed at, drudge, endeavor, exert oneself, strain, strive, struggle, work, work at, work hard

laboratory *n.* darkroom, lab, observation room, proving ground, science room, testing ground, workroom, workshop

laborer *n.* See **labor (n) 2**

lack *n.* absence, dearth, defect, deficiency, deficit, depletion, deprivation, destitution, imperfection, inadequacy, inferiority, insufficiency, meagerness, need, omission, paucity, poverty, reduction, scantiness, scarcity, shortage, shortcoming, sparsity, want

lading *n.* cargo, carload, change, contents, freight, freightage, goods, haul, load, merchandise, shipload, shipment, truckload, weight

laissez faire *n.* deregulation, free enterprise, free-enterprise system, free trade, noninterference, nonintervention, private enterprise

land *n.* acreage, acres, continent, country, countryside, earth, expanse, farmland, field, ground, grounds, homeland, lot, mainland, nation, native land, open space, parcel, plot, real estate, real property, shore, sod, soil, terrain, territory, topography, tract

land *v.* alight, arrive, bring down, bring in, check in, come ashore, come down, come in, debark, deplane, descend, disembark, dock, drop anchor, fall, go ashore, make landing, put down, put in, reach destination, set down, settle on, take down, touch down

landlord *n.* host, landowner, lessor, manager, owner, property holder, property owner, proprietor, resident manager, superintendent

landmark *n.* **1.** benchmark, distinctive feature, guide, guidepost, historic structure, marker, memorial, milepost, milestone, monument, prominent feature, promontory, ruins, vantage point, vestige **2.** crisis, critical point, decisive point, memorable event, milestone, significant event, turning point

language *n.* common speech, communication, conversation, dialect, discourse, expression, idiom, parlance, phraseology, rhetoric, speech, style, system of communication, terminology, tongue, verbal interchange, verbal intercourse, vernacular, vocabulary, words, wording

lapse *n.* **1.** break, elapse, gap, hiatus, interlude, intermission, interruption, interval, lull, passage, pause, recess **2.** blunder, breach, crime, error, failing, failure, fault, flaw, gaffe, mistake, negligence, nonfeasance, offense, omission, oversight, recidivism, relapse, sin, slip, slipup, transgression, violation, wrong

latitude *n.* breadth, compass, extent, freedom, independence, indulgence, leeway, liberty, license, margin, range, reach, room, scope, space, span, spread, stretch, unrestrictedness, width

launch *v.* begin, commence, embark, establish, found, go ahead, inaugurate, initiate, instigate, institute, introduce, open, organize, originate, set up, start, take initiative, take steps, usher in

law *n.* **1.** act, bill, bylaw, charge, charter, code, command, commandment, constitution, covenant, decree, dictate, due process, edict, enactment, equity, injunction, jurisprudence, legal code, legislated rules, legislation, mandate, measure, official rules, order, ordinance, prescription, regulation, ruling, statute, warrant, writ **2.** assumption, axiom, criterion, custom, formula, foundation, fundamental, guide, maxim, postulate, practice, precept, principle, proposition, reason, standard, tenet, theorem, theory, truism, truth

lawful *adj.* allowable, authorized, canonical, chartered, constitutional, decreed, enacted, judicial, juridical, jurisprudential, just, legal, legalized, legislated, legitimate, licensed, licit, mandated, official, ordained, ordered, permissible, right, rightful, sanctioned, statutory, valid, vested, warranted

lawsuit *n.* action, case, legal action, litigation, suit

layoff *n.* cutback, discharge, dismissal, early retirement, firing, reduction, reduction in force, unemployment, work force reduction

layout *n.* arrangement, blueprint, design, drawing, dummy, plan, schematic arrangement, sketch, spread, structure

layover *n.* break, delay, interruption, overnight stay, overnight stop, pause, rest, stay, stayover, stop, stopover

lead *v.* **1.** advise, affect, bring around, bring on, captain, cause, command, conduct, convince, direct, govern, guide, handle, head, induce, influence, manage, motivate, move, order, oversee, persuade, prescribe, preside over, prevail on, produce, prompt, regulate, reign, rule, run, spur, superintend, supervise, sway, talk into, tend, win over **2.** be ahead, exceed, excel, outdistance, outdo, outperform, outrun, outstrip, overcome, overshadow, surpass, transcend

leader *n.* boss, captain, chief, chief executive officer, commander, conductor, controller, director, executive, forerunner, general, guide, head, manager, motivator, officer, overseer, pacesetter, pilot, president, principal, ruler, superintendent, superior, supervisor

leadership *n.* administration, authority, capacity, command, control, direction, directorship, domination, dominion, governance, guidance, hegemony, influence, management, power, primacy, reign, rule, sovereignty, superintendence, superintendency, superiority, supremacy, sway

leading *adj.* best, best-known, cardinal, chief, crowning, dominant, first, foremost, greatest, highest, incomparable, initial, main, matchless, maximum, most important, outstanding, paramount, predominant, preeminent, premier, preponderant, prevailing, primary, prime, principal, prominent, ruling, superior, supreme, unrivaled, unsurpassed, uppermost

learn *v.* absorb, acquire, ascertain, assimilate, attain, commit to memory, comprehend, detect, determine, digest, discern, discover, find out, glean, grasp, memorize, pick up, realize, receive, study, take in, train in, uncover, understand

learned *adj.* academic, accomplished, conversant, cultured, educated, erudite, experienced, expert, intellectual, lettered, literary, literate, sage, scholarly, skilled, studious, versed, well-educated, well-grounded, well-informed, well-read, wise

lease *n.*   formal agreement, rental agreement, subcontract, sublease, sublet contract, use contract

lease *v.*   charter, demise, farm out, grant temporary use of, hire, hire out, lend out, let, live in, loan, loan out, pay rent on, rent, rent out, sublease, sublet

lecture *n.*   **1.** address, comment, commentary, discourse, exposition, instruction, oration, sermon, speech, talk   **2.** admonition, castigation, censure, chiding, criticism, discipline, rebuke, remonstration, reprimand, reproach, reproof, scolding

lecture *v.*   **1.** address, comment, declaim, deliver address, discourse, enlighten, expound, give address, give lesson, give speech, give talk, hold forth, instruct, orate, recite, sermonize, speak, talk   **2.** admonish, castigate, censure, chide, criticize, discipline, rebuke, reprimand, reproach, reprove, scold

leeway *n.*   extra space, extra time, freedom, latitude, liberty, margin, margin for error, play, space

legacy *n.*   ancestry, bequeathal, bequeathment, bequest, bestowal, devise, disposition, dower, endowment, gift, heritage, inheritance, patrimony, will

legal *adj.*   admissible, allowable, allowed, authorized, certified, constitutional, contractual, decreed, enforceable, granted, judicatory, judicial, juridical, just, lawful, legalized, legitimate, licit, mandated, ordained, permissible, permitted, prescribed, ratified, right, rightful, sanctioned, sound, statutory, valid, warranted

legalize *v.*   allow, approve, authorize, certify, codify, constitute, decree, enact, entitle, formalize, legislate, legitimatize, legitimize, license, ordain, pass law, permit, ratify, sanction, validate, warrant

legend *n.*   brief description, caption, cipher, code, device, epigraph, explanation, inscription, key, table of symbols

legible *adj.*   clean, clear, comprehensible, decipherable, discernible, distinct, easy-to-read, explicit, intelligible, neat, perceptible, plain, readable, recognizable, tidy, understandable, well-written

legislation *n.*   act, bill, body of law, bylaws, codification, constitution, enactment, law, lawmaking, ordinances, prescription, regulation, ruling, statutes

legitimate *adj.*   acknowledged, admissible, allowable, appropriate, approved, authentic, authorized, chartered, constitutional, correct, fair, genuine, just, lawful, legal, legislated, licensed, licit, mandated, official, permissible, permitted, prescribed, proper, right, rightful, sanctioned, statutory, true, valid, verifiable, warranted, well-founded

leisure *n.* comfort, convenience, day off, ease, freedom, free time, holiday, idle hours, inactivity, liberty, pause, quiet, recess, recreation, relaxation, repose, respite, rest, restfulness, retirement, spare time, time off, tranquility, unemployment, vacation

lend *v.* accommodate, advance, contribute, expend, extend, furnish, give, impart, loan, make a loan, provide, supply

lenient *adj.* charitable, clement, compassionate, condoning, easy, easygoing, forbearing, forgiving, good-natured, indulgent, kind, liberal, merciful, mild, moderate, patient, permissive, softhearted, sympathetic, temperate, tolerant

lessee *n.* boarder, lodger, occupant, renter, roomer, tenant

lessor *n.* creditor, landlady, landlord, lender, manager, money-lender, owner, property manager, property owner

leverage *n.* advantage, advantageous use of credit, authority, clout, control, effectiveness, enhancement, influence, positional advantage, power, purchasing power, using borrowed money, using credit, weight

levy *n.* assessment, collection, custom, dues, duty, exaction, excise, fee, impost, payment, rate, surcharge, tariff, tax, taxation, toll

levy *v.* assess, call up, charge, collect, exact, fix rate, gather, impose, lay on, put on, raise, seize, set, tax

lexicon *n.* dictionary, glossary, language, thesaurus, vocabulary, wordbook, word list, word meanings

liability *n.* **1.** amount due, amount payable, arrearage, debit, debt, due, indebtedness, loan, money owed, obligation **2.** accountability, amenability, answerability, blame, charge-ability, culpability, duty, obligation, onus, responsibility **3.** exposure, inclination, likelihood, openness, probability, proneness, susceptibility, tendency, vulnerability

liable *adj.* **1.** accountable, amenable, answerable, blamable, chargeable, culpable, obligated, responsible **2.** apt, assailable, exposed, inclined, likely, open, prone, susceptible, tending, vulnerable

liaison *n.* bond, connection, contact, interface, intermediary, link, medium, tie

liberal *adj.* **1.** advanced, broad-minded, catholic, cosmopolitan, enlightened, flexible, free-thinking, humanistic, indulgent, leftist, left-wing, lenient, modern, open-minded, permissive, progressive, reasonable, receptive, reformist, tolerant, unbiased, unbigoted, understanding, unprejudiced **2.** altruistic, beneficent, benevolent, bounteous, charitable, generous, giving, humanitarian, kind, kindhearted, magnanimous, philanthropic, sympathetic, unselfish, unstinting

license *n.* accreditation, allowance, authority, authorization, certificate, certification, charter, commission, consent, entitlement, franchise, grant, grant of permission, legal authority, pass, permission, permit, title, warrant, warranty

license *v.* accredit, allow, approve, authorize, certify, charter, commission, consent to, empower, enable, entitle, franchise, grant, grant permission, legalize, permit, sanction, validate, warrant

lien *n.* action, attachment, charge, claim, creditor's claim, deed of trust, encumbrance, garnishment, hold, mortgage, security, security agreement, security interest

lifework *n.* activity, business, calling, career, employment, interest, job, line of work, livelihood, mission, occupation, profession, pursuit, vocation, work

lightweight *adj.* incompetent, inconsequential, insignificant, lean, meritless, no-account, paltry, petty, skimpy, slight, trifling, trivial, unimportant, valueless, worthless

likeness *n.* agreement, analogousness, analogy, appearance, clone, conformity, copy, counterpart, delineation, depiction, double, duplicate, equivalence, facsimile, guise, icon, identicalness, illustration, image, model, parallelism, photocopy, photograph, picture, portrait, portrayal, replica, representation, reproduction, resemblance, sameness, semblance, similarity, similitude, study, uniformity

limit *n.* absolute, border, boundary, cap, ceiling, circumference, conclusion, confinement, deadline, destination, edge, end, end point, extremity, farthest point, finality, fringe, goal, limitation, line of demarcation, margin, maximum, partition, restraint, restriction, rim, termination, ultimate, utmost, verge

limit *v.* bar, bind, bound, cap, check, circumscribe, confine, constrict, curb, cut back, delimit, demarcate, fence in, forbid, hem in, hinder, keep in, narrow, prohibit, proscribe, ration, reduce, restrain, restrict, shut in

limitation *n.* See **limit (n)**

limitless *adj.* boundless, countless, endless, extensive, great, immeasurable, immense, indefinite, indeterminate, inexhaustible, infinite, innumerable, interminable, measureless, myriad, never-ending, numberless, perpetual, unbounded, uncircumscribed, undefined, unending, unfathomable, uninterrupted, unlimited, unrestricted, untold, vast

line *n.* **1.** activity, business, department, calling, career, employment, field, forte, job, lifework, occupation, profession, province, pursuit, specialization, specialty, trade, venture, vocation, work **2.** assortment, commodities, goods, merchandise, produce, products, stock, vendibles, wares **3.** See **lineage**

lineage *n.* ancestry, bloodline, clan, descendants, descent, extraction, family, family tree, forbears, genealogy, heritage, house, origin, parentage, pedigree, progeny, race, stock, strain, succession, tribe

linear *n.* aligned, direct, lengthwise, lineal, longitudinal, one-dimensional, straight, unbent, undeviating

link *v.* affix, associate, attach, bond, chain, combine, conjoin, connect, couple, fasten, hook up, interface, join, network, tie, tie in with, unite

lip service *n.* disingenuousness, empty gesture, falseness, hypocrisy, insincerity, phoniness, tokenism

liquid *adj.* **1.** convertible, fluid, marketable, negotiable, readily available, ready, usable **2.** dissolved, flowing, fluid, melting, liquefied, liquescent, melted, melting, moist, molten, running, runny, smooth, streaming, solvent, thin, watery, wet

liquidate *v.* abolish, break up, cash, cash out, clear, close out, convert, convert to cash, disband, discharge, dismantle, dissolve, extinguish debt, honor, pay in full, pay off, quit, redeem, satisfy, sell off, sell out, sell stock, settle, terminate, unload

list *n.* attendance, catalog, checklist, directory, docket, enumeration, file, index, inventory, lineup, listing, ordered set, outline, record, register, roll, roster, schedule, slate, syllabus, table, tabulation, tally, ticket

list *v.* alphabetize, arrange, catalog, chart, chronicle, classify, detail, docket, enlist, enroll, enter, enumerate, file, group, index, inventory, itemize, keep record, note, post, record, register, schedule, specify, spell out, tabulate, tally, write down

literacy *n.*   ability to read, articulateness, erudition, intelligence, knowledge, learning, proficiency, reading ability, scholarship

literate *adj.*   articulate, educated, grammatical, instructed, intelligible, knowledgeable, lucid, schooled, trained, well-informed, well-read

litigation *n.*   action, case, cause, contention, contest, controversy, dispute, judicial contest, lawsuit, legal action, legal proceedings, prosecution, suit, trial

livelihood *n.*   activity, business, career, craft, employment, enterprise, function, income, job, line of work, living, maintenance, occupation, office, position, profession, source of income, specialization, specialty, subsistence, support, sustenance, trade, undertaking, venture, vocation, work

living *n.*   existence, income, lifestyle, livelihood, maintenance, means of support, source of income, subsistence, support, sustenance, way of life

load *n.*   **1.** boatload, capacity, cargo, carload, charge, contents, freight, goods, lading, merchandise, sales charge, shipload, shipment, truckload, weight   **2.** affliction, burden, charge, difficulty, duty, encumbrance, hardship, liability, obligation, oppression, pressure, responsibility, strain, task, tax

loan *n.*   accommodation, advance, advancing, allowance, credit, extension, financing, lending, time payment

loan *v.*   advance money, extend financing, finance a purchase, give money, lend money, offer credit

lobby *v.*   affect, campaign for, exert influence, further, high-pressure, induce, influence, move, persuade, press, pressure, promote, push, put pressure on, request, sell, solicit, sway, talk into, urge

locate *v.*   **1.** come across, come upon, detect, determine, discover, find, get at, happen on, meet with, pinpoint, search out, spot, track down, uncover, unearth   **2.** base, establish, fix, inhabit, move in, occupy, park, place, position, reside, seat, set, settle, set up, set up in business, situate

location *n.*   area, business, environment, geographical position, locale, locality, neighborhood, place, place of business, place of residence, point, position, region, residence, site, situation, spot, station, venue, vicinity, whereabouts

log *n.* account, chart, daybook, diary, journal, listing, logarithm, logbook, record, register, tally, usage report

logic *n.* argumentation, deduction, dialectics, good sense, induction, inference, nonarithmetic computer operations, ratiocination, rationale, reason, science of reasoning, sound judgment, syllogistics, wisdom

logical *adj.* clear, deducible, deductive, inductive, inferential, ratiocinative, rational, reasonable, sensible, sound, syllogistic, valid, wise

logistics *n.* coordination, direction, execution, handling, management, maneuvers, oversight, plan, plans, strategy, supervision, tactics

logo *n.* design, figure, letterhead, logotype, masthead, mark, nameplate, representation, seal, stamp, symbol, trademark, trade name

look into *v.* ask about, check, check out, delve into, examine, explore, follow up, go into, inquire into, inspect, investigate, probe, research, scrutinize, search into, study

loss *n.* **1.** debit, debt, decrease, deficiency, deficit, downturn, financial ruin **2.** accident, casualty, catastrophe, damage, destruction, disaster, misadventure, misfortune, mishap, wreckage

lot *n.* **1.** acreage, area, block, division, field, parcel, part, patch, plat, plot, portion, property, real estate, section, square, tract **2.** allotment, allowance, apportionment, commission, dole, interest, measure, part, percentage, piece, portion, proportion, quota, ration, share, slice

low *adj.* **1.** cheap, deficient, economical, inadequate, inexpensive, inferior, marked down, meager, mediocre, moderate, modest, nominal, reasonable, reduced, slashed, small, substandard, trifling **2.** coastal, depressed, flat, ground-level, little, low-hanging, low-lying, low-set, sea-level, shallow, short, small, submerged, sunken, unelevated

low-key *adj.* easygoing, indirect, low-pitched, mellow, modulated, quiet, relaxed, restrained, softened, subdued, subtle, understated

loyal *adj.* allegiant, constant, dedicated, dependable, devoted, dutiful, faithful, firm, patriotic, reliable, staunch, steadfast, steady, true, trusted, trustworthy, unchanging, unfailing, unswerving, unwavering

lucrative *adj.* fruitful, gainful, high-paying, money-making, paying, profitable, prosperous, remunerative, rewarding, well-paid, well-paying

lukewarm *adj.* apathetic, disinterested, dispassionate, hesitant, impassive, indecisive, indifferent, neutral, noncommittal, tepid, uncertain, uncommitted, unconcerned, undecided, unenthusiastic, uninterested, unresponsive

luminary *n.* celebrity, dignitary, famous person, important person, leader, notable, personage, star, superstar

lure *n.* allurement, appeal, attraction, bait, decoy, draw, enticement, gimmick, incentive, incitement, inducement, invitation, magnet, seduction, snare, temptation, trap

lure *v.* attract, bait, beguile, cajole, captivate, charm, decoy, draw in, enchant, ensnare, entice, entrap, fascinate, induce, invite, persuade, tantalize, tempt

luxurious *adj.* comfortable, costly, deluxe, epicurean, extravagant, fancy, gorgeous, grand, gratifying, immoderate, imposing, lavish, lush, luxuriant, magnificent, opulent, ostentatious, palatial, pleasurable, plush, posh, pretentious, rich, self-indulgent, splendid, sumptuous, well-appointed

luxury *n.* affluence, bliss, comfort, delight, enjoyment, epicureanism, exorbitance, extravagance, frill, gratification, great pleasure, immoderation, indulgence, intemperance, lavishness, lushness, luxuriousness, magnificence, opulence, ostentatiousness, pleasure, pretentiousness, richness, self-indulgence, splendor, sumptuousness

M

machinations *n.* conspiracies, contrivances, designs, devices, intrigues, inventions, logistics, management, maneuvers, manipulations, moves, plans, plots, ploys, ruses, schemes, strategies, tactics, tricks, wiles

machine *n.* apparatus, appliance, contrivance, device, engine, gadget, implement, instrument, mechanism, motor, robot, stand-alone system, stand-alone unit, tool, utensil, vehicle

machinery *n.* apparatus, appliances, contrivances, devices, engines, equipment, gadgetry, gadgets, gear, implements, instruments, mechanisms, organization, structure, system, tools, utensils, vehicles, works

magnate *n.* aristocrat, baron, big business owner, business leader, capitalist, captain of industry, czar, financier, industrialist, leader, luminary, mogul, notable, personage, successful entrepreneur, top executive, tycoon

magnify *v.* **1.** add to, aggrandize, amplify, augment, blow up, boost, build up, deepen, develop, enhance, enlarge, expand, extend, heighten, increase, intensify, strengthen, swell **2.** color, dramatize, embellish, embroider, enlarge on, exaggerate, hyperbolize, inflate, overdo, overemphasize, overplay, overstate

magnitude *n.* **1.** consequence, eminence, grandeur, greatness, importance, mark, momentousness, note, significance **2.** amount, amplitude, bigness, bulk, capacity, dimension, enormity, enormousness, expanse, extent, greatness, hugeness, immensity, intensity, largeness, mass, measure, proportion, proportions, quantity, range, reach, size, space, strength, tremendousness, vastness, volume

mail *n.* communications, correspondence, deliveries, electronic messages, letters, memos, messages, packages, postcards

mail *v.* deliver, dispatch, forward, put in mail, send, send by mail, ship, transmit, transport

mailbox [*computer*]: *n.* data storage, data store, e-mail storage, message center, message storage, storage, storage location

maintain *v.* **1.** care for, conserve, continue, keep, keep going, keep up, look after, manage, nurture, preserve, prolong, protect, provide for, retain, save, support, sustain, take care of, uphold **2.** advocate, affirm, allege, argue for, assert, attest, aver, avow, certify, champion, claim, contend, declare, defend, emphasize, hold, insist, justify, plead for, profess, say, stand by, state, testify, vindicate, vouch, warrant, witness

maintenance *n.* **1.** care, conservation, continuance, continuation, keeping up, necessary care, perpetuation, preservation, prolongation, retaining, upkeep **2.** alimony, allowance, food, keep, livelihood, living, living expenses, resources, subsistence, support, sustaining, sustainment

major *adj.* **1.** better, big, bigger, extensive, extreme, greater, greatest, higher, large, larger, large-scale, oversized, supreme, uppermost, utmost **2.** chief, critical, crucial, foremost, important, influential, main, outstanding, paramount, predominant, preeminent, primary, prime, principal, serious, significant, vital

make *v.* **1.** acquire, bring in, clear, earn, gain, garner, get, glean, gross, net, obtain, procure, realize, reap, receive, secure, take in **2.** assemble, build, compose, construct, create, devise, draw, erect, fabricate, fashion, forge, form, frame, generate, invent, manufacture, mold, originate, prepare, produce, put together, put up, set up, shape **3.** accomplish, bring about, cause, coerce, compel, constrain, drive, effect, force, impel, impress, induce, insist on, necessitate, oblige, persuade, press, pressure, prevail on, provoke, require, urge

malfunction *n.* breakdown, defect, failure, fault, flaw, impairment, imperfection

man *n.* adult male, being, Homo sapiens, human, human being, humankind, human race, individual, mortal, person, soul

manage *v.* administer, be in charge, bring about, care for, carry out, command, conduct, control, deal with, direct, dominate, effect, engineer, execute, govern, guide, handle, head, influence, instruct, lead, manipulate, operate, oversee, ply, preside, regulate, rule, run, steer, superintend, supervise, take care of, take charge, train, use, watch over, wield

management *n.* **1.** administration, care, charge, command, conduct, control, direction, governance, government, guidance, handling, people, leadership, manipulation, operation, oversight, policymaking, regulation, rule, stewardship, superintendence, supervision **2.** administrators, board of directors, bosses, chief executive officer, controllers, directors, employers, executives, head, key people, officials, owners

manager *n.* administrator, boss, chief, controller, director, executive, head, leader, officer, official, organizer, overseer, proprietor, superintendent, supervisor

mandate *n.* command, court order, decree, dictate, directive, edict, injunction, order, ordinance, regulation, requirement, ruling, writ

mandatory *adj.* binding, compelling, compulsory, essential, imperative, indispensable, necessary, needed, obligatory, required, requisite

maneuver *v.* contrive, engineer, exercise, finesse, guide, handle, intrigue, machinate, manage, manipulate, move, navigate, negotiate, operate, plan, plot, scheme, work

manipulate *v.* **1.** employ, guide, handle, lead, manage, maneuver, operate, ply, shape, use, wield, work **2.** change, engineer, exploit, influence, machinate, mold, motivate, shape, take advantage of, use, work on

mankind *n.* civilization, community, Homo sapiens, human community, humanity, humankind, human race, human species, mortals, people, society, the public, the world

man-made *adj.* arranged, artificial, composed, constructed, crafted, created, handmade, manufactured, prepared, synthetic, unnatural

manual *n.* documentation, guide, guidebook, handbook, how-to book, instruction book, primer, printed guide, reference, reference book, text, textbook, workbook

manual *adj.* hand-controlled, hand-operated, nonautomatic, nonelectric, physical

manufacture *n.* assembling, assembly, construction, creation, fabrication, formation, making, manufactured product, mass-production, processing, producing, production

manufacture *v.* **1.** assemble, construct, create, fabricate, form, machine, make, make up, mass-produce, process, produce, put together **2.** concoct, contrive, create, devise, fabricate, invent, make up, think up

manuscript *n.* author's copy, computer-generated copy, draft, original copy, rough draft, source document, typed copy, typescript, written document

map *n.* chart, delineation, diagram, graph, graphic representation, guide, image, plan, plat, projection, representation

margin [*finance*]: *n.* cost of next item, deposit, good-faith deposit, gross minus net, partial payment, percentage of purchase cost, usefulness of next item

marginal *adj.* borderline, dispensable, insignificant, low, minimal, minimum, minor, negligible, nonessential, passable, peripheral, slight, small, unessential, unnecessary, weak

markdown *n.* amount subtracted, decrease in price, downward adjustment, lowered price, price cut, price decrease, price reduction, reduction in price

market *n.* bazaar, business, commerce, commercial center, demand, emporium, exchange, fair, mall, marketplace, market value, mart, outlet, price, securities markets, shopping center, stock exchange, trade, trading center, traffic

market *v.* advertise, bargain, buy and sell, consign, display, exchange, merchandise, offer for sale, retail, sell, speculate, trade, traffic, transact, transport, truck, vend, wholesale

marketable *adj.* commercial, desirable, disposable, easily sold, popular, salable

marketing *n.* advertising, moving goods and services, promoting, promotion, publicity, sales, selling

market value *n.* current value, fair value, open-market price, replacement cost, sale price

markup *n.* amount added, higher price, increase in price, price increase, price rise, raise in price, rise in price, upward adjustment

master *v.* **1.** acquire skill in, become proficient in, comprehend, excel in, grasp, learn, study, understand **2.** beat, break in, command, conquer, control, defeat, direct, dominate, govern, manage, overcome, overpower, overwhelm, prevail over, regulate, rule, subdue, subjugate, suppress, triumph over, vanquish

masterful *adj.* **1.** adept, adroit, consummate, deft, dexterous, excellent, expert, first-rate, matchless, preeminent, proficient, skilled, skillful, superior, superlative, supreme **2.** arbitrary, arrogant, authoritarian, authoritative, autocratic, bossy, commanding, controlling, demanding, despotic, dictatorial, doctrinaire, dogmatic, dominating, domineering, imperative, oppressive, overbearing, peremptory, powerful, tyrannical

mastermind *v.* conceive, contrive, design, develop, devise, dream up, engineer, establish, forge, form, found, frame, generate, initiate, instigate, mold, organize, originate, plan, shape, think up, work up

material *n.* **1.** goods, ingredients, items, matter, objects, raw materials, staples, stock, substance, supplies, things **2.** data, documents, facts, figures, information, notes, papers, written material, written matter

mathematical *adj.* algebraic, differential, exact, fractional, geometrical, numerary, numerical, precise, statistical

matriculate *v.* enlist, enroll, enter, register, sign up

matrix *n.* array, cast, die, example, exemplar, form, grid, mint, model, mold, original form, pattern, rectangular array, seal, source, stamp

matter *n.* **1.** being, body, constituents, elements, mass, material, objects, protoplasm, substance, sum, things **2.** business, concern, content, essence, event, focus, incident, issue, occurrence, point, question, situation, subject, theme, thesis, thing, topic

maturity [*finance*]: *n.* becoming due, becoming payable, due date, end of term, full value, payable date

maximum *n.* apex, apogee, bound, boundary, cap, ceiling, crest, crown, culmination, extreme, extremity, greatest amount, height, limit, most, outer limit, peak, pinnacle, summit, top, upper limit, utmost, zenith

meaning *n.* **1.** connotation, content, context, core, definition, denotation, drift, effect, essence, explanation, gist, implication, import, interpretation, message, pith, point, sense, significance, spirit, subject, substance, tenor, vein **2.** aim, end, goal, intention, interest, object, plan, purpose

means *n.* **1.** agency, apparatus, avenue, channel, course, fashion, instrument, machinery, manner, mechanism, method, mode, organization, power, process, system, tactics, technique, vehicle, way **2.** assets, backing, budget, capital, finances, funds, income, money, revenue, wherewithal

measure *n.* See **measurement**

measure *v.* appraise, assess, calculate, calibrate, check out, compute, delimit, demarcate, determine, estimate, evaluate, figure, gauge, judge, map, mark, mark off, meter, plot out, rate, rule, size, size up, survey, take account of, value, weigh

measurement *n.* amplitude, appraisal, area, assessment, calibration, capacity, computation, degree, dimensions, distance, estimation, evaluation, extent, magnitude, measure, measuring, proportions, range, scope, survey, valuation

mechanism *n.*   **1.** apparatus, appliance, component, device, engine, equipment, gadget, instrument, machine, machinery, motor, tool   **2.** See **means 1**

mediate *v.*   arbitrate, bring together, bring to terms, conciliate, intercede, intervene, make peace, moderate, negotiate, propitiate, reconcile, referee, restore harmony, settle, umpire

mediation *n.*   arbitration, bringing to agreement, bringing to terms, conciliation, intercession, intervention, making peace, moderating, negotiation, propitiation, reconciliation, refereeing, restoring harmony, settling, umpiring

meet *v.*   **1.** assemble, collect, come together, confer, congregate, convene, converge, gather, get together, hold a session, join, meet with, muster, rally   **2.** accost, chance on, clash, collide, come across, come upon, confront, contact, encounter, face, happen on, hit, run into, strike

meeting *n.*   **1.** assemblage, assembly, audioconference, computer conference, conclave, concourse, conference, congregation, congress, convention, encounter, document conference, engagement, gathering, get-together, introduction, rally, rendezvous, reunion, seminar, session, symposium, teleconference, videoconference   **2.** abutment, confluence, conjunction, conjuncture, connection, contact, convergence, crossing, intersection, joining, junction, union

member *n.*   adherent, affiliate, associate, branch, chapter, component, constituent, element, inhabitant, piece, portion, post, representative, section, segment, unit

membership *n.*   adherence, admission, allegiance, associates, association, belonging, body, club, enrollment, group, matriculation, members, participation, rolls, roster, society, sodality

memo *n.*   announcement, communication, dispatch, electronic mail, e-mail, epistle, informal letter, message, missive, note, notice, reminder

memoir *n.*   account, annals, autobiography, biography, chronicle, confessions, diary, experiences, history, journal, life history, life story, memories, personal history, personal narrative, recollection, reminiscences

memory [*computer*]: *n.*   computer storage, primary storage, RAM, random-access memory, read-only memory, ROM, storage facility, storage space

mention *v.* adduce, advise, allude to, announce, bring up, call attention to, cite, comment on, communicate, declare, disclose, divulge, hint at, impart, imply, indicate, inform, intimate, invoke, let know, make known, make mention of, make note of, name, notify, point out, quote, recount, refer to, remark on, report, reveal, say, speak about, speak of, specify, state, suggest, tell, touch on

menu [*computer*]: *n.* available choices, list of choices, list of functions, list of options, on-screen display, on-screen list, options

merchandise *n.* commodities, goods, hardware, material, produce, products, staples, stock, supplies, wares

merchandise *v.* advertise, buy and sell, deal in, distribute, market, promote, publicize, retail, trade, vend

merchant *n.* businessperson, dealer, exporter, jobber, marketer, retailer, salesperson, seller, shopkeeper, storekeeper, trader, tradesperson, vendor, wholesaler

merge *v.* absorb, amalgamate, assimilate, blend, bring together, centralize, coalesce, combine, come together, concentrate, conglomerate, consolidate, converge, fuse, homogenize, incorporate, interface, intermingle, intermix, join, join forces, meld, mix, submerge, syndicate, synthesize, unify, unite

merger *n.* alliance, amalgamation, association, coalition, combination, conglomeration, consolidation, fusion, incorporation, joining, melding, merging, takeover, unification, union

merit *n.* advantage, asset, benefit, credit, due, excellence, good, goodness, integrity, quality, recompense, reward, strong point, value, virtue, worth, worthiness

merit *v.* be entitled to, be qualified for, be worthy of, deserve, earn, have a claim to, have a right to, justify, rate

message *n.* **1.** bulletin, coded signals, communication, directive, dispatch, electronic communication, epistle, group of characters, information, instruction, letter, memo, missive, news, note, notice, report, signal, transmission, word, written communication **2.** aim, idea, intent, intimation, meaning, moral, point, purport, sense, significance, theme

method *n.* approach, arrangement, classification, code, design, discipline, fashion, form, formula, function, guide, manner, means, mechanism, mode, order, organization, pattern, plan, practice, principle, procedure, process, recipe, routine, scheme, standard, structure, style, system, tactic, technique, way

methodical *adj.* businesslike, constant, deliberate, disciplined, exact, logical, methodic, methodized, meticulous, ordered, orderly, organized, painstaking, precise, regular, regulated, structured, systematic, uniform

meticulous *adj.* accurate, conscientious, correct, detailed, exact, fastidious, fussy, painstaking, particular, precise, scrupulous, strict, thorough

middleman/woman *n.* agent, broker, dealer, distributor, interceder, intercessor, intermediary, mediator, negotiator, representative, wholesaler

mileage *n.* **1.** allotment, allowance, charge, compensation, exaction, fee, freightage, levy, price, rate, recompense, reimbursement, tax, toll **2.** distance, extent, kilometers, length, miles, range, space **3.** advantage, benefit, coverage, gain, profit, publicity, service, usage, use, usefulness, wear

milestone *n.* accomplishment, achievement, breakthrough, discovery, landmark, marker, milepost, special occasion, turning point

milieu *n.* air, ambience, arena, atmosphere, aura, backdrop, background, climate, condition, element, environment, locale, medium, neighborhood, place, scene, setting, sphere, stage, surroundings

mind-set *n.* attitude, disposition, fixed disposition, fixed state of mind, habit, mental attitude, mental habit, mental inclination, state of mind, strong opinion

minimize *v.* abbreviate, abridge, attenuate, belittle, condense, curtail, cut down, decrease, deemphasize, deprecate, depreciate, detract, diminish, discount, disparage, downgrade, lessen, make smaller, prune, reduce, shorten, underestimate, underrate

minimum *n.* **1.** least amount, limit, lowest amount, lowest limit, margin, minimal amount, slightest amount, smallest amount **2.** admission, cover charge, fee, service charge

minimum *adj.* least, limited, littlest, lowest, marginal, minimal, slightest, smallest, tiniest

minor *adj.* ancillary, inconsequential, inconsiderable, insignificant, lesser, light, little, low, lower, middling, minus, negligible, paltry, petty, piddling, secondary, slight, small, smaller, subordinate, subsidiary, trifling, trite, trivial, unimportant

minority *n.* contingent, faction, section, smaller group, smaller number, smaller part, splinter group

miscalculate *v.* blunder, err, make mistake, miscompute, misconstrue, miscount, misestimate, misinterpret, misjudge, misread, misunderstand, misvalue, overestimate, overrate, overvalue, slip up, underestimate, underrate, undervalue

miscellaneous *adj.* assorted, different, disparate, divergent, diverse, diversified, heterogeneous, manifold, mixed, multifarious, multiform, odd, selected, sundry, varied, variegated, various

misconception *n.* delusion, false belief, false impression, misapprehension, miscalculation, misconstruction, misinterpretation, misjudgment, mistaken belief, misunderstanding, wrong idea, wrong impression

misfortune *n.* accident, adversity, affliction, bad luck, calamity, causality, catastrophe, disadvantage, disaster, failure, hardship, harm, ill fortune, loss, misadventure, mischance, mishap, setback, tragedy, trial, tribulation, trouble

misguided *adj.* deceived, deluded, erroneous, ill-advised, imprudent, injudicious, misdirected, misinformed, misinstructed, misled, mistaken, wrong

mishandle *v.* abuse, blunder, bungle, deal with ignorantly, deal with wrongly, fumble, maladminister, misapply, misappropriate, misconduct, misdirect, misemploy, misgovern, mismanage, mistreat, misuse, squander, waste

misjudge *v.* be wrong, err, judge wrongly, misapprehend, miscalculate, misconstrue, misevaluate, misinterpret, misread, misunderstand, overestimate, overrate, underestimate, underrate

misleading *adj.* ambiguous, confusing, deceitful, deceiving, deceptive, deluding, delusive, disingenuous, evasive, fallacious, false, fraudulent, inaccurate, tricky, wrong

mismanage *v.* See **mishandle**

misplace *v.* dislocate, displace, file incorrectly, lose, misfile, mislay, place wrongly

misrepresent *v.* color, deceive, disguise, distort, embroider, exaggerate, fabricate, falsify, mislead, misstate, overstate, prevaricate, understate

mistake *n.* blunder, bungle, error, error in judgment, fallacy, fault, gaffe, inaccuracy, indiscretion, misapprehension, miscalculation, misconception, misconduct, misdeed, misestimation, misinterpretation, misjudgment, misstatement, misstep, misunderstanding, omission, oversight, slip, transgression, typographical error, wrong impression

mistake *v.* be mistaken, be wrong, blunder, bungle, confound, confuse, err, make mistake, misapprehend, miscalculate, misconceive, misinterpret, misjudge, misread, misunderstand, mix up, overlook

mistrust *v.* be skeptical of, be wary of, disbelieve, distrust, doubt, have doubts about, have reservations about, question, suspect

misunderstand *v.* be confused, get false impression, get wrong idea, misapprehend, miscalculate, miscomprehend, misconstrue, misinterpret, misjudge, misread

misunderstanding *n.* **1.** argument, clash, conflict, difference, disagreement, discord, dissension, feud, quarrel, rift, split, variance **2.** confusion, false impression, misapprehension, miscalculation, misconception, misconstruction, misinterpretation, misjudgment, misreading, mix-up, wrong idea

misuse *n.* abuse, corruption, exploitation, ill-treatment, maltreatment, misapplication, misappropriation, misemployment, mishandling, mistreatment, misusage, squandering, waste, wasting, wrong application

mobile *adj.* ambulatory, changeable, fluid, movable, moving, portable, roaming, roving, transportable, traveling, unstationary, wandering

model *n.* abstract version, archetype, characterization, criterion, design, embodiment, epitome, example, exemplar, formal representation, gauge, graphical representation, ideal, mathematical representation, mold, original, paradigm, paragon, pattern, physical representation, pictorial representation, prototype, quintessence, role model, sample, schematic representation, standard, symbol, type

model *adj.* archetypal, classic, classical, commendable, exemplary, flawless, ideal, illustrative, imitation, inimitable, paradigmatic, perfect, prototypical, quintessential, representative, standard, typical, unparalleled

model *v.* **1.** demonstrate, display, exhibit, parade, pose, represent, show, wear **2.** base, carve, cast, create, design, fashion, form, lay out, mold, pattern, plan, sculpt, shape, sketch

modern *adj.* advanced, contemporary, current, existent, existing, fresh, immediate, latest, modernistic, modernized, new, newest, new-fashioned, present, present-day, prevailing, progressive, recent, reshaped, stylish, topical, up-to-date, up-to-the-minute

modernize *v.* bring up to date, make modern, make new, redesign, refresh, regenerate, rejuvenate, remodel, renew, renovate, revive, update

modify *v.* **1.** accommodate, adapt, adjust, alter, change, convert, customize, make changes, make modifications, recast, reconstruct, redo, refashion, re-form, remodel, reorganize, reshape, revise, rework, transfigure, transform, vary **2.** abate, curb, decrease, diminish, lessen, limit, lower, moderate, modulate, qualify, reduce, restrain, restrict, soften, temper

modulate *v.* adapt, adjust, attune, change, harmonize, inflect, lower, moderate, modify, regulate, relax, soften, subdue, temper, tune, vary

momentum *n.* drive, driving power, energy, force, impetus, impulse, power, push, rate of acceleration, speed, thrust

monetary *adj.* budgetary, capital, cash, financial, fiscal, monied, pecuniary

money *n.* affluence, assets, bank notes, bills, capital, cash, checks, coinage, coins, currency, exchange, exchange medium, finances, funds, legal tender, means, medium of exchange, profit, prosperity, riches, specie, unit of value, wealth, wherewithal

moneymaking *adj.* advantageous, gainful, lucrative, paying, productive, profitable, remunerative, successful, well-paying, worthwhile

monitor *n.* **1.** cathode-ray tube, display, display screen, display unit, screen, video display unit, visual display **2.** advisor, computer control program, control program, counselor, director, guide, instructor, overseer, proctor, superintendent, supervisor

monitor *v.* advise, check, counsel, examine, listen, observe, oversee, record, scan, study, superintend, supervise, survey, track, watch

monopoly *n.* cartel, control, corner, domination, exclusive possession, margin, power, trust

morale *n.* attitude, confidence, disposition, drive, emotion, feelings, humor, mood, outlook, spirit, state, temper, temperament

mortgage *n.* bond, collateral, guaranty, lien, pledge, security, warranty

motion *n.* **1.** formal proposal, formal suggestion, meeting transaction, plan, proposal, proposition, recommendation, submission, suggestion **2.** act, action, activity, agitation, change, changing place, changing position, drift, flow, fluctuation, flux, gesture, locomotion, mobility, movement, oscillation, passage, progress, signal, stir, stirring, stream, transit, travel, wave, wavering

motivate *v.* actuate, arouse, bring on, cause, drive, encourage, excite, force, galvanize, goad, impel, incite, induce, influence, inspire, lead, manipulate, move, persuade, prevail on, prod, prompt, propel, provoke, push, rouse, spur, stir, sway, trigger, urge on

motivation *n.* actuation, ambition, arousal, catalyst, cause, desire, drive, encouragement, impetus, impulse, incentive, incitement, inducement, inner striving, inspiration, instigation, interest, motive, persuasion, provocation, push, reason, spur, stimulus

motto *n.* adage, aphorism, apothegm, byword, catch phrase, epigram, formula, guide, inscription, maxim, moral, precept, proverb, saying, slogan, watchword

movable *adj.* adjustable, changeable, conveyable, deployable, detachable, mobile, portable, removable, transferable, transportable, unattached, unfastened, unstationary

move *v.* **1.** advance, be in motion, budge, change address, change place, change position, depart, drive, fly, go, go ahead, go away, jump, leap, leave, march, migrate, offload, proceed, progress, pull out, put in motion, relocate, remove, run, shift, stir, switch, transfer, transport, travel, walk, withdraw, yield **2.** activate, actuate, advise, advocate, arouse, call on, convert, counsel, electrify, excite, exhilarate, exhort, galvanize, give rise to, impel, impress, incite, induce, inspire, instigate, lead, persuade, prevail on, prod, prompt, propel, propose, provoke, push, put forward, recommend, rouse, spur, stimulate, stir, submit, suggest, sway, urge

movement *n.* **1.** act, action, activity, advance, advancement, change, development, evolution, exercise, flow, fluctuation, flux, gesture, journey, maneuver, migration, mobility, motion, move, operation, passage, proceedings, progress, progression, stir, transferal, transit, velocity **2.** campaign, coalition, crusade, demonstration, faction, front, fund-raiser, group, march, mobilization, organization, party, patrol, political action, undertaking, wing

multiply *v.*   accumulate, add, aggrandize, augment, boost, build up, compound, double, duplicate, enlarge, expand, generate, heighten, increase, intensify, magnify, make greater, make larger, produce, proliferate, propagate, raise, repeat, reproduce, redouble, repeat, spread

municipal *adj.*   borough, city, civic, civil, community, local, metropolitan, public, town, urban

mutual *adj.*   associated, common, connected, interactive, interchangeable, joint, reciprocal, related, shared

myth *n.*   allegory, fabrication, false notion, fancy, fantasy, fiction, figment, illusion, imagination, invention, legend, parable, popular belief, saga, story, superstition, tale, tradition

naive *adj.* artless, candid, childlike, confiding, credulous, frank, gullible, innocent, nonexpert, open, plain, simple, simple-minded, sincere, trustful, trusting, unaffected, unsophisticated, unspoiled, unsuspecting, unsuspicious, unworldly

name *v.* **1.** address, call, characterize, christen, classify, denominate, designate, dub, entitle, give a title, identify, label, nickname, style, tag, term, title **2.** announce, appoint, assign, authorize, charge, choose, cite, commission, declare, delegate, denote, designate, elect, employ, empower, engage, entrust, hire, identify, mention, nominate, pick, refer to, relegate, select, specify, suggest, vote in

national *adj.* countrywide, domestic, federal, governmental, nationalistic, nationwide, sovereign

nationality *n.* ancestry, birthplace, citizenship, country, descent, extraction, nation, native land, origin, roots

natural *adj.* **1.** artless, authentic, candid, childlike, direct, frank, genuine, guileless, ingenuous, innocent, naive, open, plain, real, simple, sincere, spontaneous, straightforward, trusting, unaffected, unassuming, unpretentious, unsophisticated, unstudied **2.** accepted, accustomed, characteristic, common, commonplace, customary, everyday, habitual, inborn, innate, instinctive, logical, native, normal, ordinary, prevalent, reasonable, regular, routine, standard, typical, universal, usual

necessary *adj.* basic, binding, compelling, compulsory, crucial, elementary, essential, exigent, fundamental, imperative, indispensable, mandatory, needed, needful, obligatory, prerequisite, pressing, required, requisite, unavoidable, urgent, vital

negative *adj.* adverse, complaining, contradictory, contrary, counteractive, cynical, disavowing, dissenting, gloomy, faultfinding, invalidating, neutralizing, nullifying, opposing, pessimistic, refusing, rejecting, repugnant, resisting, resistive, unenthusiastic, uninterested, unwilling

negligent *adj.* careless, delinquent, derelict, disregardful, forgetful, heedless, inadvertent, inattentive, inconsiderate, indifferent, lax, neglectful, reckless, remiss, sloppy, slovenly, thoughtless, unheedful, unmindful, unthinking

negligible *adj.* imperceptible, inappreciable, inconsequential, insignificant, minor, petty, small, trifling, trivial, unimportant, worthless

negotiate *v.* **1.** accommodate, adjudicate, arbitrate, arrange, bargain, conciliate, confer, deal, debate, discuss, haggle, intercede, make a deal, make an offer, manage, mediate, moderate, referee, settle, work out **2.** clear, cross, get around, get over, get past, hurdle, jump over, leap over, pass, pass over, pass through, surmount, traverse, vault over

negotiation *n.* adjudication, agreement, arbitration, bargaining, collective bargaining, compromise, conflict resolution, deal, debate, diplomacy, discussion, dispute resolution, intervention, mediation, refereeing, settlement, transaction, umpiring

neophyte *n.* amateur, apprentice, beginner, convert, disciple, entrant, intern, learner, newcomer, new member, novice, novitiate, proselyte, protégé, pupil, student, student teacher, trainee

net *v.* bring in, clear, earn, gain, make, realize, realize net profit, yield

network *n.* communications link, communications structure, communications system, grid, hookup, interconnection, net, organizational link, set of computers, structure, system, system of computers, web

networking *n.* developing a network, developing professional contacts, establishing a computer network, exchanging information, exchanging services, making use of contacts, using a computer network, using professional contacts

neutral *adj.* **1.** conciliatory, detached, disengaged, disinterested, dispassionate, evenhanded, fair-minded, impartial, independent, indifferent, nonaligned, noncommittal, nonparticipating, nonpartisan, objective, open-minded, unaffiliated, unaligned, unallied, unbiased, uncommitted, undecided, uninvolved, unprejudiced **2.** abstract, achromatic, colorless, drab, dull, expressionless, flat, hueless, indistinct, pale, toneless, undefined, vague

neutralize *v.* annul, balance out, cancel out, compensate for, counteract, counterbalance, countercheck, counterpoise, invalidate, negate, nullify, offset, overcome, subdue, undo

newcomer *n.* alien, amateur, apprentice, arrival, beginner, entrant, immigrant, initiate, intruder, late arrival, learner, naturalized citizen, neophyte, new arrival, novice, novitiate, outsider, recruit, settler, stranger

news *n.* **1.** account, announcement, bulletin, communication, copy, data, disclosure, dispatch, enlightenment, exposé, facts, headlines, information, intelligence, message, publication, release, report, revelation, rumor, scandal, statement, story, word **2.** broadcast, newscast, radio broadcast, radio program, telecast, television program

node [*computer*]: n. computer, connecting point, connection, connection point, endpoint, event, intersection, joint, junction, juncture, link, peripheral, point, terminal

nomenclature *n.* classification, codification, designation, glossary, name, phraseology, set of terms, taxonomy, terminology, vocabulary

nominal *adj.* **1.** inexpensive, insignificant, low, low-priced, meaningless, minimal, small, symbolic, token, trifling, trivial, unnecessary **2.** alleged, apparent, formal, ostensible, pretended, professed, puppet, purported, represented, self-styled, so-called, suggested, supposed, theoretical, titular

nominate *v.* appoint, assign, choose, designate, draft, elect, name, offer, place, present, propose, put up, recommend, select, specify, submit, suggest, vote in

nomination *n.* appointment, choice, designation, induction, investment, naming, proposal, recommendation, selection, submission, suggestion

nonessential *adj.* dispensable, expendable, gratuitous, immaterial, inapplicable, insignificant, irrelevant, needless, peripheral, redundant, superfluous, trivial, unimportant, unnecessary, unneeded

nonpartisan *adj.* disinterested, equitable, fair, impartial, independent, just, neutral, nonaligned, objective, unaffiliated, unassociated, unbiased, uncommitted, uninfluenced, unprejudiced, unswayed

nonpayment *n.* default, delinquency, dishonor, evasion, nonremittal

nonprofit *adj.* charitable, eleemosynary, funded, not-for-profit, philanthropic, public-service, sponsored, supported

norm *n.* average, barometer, benchmark, check, criterion, gauge, general level, mean, measure, median, medium, model, normal rate, par, pattern, rule, scale, standard, test, type, usual, yardstick

normal *adj.* **1.** accepted, accustomed, acknowledged, average, common, commonplace, conventional, current, customary, established, general, habitual, mean, median, middle, natural, ordinary, orthodox, popular, prevailing, prevalent, recurrent, regular, routine, standard, traditional, typical, universal, usual, widespread, worldwide **2.** healthy, rational, reasonable, sane, sound, well-adjusted, wholesome

notable *n.* celebrity, dignitary, important person, leader, luminary, mogul, name, personage, powerful person, star, superstar

notable *adj.* celebrated, distinct, distinguished, eminent, exceptional, extraordinary, famed, famous, great, illustrious, important, imposing, impressive, marked, memorable, noteworthy, noticeable, outstanding, preeminent, prominent, remarkable, renowned, singular, special, striking, uncommon, unique, unusual, well-known

notarize *v.* acknowledge, attest, certify, take affidavit, take deposition, witness

notation *n.* characters, cipher, code, figures, memo, note, record, signs, symbols, system of symbols, written remarks

note *n.* **1.** annotation, brief comment, brief record, bulletin, comment, commentary, communication, correspondence, dispatch, entry, epistle, gloss, inscription, item, letter, memo, message, missive, notation, observation, postcard, record, register, remark, reminder, short letter, word, written communication **2.** bank draft, bank note, bill, bill of exchange, certificate, check, currency, draft, legal tender, money, paper money, promise to pay, promissory note, receipt, treasury note, voucher

notebook *n.* address book, album, calendar, catalog, chronicle, diary, dossier, journal, ledger, log, logbook, memoir, minute book, portable computer, record, record book, register, roll, schedule, scrapbook, yearbook

noted *adj.* acclaimed, celebrated, distinguished, eminent, esteemed, exalted, famed, famous, great, honored, illustrious, leading, legendary, named, notable, popular, preeminent, prominent, renowned, respected, venerable, well-known

notes *n.* brief, outline, preliminary draft, research, rough account, rough draft, skeleton, sketchy report, summary, synopsis

noteworthy *adj.* acclaimed, distinguished, eminent, esteemed, exceptional, extraordinary, famous, illustrious, important, memorable, notable, outstanding, preeminent, prominent, remarkable, renowned, respected, significant, unique, unusual

notice *n.* account, admonition, advertisement, announcement, broadcast, bulletin, caution, caveat, circular, comment, communication, criticism, critique, data, declaration, directive, facts, information, intelligence, knowledge, leaflet, manifesto, memo, mention, message, news, note, notification, order, pamphlet, poster, proclamation, publication, reference, report, review, statement, warning

notify *v.* advise, air, alert, announce, apprise, brief, broadcast, call, caution, circulate, communicate, convey, declare, disclose, disseminate, divulge, fax, inform, let know, make known, proclaim, publish, relate, remind, report, reveal, send word, telephone, tell, write

notion *n.* **1.** apprehension, assumption, belief, concept, conception, conceptualization, conjecture, idea, impression, inclination, intuition, judgment, observation, opinion, perception, sentiment, supposition, theory, thought, understanding, view **2.** bauble, knickknack, merchandise, small item, sundry, trifle

novelty *n.* **1.** fad, freshness, innovation, modernity, newness, novelness, oddity, originality, peculiarity, rarity, specialty, strangeness, unfamiliarity, uniqueness, unusualness, variety **2.** curio, curiosity, gadget, gimmick, knickknack, oddity, plaything, souvenir, toy, trifle, trinket

nucleus *n.* basis, center, core, crux, essence, essential point, focus, foundation, gist, heart, kernel, main point, nub, pith, premise, principle, seed

nullify *v.* abolish, abrogate, annul, cancel, counterbalance, countervail, declare null and void, disannul, discontinue, invalidate, negate, neutralize, repeal, rescind, revoke, set aside, stop, suspend, terminate, undo, veto, vitiate, void

number *n.* **1.** Arabic number, cardinal number, character, cipher, denominator, digit, digital number, figure, folio, fraction, integer, mathematical entity, numeral, numerator, ordinal number, Roman numeral, set of digits, statistic, sum, whole number **2.** aggregate, amount, difference, estimate, exponent, multitude, power, product, quantity, quotient, sum, summation, total, volume

number *v.*   add, add up, calculate, cipher, compute, count, count off, enumerate, estimate, figure, include, numerate, paginate, sum, sum up, tally, tell, total

numeral *n.*   cipher, digit, figure, integer, mathematical character, number, symbol

numerical *adj.*   algebraic, arithmetic, binary, differential, digital, exponential, fractional, integral, logarithmic, mathematical, numeral, numerary, statistical

numerous *adj.*   abundant, countless, diverse, large, many, multifarious, multitudinous, plentiful, populous, profuse, several, sundry, untold, various, voluminous

oath *n.* affirmation, attestation, avowal, deposition, pledge, promise, sworn declaration, sworn statement, vow, word, word of honor

object *n.* **1.** aim, design, desire, destination, end, goal, idea, intent, intention, mark, mission, motive, objective, plan, point, purpose, pursuit, reason, scheme, target, view, wish **2.** article, body, commodity, device, entity, gadget, item, material, matter, phenomenon, product, substance, thing, unit, variable

objection *n.* argument, challenge, complaint, counterargument, criticism, demur, disagreement, disapprobation, disapproval, disinclination, dislike, dissatisfaction, dissent, exception, grievance, hesitation, objecting, opposition, protest, rejection, remonstrance, scruple, unwillingness

objective *n.* aim, ambition, aspiration, design, desire, destination, end, goal, intent, intention, mark, mission, object, plan, plot, point, purpose, pursuit, target, vision

obligation *n.* accountability, agreement, bond, burden, business, charge, commitment, contract, debt, dues, duty, function, liability, necessity, onus, pledge, promise, requirement, responsibility, trust, understanding

observance *n.* **1.** anniversary, celebration, ceremonial, ceremony, commemoration, dedication, festivity, form, holiday, performance, rite, ritual, service, vigil **2.** convention, custom, fashion, form, formality, habit, practice, style, tradition, usage, way **3.** acknowledgment, adherence, attention to, awareness, carrying out, cognizance of, compliance, conformity, discharge, fidelity to, fulfillment of, heed, honoring, keeping, knowledge of, mark, obedience, observation, performance, regard for

observation *n.* **1.** attention, cognition, cognizance, consideration, detection, examination, heed, heedfulness, inspection, investigation, measurement, monitoring, note, notice, noticing, observing, overseeing, perception, probing, recognition, regard, research, review, scrutiny, seeing, study, supervision, surveillance, viewing, watching, witnessing **2.** account, comment, commentary, depiction, description, expression, impression, mention, note, notion, opinion, pronouncement, reflection, remark, report, statement, thought, viewpoint

observe *v.* **1.** celebrate, commemorate, dedicate, formalize, honor, mark, memorialize, remember, respect, revere, solemnize, venerate **2.** abide by, acquiesce in, adhere to, adopt, be faithful to, carry out, comply, comply with, conform to, defer to, discharge, execute, follow, fulfill, heed, honor, mind, obey, perform, satisfy **3.** behold, detect, discern, discover, distinguish, examine, inspect, look at, monitor, note, notice, pay attention to, perceive, recognize, regard, scrutinize, see, study, view, watch, witness

obsolete *adj.* abandoned, ancient, antiquated, antique, archaic, dead, defunct, depreciated, discarded, discontinued, disused, expired, extinct, old, old-fashioned, outdated, outmoded, out-of-date, out-of-fashion, out-of-style, primitive, retired, superannuated, timeworn, useless

obstacle *n.* bar, barricade, barrier, block, blockade, catch, check, deterrent, encumbrance, handicap, hindrance, hurdle, obstruction, restriction, snag

occasion *n.* **1.** adventure, affair, celebration, commemoration service, episode, event, experience, function, happening, incident, observance, occurrence **2.** basis, cause, circumstance, determinant, excuse, foundation, ground, grounds, incentive, inducement, influence, inspiration, justification, motivation, motive, provocation, purpose, reason, stimulus, warrant

occupation *n.* business, activity, calling, career, craft, employment, field, job, line of work, livelihood, position, profession, pursuit, trade, vocation, work

occupy *v.* be established, dwell in, engross, establish, hold, inhabit, keep, live in, locate, maintain, move into, own, possess, preoccupy, remain in, reside in, settle in, stay in, take up residence, use, utilize

occurrence *n.* accident, adventure, affair, case, circumstance, deed, episode, event, experience, incidence, incident, instance, matter, occasion, phenomenon, proceeding, situation

odds *n.* **1.** chances, likelihood, probability **2.** advantage, benefit, edge, handicap, lead, preeminence, predominance, superiority, supremacy

offend *v.* affront, aggravate, annoy, disgust, displease, distress, disturb, exasperate, gall, harm, humiliate, hurt, incense, infringe on, insult, irk, irritate, malign, nauseate, nettle, outrage, pique, provoke, repel, repulse, rile, sicken, slight, transgress, trespass, vex, wound

offer *n.* application, asked price, bid, commitment, motion, offering, offering price, overture, presentation, proffer, promise, proposal, proposition, submission, suggestion

offer *v.* advance, display, donate, exhibit, extend, furnish, give, grant, hold out, make a motion, make available, move, pose, present, proffer, promise, propose, propound, provide, put forth, put forward, put on the market, put up, put up for sale, recommend, set before, show, submit, suggest, tender, volunteer

office *n.* **1.** building, center, cubicle, department, facility, location, place, place of business, room, suite, workstation **2.** appointment, assignment, business, capacity, care, charge, commission, duty, employment, function, job, mission, obligation, occupation, position, post, responsibility, role, situation, station, task, trust, work

officer *n.* bureaucrat, chief, civil servant, commissioned officer, dignitary, director, leader, manager, official, police officer, president, public servant, secretary, treasurer, trustee, vice president

official *n.* See **officer**

official *adj.* accredited, approved, authentic, authenticated, authoritative, authorized, certified, customary, endorsed, definitive, established, formal, genuine, lawful, legal, legitimate, licensed, orthodox, proper, real, recognized, rightful, sanctioned, true, valid, validated, verified

officiate *v.* administer, be in charge of, chair, conduct, control, direct, emcee, govern, lead, manage, moderate, oversee, preside over, run, superintend

off-line *adj.* disconnected, independently functioning, noninteracting, turned-off, unconnected, unhooked

offset *v.* balance, cancel out, compensate for, counteract, counterbalance, counterpoise, equalize, even out, handicap, make amends, make up for, neutralize, nullify, recompense, reimburse, set off

omission *n.* **1.** cancellation, deletion, disregard, elimination, erasure, exception, excluding, exclusion, failure, gap, ignoring, lapse, neglect, noninclusion, overlooking, oversight, passing over, preclusion, withholding **2.** dereliction, disregard, exception, exclusion, failure, failure to act, inactivity, neglect, negligence, nonfeasance, nonfulfillment, omitting, overlooking, oversight, wrongful inaction

omit *v.* bypass, cancel, cut out, delete, discard, disregard, drop, edit out, eliminate, except, exclude, expunge, fail to mention, forget, ignore, leave out, neglect, overlook, pass by, pass over, reject, skip, withhold

on-line *adj.* connected, directly connected, hooked-up, interacting, turned-on

open *adj.* **1.** accessible, admissible, allowable, approachable, attainable, available, free, general, inclusive, nondiscriminatory, nonexclusive, obtainable, permitted, public, reachable, securable, unqualified, unrestricted, usable **2.** amenable, broad-minded, candid, disinterested, fair, frank, honest, impartial, innocent, objective, open-minded, reasonable, receptive, sincere, straightforward, unbiased, undisguised **3.** agape, ajar, exposed, gaping, navigable, passable, unbarred, unblocked, unbolted, unclosed, uncovered, unfastened, unimpeded, unlatched, unlocked, unobstructed, unplugged, unsealed, vacant, vacated **4.** arguable, contestable, controversial, debatable, disputable, doubtful, dubious, indecisive, indeterminate, problematic, questionable, uncertain, undecided, undetermined, unresolved, unsettled

operate *v.* **1.** administer, be in charge, carry on, command, conduct, direct, employ, handle, manage, maneuver, manipulate, pilot, run, steer, use, work **2.** act, act on, bring about, cause, compel, effect, engage, exert, exert influence, exert power, function, go, influence, perform, proceed, produce, produce result, progress, promote, serve, work

operation *n.* **1.** business concern, business deal, enterprise, project, task, undertaking, venture **2.** act, action, activity, agency, application, conveyance, deed, discharge, doing, effect, effectuation, effort, employment, engagement, execution, exercise, exertion, force, functioning, influence, labor, manipulation, motion, movement, performance, procedure, proceeding, process, progress, progression, work, working

operative *adj.* acting, active, current, effective, effectual, efficient, employed, functional, functioning, influential, instrumental, key, operating, operational, performing, practicable, relevant, running, serviceable, significant, usable, workable, working

opinion *n.* assessment, assumption, attitude, belief, concept, conception, conclusion, conjecture, estimate, estimation, fancy, feeling, guess, idea, image, impression, inference, judgment, notion, observation, perception, persuasion, sentiment, speculation, supposition, surmise, theory, thought, view, viewpoint

opportunity *n.* contingency, favorable circumstances, favorable moment, favorable time, fortuity, good fortune, good luck, happening, occasion, opening

opposition *n.* **1.** antagonism, antithesis, aversion, brush, clash, conflict, confrontation, contention, contest, contraposition, contravention, counteraction, defense, defiance, disagreement, disapproval, hostility, obstruction, obstructiveness, prevention, repulsion, resistance, rivalry **2.** adversary, antagonist, competition, enemy, foe, iconoclast, opponent, rival

option *n.* ability to choose, alternative, choice, election, license, opportunity, possibility, preference, prerogative, replacement, right to buy, right to choose, right to sell, selection, substitute

orchestrate *v.* arrange, bring about, coordinate, integrate, manage, organize, present, put together, set up

order *n.* **1.** application, booking, engagement, goods, materials, purchase, purchasing agreement, request, requisition, reservation, shipment, stipulation, supplies **2.** arrangement, array, assortment, categorization, classification, codification, composition, disposition, distribution, form, grouping, harmony, method, neatness, ordering, orderliness, organization, pattern, placement, regularity, scheme, sequence, series, setup, structure, succession, symmetry, system, systemization, uniformity **3.** act, authorization, behest, charge, command, commandment, decree, direction, directive, edict, injunction, instruction, law, mandate, manifesto, ordinance, precept, proclamation, regulation, request, rule, statute, stipulation, subpoena, summons, ultimatum, writ **4.** affiliation, alliance, association, church, club, community, company, denomination, faction, league, organization, sect, society, sodality, union

order *v.* **1.** book, buy, commission, engage, purchase, request, requisition, reserve, select, stipulate **2.** alphabetize, arrange, array, assign, assort, catalog, categorize, class, classify, codify, dispose, distribute, file, formalize, group, index, lay out, methodize, neaten, normalize, organize, pattern, place, regularize, regulate, set guidelines, set in order, set up, sort out, standardize, systematize, tabulate **3.** adjure, authorize, call for, charge, command, compel, decree, demand, dictate, direct, enjoin, instruct, mandate, ordain, prescribe, regulate, request, require, rule, stipulate, tell

orderly *adj.* arranged, businesslike, careful, conventional, correct, exact, formal, harmonious, methodical, meticulous, neat, organized, precise, regular, scientific, symmetrical, systematic, systematized, tidy, trim, uncluttered, uniform, well-arranged, well-balanced, well-designed, well-groomed

ordinance *n.* act, authorization, bill, canon, code, command, declaration, decree, dictum, edict, fiat, injunction, law, legislative enactment, local law, mandate, measure, order, precept, prescript, regulation, rule, ruling, statute

ordinary *adj.* **1.** accustomed, average, common, conventional, current, customary, established, everyday, familiar, general, habitual, natural, popular, prevailing, prevalent, regular, routine, standard, stock, traditional, typical, usual **2.** common, commonplace, domestic, dull, fair, homespun, inferior, informal, mediocre, middle-class, modest, pedestrian, plain, simple, stereotyped, undistinguished, unexceptional, unimpressive, uninspired, unpretentious, unremarkable

organ *n.* **1.** forum, journal, magazine, newspaper, paper, periodical, publication, review **2.** agency, agent, channel, component, constituent, device, element, factor, implement, ingredient, instrument, means, medium, member, part, process, structure, tool, unit, vehicle, way

organization *n.* **1.** alliance, association, bloc, business, cartel, club, coalition, combination, combine, company, concern, confederation, conglomerate, consolidation, consortium, cooperative, corporation, establishment, federation, guild, institute, institution, league, order, partnership, party, society, syndicate, trust, union **2.** arrangement, array, assembly, assortment, chemistry, classification, composition, configuration, conformation, constitution, construction, coordination, design, disposal, form, format, formation, formulation, framework, grouping, harmony, make-up, methodology, order, ordering, pattern, plan, selection, standardization, structure, symmetry, system, unity

organize *v.* adjust, arrange, array, assort, catalog, categorize, classify, codify, construct, coordinate, correlate, create, develop, devise, dispose, establish, file, form, formulate, frame, group, harmonize, line up, make up, marshal, methodize, mold, order, put in order, put together, regulate, set up, shape, sort out, standardize, straighten out, systematize, unify

orient *v.* acclimate, acclimatize, adapt, adjust, break in, condition, direct, familiarize, locate, orientate, season, settle, situate, train

orientation *n.* acclimation, acclimatization, adaptation, adjustment, assimilation, breaking in, briefing, coordination, direction, familiarization, initial directions, initial instructions, initiation, introduction, location, orientating, placement, preparation, program for newcomers, receiving, setting up, training, welcoming

origin *n.* **1.** alpha, ancestry, antecedent, beginning, birth, commencement, conception, creation, dawn, dawning, descent, emergence, entry, extraction, foundation, genesis, germ, germination, heritage, inception, lineage, nativity, origination, outset, pedigree, seed, start, stock **2.** agent, base, basis, cause, derivation, determinant, fountainhead, generator, inception, inducement, inspiration, motive, occasion, producer, progenitor, provenance, root, source, wellspring

original *n.* archetype, creation, exemplar, first, forerunner, invention, model, paradigm, pattern, precedent, precursor, primary, prototype, type

originality *n.* creativeness, creativity, freshness, imagination, imaginativeness, individuality, ingeniousness, ingenuity, innovativeness, inventiveness, new idea, newness, nonconformity, novelty, resourcefulness, unconventionality, unorthodoxy

originate *v.* **1.** bring about, cause, compose, conceive, create, develop, evolve, form, formulate, generate, inaugurate, initiate, innovate, institute, introduce, invent, launch, make, pioneer, procreate, produce, set in motion, set up, start, think up, usher in **2.** arise, begin, come from, commence, dawn, derive, emanate, emerge, flow, germinate, grow, issue, proceed, result, rise, root, spring, start, stem

orthodox *adj.* accepted, accustomed, acknowledged, admitted, approved, authoritative, conformist, conservative, conventional, correct, customary, doctrinal, established, faithful, fixed, fundamentalist, official, prevailing, proper, recognized, regular, right, sanctioned, set, sound, standard, traditional, traditionalist, true, usual, well-established

outcome *n.* aftereffect, aftermath, conclusion, consequence, development, effect, end, issue, outgrowth, product, reaction, result, sequel, yield

outdated *adj.* antiquated, antique, archaic, dated, extinct, obsolescent, obsolete, old, old-fashioned, outmoded, out-of-date, out-of-style, tired, unfashionable, vintage

outlay *n.* allowance, amount, charge, compensation, cost, damage, disbursement, expenditure, expense, expenses, fee, figure, investment, outgo, payment, price, rate, recompense, spending

outlet *n.* **1.** auction room, bazaar, chain store, concession, cooperative, department store, distribution center, emporium, factory store, farmers' market, flea market, mall, market, marketplace, mart, mill store, open market, plaza, retail market, salesroom, shopping center, store, street market, trading post, wholesale market **2.** aperture, avenue, channel, conduit, door, drain, duct, egress, escape, exit, fire door, gate, hole, nozzle, opening, orifice, passageway, safety valve, spout, trench, vent, way

outline *n.* blueprint, diagram, draft, framework, layout, list, main features, plan, rough draft, skeleton, sketch, summary, synopsis

outline *v.* draft, frame, highlight, lay out, list, list main features, plan, rough out, sketch, summarize, synopsize

outlook *n.* **1.** anticipation, assumption, calculation, chance, expectancy, expectation, forecast, hope, likelihood, opportunity, possibility, probability, probable future, promise, prospect, prospects, risk **2.** attitude, disposition, frame of mind, mood, perspective, point of view, position, standpoint, view, viewpoint, vision

outmoded *adj.* See **outdated**

out-of-date *adj.* See **outdated**

output *n.* accomplishment, achievement, amount, crop, data, display, document, end product, final product, harvest, information, manufacture, manufacturing, printout, produce, product, production, productivity, readout, result, signals, turnout, yield

outright *adj.* absolute, all, all-out, categorical, clear, complete, definite, direct, downright, entire, flat, full, incontestable, manifest, straightforward, thorough, thoroughgoing, total, unconditional, undeniable, unequivocal, unmitigated, unqualified, wholesale

outstanding *adj.* **1.** due, mature, overdue, owing, payable, pending, remaining, uncollected, undissolved, unpaid, unresolved, unsettled **2.** distinguished, eminent, excellent, exceptional, first-class, great, important, impressive, magnificent, major, meritorious, phenomenal, preeminent, special, superior, superlative **3.** arresting, bold, conspicuous, extruding, eye-catching, leading, marked, notable, noteworthy, noticeable, overhanging, projecting, prominent, pronounced, remarkable, salient, striking, unmistakable

overcharge *v.*   charge excess, charge excessive price, charge too much, exaggerate, make excessive charge, overdraw, overfill, overload, overstate

overdraft *n.*   amount overdrawn, loan, maximum credit, negative balance, overdrawing

overdue *adj.*   behind-schedule, belated, delinquent, due, late, long-delayed, mature, outstanding, owing, past-due, payable, tardy, unpaid, unsettled

overflow *v.*   be congested, be inundated, discharge, exceed capacity, exceed limits, flood, flow over, overburden, run over, spill over, spread over, surge, swell

overhaul *v.*   check over, debug, examine, fix, improve, inspect, mend, modernize, patch up, rebuild, recondition, reconstruct, redo, renew, renovate, repair, restore, revamp, service

overhead *n.*   burden, cost, costs, disbursement, expenses, indirect costs, indirect expenses, operating costs, outlay

overload *v.*   burden, encumber, be in excess, be overweight, exceed capacity, exceed limits, overburden, overcharge, overtax, saturate, strain, weigh down

overlook *v.*   **1.** fail to notice, forget, ignore, leave out, leave undone, miss, neglect, omit, pass by, pass up, skip, slight **2.** condone, disregard, excuse, extenuate, forget about, forgive, gloss over, go along with, ignore, let go, make allowances for, pardon **3.** front on, have view of, look down on, look out, look out on, look over, oversee, soar above, surmount, top, tower over, watch over **4.** See **oversee**

overproduce *v.*   See **overrun**

overrate *v.*   assess too highly, build up, exaggerate worth, exceed, expect too much of, magnify importance of, overassess, overestimate, overpraise, overprize, oversell, overvalue, rate too highly

overrun *v.*   exceed, extend past, go beyond, overextend, overproduce, overreach, produce excess, produce excessively, produce in excess, produce more, run beyond, run over, surmount, surpass, transcend

oversee *v.*   administer, be in command, be in control, boss, carry out, command, conduct, control, direct, govern, guide, handle, have control over, lead, look after, manage, navigate, operate, pilot, preside over, regulate, rule, run, superintend, supervise, take charge, watch over

oversight *n.* **1.** blunder, carelessness, default, delinquency, dereliction, disregard, error, failure, fault, forgetfulness, heedlessness, inattention, lapse, laxity, mistake, neglect, negligence, nonperformance, omission, slight, thoughtlessness **2.** administration, auspices, care, charge, command, control, custody, guardianship, jurisdiction, keeping, maintenance, management, ministry, protection, stewardship, superintendence, supervision, surveillance, tutelage, watchful care

overt *adj.* apparent, clear, conspicuous, definite, explicit, exposed, manifest, observable, obvious, open, patent, plain, prominent, public, unconcealed, undisguised, unhidden, unmistakable, unobscured, unveiled, visible

overtime *n.* additional hours, additional working hours, extra, extra working hours, payment for additional hours, time beyond normal, wage for additional hours

overvalue *v.* See **overrate**

owe *v.* be in arrears, be in debt to, be indebted to, be obligated to, be under obligation to, have a loan from, have debts, have obligation, have unpaid bills

owner *n.* buyer, entrepreneur, heir, holder, keeper, landlady, landlord, landowner, partner, property holder, proprietor, purchaser, shareholder, stockholder, titleholder

ownership *n.* buying, claim, dominion, holding, occupancy, partnership, property holding, proprietary rights, proprietorship, purchase, purchasing, title, use

P

package *n.* bag, batch, box, bundle, carton, case, collection of related items, collection of software, combination, container, crate, deal, direct-mail piece, pack, packet, parcel, preassembled unit, program, set of items, special deal, travel arrangement, unit, wrapper

pamphlet *n.* booklet, brochure, bulletin, circular, folder, handout, leaflet, monograph, program, tract, treatise

panic *n.* **1.** crash, depression, economic disaster, slump, sudden decline **2.** alarm, confusion, consternation, dread, extreme fright, fear, frenzy, fright, horror, hysteria, scare, terror, trepidation

paper *n.* **1.** bond, cardboard, card stock, cover stock, gift wrapping, letterhead, manila, newsprint, note, note card, note pad, papyrus, parchment, poster, rag, stationery, tissue, vellum, wrapper **2.** bulletin, circular, house organ, newsletter, newspaper, publication **3.** bill, certificate, document, file, instrument, legal document, legal paper, official paper, order, record, writings **4.** article, commentary, composition, critique, discourse, discussion, dissertation, essay, exposition, manuscript, monograph, report, script, study, theme, thesis, treatise, white paper

par *n.* average, balance, coequality, constant, equality, equilibrium, equivalence, established value, face amount, face value, mean, median, nominal value, norm, normal, parity, rule, sameness, standard, usual

paradigm *n.* archetype, criterion, design, example, exemplar, ideal, model, original, pattern, prototype, sample, specimen, standard

paragon *n.* archetype, best example, champion, epitome, essence, example, exemplar, good example, ideal, masterpiece, model, outstanding example, paradigm, pattern, perfection, prototype, quintessence, standard, ultimate example

parallel *n.* analog, analogy, complement, correlation, correspondence, correspondent, counterpart, duplication, equivalent, likeness, match, parallelism, resemblance, similarity

parameter *n.* boundary, criterion, framework, guideline, limit, limitation, measure, option, restriction, specifications, value, variable

parity *n.* affinity, agreement, analogy, approximation, balance, closeness, coequality, comparison, conformity, congruence, congruity, consistency, correspondence, equality, equal terms, equilibrium, equivalence, equivalency, evenness, levelness, likeness, odd or even number, par, parallelism, resemblance, sameness, semblance, similarity, uniformity, unity

parochial *adj.* biased, bigoted, confined, conservative, constricted, illiberal, insular, intolerant, limited, local, narrow, narrow-minded, petty, prejudiced, provincial, regional, restricted, shortsighted, small-minded, small-town, unsophisticated, unsympathetic

participant *n.* associate, colleague, contributor, helper, member, partaker, participator, partner, player, shareholder, sharer

participate *v.* be participant, be part of, be party to, compete, contribute, cooperate, engage in, enter into, help, join in, partake in, play, share in, take part in

partition *n.* allocation, allotment, apportionment, barrier, compartment, detachment, disk storage area, divider, dividing line, dividing wall, division, judicial separation, part, parting, section, separation, separating device, separator, splitting, storage area, subdivision, subsection

partner *n.* accomplice, aide, ally, assistant, associate, cohort, collaborator, colleague, comrade, confederate, consort, contributor, coworker, friend, helper, participant, principal, teammate

partnership *n.* affiliation, alliance, association, business, business arrangement, cartel, collaboration, combination, combine, company, conglomerate, connection, cooperation, co-ownership, firm, friendship, interest, joining, organization, participation, sharing, union

party *n.* **1.** company, defendant, entity, group, individual, litigant, member, participant, person, plaintiff, signatory **2.** entertainment, festive event, festive occasion, festivities, gathering, social event, social gathering

passage *n.* **1.** citation, clause, excerpt, extract, line, paragraph, part, phrase, piece, portion, quotation, reading, section, selection, sentence, text, transition, verse **2.** acceptance, adoption, allowance, approval, authorization, enactment, endorsement, establishment, legalization, legislation, permission, ratification, right, validation, warrant **3.** change, conversion, crossing, journey, motion, movement, passing, progress, tour, transit, transition, transportation, travel, traverse, trek, trip, voyage   **4.** aperture, avenue, canal, channel, conduit, corridor, course, entrance, exit, hall, lobby, opening, pathway, road, route, shaft, thoroughfare, track, trail, tunnel

password *n.*   access code, entry code, identification, key, keyword, secret character string, secret identification, security code, special word, watchword

path *n.*   **1.** command sequence, file hierarchy, hierarchy of files, link, link between points, list, list of directories, programming route, programming track, sequence of commands   **2.** course, passageway, pathway, revolution, track, trajectory, way of life

patron *n.*   **1.** buyer, client, customer, frequenter, prospect, purchaser, regular, shopper, subscriber   **2.** advocate, backer, benefactor, booster, champion, encourager, friend, guarantor, guardian, helper, partisan, philanthropist, promoter, sponsor, supporter, sympathizer, well-wisher

patronage *n.*   **1.** business, buying, clientele, commerce, custom, shopping, trade, trading, traffic   **2.** advocacy, aid, assistance, auspices, backing, championship, encouragement, financing, guardianship, help, promotion, protection, sponsorship, subsidy, support, sympathy

patronize *v.*   **1.** be a client, be a customer, buy, buy from, deal with, do business at, do business with, frequent, give business to, purchase from, shop at, trade with   **2.** advocate, assist, back, champion, defend, espouse, finance, foster, fund, help, maintain, promote, protect, sponsor, subscribe to, support, sustain, sympathize with, uphold   **3.** be lofty, condescend, deign, humor, indulge, look down on, talk down to, treat as inferior, treat condescendingly

pattern *n.*   **1.** archetype, copy, criterion, example, exemplar, guide, ideal, mirror, model, original, paradigm, paragon, prototype, sample, specimen, standard, template   **2.** cast, arrangement, classification, form, format, kind, method, order, orderliness, plan, shape, sort, style, system, type, variety   **3.** decoration, design, device, engraving, etching, figure, impression, marking, motif, ornamentation, patterning

pause *n.*   abeyance, break, cessation, deadlock, delay, discontinuance, gap, halt, hesitancy, hesitation, hiatus, interim, interlude, intermission, interruption, lapse, lull, recess, respite, rest, rest period, standstill, stay, stop, stoppage, suspension, temporary stop, wait

pay *n.* commission, compensation, consideration, earnings, fee, honorarium, income, payment, perquisites, proceeds, profit, reimbursement, remuneration, salary, settlement, stipend, wages

pay *v.* **1.** advance, clear, compensate, contribute, disburse, discharge, expend, extend, give, honor, indemnify, liquidate, make payment, meet, prepay, recompense, refund, reimburse, remit, remunerate, render, repay, reward, satisfy, settle, spend **2.** benefit, be profitable, be worthwhile, bring in, make money, pay dividends, produce, produce return, profit, provide living, return, serve, show gain, show profit, yield, yield profit **3.** answer for, atone, avenge oneself, be punished, compensate, make amends, make up for, pay back, punish, reap consequences, reciprocate, recompense, repay, requite, retaliate, settle, suffer, suffer consequences

payable *adj.* due, mature, outstanding, overdue, owed, past-due, receivable, unpaid, unsettled

payment *n.* advance, alimony, annuity, award, cash, compensation, contribution, damages, defrayal, deposit, disbursement, discharge, earnest money, earnings, expenditure, fee, fulfillment, grant, gratuity, honorarium, indemnification, indemnity, installment, liquidation, maintenance, money, outlay, pay, pension, premium, rebate, refund, reimbursement, remittance, remuneration, repayment, restitution, retainer, reward, salary, satisfaction, settlement, stipend, subsidy, support wage

payoff *n.* **1.** discharge, final payment, fulfillment, judgment, liquidation, payment, reimbursement, settlement **2.** climax, conclusion, consequence, culmination, finale, outcome, result, retribution

payroll *n.* aggregate labor costs, amount due, amount paid, employees, labor, labor costs, list of employees and compensation, money to be distributed, record of compensation, roster of employees and compensation, sum for distribution

pedantic *adj.* conceited, didactic, doctrinaire, egotistical, formal, fussy, haughty, narrow, ostentatious, pedagogic, pedestrian, pompous, precise, pretentious, scholastic, unimaginative

peer *n.* coequal, counterpart, equal, equivalent, match, rival

penalize *v.* castigate, chasten, chastise, correct, discipline, encumber, fine, handicap, impair, impose fine, impose penalty, inflict penalty on, judge, pass sentence on, punish, sentence

penalty *n.* amends, corrective action, cost, damages, discipline, fine, forfeiture, handicap, loss, payment, price, punishment, punitive action, retribution, sentence

pending *adj.* forthcoming, imminent, impending, indefinite, indeterminate, inescapable, inevitable, undecided, undetermined, unfinished, unresolved, unsettled

people *n.* citizens, common people, community, constituency, general public, human beings, humanity, humankind, human race, humans, individuals, inhabitants, masses, mortals, multitude, persons, populace, population, proletariat, public, residents, voters

percentage *n.* allotment, allowance, commission, discount, duty, fee, interest, percent, portion, proportion, quota, rate, ratio

perception *n.* appreciation, awareness, cognition, comprehension, concept, conception, discernment, feeling, grasp, image, impression, insight, mental image, notion, observation, perspicacity, realization, recognition, sagacity, sensation, sense, understanding, view, viewpoint

perceptive *adj.* alert, astute, aware, cognizant, conscious, discerning, discriminating, incisive, insightful, intuitive, knowing, observant, open, penetrating, perspicacious, responsive, sagacious, sensitive, understanding

perfect *adj.* **1.** accurate, certain, correct, definite, exact, faithful, precise, proper, required, requisite, right, strict, suitable, true, unerring **2.** classical, consummate, excellent, exemplary, faultless, ideal, immaculate, impeccable, incomparable, inimitable, matchless, peerless, pure, splendid, superb, superlative, supreme, unequaled **3.** complete, consummate, entire, flawless, full, intact, spotless, stainless, unadulterated, unalloyed, unblemished, unbroken, undamaged, unimpaired, unmarred, untainted, untarnished

perfection *n.* achievement, completeness, completion, consummation, correctness, entirety, exactness, excellence, exquisiteness, faultlessness, fulfillment, ideal, impeccability, paragon, perfectness, precision, purity, quality, realization, rightness, sublimity, superiority, supremacy, transcendence, wholeness

perform *v.* accomplish, achieve, act, bring about, carry out, carry through, complete, conduct, discharge, do, effect, execute, fulfill, function, implement, meet, operate, take on, transact, work

performance *n.* accomplishment, achievement, action, attainment, completion, conduct, consummation, deed, discharge, doing, effectiveness, execution, exercise, exploit, feat, fulfillment, functioning, level of capability, operation, practice, pursuit, realization, work, working

peril *n.* danger, endangerment, exposure, hazard, insecurity, jeopardy, liability, menace, openness, risk, susceptibility, uncertainty, vulnerability

period *n.* aeon, age, days, duration, eon, epoch, era, generation, interval, season, space, span, spell, stage, stretch, term, time, years

periodic *adj.* alternate, alternating, annual, biennial, bimonthly, centennial, cyclic, cyclical, daily, diurnal, hourly, infrequent, intermittent, isochronal, isochronous, monthly, occasional, perennial, periodical, recurrent, recurring, regular, remittent, repeating, rhythmic, seasonal, semiannual, semimonthly, semiweekly, spasmodic, weekly, yearly

peripheral *n.* add-on, auxiliary equipment, connected device, dependent device, external device, supplementary device, supplementary equipment

peripheral *adj.* borderline, encircling, exterior, external, incidental, marginal, minor, outer, outside, secondary, superficial, surrounding, unessential, unimportant

permanent *adj.* abiding, changeless, constant, continual, durable, endless, enduring, eternal, everlasting, fixed, imperishable, indestructible, lasting, long-lasting, perennial, perpetual, persistent, stable, steadfast, unchanging, unending

permission *n.* acquiescence, admission, agreement, allowance, approval, assent, authorization, concession, concurrence, consent, dispensation, empowerment, endorsement, franchise, indulgence, leave, liberty, license, permit, privilege, sanction, sufferance, tolerance, toleration, warrant

permit *n.* admittance, allowance, authority, authorization, charter, concession, consent, edict, entitlement, franchise, leave, legalization, license, permission, sanction, warrant

permit *v.* accede to, accept, acquiesce in, agree to, allow, assent to, authorize, commission, condone, consent to, empower, enable, endorse, endure, entitle, franchise, give permission, grant, indulge, let, license, sanction, say yes, suffer, tolerate, warrant, yield

perquisite *n.* advantage, benefit, bonus, compensation, extra, fringe benefit, gain, gift, gratuity, privilege, profit, reward, tip

perseverance *n.* constancy, continuance, dedication, determination, diligence, drive, endurance, indefatigability, patience, persistence, pertinacity, purposefulness, pursuance, resolve, stamina, steadfastness, tenacity

persevere *v.* be determined, be resolute, be resolved, be steadfast, be tenacious, be unyielding, continue, endure, keep at, keep going, keep on, labor, maintain, persist, press on, pursue, pursue relentlessly, strive, struggle, sustain, work hard

persistent *adj.* ambitious, assiduous, constant, continual, continuous, diligent, enduring, firm, fixed, immovable, incessant, indefatigable, industrious, insistent, obdurate, obstinate, perpetual, persevering, persisting, pertinacious, relentless, resolute, sedulous, steadfast, tenacious, tireless, undistracted, unflagging, unrelenting, unshakable, untiring, zealous

personnel *n.* crew, employees, help, human resources, laborers, labor force, members, office staff, staff, workers, work force

perspective *n.* angle, aspect, attitude, frame of mind, horizon, landscape, mental outlook, outlook, overview, panorama, picture, point of view, position, prospect, scene, sentiment, stand, standpoint, view, viewpoint, vista, way of looking

persuade *v.* affect, allure, assure, bend, cajole, cause, coax, compel, convert, convince, enlist, entice, exhort, impel, incite, incline, induce, influence, inspire, inveigle, lead to believe, lead to do, lure, motivate, move, prevail on, prompt, rouse, satisfy, seduce, sell, stimulate, sway, talk into, tempt, urge, win over

persuasion *n.* **1.** alluring, cajolery, coercion, conversion, enlistment, enticement, exhortation, force, inducement, inveiglement, persuasiveness, potency, power, promotion, seduction, temptation, winning over **2.** belief, church, connection, conviction, credo, creed, cult, denomination, faith, opinion, religion, school, sect, tenet, view

persuasive *adj.* alluring, authoritative, cogent, compelling, conclusive, convincing, effective, effectual, efficacious, enticing, exhortative, forceful, impelling, impressive, inducing, influential, inveigling, luring, plausible, powerful, seductive, stimulating, strong, swaying, telling, valid, weighty, winning

pertinent *adj.* applicable, apposite, appropriate, apropos, apt, correct, fit, fitting, germane, proper, related, relevant, right, seemly, suitable, suited, well-suited

petition *n.* address, adjuration, appeal, application, entreaty, formal request, invocation, plea, prayer, request, solicitation, suit, supplication, written application, written request

petition *v.* address, adjure, appeal, apply to, beg for, bid, call, entreat, implore, plead, plead for, pray for, request, seek, solicit, sue, supplicate

phase *n.* appearance, aspect, chapter, condition, development, facet, juncture, moment, occasion, part, period, point, portion, position, posture, stage, state, step, time

philanthropic *adj.* altruistic, beneficent, benevolent, bountiful, charitable, eleemosynary, generous, giving, gracious, helpful, humane, humanitarian, kind, kindhearted, liberal, magnanimous, munificent, openhanded, philanthropical, public-spirited, unselfish

philosophy *n.* aesthetics, attitude, beliefs, conception, convictions, doctrine, idea, ideology, logic, moral code, opinion, outlook, point of view, principles, rationalism, reason, reasoning, school of thought, study of truth, tenet, theory, thinking, thought, truth, values, view, viewpoint

phonetic *adj.* articulated, enunciated, intonated, oral, pronounced, spoken, sounded, unwritten, verbal, vocal, vocalized, voiced

photocopy *n.* copy, duplicate, image, photographic reproduction, reproduction

picket *v.* demonstrate, demonstrate against, demonstrate for, dissent, protest, rebel, sit down, sit in, strike, strike against, strike for, walk out, walk picket line

picture *n.* **1.** artwork, copy, depiction, description, drawing, duplicate, engraving, etching, facsimile, figure, icon, illustration, image, likeness, line drawing, oil painting, painting, pastel, photograph, portrait, portrayal, print, replica, report, representation, reproduction, semblance, similitude, sketch, watercolor **2.** archetype, embodiment, epitome, essence, incarnation, model, perfect example, personification, prototype, typification

piece *n.* **1.** allotment, bit, chunk, component, division, dole, fraction, fragment, ingredient, item, lot, lump, morsel, parcel, part, particle, percentage, portion, quota, remnant, sample, scrap, section, segment, share, shred, slice, specimen

2. arrangement, artistic production, art object, composition, creation, dissertation, engraving, exposition, music, painting, paper, photograph, print, production, song, statue, thesis, treatise, work of art, writing

pinpoint *v.* aim, define, determine, diagnose, distinguish, fix, highlight, identify, locate, place, recognize, spot

pioneer *n.* antecedent, developer, explorer, forerunner, founder, groundbreaker, guide, immigrant, innovator, leader, pacesetter, pathfinder, precursor, predecessor, settler, trailblazer, trailbreaker, trendsetter

pioneer *v.* begin, create, develop, discover, establish, explore, found, guide, inaugurate, initiate, instigate, institute, invent, launch, lay groundwork, lead, lead the way, make start, open up, originate, set in motion, set up, start, take initiative, take the lead

pitfall *n.* danger, difficulty, drawback, entanglement, hazard, peril, risk, snare, trap, web

pivotal *adj.* basic, cardinal, central, chief, critical, crucial, decisive, essential, focal, fundamental, main, momentous, overriding, paramount, primary, prime, principal, significant, supreme, underlying, urgent, very important, vital

place *n.* **1.** accommodations, area, city, community, corner, country, district, division, habitat, housing, latitude, locale, locality, location, neighborhood, point, property, province, quarter, realm, region, scene, section, sector, setting, site, spot, station, territory, town, venue, vicinity, zone **2.** appointment, capacity, charge, concern, duty, employment, function, grade, job, occupation, office, position, post, profession, rank, responsibility, role, situation, standing, station, status

placement *n.* **1.** appointment, assignment, commission, deputation, employment, engagement, hiring, installment **2.** arrangement, classification, deployment, disposition, grouping, locating, positioning, ranking, sorting, stationing

plan *n.* **1.** aim, angle, arrangement, aspiration, course, disposition, gimmick, idea, intent, intention, means, method, plot, policy, procedure, program, project, proposal, proposition, purpose, scenario, scheme, strategy, suggestion, system, tactics, treatment, trick, undertaking, view, way **2.** agenda, blueprint, chart, delineation, design, diagram, draft, drawing, form, illustration, layout, map, mockup, model, outline, pattern, projection, prospectus, representation, scale drawing, sketch, written description

plan *v.* aim for, arrange, calculate, concoct, contrive, design, develop, devise, draft, fabricate, fashion, figure out, form, formulate, frame, intend, invent, make arrangements, make ready, map, mold, organize, outline, plot, prepare, prepare for, project, propose, represent, schedule, scheme, shape, sketch, think out, work out

plant *n.* buildings and equipment, factory, foundry, industrial site, laboratory, metalworks, mill, shop, works, workshop

platform *n.* **1.** basic standard, computer hardware, computer standard, major software, software library **2.** campaign promises, creed, declaration of principles, line, party declaration, party policies, party principles, plan, plank, policies, position, principles, program

plea *n.* **1.** alibi, apology, argument, defense, excuse, explanation, extenuation, justification, palliation, pleading, pretext, reason, vindication **2.** appeal, begging, entreaty, imploring, overture, petition, prayer, request, solicitation, suit, supplication

pledge *n.* **1.** bail, bond, collateral, delivery of goods, deposit, earnest money, security, surety **2.** agreement, assurance, attestation, covenant, endorsement, guarantee, oath, promise, sworn statement, vow, warrant, warranty, word, word of honor

plot *v.* **1.** blueprint, chart, depict, diagram, draw, draw in, draw to scale, graph, lay out, map, map out, mark, outline, represent **2.** concoct, conspire, contrive, devise, dream up, fabricate, fashion, formulate, machinate, make plans, mold, plan secretly, scheme, shape, think up

point *n.* **1.** aim, argument, attribute, characteristic, component, detail, essence, facet, feature, gist, goal, idea, import, intent, main idea, meaning, motive, nub, object, objective, pith, property, proposition, question, significance, subject, theme, thrust, topic, trait **2.** circumstance, condition, date, degree, duration, extent, instant, juncture, limit, limited time, locality, location, moment, period, place, position, site, situation, spot, stage, threshold, time

pointer *n.* **1.** admonition, advice, caution, hint, motto, recommendation, rule, suggestion, tenet, tip, useful information, warning, wise saying **2.** connection, cursor, device, indicator, input device, on-screen symbol, pointing device

point out *v.* allude to, bring up, call attention to, denote, designate, explain, identify, illustrate, indicate, mention, refer to, show, specify, tell about

policy *n.* approach, behavior, code, contract, course, custom, design, guidelines, insurance contract, management style, method, plan, practices, procedure, program, rule, scheme, strategy, system, tactics, way of managing, written agreement

polish *v.* **1.** better, correct, cultivate, enhance, finish, improve, make better, make improvements, mend, perfect, refine, smooth out, style, touch up **2.** brighten, buff, burnish, clean, rub, rub down, scour, shine, smooth, wax

polite *adj.* affable, amiable, attentive, civil, civilized, conciliatory, considerate, cordial, courteous, cultured, deferential, diplomatic, genial, gracious, mannerly, obliging, pleasant, polished, politic, refined, respectful, sociable, thoughtful, urbane, well-behaved, well-bred, well-mannered

popular *adj.* **1.** accepted, accustomed, approved, catholic, common, commonplace, conventional, current, customary, demanded, everyday, extensive, familiar, general, normal, ordinary, predominant, prevailing, prevalent, public, rampant, routine, secular, standard, stock, universal, usual, vernacular, well-known, widespread, working-class **2.** attractive, celebrated, desired, famous, fashionable, favored, favorite, leading, likable, liked, lovable, noted, pleasing, preferred, sought-after, stylish, trendy, wanted, well-liked, well-received

population *n.* citizenry, citizens, community, dweller, inhabitants, natives, people, populace, public, residents, society

portable *adj.* conveyable, movable, portative, transferable, transmittable, transportable, unattached, unfixed

portfolio *n.* **1.** account, bonds, combined holdings, debentures, group of securities, investments, shares, stocks, total investments **2.** attache case, bag, briefcase, case, container, envelope, folder, notebook, valise **3.** credentials, documents, dossier, papers

position *n.* **1.** activity, appointment, assignment, business, capacity, commission, duty, employment, function, job, livelihood, occupation, office, place, profession, responsibility, role, situation **2.** caste, class, degree, footing, grade, importance, level, place, rank, situation, standing, station, stature, status **3.** attitude, circumstances, condition, deportment, financial condition, manner, predicament, situation, stance, state, status **4.** bearings, fix, latitude and longitude, locale, location, place, point, seat, site, situation, spot, station

possession *n.* care, control, custody, dominion, habitation, having property, holding property, interest, occupancy, occupation, ownership, proprietary rights, proprietorship, residence, retention, tenancy, tenure, title, vested interest

possessions *n.* accessories, assets, belongings, chattel, effects, equipment, fixtures, furnishings, goods, holdings, inventories, personal effects, properties, property, real estate, real property, resources, tangibles, things, worldly goods

possibility *n.* chance, conceivability, contingency, feasibility, hazard, liability, likelihood, opportunity, plausibility, potentiality, practicability, probability, prospect, risk, workability

post *v.* advertise, affix, announce, assign, carry to, display, enter, establish, exhibit, give notice, give public notice, list, locate, log, make transfer entries, place, position, publish, summarize, transfer, transfer entries

postpone *v.* defer, delay, dispense with, hold in abeyance, hold off, put aside, put off, shelve, suspend, table, wait, waive

potential *n.* ability, aptitude, capability, capacity, endowment, gift, likelihood, possibility, potentiality, power, probability, promise, prospect, talent

potential *adj.* conceivable, dormant, hidden, imaginable, latent, likely, passive, possible, probable, prospective, quiescent, unapparent, undeveloped, unrealized

poverty *n.* barrenness, dearth, debt, deficiency, depletion, destitution, distress, extreme need, financial exhaustion, hardship, impoverishment, inadequacy, indigence, insolvency, insufficiency, lack, meagerness, narrow circumstances, neediness, paucity, pauperism, penury, privation, scarcity, shortage, starvation, straits, want

power *n.* **1.** ascendancy, authority, clout, command, control, dominance, domination, dominion, hegemony, influence, license, might, omnipotence, predominance, primacy, rule, sovereignty, strength, superiority, supremacy, sway, unconditional authority, weight **2.** ability, aptitude, bent, capability, capacity, competence, competency, effectiveness, efficacy, faculty, forcefulness, genius, influence, potential, potentiality, powerfulness, skill, talent, turn

powerful *adj.* all-powerful, authoritarian, authoritative, cogent, commanding, compelling, controlling, dominant, dominating, effective, effectual, efficacious, forceful, forcible, incontestable, influential, invincible, mighty, omnipotent, paramount, persuasive, potent, prevailing, ruling, strong, unyielding

practical *adj.* **1.** businesslike, commonsensical, constructive, down-to-earth, effective, efficient, feasible, functional, handy, operative, practicable, pragmatic, rational, realistic, reasonable, sensible, serviceable, sound, unsentimental, usable, useful, utilitarian, workable   **2.** able, accomplished, capable, competent, effective, efficient, experienced, practiced, proficient, qualified, skilled, skillful, trained, versed

practice *n.* **1.** common procedure, convention, custom, fashion, habit, manner, manner of operation, method, method of operation, mode of operation, procedure, routine, rule, rules, tradition, usage, use, usual procedure, way   **2.** action, application, assignment, discipline, drill, exercise, experience, operation, performance, preparation, rehearsal, repetition, study, training, warm-up, workout   **3.** business, clientele, clients, conduct, patients, patronage, profession, pursuit, trade, vocation, work

practice *v.* **1.** carry on, engage in, follow, function, observe, perform, pursue, put into effect, specialize in, work at   **2.** do again, do regularly, drill, exercise, go over, polish, prepare, rehearse, repeat, study, train, warm up, work out

precaution *n.* anticipation, apprehension, attentiveness, care, carefulness, caution, discretion, foresight, forethought, insurance, preventive measure, provision, prudence, readiness, safeguard, safety measure, vigilance, wariness, watchfulness

precedent *n.* antecedent, authority, classic example, criterion, example, exemplar, measure, model, paradigm, pattern, previous case, prototype, rule, yardstick

precision *n.* accurateness, accuracy, care, carefulness, closeness, correctness, exactitude, exactness, fidelity, flawlessness, meticulousness, particularity, preciseness, rectitude, rightness, rigor, scrupulousness, strictness, thoroughness

prediction *n.* conjecture, forecast, forecasting, foretelling, guess, prognosis, prognostication, projection, prophecy, speculation, supposition, surmising

predominant *adj.* absolute, all-powerful, authoritative, chief, controlling, dominant, governing, leading, main, most important, official, overpowering, paramount, prevailing, prevalent, primary, prime, principal, prominent, ranking, reigning, ruling, sovereign, superior, supreme, transcendent, weighty

preeminent *adj.* chief, distinguished, dominant, foremost, incomparable, inimitable, leading, main, matchless, most important, most influential, outstanding, paramount, peerless, predominant, renowned, superior, supreme, towering, transcendent, unequaled, unmatched, unparalleled, unrivaled, unsurpassed

preface *n.* beginning, front matter, introduction, opening, opening remarks, opening statement, preliminaries, preliminary, prelude, prelusion

premise *n.* assertion, assumption, basis, conjecture, foundation, ground, hypothesis, inference, postulate, postulation, presupposition, proposition, supposition, surmise, thesis

premises *n.* building, buildings, campus, establishment, grounds, grounds and buildings, land, office, place, plant, property, site

premium *n.* award, benefit, bonus, cut, deduction, discount, excess, extra payment, fee, gift, incentive, inducement, insurance payment, payment, periodic payment, perquisite, price, price reduction, prize, promotional gift, rate, rebate, recompense, refund, reward, rollback

prepare *v.* arrange, assemble, brief, compose, concoct, construct, develop, devise, draw up, equip, fashion, fix up, form, formulate, furnish, get ready, groom, invent, lay groundwork, make, make preparations for, make provisions for, make ready, make up, order, outfit, practice, prime, produce, provide, put in order, put together, ready, rehearse, set up, supply, take steps, teach, train, turn out

prescribe *v.* advocate, appoint, authorize, command, decree, define, designate, dictate, direct, enact, enjoin, establish, impose, institute, instruct, lay down, legislate, ordain, order, recommend, require, specify, stipulate, urge, write prescription

present *v.* **1.** award, bestow, confer, contribute, dispense, donate, endow, entrust, furnish, give, give away, grant, hand out, hand over, offer, proffer, put forth, turn over **2.** cite, declare, demonstrate, disclose, display, exhibit, expose, expound, give, give introduction, indicate, introduce, make a production, make introductions, make known, offer, open to view, perform, produce, put forward, put on, put on display, put on a show, relate, set forth, show, sponsor, stage, submit

presentation *n.* **1.** award, bequeathal, bestowal, conferral, contribution, dispensation, donation, endowment, gift, giving, giving away, grant, offering, present, proffering, putting forth, reward, turning over **2.** act, appearance, debut, delivery, demonstration, disclosure, display, enactment, exhibit, exhibition, exposition, introduction, launching, overture, performance, portrayal, production, proposal, proposition, reception, rendition, representation, show, submission, unveiling

preside over *v.*   administer, be in control, carry out, chair, command, conduct, conduct meeting, control, direct, govern, head, lead, manage, moderate, oversee, regulate, rule, run, superintend, supervise

prevent *v.*   abort, arrest, avert, avoid, balk, bar, block, check, constrain, counteract, deflect, delay, foil, forbid, forestall, frustrate, halt, hamper, hinder, hold back, hold off, impede, inhibit, intercept, interfere, interrupt, intervene, obstruct, obviate, preclude, prohibit, put an end to, put a stop to, repress, restrain, restrict, retard, stop, thwart, turn aside, veto, ward off

preview *n.*   advance showing, examination, on-screen viewing, preliminary showing, preliminary study, preprint viewing, previous view, private viewing

price *n.*   amount, appraisal, assessment, bill, charge, check, compensation, consideration, cost, damages, expenditure, expense, fare, fee, figure, financial value, money paid, pay, payment, rate, toll, valuation, value, worth

price *v.*   appraise, assess, determine price, estimate, evaluate, fix price, judge value, put price on, rate, set price

primary *adj.*   **1.** best, capital, cardinal, chief, dominant, leading, main, major, most important, paramount, prime, principal, stellar, top   **2.** aboriginal, beginning, earliest, first, initial, original, premier, primal, primeval, primitive, primordial, pristine   **3.** basal, basic, central, elemental, elementary, essential, fundamental, radical, rudimentary, underlying

prime *adj.*   See **primary**

principal *n.*   **1.** amount of debt, amount invested, assets, capital, capital funds, carrying value, cash reserves, face amount, face value, investments, noninterest balance, nonliquid funds, reserves, resources, savings   **2.** administrator, boss, captain, chief, contractor, dean, director, leader, major party, owner, ruler, superintendent, supervisor

principal *adj.*   cardinal, chief, controlling, crowning, dominant, essential, first, foremost, greatest, highest, key, leading, main, major, matchless, most important, paramount, peerless, predominant, preeminent, prevailing, primary, prime, sovereign, star, strongest, superior, supreme, unequaled, unparalleled

principle *n.* axiom, canon, criterion, doctrine, ethic, formula, fundamental, general standard, guideline, law, maxim, postulate, precept, proposition, rule, standard, tenet, theorem, truth

principles *n.* belief, code, conduct, conscience, ethical code, ethics, ideals, integrity, moral code, morality, morals, personal code, probity, scruples, sense of honor, standards, uprightness

procedure *n.* approach, computer program, computer subroutine, course, custom, fashion, formula, guidelines, line, maneuver, means, measure, method, mode, move, operation, plan, policy, practice, proceeding, routine, step, strategy, style, transaction

proceedings *n.* account, affairs, dealings, matters, minutes, record, records, report, transactions

proceeds *n.* benefits payable, earnings, funds given, income, money received, net amount, profits, receipts, returns, total amount

processing *n.* change, changing, examination, handling, manipulating, manipulation, preparation, preparing, prosecuting, prosecution, refining, treating, treatment, transformation, transforming

produce *v.* **1.** assemble, build, compose, construct, create, design, develop, devise, draw up, effectuate, engender, erect, fabricate, fashion, form, formulate, frame, generate, invent, make, manufacture, originate, propagate, provide, put together, render, reproduce, shape, supply, turn out, work out, work up, write, yield **2.** bring forth, bring forward, bring out, bring to light, demonstrate, display, exhibit, mount, offer, present, put forward, put on, set forth, show, stage, unfold

product *n.* artifact, by-product, commodity, consequence, creation, device, effect, end result, fabrication, goods, handiwork, invention, manufacture, merchandise, outcome, output, produce, production, result, work, yield

production *n.* **1.** assembly, building, composition, construction, creation, design, development, direction, drawing up, engendering, fabrication, fashioning, formation, formulation, framing, generation, invention, making, manufacture, manufacturing, origination, preparation, producing, propagation, provision, putting together, rendering, reproduction, shaping, turning out, working out, working up, writing, yielding **2.** bringing forth, bringing forward, bringing out, bringing to light, demonstration, display, exhibition, mounting, offering, presentation, putting forward, putting on, setting forth, unfolding

productivity *n.* capacity, creativeness, creativity, fertility, ingenuity, inventiveness, measure of production, production, productiveness

profession *n.* **1.** art, calling, career, chosen work, craft, employment, engagement, field, lifework, line of work, livelihood, occupation, office, position, post, professional activity, pursuit, service, situation, specialty, sphere, vocation, work **2.** acknowledgment, affirmation, assertion, attestation, avowal, confession, declaration, deposition, pledge, proclamation, statement, testimony, vow

professional *n.* adept person, businesslike person, competent person, conscientious person, expert, maven, proficient person, skilled person, specialist, trained person

professional *adj.* able, accomplished, adept, competent, conscientious, efficient, experienced, expert, knowledgeable, practiced, proficient, skilled, skillful, trained, well-qualified

profit *n.* **1.** See **profits** **2.** advancement, advantage, augmentation, avail, benefit, convenience, desirability, help, service, suitability, use, usefulness, value, worth

profit *v.* advance, avail oneself, benefit, be of advantage, better, capitalize on, contribute to, exploit, further, gain, gain advantage, help, improve, learn from, make good use of, make money, promote, prosper, realize from, serve, take advantage of, turn to advantage, use

profitable *adj.* advantageous, beneficial, conducive, contributive, convenient, cost-effective, desirable, favorable, fruitful, gainful, helpful, lucrative, money-making, paying, productive, remunerative, rewarding, serviceable, successful, useful, valuable, well-paying, worthwhile

profits *n.* earnings, excess, gain, income, income less expenses, interest, proceeds, receipts, remuneration, return, revenue, savings, surplus, winnings, yield

program *n.* **1.** agenda, arrangements, calendar, curriculum, docket, lineup, list, listing, list of instructions, order of the day, outline, plan, plans, preparations, protocol, schedule, series of events, set of instructions, syllabus, timetable **2.** broadcast, organized event, performance, play, presentation, production, radio show, show, telecast, television show

progress *n.* advance, advancement, betterment, breakthrough, development, evolution, forward movement, furtherance, gain, going forward, growth, headway, improvement, momentum, movement, movement forward, movement upward, process, progression, promotion, rise, stride, upgrading, upward movement

project *n.* activity, assignment, campaign, contract, deal, design, effort, engagement, enterprise, game, intention, job, operation, plan, program, proposal, proposition, scheme, strategy, task, undertaking, venture, work

project *v.* **1.** aim, arrange, calculate, chart, conceive, contemplate, contrive, design, devise, draft, estimate, extrapolate, figure, forecast, gauge, invent, map out, outline, plan, plan ahead, predetermine, predict, present, propose, put forth, scheme, set forth, shape course, take steps, visualize **2.** display, display image, display on screen, impart, put on, show, transfer, transfer image, transmit

promote *v.* **1.** advance, better, elevate, give better position, give raise, graduate, improve position, improve rank, improve standing, increase pay, move up, upgrade **2.** advertise, advocate, aid, assist, back, benefit, be of service to, boost, call attention to, champion, encourage, endorse, espouse, facilitate, foster, further, get behind, help, nourish, nurture, patronize, publicize, push, recommend, sponsor, support, work for

promotion *n.* **1.** advance, advancement, betterment, better position, elevation, graduation, higher position, improvement, improvement in position, improvement in rank, improvement in standing, moving up, pay increase, progress, raise, rise, step up, upgrade, upgrading **2.** advertisement, advertising campaign, advocacy, aid, assistance, backing, benefit, boost, buildup, encouragement, endorsement, espousal, fostering, furtherance, preference, propaganda, publicity, public relations, pushing, sponsorship, support, working for

propaganda *n.* advertisement, advertising, brainwashing, disinformation, doctrine, inculcation, indoctrination, information, promotion, promulgation, proselytizing, publicity

proper *adj.* **1.** applicable, appropriate, apt, befitting, desired, fit, fitting, just, legitimate, qualified, right, suitable, suited, useful **2.** accepted, accurate, conventional, correct, customary, established, exact, formal, normal, orthodox, precise, right, routine, usual **3.** becoming, decent, decorous, demure, fastidious, mannerly, moral, polite, refined, respectable, seemly, tasteful

property *n.* **1.** acreage, assets, belongings, buildings, capital, chattel, chose, effects, equity, estate, goods, grounds, holdings, investments, land, means, ownership, personal effects, personal property, personalty, plot, possession, possessions, premises, real estate, real property, realty, resources, things, worth **2.** attribute, character, characteristic, distinction, idiosyncrasy, mark, note, peculiarity, quality, trademark, trait

proponent *n.* adherent, advocate, backer, champion, defender, enthusiast, exponent, partisan, patron, promoter, propagandist, spokesperson, subscriber, supporter, sympathizer

proportion *n.*   allotment, comparative extent, comparative size, correlation, correspondence, distribution, division, extent, measure, part, percentage, portion, quota, ratio, ration, relationship, relative amount, relative size, share

proposal *n.*   arrangement, bid, conditions, idea, meeting motion, offer, overture, plan, presentation, proffer, program, project, proposition, prospectus, recommendation, scheme, suggestion, terms

propose *v.* **1.** advance, bid for, bring before, introduce, make a motion, make offer, make recommendation, make suggestion, move, nominate, offer, offer resolution, pose, prefer, present, proffer, put forward, recommend, set forth, submit, suggest, tender **2.** aim for, aspire to, design, expect, have in mind, intend, mean, plan, purport, resolve

proposition *n.* hypothesis, invitation, motion, offer, overture, plan, premise, proposal, recommendation, scheme, submission, suggestion

proprietor *n.* deed holder, holder, landholder, landlady, landlord, landowner, manager, owner, property owner, titleholder

prorate *v.* assess, assess proportionately, distribute, distribute proportionately, divide, divide proportionately, make pro rata distribution

prosecute *v.* **1.** accuse, arraign, bring action against, bring suit, bring to trial, charge, contest, indict, involve in litigation, litigate, prefer charges, put on trial, seek redress, sue, summon, take to court, try **2.** carry on, carry through, conduct, continue, deal with, direct, dispose of, end, engage in, execute, finish, follow through, follow up, handle, manage, perform, persevere, persist at, practice, proceed with, pursue, work at

prospects *n.* anticipation, calculation, chance, contemplation, distinct possibility, expectation, forecast, hope, likelihood, odds, outlook, outlook for future, plan, possibility, presumption, probability, speculation, thought

prosperity *n.* abundance, affluence, fortune, good times, growth, luxury, opulence, plenty, prosperousness, riches, success, wealth, well-being

protest *n.* **1.** challenge, complaint, demur, demurral, disagreement, dissent, exception, formal complaint, formal objection, formal statement, grievance, remonstration, stated complaint, stated objection **2.** boycott, demonstration, march, public demonstration, rally, revolt, riot, shutdown, sit-in, strike, walkout

protocol *n.* code, code of behavior, conventional practice, conventional usage, conventions, courtesy, customs, decorum, diplomatic code, etiquette, formalities, good form, manners, prevailing form, rules, rules of behavior, rules of conduct, set of conventions, standards

prototype *n.* antecedent, archetype, cast, example, forerunner, initial version, model, mold, original, paradigm, pattern, pilot, precursor, predecessor, source, standard

proverb *n.* adage, aphorism, apothegm, axiom, byword, catch phrase, dictum, epigram, gnome, maxim, moral, motto, platitude, precept, saying, slogan, truism, witticism

provide *v.* accommodate, administer, afford, bestow, cater, confer, contribute, dispense, donate, endow, equip, furnish, give, grant, hand over, impart, lend, maintain, minister, outfit, present, produce, proffer, provision, replenish, serve, stock, supply, support, sustain, take care of, yield

provision *n.* agreement, clause, condition, exception, exemption, limitation, prerequisite, proviso, qualification, requirement, reservation, restriction, specifications, stipulation, term, terms

proviso *n.* See **provision**

public *n.* audience, buyers, citizens, clientele, common people, community, electorate, masses, multitude, nation, patronage, people, populace, population, society, supporters, voters

public *adj.* **1.** accessible, civic, common, communal, community, general, governmental, municipal, national, nationwide, open, popular, publicly financed, social, universal, unrestricted, widespread **2.** acknowledged, admitted, apparent, conspicuous, exposed, general, known, obvious, open, overt, plain, prevalent, published, recognized, unconcealed, usual, widely known, widespread

publicity *n.* advertising, announcement, announcing, attention, broadcasting, dissemination, information, press, promotion, propaganda, public attention, public notice, public relations

publicize *v.* advertise, announce, bring to attention of, broadcast, disseminate, make known, make public, promote, promulgate, propagandize, spread about

purchase *v.* acquire, attain, bargain for, buy, come by, earn, gain, get hold of, gain, invest in, make purchase, obtain, pay for, procure, put money into, secure, shop for, take possession of

purpose *n.* **1.** aim, aspiration, design, desire, destination, direction, dream, end, expectation, goal, hope, idea, ideal, intent, intention, justification, mark, meaning, mission, motive, object, objective, plan, point, principle, proposal, proposition, prospect, rationale, reason, scheme, target, wish **2.** ambition, ardor, determination, devotion, diligence, drive, enthusiasm, fervor, firmness, industry, perseverance, persistence, resoluteness, resolution, resolve, single-mindedness, steadfastness, tenacity, will **3.** advantage, avail, benefit, effect, enjoyment, gain, outcome, profit, result, return, use, utility, well being, welfare

pursuit *n.* activity, assignment, business, calling, career, craft, employment, field, forte, interest, job, lifework, line of work, mission, occupation, practice, profession, project, specialty, trade, undertaking, venture, vocation, work

Q

quagmire *n.* bad situation, crisis, difficulty, dilemma, entanglement, fix, imbroglio, impasse, involvement, perplexity, plight, predicament, quandary, trouble, stalemate

qualification *n.* **1.** ability, accomplishment, adequacy, aptitude, attributes, capability, competence, competency, eligibility, experience, fitness, know-how, skill, suitability, suitableness, technical competence **2.** caveat, condition, contingency, criterion, exception, limitation, modification, prerequisite, provision, proviso, requirement, requisite, reservation, restriction, stipulation

qualified *adj.* **1.** able, accomplished, adept, adequate, capable, certified, competent, eligible, equipped, experienced, expert, fit, fitted, knowledgeable, licensed, prepared, proficient, ready, skillful, suitable, tested, trained **2.** altered, changed, circumscribed, conditional, contingent, dependent, limited, modified, provisional, restricted, restrictive

qualify *v.* **1.** authorize, become ready, be prepared, capacitate, certify, commission, empower, enable, endow, entitle, equip, get ready, license, make ready, pass, permit, prepare, ready, train **2.** abate, adapt, adjust, alter, assuage, change, circumscribe, diminish, ease, lessen, limit, make conditions, make exceptions, make provisions, mitigate, moderate, modify, reduce, regulate, restrain, restrict, soften, temper

quality *n.* **1.** aspect, attribute, basic character, character, characteristic, condition, description, detail, element, endowment, factor, feature, genius, kind, mark, measure of excellence, nature, peculiarity, property, trait, virtue **2.** character, class, distinction, excellence, grade, merit, perfection, place, position, preeminence, rank, social position, standing, station, status, superiority, value, worth

quantity *n.* aggregate, allotment, amount, capacity, extent, load, lot, magnitude, measure, number, portion, positive or negative number, quota, share, sum, total, volume

quasi *adj.* apparent, fake, near, partial, pretended, pseudo-, seeming, semi-, similar, so-called, synthetic, virtual

query *v.* ask, ask for, challenge, cross-examine, dispute, examine, inquire, interrogate, make a request, probe, question, quiz, raise objection, request information, test

question *n.* **1.** examination, inquest, inquiry, inquisition, interrogation, interrogatory, investigation, poll, query, questioning **2.** argument, challenge, confusion, contention, controversy, debate, demur, demurral, difficulty, discussion, dispute, doubt, enigma, issue, meeting motion, misgiving, motion, mystery, objection, problem, point, proposal, proposition, protest, puzzle, query, remonstrance, remonstration, riddle, theme, topic

questionable *adj.* ambiguous, ambivalent, arguable, contingent, controvertible, debatable, disputable, doubtful, dubitable, duplicitous, equivocal, indefinite, moot, obscure, paradoxical, problematic, problematical, provisional, suspect, suspicious, tentative, uncertain, unconfirmed, undecided, unproven, unreliable, unsettled, unsure, vague

queue *n.* chain, cordon, data structure, file, group of items, line, order, progression, range, rank, row, sequence, series, string, succession, train, waiting line

quintessence *n.* core, essence, essential part, extract, gist, heart, import, kernel, lifeblood, marrow, pith, sense, significance, soul, spirit, substance

quota *n.* allocation, allotment, allowance, apportionment, assignment, lot, measure, part, percentage, portion, predetermined goal, proportion, quantity, ration, share

quotation *n.* **1.** citation, citing, excerpt, extract, passage, quote, reference, selection **2.** asked price, asking price, bid price, bid and asked price, charge, cost, current price, financial estimate, highest bid, lowest offer, market price, price estimate, published price, quote, quoted price, stated price

quote *n.* See **quotation**

quote *v.* **1.** adduce, cite, excerpt, extract, give example, make reference to, recite, reference, refer to, repeat, repeat verbatim, retell, select passage **2.** charge, fix price, place value on, price, value, valuate

radical *adj.* **1.** basal, basic, cardinal, constitutional, elementary, essential, foundational, fundamental, inherent, intrinsic, main, necessary, primary, primitive, principal, underlying, vital **2.** anarchistic, excessive, extremist, fanatical, iconoclastic, immoderate, insubordinate, insurgent, insurrectionary, intransigent, lawless, militant, mutinous, nihilistic, rebellious, recalcitrant, revolutionary, riotous, seditious, underground, violent

raise *n.* additional income, augmentation, boost, hike, increase, increase in salary, increase in wages, pay increase, pay raise, promotion, salary increase

rally *v.* arouse, assemble, bring together, call together, call up, collect, come together, convene, gather, get together, marshal, mobilize, muster, organize, reassemble, regroup, reorganize, round up, rouse, summon, unite

ramification *n.* aftermath, complication, configuration, consequence, development, effect, end, implication, offshoot, outcome, outgrowth, product, result, upshot

random *adj.* accidental, aimless, arbitrary, casual, chance, desultory, fortuitous, haphazard, incidental, indiscriminate, irregular, orderless, purposeless, stray, unconsidered, unmethodical, unordered, unplanned, unpremeditated

range *n.* **1.** class, collection, file, kind, line, order, queue, rank, row, sequence, series, set of cells, sort, string, tier, variety **2.** area, dimensions, domain, expanse, extent, field, high and low ends, latitude, length, limits, magnitude, parameters, province, radius, reach, realm, scope, space, span, sphere, spread, stretch, sweep, territory, vicinity, width

rank *n.* **1.** arrangement, array, classification, column, file, formation, group, hierarchy, level, line, order, organization, position, queue, range, relative position, row, sequence, series, string, tier **2.** ancestry, authority, birth, capacity, caste, circumstances, class, degree, dignity, division, echelon, estate, footing, grade, hierarchy, level, nobility, order, pedigree, place, position, seniority, situation, sovereignty, state, station, stature, status, stratum, supremacy

rank *v.* **1.** align, arrange, array, assort, class, classify, dispose, establish, fix, grade, group, label, line up, list, locate, marshal, order, organize, place, position, put in a row, put in line, queue up, range, rate, set, size, sort, type **2.** be classed above, be influential, be powerful, come first, go ahead of, go before, have advantage, have supremacy, have weight, outrank, precede, rank above, take precedence, take the lead

rate *n.* **1.** charge, commission, cost, cost per unit, dues, duty, fare, fee, fixed price, freightage, price, quotation, stated price, tariff, tax, toll, valuation **2.** comparison, degree, percentage, proportion, ratio, relation, relationship, scale, standard **3.** flow, gait, measure, motion, movement, pace, speed, stride, tempo, time, velocity

ratify *v.* accredit, affirm, approve, authenticate, authorize, bear out, bind, certify, confirm, corroborate, endorse, establish, evidence, guarantee, license, prove, sanction, substantiate, underwrite, uphold, validate, verify, warrant

rating *n.* assigning ranks, assignment, classification, designation, evaluation, grade, grading, rank, ranking, rate basis, rate making, relegation, valuation, valuation of risk

ratio *n.* comparative size, correlation, correspondence, fraction, fractional relationship, percentage, proportion, proportional relationship, rate, relation, relationship, relativity

reason *n.* **1.** acumen, apprehension, cognition, comprehension, deduction, discernment, induction, inference, intellect, intellectuality, judgment, logic, mental analysis, mentality, perception, rationality, reasonableness, reasoning, sensibleness, understanding, wisdom **2.** aim, basis, cause, consideration, end, goal, impetus, incentive, inducement, intention, motivation, motive, object, occasion, purpose, rationale **3.** account, apology, argument, defense, excuse, explanation, exposition, grounds, justification, proof, rationalization, vindication

reason *v.* **1.** analyze, conclude, contemplate, decide, deduce, deliberate, draw conclusion, examine, explain, explicate, figure out, find, gather, generalize, glean, intellectualize, infer, philosophize, ponder, rationalize, reflect, resolve, solve, speculate, study, think, think through, understand, work out **2.** argue, bring around, coax, contend, debate, demonstrate, discuss, dispute, dissuade, exchange views, expostulate, justify, lead to believe, move, point out, persuade, plead with, prevail, prove, remonstrate, show, talk into, talk out of, talk over, urge, win over

rebate *n.* abatement, allowance, amount credited, amount paid back, amount returned, decrease, deduction, discount, incentive payment, partial refund, payment, reduction, refund, reimbursement, repayment

recall *v.* **1.** abjure, annul, ask for return, bring back, call back, call in, cancel, countermand, disavow, nullify, recant, remove, repeal, rescind, retract, reverse, revoke, summon, take back **2.** awaken, bring to mind, call to mind, call up, evoke, look back on, muse, recognize, recollect, remember, remind, reminisce, retrace, review, think back to, think of

receipt *n.* **1.** acknowledgment, check, proof of purchase, sales slip, sales ticket, slip, stub, voucher **2.** acceptance, acquisition, arrival, delivery, receiving, reception, taking

receipts *n.* advance, amount received, assets received, cash, cash flow, cash receipts, commission, compensation, earnings, gross income, income, money earned, payment received, proceeds, profit, receivables, return, revenue, wages

receivables *n.* amount billed, amount receivable, billings, claims, collectables, current assets, expected income, noncurrent assets, unpaid income, unreceived income

recess *n.* break, cessation, halt, hiatus, holiday, interlude, intermission, interval, letup, lull, pause, refreshment break, respite, rest, temporary adjournment, time out, vacation

recession *n.* economic collapse, economic crisis, economic decline, depression, downturn, reduction, reversal, slowdown, slump, stagnation

recision *n.* abrogation, annulling, canceling, cancellation, nullification, release, rescinding, return to prior state, vacating, voidance

recognition *n.* **1.** acceptance, acknowledgment, admission, apprehension, awareness, cognizance, consciousness, detection, discovery, identification, memory, notice, perception, realization, recall, recognizance, recollection, remembering, remembrance, sensibility, understanding, verifying **2.** acknowledgment, appreciation, approval, attention, credit, gratitude, honor, paying respects, regard, salute

recognize *v.* **1.** be familiar with, call on, detect, diagnose, distinguish, give floor to, identify, introduce, know, make out, notice, observe, perceive, pinpoint, place, recall, recollect, remark, remember, spot, verify, yield to **2.** accept, acknowledge, agree, allow, appreciate, approve, endorse, grant, greet, honor, pay respects to, ratify, respect, reward, salute, sanction, support, validate

recommend *v.* advise, advocate, approve, back, commend, confirm, counsel, encourage, endorse, enjoin, exalt, exhort, extol, favor, guarantee, justify, laud, mention favorably, offer, praise, prescribe, promote, propose, propound, put forward, sanction, second, speak well of, suggest, support, think highly of, uphold, urge, value, vouch for

recommendation *n.* advice, approbation, approval, character reference, commendation, counsel, endorsement, favorable letter, favorable mention, guidance, honorable mention, instruction, letter of support, praise, reference, referral, sanction, suggestion, support, testimonial, tribute

recompense *n.* **1.** amends, atonement, compensation, damages, expiation, indemnification, indemnity, quittance, recovery, redress, reparation, repayment, requital, restitution, return, satisfaction **2.** consideration, earnings, income, pay, payment, remuneration, revenue, reward, salary, tip, wages

record *n.* **1.** account, almanac, annals, catalog, certificate, chronicle, chronology, collection, collection of fields, data collection, data structure, diary, directory, file, history, inventory, journal, ledger, log, logbook, memoir, minutes, notes, register, registry, report, set of data, transactions, transcript, yearbook **2.** accomplishments, achievements, background, case history, curriculum vitae, education, experience, performance highlights, personal history, personnel file, résumé, training

record *v.* affirm, catalog, certify, chronicle, document, enter, enumerate, file, inscribe, insert, itemize, keep account, keep log, list, log, make computer entry, make entry, make recording, mark down, note, post, preserve, put down, put in writing, put on disk, register, report, set down, store information, store on disk, take down, tape, tape-record, videotape, write, write down

recruit *n.* apprentice, beginner, convert, enlisted person, fledgling, initiate, learner, neophyte, newcomer, novice, novitiate, rookie, trainee, volunteer

recruit *v.* acquire, build up, call up, draft, engage, enlist, enroll, find help, gather, impress, induct, levy, mobilize, muster, obtain, procure, refresh, regain, reinforce, renew, replace, replenish, restore, revive, round up, select, sign up, strengthen, take in, take on

redemption *n.* paying in full, paying off, purchasing back, recovery by payment, reestablishment, regaining possession, reinstatement, repayment of bonds, repayment of mutual funds, restitution, restoration, right to call stock, right to redeem stock

reference *n.* **1.** citation, credit line, note, quotation, source, source note **2.** affirmation, attestation, certification, character witness, credentials, endorsement, recommendation, testimonial, tribute, witness **3.** allusion, attribution, hint, implication, innuendo, insinuation, intimation, mention, mentioning, pointing out, remark, source, suggestion

referral *n.* See **reference 2**

refund *n.* allowance, discount, payment, rebate, reimbursement, repayment, return, returned money, returned payment, settlement

refund *v.* adjust, compensate, give back, indemnify, make amends, make repayment, make restitution, pay back, rebate, recompense, redeem, redress, refinance, reimburse, remit, remunerate, repay, restore, return

refurbish *v.* brighten up, clean up, fix up, modernize, overhaul, recondition, redo, refit, refreshen, rejuvenate, remodel, renew, renovate, repair, restore, revamp, update

refuse *v.* be unwilling, decline, demur, deny, disallow, disapprove, dissent, do not accept, do not allow, do not permit, pass up, prohibit, protest, rebuff, reject, repel, say no, send back, shun, spurn, turn away, turn down, withhold consent

regeneration *n.* conversion, improvement, positive feedback, rebirth, rebuilding, reclamation, reconditioning, reconstitution, reconstruction, redemption, reformation, rehabilitation, renewal, renovation, repair, restoration, restoring, revival, rewriting, salvation

register *n.* annals, archives, catalog, chronicle, chronology, computer storage area, diary, directory, guest book, guest list, journal, ledger, list, log, notebook, record, records, registry, roll, roster, schedule, storage area, temporary storage, yearbook

register *v.* **1.** catalog, check in, chronicle, enlist, enroll, enter, inscribe, insert, join, list, log, make entry, matriculate, put on record, record, record formally, schedule, set down, sign up, tape, write down **2.** denote, disclose, display, divulge, exhibit, express, indicate, manifest, mark, point out, read, represent, reveal, say, show, signify

regret *n.* contriteness, contrition, disappointment, grief, lamentation, misgiving, qualms, regretfulness, remorse, repentance, self-accusation, self-condemnation, self-reproach, sorrow, worry

regret *v.* apologize for, be disturbed about, bemoan, be sorry for, be upset about, deplore, deprecate, feel remorse, feel sorry, grieve, lament, mourn, repent

regular *adj.* **1.** common, commonplace, conventional, customary, daily, established, everyday, familiar, general, habitual, natural, normal, ordinary, prevailing, prevalent, routine, standard, traditional, typical, unchanging, unvarying, usual **2.** arranged, balanced, classified, consistent, constant, cyclic, dependable, efficient, established, even, fixed, flat, harmonious, level, methodical, ordered, orderly, organized, periodic, recurrent, regulated, rhythmical, routine, smooth, standardized, steady, straight, symmetrical, systematic, uniform

regulate *v.* adjust, administer, arrange, balance, classify, conduct, control, coordinate, direct, dispose, establish, fix, govern, guide, handle, manage, methodize, monitor, order, organize, oversee, put in order, rule, run, set, standardize, superintend, supervise, systematize, time, tune

regulation *n.* **1.** book, canon, code, commandment, decree, dictate, edict, law, order, ordinance, precept, requirement, rule, standing order, statute **2.** adjustment, administration, classification, codification, control, coordination, direction, government, guidance, handling, management, organization, regimentation, standardization, superintendence, supervision

rehabilitate *v.* adjust, alter, change, change views, convert, fix up, improve, make whole again, mend, rebuild, reclaim, recondition, reconstitute, reconstruct, redecorate, reeducate, reestablish, reform, refurbish, reinstate, reintegrate, rejuvenate, renew, renovate, reorient, restore, return to normal, transform

reimburse *v.* compensate, indemnify, make repayment, make restitution, pay, pay back, recompense, refund, repay, return

reinstate *v.* bring back, place again, put back, put in power again, reelect, reenroll, reestablish, rehire, reinstall, reintroduce, reinvest, renew, replace, restore, return, return responsibility

relationship *n.* accord, affiliation, affinity, alliance, ancestry, association, bond, closeness, connection, consanguinity, contingency, dependency, descent, extraction, friendship, interconnection, interdependence, interrelation, kinship, liaison, link, nearness, parallel, pertinence, rapport, relatedness, relation, relativity, relevance, similarity, tie, union

release *n.* **1.** announcement, broadcasting, declaration, disclosure, news, notice, proclamation, propaganda, publication, publicity, statement **2.** acquittal, clemency, deliverance, delivery, detachment, discharge, disconnection, disengagement, dismissal, dispensation, exemption, exoneration, freedom, giving up, letting go, liberation, redemption, relief, relinquishing, separation, unfastening, vindication, walkout

release *v.* acquit, clear, commute sentence, deliver, detach, discharge, disconnect, disengage, dismiss, dispense with, except from, exclude from, exculpate, excuse, exempt, exonerate, extricate, franchise, free, let go, let off, liberate, loosen, relieve of, separate, set free, set loose, surrender, turn loose, turn out, unbind, undo, unfasten, unhook, unleash, unshackle, untie, vindicate

reliability *n.* **1.** assuredness, authenticity, authoritativeness, believability, certainty, confidence generated, credibility, dependability, genuineness, guarantee, probability of being reliable, reputability, soundness, substantiation **2.** conscientiousness, dependableness, faithfulness, honesty, responsibleness, steadfastness, steadiness, trustworthiness, uprightness

relocate *v.* change address, change location, establish new location, locate again, locate elsewhere, move, move business, move offices, move to new location, move to new place

remainder *n.* balance, carryover, excess, fragment, leftover, remains, remnant, residue, rest, salvage, surplus, waste

reminder *n.* **1.** admonition, clue, cue, hint, intimation, memo, memorial, note, notice, suggestion, warning **2.** favor, gift, keepsake, promotional gift, remembrance, souvenir, token, trophy

remit *v.* **1.** dispatch, forward, mail, make payment, pay, route, send, settle, ship, transfer, transmit **2.** absolve, alleviate, cancel, cease, check, condone, decrease, defer, delay, desist, diminish, ease up, excuse, exonerate, forgive, halt, hold up, interrupt, make allowances for, nullify, pardon, postpone, reduce, refrain, relax, release, relieve, reschedule, set free, slacken, soften, stay, stop, void, waive, weaken

remote *adj.* **1.** distant, far, faraway, far-off, inaccessible, isolated, lonely, obscure, outlying, out-of-the-way, private, removed, secluded, secret, undiscovered, unsettled, wild

2. doubtful, dubious, implausible, improbable, negligible, questionable, slight, slim, small, unlikely

remunerate *v.* award, grant, indemnify, pay, recompense, redress, reimburse, repay, reward, yield

remuneration *n.* allowance, compensation, consideration, direct compensation, earnings, fee, fringe benefits, gain, gratuity, honorarium, income, indirect compensation, pay, payment, proceeds, profits, revenue, salary, stipend, wages, yield

renowned *adj.* acclaimed, celebrated, distinguished, eminent, esteemed, extolled, famed, famous, illustrious, important, notable, noted, outstanding, popular, preeminent, prominent, respected, revered, well-known

rent *n.* amount, cost, fee, lease, payment, price, property, rental, rental cost, return, sum

rent *v.* allow possession, allow use of, charge fee for, contract for, grant possession, lease, make available, obtain possession, obtain use of, sublet, take possession

repay *v.* compensate, give back, indemnify, make amends, make restitution, make up for, pay back, rebate, reciprocate, recompense, refund, reimburse, return, reward, settle up

repeal *v.* abolish, abrogate, annul, cancel, countermand, invalidate, nullify, recall, remove, rescind, reverse, revoke, set aside, vacate, void, withdraw

reply *n.* acknowledgment, answer, defensive pleading, echo, rejoinder, response, retort, return

reply *v.* acknowledge, answer, echo, resound, respond, retort, return, write back

report *n.* account, analysis, chronicle, commentary, computer output, critique, database output, data presentation, detailed statement, dissertation, exposition, formal presentation, indepth account, information, memo, output, paper, piece, presentation of data, presentation of information, release, review, summary, thesis, transcription, written presentation

report *v.* advise, announce, brief, broadcast, characterize, circulate, communicate, critique, depict, describe, detail, disclose, discuss, divulge, document, enlighten, give account of, give facts, impart, inform, make known, make public, narrate, notify, pass on, portray, present, print, provide details, publicize, publish, recapitulate, recite, recount, rehearse, relate, relay, reveal, review, send out, set forth, sketch, spread, state, summarize, tell

represent *v.* **1.** act as broker, act for, act in place of, appear as, assume role of, be agent for, be spokesperson for, correspond to, do business for, embody, epitomize, exemplify, express, perform as, personify, present image of, produce, sell for, serve, serve as example for, serve constituents, speak for, stand for, symbolize, typify, vote proxy for **2.** characterize, delineate, denote, depict, describe, designate, display, draw, exhibit, express, illustrate, interpret, paint, picture, portray, reproduce, show, sketch

representative *n.* **1.** agent, appointed official, attorney, broker, delegate, deputy, elected representative, lawyer, legislator, proxy, public servant, salesperson, spokesperson, stand-in, substitute, understudy **2.** case, case in point, epitome, exemplar, exemplification, illustration, instance, personification, sample, specimen, typical example

reproduce *v.* clone, copy, duplicate, emulate, imitate, make copy of, make over, match, model after, offset, parallel, pattern after, photocopy, photograph, print, print out, remake, remodel

reproduction *n.* clone, copy, duplicate, duplication, facsimile, fake, imitation, photocopy, photograph, picture, portrayal, print, printout, propagation, replica, replication, reprint

reputable *adj.* conscientious, dependable, distinguished, eminent, esteemed, fair, honest, honorable, honored, just, legitimate, principled, prominent, reliable, renowned, respectable, respected, righteous, sincere, straightforward, trustworthy, upright

reputation *n.* acceptability, approval, authority, character, consideration, credit, dependability, distinction, eminence, esteem, estimation, honor, name, position, prestige, prominence, regard, reliability, renown, reputability, repute, respect, respectability, standing, stature, trustworthiness

requirement *n.* claim, command, condition, constraint, contingency, demand, directive, essential, exaction, exigency, fulfillment, fundamental, imperative, injunction, mandate, necessity, need, obligation, precondition, prerequisite, provision, proviso, qualification, requisite, specification, stipulation, terms, vital part

rescind *v.* abolish, abrogate, annul, call off, cancel, countermand, end, invalidate, negate, nullify, overturn, recall, recant, repeal, retract, reverse, revoke, set aside, terminate, undo, veto, void

research *n.* analysis, appraisal, assessment, examination, experimentation, exploration, fact finding, inquiry, inquisition, inspection, investigation, probe, review, scrutiny, survey

reservation *n.* **1.** condition, demur, doubt, exception, hesitancy, misgiving, provision, proviso, qualification, qualm, restriction, scruple, skepticism, stipulation, terms **2.** appointment, booking, exclusive possession, reserving, setting aside, temporary possession, temporary use, use, withholding

reserve *n.* **1.** accrued liability, accumulation, assets, backlog, cache, capital, deposits, Federal Reserve deposits, fund, holdings, inventory, reservoir, resources, savings, segregated earnings, stock, stockpile, store, supply, supply on hand, wealth **2.** aloofness, caution, coolness, detachment, formality, inhibition, modesty, restraint, reticence, self-restraint, unresponsiveness

resign *v.* abdicate, cease work, cede, end employment, end service, give notice, give up, hand in resignation, hand over, leave, quit, relinquish, renounce, retire, stand aside, step down, surrender, terminate employment, turn in resignation, turn over, vacate, walk out, yield

resignation *n.* **1.** abdication, ceasing work, ceding, departure, ending employment, ending service, giving notice, giving up, handing in resignation, handing over, leaving, notice, quitting, relinquishing, relinquishment, renunciation, retirement, standing aside, stepping down, surrender, tendering, terminating employment, termination, turning in resignation, turning over, vacating, walking out, withdrawal, yielding **2.** acceptance, acquiescence, compliance, docility, endurance, forbearance, humbleness, humility, meekness, nonresistance, passivity, patience, submission, submissiveness, sufferance

resolution *n.* **1.** answer, assertion, decision, declaration, decree, directive, expression of desire, expression of intent, finding, formal statement, interpretation, judgment, legal order, meeting motion, motion, opinion, outcome, parliamentary motion, proclamation, proposal, proposition, ruling, solution, statement, upshot, verdict **2.** clarity of detail, fineness of detail, measure of detail, measure of sharpness **3.** aim, courage, dauntlessness, decision, declaration, dedication, determination, earnestness, firmness, fixed purpose, fortitude, intent, intention, perseverance, purpose, purposefulness, resoluteness, resolve, spirit, steadfastness, tenacity, willpower

resources *n.* accounts receivable, assets, belongings, capital, cash, chattel, effects, finances, fixtures, frozen assets, funds, gains, goods, goodwill, holdings, income, inventories, liquid assets, machinery, material goods, means, money, notes, possessions, profits, property, real estate, real property, reserves, revenue, savings, securities, supplies, wealth

responsibility *n.* **1.** accountability, answerability, blame, burden, care, culpability, duty, fault, guilt, jurisdiction, liability, obligation, onus, trust **2.** competency, conscientiousness, dependability, dependableness, faithfulness, honesty, reliability, steadfastness, trustworthiness, uprightness

responsible *adj.* **1.** accountable, answerable, blamable, chargeable, culpable, guilty, liable, obligated, trusted **2.** competent, conscientious, dependable, faithful, honest, reliable, steadfast, trustworthy, upright

restitution *n.* amends, compensation, indemnification, indemnity, payment, recompense, redress, refund, reimbursement, remuneration, reparation, repayment, requital, restoration, satisfaction

restore *v.* bring back, convert, fix, give back, go back to, mend, put back, recall, recondition, reconstitute, reconstruct, reconvert, reestablish, rehabilitate, reinstall, reinstate, renew, replace, return, reverse, revive, send back

restriction *n.* check, condition, confinement, constraint, curb, demarcation, handicap, inhibition, limit, limitation, qualification, regulation, reservation, restraint, rule, stipulation

result *n.* aftereffect, aftermath, answer, by-product, completion, conclusion, consequence, crop, decision, deduction, denouement, determination, development, effect, end, event, eventuality, finding, finish, fruition, harvest, issue, judgment, offshoot, outcome, outgrowth, proceeds, product, reaction, repercussion, resolution, returns, sequel, settlement, solution, upshot, verdict, yield

retire *v.* abdicate, call in, cancel, cease employment, depart from activity, exit, leave, leave active employment, leave company, recover, redeem, regain, remove, remove from service, repay, repay debt, resign, stop working, terminate employment, terminate employment voluntarily, withdraw, withdraw permanently, withdraw voluntarily

retirement *n.* cancellation, cessation of employment, departing from activity, departure from activity, exiting, leaving, leaving active employment, leaving company, permanent withdrawal, removal, removal from service, repayment, repayment of debt, resignation, stopping work, termination of employment, voluntary termination of employment, voluntary withdrawal, withdrawal, withdrawing

retrieve *v.* access file, access information, get back, liberate, obtain, put back, recall, recapture, reclaim, recoup, recover, reestablish, regain, reinstate, rescue, restore, return, salvage, save, take back

return *n.* **1.** compensation, consideration, earnings, exchange, exchange of merchandise, gain, income, increase, indemnification, interest, monetary gain, proceeds, profits, recompense, redress, reimbursement, reparation, repayment, results, revenue, reward, tax form, taxpayer information form, yield **2.** arrival, coming again, coming back, entry, homecoming, reappearance, rebound, reconsidering, recovery, recurrence, reentry, reestablishment, regression, rehabilitation, reinstatement, renewal, recurrence, repetition, replacement, restoration, reversion, revisitation **3.** acknowledgment, answer, countercharge, rebuttal, rejoinder, reply, response, retort

return *v.* **1.** compensate, make payment, make repayment, make restitution, pay, pay back, pay dividend, pay off, rebate, refund, reimburse, repay, yield **2.** carry back, convey, give, give back, put back, replace, reseat, restore, roll back, send, send back, take back, transmit **3.** arrive, come again, come back, come home, enter, move back, reappear, rebound, reconsideration, recover, recur, reenter, reestablish, reexamine, regress, rehabilitate, reinstate, renew, recur, repeat, replace, restore, retrace steps, revert, revisit, turn back

revenue *n.* amount earned, cash, earnings, finances, gain, gross income, income, money, pay, proceeds, profit, receipts, return, wages, wealth, yield

review *n.* abstract, analysis, appraisal, assessment, audit, check, commentary, criticism, discourse, discussion, essay, evaluation, examination, inspection, investigation, journal, judicial reexamination, magazine, organ, periodical, publication, reassessment, recapitulation, reconsideration, reexamination, report, scrutiny, second look, second thought, second view, survey, synopsis, treatise, view

review *v.* abstract, analyze, appraise, assess, audit, check, comment on, correct, criticize, discuss, evaluate, examine, give opinion, give second look, give second thought, give second view, go over again, inspect, investigate, judge, prepare treatise, rave, read through, reassess, recapitulate, reconsider, reedit, reevaluate, reexamine, report on, revise, scrutinize, study, summarize, survey, synopsize, view, weigh, write critique

revise *v.* alter, amend, change, correct, develop, edit, emend, improve, modify, overhaul, perfect, polish, reconsider, redo, redraft, reorganize, restyle, review, rework, rewrite, update

revision *n.* alteration, amendment, change, correction, development, editing, emendation, improvement, modification, overhauling, perfecting, polishing, reconsideration, rectification, redoing, redrafting, reorganization, restyling, review, revising, reworking, rewriting, updating

revoke *v.* abjure, abolish, abrogate, annul, call back, cancel, countermand, counterorder, disclaim, dismiss, dissolve, disown, expunge, invalidate, negate, nullify, recall, recant, remove, renounce, repeal, repudiate, rescind, retract, reverse, set aside, terminate, vacate, veto, void, withdraw

rewarding *adj.* advantageous, fulfilling, gratifying, profitable, satisfying, valuable, worthwhile

rider *n.* addendum, addition, additional clause, adjunct, amendment, appendix, attachment, codicil, suffix, supplement

right *n.* **1.** authority, birthright, claim, concern, due, freedom, heritage, holding, immunity, inheritance, interest, just claim, legal claim, liberty, license, moral claim, ownership, permission, possession, power, prerogative, privilege, share, title **2.** equitableness, equity, fairness, good, goodness, honesty, honor, impartiality, integrity, justice, lawfulness, legality, morality, nobility, propriety, reasonableness, righteousness, rightness, scrupulousness, truth, uprightness, virtuousness **3.** absoluteness, accuracy, actuality, authenticity, certainty, correctness, exactness, factuality, faithfulness, faultlessness, perfection, precision, truth, validity, veracity

risk *n.* chance, chance of loss, contingency, danger, exposure, exposure to destruction, exposure to disadvantage, exposure to injury, exposure to loss, gamble, hazard, jeopardy, liability, measurable possibility of loss, peril, possibility of loss, possibility of problem, speculation, susceptibility, uncertainty, unpredictability, vulnerability, wager

risk *v.* brave, chance, dare, defy, defy danger, endanger, expose to danger, gamble, hazard, imperil, jeopardize, menace, put in jeopardy, run the risk, speculate, take chance, venture, wager

ritual *n.* act, celebration, ceremonial act, ceremony, convention, custom, exercise, form, formal act, formality, observance, practice, procedure, protocol, rite, rites, service, solemnity, system of rites, tradition, usage

role *n.* **1.** capacity, duty, function, operation, place, position, posture, province, purpose, situation, status, task **2.** acting, character, characterization, guise, impersonation, part, performance, personification, portrayal, presentation, representation

roll *n.* **1.** address list, attendance list, census, directory, index, list, muster, names, panel, register, roll call, roster, scroll, slate, ticket **2.** coil, cone, cycle, cylinder, reel, revolution, roller, rotation, spool, turn, wheel

rollover *n.* buffer, delay in payment, movement of funds, moving funds, refinancing, refunding, renewal of obligation, replacing loan, storage buffer

root *n.* base, basic element, basis, beginning, bottom, cause, conception, core, crux, derivation, essence, foot, footing, foundation, fountain, fundamental, germ, ground, heart, hypothesis, inception, lower part, mainspring, motive, nucleus, occasion, origin, pith, premise, proposition, quintessence, radical, rationale, reason, seat, seed, source, starting point, substratum, substructure, thesis, wellspring

roster *n.* See **roll 1**

rotate *v.* **1.** alternate, change places, exchange, exchange places, interchange, move around, replace, switch, take turns, trade places **2.** circle, circumrotate, go in circle, gyrate, move around, pivot, reel, revolve, roll, shift, spin, swivel, turn, whirl

route *v.* convey, direct, dispatch, forward, mail, remit, send, ship, transmit, transport

routine *n.* computer program, convention, custom, formality, instructions, method, ordered set of instructions, pattern, practice, program, program code, protocol, regular course, rule, set of instructions, set of programming instructions

row *n.* chain, column, file, line, order, progression, queue, range, rank, sequence, series, string, succession, tier, train

rule *n.* **1.** bylaw, canon, code, command, commandment, conditional statement, control, corollary, criterion, decree, dictum, directive, doctrine, dogma, edict, formula, general truth, guide, guideline, instruction, law, mandate, maxim, model, natural law, order, ordinance, precept, principle, proposition, regulation, restriction, standard, statute, tenet, theorem, truism **2.** administration, ascendancy, authority, command, control, direction, dominance, domination, dominion, government, influence, jurisdiction, leadership, oversight, power, regulation, reign, sovereignty, supervision, supremacy, sway **3.** convention, custom, customary practice, habit, policy, practice, procedure, routine, usual occurrence, way

rule *v.* **1.** administer, be in authority, be in charge, be in control, be in power, command, control, decree, dictate, direct, dominate, govern, guide, have control of, head, lead, manage, order, oversee, predominate, preside over, prevail, regulate, reign, run, wield power **2.** adjudge, decide, decree, determine, hand down decision, hold, judge, lay down, make judgment, order, pass upon, prescribe, pronounce, resolve, settle

rule out *v.* ban, cancel, dismiss, disregard, do not consider, eliminate, except, exclude, ignore, leave out, prohibit, reject, revoke, suspend

run *v.* **1.** administer, be in charge, carry out, command, conduct, control, coordinate, direct, govern, handle, head, lead, maintain, manage, manipulate, navigate, operate, order, oversee, prescribe, regulate, superintend, supervise **2.** be candidate, campaign for, challenge, compete, contend, enter race, oppose, seek election to, seek office

rural *adj.* agrarian, agricultural, agronomical, country, farming, natural, nonurban, pastoral, provincial, rough, rustic, simple, unsophisticated

safeguard *n.* aegis, buffer, bulwark, defense, escort, guard, password, precaution, precautionary measure, security, security guard, shield

safeguard *v.* care for, defend, escort, guard, preserve, prevent access, save, secure, shield, take precautions, watch over

salary *n.* compensation, earnings, emolument, fixed compensation, income, pay, payment, payroll, regular compensation, remuneration, stipend, wage, wages

sale *n.* agreement, auction, clearance, closeout, contract, discount, exchange, income, markdown, market, marketing, outlet, reduction, selling, trade, transaction, vending

sample *n.* case history, cross section, example, exemplification, illustration, instance, model, pattern, piece, representation, representative, sampling, selected items, specimen, type

sanction *v.* accredit, agree to, allow, approve, authorize, back, certify, commission, consent to, countenance, empower, endorse, license, permit, subscribe to, support, uphold, warrant

satellite *n.* auxiliary, dependency, electronic system, orbiting device, orbiting system, remote installation, spacecraft, terminal, workstation

satisfaction *n.* **1.** amends, atonement, compensation, expiation, indemnification, indemnity, payment, recompense, redress, reimbursement, remuneration, reparation, repayment, resolution, restitution, reward, settlement **2.** bliss, cheerfulness, comfort, conciliation, contentedness, contentment, delight, enjoyment, fulfillment, gladness, gratification, happiness, indulgence, joy, justice, pleasure, serenity, well-being

satisfactory *adj.* able, acceptable, adequate, all right, average, capable, competent, decent, fair, fit, good, passable, satisfying, sufficient, suitable, tolerable, unexceptional, valid

satisfy *v.* **1.** atone for, compensate, discharge, indemnify, liquidate, make reparation, meet, pay, pay back, recompense, reimburse, remunerate, repay, requite, reward, settle **2.** amuse, appease, assuage, cheer, comfort, delight, entertain, fill, gladden, gratify, indulge, pacify, placate, please, satiate, suit

save *v.* **1.** amass, be frugal, be thrifty, conserve, economize, hoard, hold back, keep, lay aside, lay away, maintain, pile up, reserve, stockpile, store up, stow away   **2.** conserve, copy, guard, keep safe, keep up, look after, maintain, preserve, protect, safeguard, screen, secure, shield, store, sustain, take care of   **3.** come to rescue, defend, deliver, extricate, free, help out, liberate, recover, redeem, salvage, set free, unchain, unshackle

savings *n.* accumulation, assets, cache, capital, finances, funds, hoard, investment, means, money, provision, provisions, reserve, reserves, resources, stockpile, store

scale *n.* amount of production, calibration, degrees, gradations, graduated system, hierarchy, levels, order, progression, range, range of values, register, scope, sequence, series, spectrum, steps, succession, value range, wage rate

scan *v.* browse, check, examine, examine sequentially, glance at, inspect, look over, peruse, read over, review, scrutinize, search, skim

schedule *n.* agenda, appointment list, calendar, detailed statement, docket, itinerary, lineup, list, order of business, program, register, timetable

schedule *v.* allot, appoint, appropriate, arrange, assign, book, budget, make arrangements, make plans, make reservations, organize, plan, program, record, register, reserve, set aside, set up

schematic *n.* block diagram, blueprint, chart, design, diagram, drawing, flow chart, graph, layout, line graph, plan, sketch

scheme *n.* **1.** aim, arrangement, course of action, end, idea, intent, object, objective, order, order of business, organization, plan, procedure, program, project, proposal, proposition, purpose, schedule, strategy, suggestion, system, tactics   **2.** blueprint, chart, delineation, design, diagram, draft, drawing, layout, map, outline, pattern, projection, schema, sketch   **3.** collusion, connivance, conspiracy, contrivance, device, gimmick, intrigue, machination, maneuver, plot, ploy, ruse, strategy, subterfuge, tactics, trick

scholarly *adj.* academic, bookish, cultured, educated, erudite, intellectual, intelligent, knowledgeable, learned, lettered, literary, literate, professorial, scholastic, studious, well-educated, well-read

scientific *adj.*   accurate, controlled, deductive, empirical, exact, experimental, logical, mathematical, methodical, objective, observable, precise, provable, sound, systematic, verifiable

scope *n.*   area, breadth, compass, comprehensiveness, confines, depth, expanse, extension, extent, field, influence, latitude, length, margin, orbit, purview, radius, range, reach, realm, space, span, sphere, spread, stretch, width

screen *n.*   See **monitor (n) 1**

screen *v.*   choose, clarify, clean, cull, eliminate, evaluate, examine, filter, filtrate, grade, interview, look over, order, pick out, process, rank, riddle, scan, select, separate, separate out, sift, sort, sort through, strain

script *n.*   **1.** book, computer file, dialog, lines, manuscript, screenplay, series of instructions, story, text, typescript   **2.** calligraphy, cursive writing, handwriting, longhand, penmanship, style of writing, writing

seal *n.*   assurance, authentication, authorization, confirmation, guarantee, imprint, insignia, oath, permit, pledge, promise, stamp, surety, vow, warrant, warranty

seat *n.*   **1.** capital, center, central location, focal point, headquarters, heart, hub, location, place, site, source, station   **2.** base, basement, bed, foot, footing, foundation, groundwork, pedestal, post, stand, substructure

secondary *adj.*   **1.** accessory, alternate, alternative, ancillary, auxiliary, backup, extra, inferior, insignificant, lesser, less important, lower, minor, next, nonessential, reserve, second, smaller, subordinate, subsidiary, supporting, trivial, unimportant   **2.** borrowed, consequent, dependent, derivative, derived, developed, eventual, indirect, resultant, resulting, second-hand, subsequent

sectarian *adj.*   bigoted, confined, denominational, doctrinaire, exclusive, factional, fanatical, insular, limited, narrow, narrow-minded, parochial, partisan, prejudicial, provincial, rigid

sector *n.*   area, category, division, economic area, group of stocks, part, portion, region, segment, smallest block of storage, smallest disk space, subdivision, zone

secure *v.*   cover, defend, fortify, guarantee, guard, insure, make certain, make safe, make sound, protect, reinforce, safeguard, shield, strengthen, support, underwrite, watch over

security *n.* **1.** agreement, bail, bond, collateral, contract, covenant, earnest money, guarantee, immunity, instrument of ownership, insurance, pact, pledge, precaution, promise, protection, refuge, retreat, safeguard, safekeeping, safeness, safety, safety measure, sanctuary, shelter, shield, surety, use of safeguards, verbal agreement, warrant, warranty **2.** assurance, certainty, confidence, conviction, definiteness, ease, faith, peace of mind, positiveness, reassurance, reliance, sureness, trust

segment *n.* area of responsibility, compartment, component, division, element, excerpt, factor, fragment, member, parcel, part, piece, portion, section, sector, slice, subdivision, wedge

segregate *v.* banish, close off, cut off, disconnect, discriminate, dissociate, divide, exclude, exile, insulate, isolate, leave out, lock up, ostracize, quarantine, select, separate, sequester, set apart, sever, single out, split up

selection *n.* **1.** citation, excerpt, extract, quote, quotation, passage, piece, text, unit of text **2.** alternative, choice, choosing, collection, culling, election, opting for, option, pick, picking, preference, separation, setting apart, singling out, sorting out

self-confident *adj.* assured, confident, poised, secure, self-assured, self-reliant, steady, undoubting, unhesitating

sell *v.* auction, carry, close deal, convince, deal in, dispose of, exchange, furnish, handle, liquidate, make available, market, merchandise, offer, persuade, put up for sale, retail, supply, trade, trade in, unload, vend, wholesale

send *v.* address to, assign, broadcast, circulate, commission, communicate, consign, convey, delegate, deliver, direct, dispatch, emit, expedite, express, forward, impart, issue, mail, pass along, post, propel, put out, radiate, radio, relay, remit, route, ship, telecast, televise, transfer, transmit

seniority *n.* being senior, preference, priority, rank, ranking, privileged status, service-based system, service preference, service status, standing, superiority, status, time-based system

sequence *n.* arrangement, array, classification, consecutiveness, continuity, continuousness, cycle, distribution, file, flow, graduation, grouping, line, nonrandom order, order, ordered set, ordering, organization, placement, progression, queue, rank, row, series, succession, successiveness, tier

sequential *adj.* consecutive, ensuing, following, next, sequent, serial, subsequent, subsequential, succeeding, successive

serial *adj.* consecutive, continual, ensuing, following, sequent, sequential, succeeding, successive

series *n.* arrangement, consecution, division, group, line, order, procession, progression, run, sequel, sequence, set, string, succession

service *n.* **1.** aid, assistance, benefit, contribution, courtesy, duty, employ, employment, favor, help, kindness, labor, maintenance, ministration, serviceability, servicing, usefulness, utility, work **2.** ceremonial, ceremony, formal ceremony, observance, ritual, sacrament, sermon, worship

session *n.* assembly, conference, court activity, discussion, gathering, hearing, legislative activity meeting, period, series of meetings, sitting, term

setback *n.* defeat, delay, difficulty, disappointment, failure, hindrance, impediment, loss, misfortune, mishap, obstacle, rebuff, recurrence, regression, rejection, relapse, reversal, reverse, slowdown, upset

settlement *n.* **1.** accommodation, adjustment, agreement, appeasement, arbitration, closing, compensation, completion, compromise, conclusion, contract, covenant, decision, defrayal, discharge, disposition, distribution, liquidation, mollification, pay, payment, payoff, placation, real estate closing, recompense, reconciliation, reimbursement, release, resolution, satisfaction, trade-off **2.** community, development, encampment, habitation, occupancy, occupation, outpost, possession, post, residence, satellite, village

set up *v.* arrange, assemble, begin, build, compose, configure, constitute, construct, create, design, draft, erect, establish, form, format, found, frame, implement, initiate, install, institute, introduce, launch, lay out, make up, organize, originate, plan, prepare, put together, raise, start, structure

shape *n.* appearance, arrangement, aspect, build, cast, configuration, construction, contour, cut, figure, form, format, formation, frame, guise, image, likeness, lines, look, model, outline, pattern, profile, semblance, silhouette, structure, style

shape *v.* **1.** accommodate, adapt, adjust, align, alter, arrange, assort, change, define, devise, lay out, line up, modify, order, organize, plan, regulate, sort out, tailor, transform **2.** assemble, block out, build, carve, cast, chisel, construct, create, design, fabricate, fashion, forge, form, frame, make, model, mold, pattern, produce, put together, sculpture, trim, whittle

share *n.* allocation, allotment, allowance, apportionment, appropriation, claim, commission, consignment, dispensation, dividend, division, dole, equity, equity ownership, fraction, grant, helping, interest, lot, measure, ownership, parcel, part, percentage, piece, proportion, quota, ration, segment, serving, slice, split, unit of equity

share *v.* allocate, allot, apportion, be party to, deal out, dispense, distribute, divide, divide with, dole out, give out, measure out, mete out, parcel out, participate in, partition, portion out, ration, slice up, split up, subdivide

shelve *v.* defer, delay, dismiss, dispense with, hang up, hold, hold off, lay aside, postpone, prorogue, put aside, put off, put on hold, retire, suspend, table, waive

shift *n.* alteration, change, change of direction, hours of work, maneuver, move, rearrangement, reassignment, relocation, swerve, transfer, transposition, work hours

ship *v.* address to, carry, consign, convey, direct, dispatch, export, ferry, forward, haul, move, remit, route, send, transfer, transmit, transport

shop *n.* boutique, business, factory, factory workforce, gift store, market, office, outlet, plant, production area, retail business, retail store, showroom, small store, store, workforce, workshop

shop *v.* be in market for, buy, go shopping, hunt for, look for, purchase, search for, try to buy

short *adj.* **1.** abbreviated, abridged, bare, brief, compact, compressed, concise, condensed, contracted, curtailed, decreased, diminished, epigrammatic, laconic, lessened, little, momentary, pithy, pointed, precise, sententious, shortened, short-lived, short-term, succinct, small, summarized, summary, terse **2.** below-standard, deficient, inadequate, insufficient, lacking, lean, limited, low, meager, poor, scarce, short-handed, skimpy, slender, slim, sparse, tight, wanting

shortage *n.* dearth, deficiency, deficit, failure, inadequacy, insufficiency, lack, leanness, limitation, meagerness, paucity, poverty, scantiness, scarcity, shortfall, short supply, sparseness, want

shortcoming *n.* defect, deficiency, drawback, failing, failure, fault, flaw, frailty, imperfection, infirmity, lack, lapse, liability, weakness, weak point

short-lived *adj.* brief, cursory, ephemeral, evanescent, fleeting, hasty, impermanent, momentary, mortal, passing, perishable, short-run, short-term, temporary, transient, transitory

show *n.* arrangement, array, demonstration, display, entertainment, exhibit, exhibition, exposition, fair, manifestation, motion picture, movie, pageant, pageantry, parade, play, presentation, production, program, representation, revelation, showing

show *v.* **1.** air, demonstrate, display, exhibit, mount, offer, present, produce, put on, showcase, show off, stage, unfold, unveil **2.** assert, clarify, confirm, corroborate, define, disclose, divulge, document, elucidate, establish, exemplify, explain, explicate, expound, express, illustrate, indicate, inform, instruct, interpret, make known, manifest, note, point out, proclaim, prove, reveal, substantiate, teach, testify to, verify **3.** accompany, chaperon, conduct, direct, escort, guide, lead, pilot, steer, usher

sign *n.* **1.** badge, cipher, crest, device, emblem, ensign, initials, insignia, logo, logotype, mark, nameplate, placard, representation, symbol, token, type **2.** auspice, caution, clue, evidence, foreboding, forecast, foreknowledge, foreshadowing, forewarning, harbinger, hint, indication, manifestation, omen, portent, prediction, premonition, presage, prognostication, proof, suggestion, symptom, trace, warning

sign *v.* authorize, autograph, certify, cosign, countersign, endorse, initial, inscribe, notarize, subscribe, underwrite, validate, witness, write name, write on

significant *adj.* **1.** cogent, compelling, deep, expressive, forceful, important, informative, meaningful, noteworthy, pithy, powerful, primary, profound, representative, suggestive, telling, valid, weighty **2.** consequential, critical, crucial, decisive, essential, foreboding, momentous, necessary, ominous, portentous, serious, urgent, vital, weighty

similarity *n.* agreement, analogy, approximation, coincidence, comparability, concordance, conformity, congruity, consistency, correspondence, equivalence, harmony, homogeneity, likeness, parallel, parallelism, relationship, resemblance, sameness, similitude, uniformity

simulate *v.* act like, copy, do like, duplicate, equivocate, feign, imitate, impersonate, make believe, mimic, mirror, model, parallel, pose as, pretend, pretend to be, reflect, replicate, represent, reproduce, resemble, take on appearance of

sincere *adj.* aboveboard, artless, candid, earnest, forthright, frank, genuine, guileless, honest, natural, open, plain-spoken, real, serious, straightforward, true, trustworthy, unaffected, unassuming, undeceptive, undisguised, unequivocal, unpretentious, upright, wholehearted

sincerity *n.* artlessness, candidness, candor, earnestness, forthrightness, frankness, genuineness, good faith, guilelessness, honesty, honorableness, naturalness, openheartedness, openness, plain-speaking, seriousness, straightforwardness, trustworthiness, truthfulness, undeceptiveness, unequivocalness, unpretentiousness, uprightness, wholeheartedness

site *n.* area, environment, layout, locale, locality, location, lot, place, placement, plot, point, position, setting, spot, station, vicinity

situation *n.* **1.** See **site** **2.** case, circumstances, condition, picture, plight, position, predicament, standing, state, state of affairs, status **3.** appointment, capacity, employment, employment status, job, office, placement, position, post, profession, trade

sketch *n.* blueprint, compendium, copy, delineation, depiction, description, design, diagram, digest, draft, drawing, illustration, outline, portrayal, précis, preliminary drawing, report, representation, skeleton, study, summary, syllabus, synopsis

skill *n.* **1.** ability, adeptness, adroitness, aptitude, artistry, capability, competence, craftsmanship, deftness, dexterity, expertise, expertness, facility, faculty, finesse, forte, gift, handiness, ingenuity, knack, know-how, proficiency, skillfulness, talent, technique **2.** activity, art, craft, handicraft, industrial art, line of work, occupation, profession, trade, vocation

skillful *adj.* able, accomplished, adept, adroit, capable, dexterous, endowed, experienced, expert, gifted, handy, knowledgeable, polished, practiced, professional, proficient, seasoned, skilled, talented, veteran, well-versed, whiz

slant *n.* angle, approach, attitude, bent, bias, direction, distortion, emphasis, judgment, leaning, one-sidedness, opinion, outlook, partiality, point of view, position, predilection, predisposition, prejudice, proclivity, sentiment, stance, standpoint, tendency, turn, view, viewpoint

slip *n.* **1.** blunder, error, gaffe, imprudence, indiscretion, lapse, misdeed, misstep, mistake, oversight, trip **2.** admission, card, note, notepaper, paper, pass, sheet, strip, stub, ticket

slogan *n.* byword, catch phrase, expression, jingle, motto, pet phrase, phrase, proverb, saying, shibboleth, watchword

slot *n.* aperture, channel, crack, groove, hole, keyhole, mail receptacle, niche, notch, opening, position, slit, space, time, vacancy

slowdown *n.* deceleration, decline, de-escalation, downswing, downtrend, downturn, drop-off, downslide, ebbing, gradual decrease, inactivity, recession, retardation, slackening, slackening off, stagnation, stoppage, strike, subsiding, tapering off, winding down

slump *n.* collapse, decline, decrease, depreciation, depression, descent, devaluation, downslide, downswing, downtrend, downturn, drop-off, failure, lapse, recession, rut, slide, slowdown, stagnation

small *adj.* **1.** abbreviated, brief, compact, concise, condensed, cramped, diminutive, limited, little, meager, microscopic, miniature, minuscule, minute, modest, narrow, petite, scanty, short, slight, small-scale, tiny, undersized, unpretentious **2.** immaterial, inconsequential, insignificant, lesser, limited, lower, minor, negligible, nonessential, obscure, secondary, trifling, trivial, unimportant

smart *adj.* **1.** adept, adroit, apt, astute, bright, brilliant, clever, deft, discerning, educated, ingenious, intellectual, intelligent, knowledgeable, logical, perceptive, quick-witted, resourceful, sage, sharp-witted, shrewd, well-read, wise **2.** chic, dapper, dashing, elegant, fashionable, modish, neat, spruce, stylish, trendy, trim, well-groomed

social *adj.* **1.** civil, collective, common, communal, community, human, municipal, popular, public, societal **2.** affable, amiable, communicative, companionable, convivial, cordial, entertaining, friendly, gracious, gregarious, hospitable, mannerly, pleasant, sociable

socialize *v.* associate with, attend social events, be friendly, consort with, entertain, get together, go out, join, keep company with, mingle, mix, talk

society *n.* **1.** civilization, community, culture, general public, humanity, humankind, human race, nation, people, population, public, social order, the world **2.** alliance, association, club, federation, group, guild, institute, institution, league, order, organization, sodality, syndicate, union **3.** aristocracy, gentry, high society, nobility, privileged classes, the elite, the rich, upper classes

solicit *v.* accost, appeal to, apply for, approach, ask, ask for, beg, call on, canvass, demand, entice, entreat, implore, importune, inquire, invite, petition, plead for, pray, promote, question, request, seek, supplicate, try to sell

solution *n.* **1.** answer, clarification, discovery, elucidation, exegesis, explanation, explication, key, resolution, result, unfolding, unraveling **2.** compound, elixir, emulsion, extract, fluid, liquid blend, liquid mixture, mix, mixture, solvent, suspension

solve *v.* answer, clarify, clear up, decipher, decode, determine, disentangle, elucidate, explain, fathom, figure out, find answer, find out, interpret, reason out, resolve, settle, think out, unfold, unlock, unravel, untangle, work out

sophistication *n.* civility, culture, elegance, finesse, graciousness, knowledgeability, poise, polish, social grace, style, suaveness, tact, urbanity, wide experience

sort *n.* array, brand, breed, category, character, class, denomination, family, genre, genus, group, kind, lot, make, nature, order, phylum, race, set, species, stamp, strain, style, suite, type, variety

sort *v.* arrange, arrange in order, assort, catalog, categorize, class, classify, cull, divide, file, group, index, list, methodize, order, organize, place in order, put in order, rank, rearrange, reorder, screen, segregate, select, separate, sift, systematize

source *n.* ancestry, antecedent, authority, beginning, cause, commencement, dawn, dawning, derivation, embryo, fountain, fountainhead, genesis, germ, inception, onset, origin, origination, originator, outset, provenance, root, seed, start, starting point, supply point, wellspring

souvenir *n.* gift, keepsake, memento, memorial, relic, remembrance, reminder, token, trophy

sovereign *n.* autocrat, chief, crowned head, czar, dictator, emperor, empress, head of state, king, majesty, monarch, potentate, queen, royal head of state, ruler, supreme ruler

span *n.* distance, extent, interval, length, maximum distance, measure, period, portion, reach, space, spread, stretch, time

span *v.* arch over, bridge, connect, cross, extend, extend across, extend over, go over, join, link, pass over, range over, reach across, stretch over, tie, traverse, unite

speak *v.* **1.** address, deliver address, discourse, give lecture, give talk, hold forth, lecture, make speech, orate, recite, sermonize **2.** advise, articulate, chat, communicate, converse, convey, declare, disclose, discuss, enunciate, express, inform, mention, mumble, point out, pronounce, put into words, relate, say, shout, signify, state, talk, tell, utter, verbalize, vocalize, voice

speak out *v.* affirm, assert, avow, declare, insist, make oneself heard, make position known, proclaim, protest, say clearly, speak loudly, stand up for

specialist *n.* aficionado, authority, connoisseur, devotee, expert, maven, professional, sage, scholar, technical expert, technician, veteran

specialize *v.* concentrate efforts, concentrate on, develop skill in, focus on, limit to, particularize, practice, practice exclusively, pursue, study intensively, train for, work in

specialty *n.* ability, career, craft, distinction, distinguishing feature, featured item, field of concentration, field of study, forte, hallmark, line of work, major, object of attention, object of study, occupation, practice, profession, professional practice, pursuit, skill, specialization, special quality, sphere, strength, talent, trade

specifications *n.* blueprint, checklist, conditions, delineation, description, designation, details, drawings, explanation, itemization, listing, particulars, qualifications, requirements, stipulation, terms

specify *v.* be specific, cite, define, designate, detail, enumerate, establish, exemplify, identify, indicate, itemize, limit, list, make clear, make list of, mention, name, particularize, point out, prescribe, set conditions, show clearly, spell out, stipulate

specimen *n.* case, example, exemplar, exemplification, exhibit, illustration, instance, model, representation, representative, sampling, type

speculate *v.* **1.** assume risk, buy and sell, buy futures, exchange, gamble, hazard, play the market, risk, take a chance, trade, venture **2.** cogitate, conjecture, consider, contemplate, deliberate, evaluate, examine, guess, hypothesize, imagine, meditate, ponder, postulate, reflect on, suppose, surmise, theorize, think about, weigh

speculation *n.* **1.** assumption of risk, buying and selling, buying futures, exchanging, gamble, gambling, hazard, playing the market, risk, taking chances, taking risks, trading, venture, venturing **2.** belief, cogitation, conjecture, consideration, contemplation, deliberation, evaluation, examination, guess, guesswork, hypothesis, imagining, meditation, musing, pondering, postulation, reflection, shot, supposition, surmise, theorizing, theory, thinking about, thought, weighing

speech *n.* **1.** address, commentary, discourse, eulogy, formal talk, keynote address, lecture, oration, oratory, remarks, sermon, valedictory **2.** accent, communication, conversation, dialect, dialog, diction, discussion, elocution, enunciation, expression, language, oral communication, pronunciation, remark, speaking, talk, tongue, utterance, verbalization, vernacular, vocal expression, vocalization

spend *v.* allocate, apply, consume, contribute, deplete, devote, disburse, dispense, dissipate, donate, drain, employ, empty, exhaust, expend, fill, finish, give, hand out, invest, lay out, pass out, pay, pay out, put in, squander, use, use up, waste

sphere *n.* **1.** capacity, circumstances, class, department, discipline, district, domain, dominion, environment, field, forte, function, jurisdiction, level, office, position, province, range, rank, realm, responsibility, scope, situation, specialization, specialty, standing, status, territory **2.** ball, celestial body, circle, earth, globe, globule, oval object, planet, round object, spheroid

spokesperson *n.* advocate, agent, attorney, champion, delegate, deputy, intermediary, mediator, press agent, public relations person, representative, voice

sponsor *n.* advocate, backer, benefactor, financer, guarantor, important investor, patron, promoter, supporter, underwriter

sponsor *v.* advocate, aid, answer for, back, be responsible for, finance, fund, help, patronize, promote, put up money, recommend, speak for, subsidize, support, vouch for

spotlight *n.* attention, center stage, fame, interest, light, limelight, notoriety, observation, popularity, public attention, public consciousness, public eye, publicity

spread *v.* **1.** advertise, air, announce, broadcast, cast, circulate, diffuse, dispense, disperse, disseminate, distribute, give out, hand out, make known, make public, pass out, promulgate, propagate, publicize, publish, scatter, send out, sow, strew, televise, tell about, throw out, transmit **2.** branch out, broaden, coat, cover, develop, elongate, enlarge, expand, extend, fan out, flow, increase, lengthen, multiply, mushroom, open, open out, open up, outstretch, overlay, pervade, proliferate, radiate, roll out, sprawl, stretch, unfold, unfurl, unroll, untwist, unwind, widen

stability *n.* balance, cohesion, constancy, continuity, dependability, durability, endurance, equilibrium, firmness, immobility, immovability, maturity, permanence, perseverance, resistance, solidity, soundness, stableness, steadfastness, steadiness

stabilize *v.* anchor, balance, bolt, brace, counterbalance, equalize, fasten, fix, fortify, immobilize, maintain, make steady, preserve, secure, steady, strengthen, support, sustain, uphold

stable *adj.* abiding, anchored, balanced, constant, continuing, dependable, durable, enduring, established, firm, fixed, immovable, immutable, lasting, long-lasting, long-standing, permanent, reliable, resistant, resolute, secure, solid, sound, stalwart, staunch, steadfast, steady, sturdy, substantial, unchangeable, uniform, unwavering, well-built

staff *n.* assistants, crew, employees, faculty, help, hired help, office workers, operatives, personnel, support, team, workers, workforce

stalemate *n.* check, deadlock, draw, gridlock, impasse, standoff, standstill

stall *v.* consume time, delay, evade issue, filibuster, gain time, hamper, hinder, hold off, lag, postpone, put off, slow down, stand still, stave off, use up time, waste time

stamp *n.* badge, block, brand, cast, crest, design, die, emblem, engraving, hallmark, impression, imprint, inscription, insignia, label, legend, logo, mark, matrix, medallion, mold, pattern, plate, print, representation, seal, sign, signature, symbol, trademark

stand *n.* **1.** angle, attitude, belief, contention, opinion, philosophy, plan, point of view, policy, position, sentiment, slant, stance, standpoint, strategy, view, viewpoint, way of thinking **2.** base, booth, counter, dais, grandstand, lectern, platform, podium, pulpit, reviewing stand, stall, support, witness box

standard *n.*   archetype, average, axiom, barometer, canon, code, criterion, established measure, example, exemplar, fixed measure, fundamental, gauge, grade, guide, guideline, ideal, law, mean, measure, median, mirror, model, norm, par, paradigm, paragon, pattern, principle, prototype, rule, test, yardstick

standard *adj.*   accepted, approved, authoritative, average, basic, classic, common, conventional, customary, definitive, established, everyday, general, normal, official, orthodox, popular, prevailing, prevalent, recognized, regular, set, stock, traditional, typical, universal, usual, widespread

standardize *v.*   equalize, homogenize, make regular, make similar, make uniform, mass produce, normalize, regulate, systematize

stand-by *n.*   alternate, backup, fill-in, replacement, second, substitute, understudy

standing *n.*   capacity, character, circumstance, class, condition, credit, echelon, eminence, footing, level, name, order, place, position, prestige, rank, reputation, repute, situation, state, station, stature, status

start *n.*   **1.** beginning, birth, commencement, creation, dawn, dawning, departure, embarkation, emergence, first step, foundation, founding, genesis, inauguration, inception, initiation, institution, leaving, onset, opening, origin, outset, source, takeoff   **2.** advantage, backing, break, chance, financing, guidance, head start, helping hand, introduction, lead, odds, opening, opportunity, patronage, sponsorship, upper hand, vantage

start *v.*   activate, begin, come into being, commence, create, depart, embark, emerge, engender, establish, found, inaugurate, initiate, instigate, institute, introduce, issue, launch, lay foundation, leave, make beginning, open, originate, pioneer, set in motion, set up, spring, take first step, take off

state *n.*   **1.** commonwealth, country, dominion, federation, government, kingdom, nation, republic, territory, union   **2.** attitude, character, circumstance, circumstances, class, condition, echelon, environment, estate, footing, form, frame of mind, mood, nature, order, outlook, phase, place, plight, position, posture, predicament, rank, shape, situation, stage, standing, state of affairs, station, status

statement *n.*   **1.** account, bill, charge, financial summary, invoice, list of charges, list of expenses, record   **2.** account, affidavit, affirmation, announcement, assertion, command, comment, communication, declaration, explanation, expression, formal document, formal notice, manifesto, message, observation, opinion, presentation, proclamation, profession, promulgation, pronouncement, remark, report, set of instructions, testimony, word

station *n.* **1.** appointment, capacity, caste, character, circumstances, class, condition, distinction, duty, eminence, employment, estate, footing, grade, importance, level, occupation, occupational status, order, place, position, prominence, rank, situation, social status, standing, state, status **2.** base, base of operations, bureau, center, central office, command post, headquarters, home office, location, main office, office, place, seat, site, terminal, workstation

stationary *adj.* anchored, attached, fixed, immobile, immovable, inactive, inert, moored, motionless, permanent, rooted, secure, stable, static, unmoving

stature *n.* capacity, consequence, eminence, importance, place, position, posture, prestige, prominence, rank, standing, state, station, status, value, worth

status *n.* caliber, capacity, case, circumstances, class, condition, degree, distinction, eminence, footing, grade, level, merit, place, position, posture, prominence, rank, rating, reputation, situation, standing, state, station, stature

stimulate *v.* activate, agitate, animate, arouse, encourage, energize, enliven, exhilarate, excite, foment, galvanize, goad, impel, incite, inflame, inspire, instigate, motivate, move, prod, prompt, provoke, rouse, spur, trigger, urge, whet

stimulus *n.* catalyst, encouragement, impetus, incentive, incitement, inducement, inspiration, instigation, motivation, motive, propellant, provocation, spur, stimulant, stimulation, urging

stipend *n.* allotment, allowance, award, earnings, fee, grant, gratuity, honorarium, pay, payment, remuneration, salary, wages

stipulate *v.* contract, covenant, designate, detail, determine, impose, insist on, lay down, provide, require, set, set conditions, set terms, specify, spell out, state, state conditions

stipulation *n.* admission, agreement, arrangement, concession, condition, contingency, contract, demand, designation, limitation, obligation, precondition, prerequisite, provision, proviso, qualification, requirement, reservation, restriction, specification, terms

stock *n.* **1.** array, articles, assortment, backlog, commodities, fund, goods, inventory, lot, merchandise, produce, products, provisions, quantity, reserve, selection, stockpile, store, supplies, supply, variety, wares **2.** assets, blue chips, funds, investment, number of shares, ownership, share, shares, transferable certificate **3.** ancestry, background, breed, descent, ethnic group, extraction, family, heritage, lineage, line of descent, parentage, pedigree, primogenitor, progenitor, race, species, strain, type, variety

stock *v.* accumulate, amass, carry, collect, deal in, equip, fill up, furnish, gather, handle, have, hoard, hold, keep, keep on hand, lay in, market, offer, outfit, provide, put away, ration, reserve, retain, save, sell, stockpile, store, store up, stow away, supply, trade in

stopgap *n.* alternate, emergency action, expediency, fill-in, makeshift arrangement, replacement, substitute, temporary expedient, temporary help

storage *n.* archives, area, capacity, holding area, holding capacity, space, storehouse, storeroom, stowage, warehouse

store *n.* **1.** booth, business, business establishment, concession, co-op, counter, establishment, franchise, market, mart, outlet, shop, showroom, stall, stand, storehouse **2.** accumulation, assortment, backlog, cache, collection, commodities, fund, goods, hoard, holdings, inventory, lot, provision, provisions, quantity, reserve, savings, staples, stock, stockpile, supply, treasure, wares

store *v.* accumulate, amass, collect, cumulate, deposit, gather, hide, hoard, hold, keep, keep in reserve, lay away, lay in, preserve, put aside, put away, put in storage, reserve, retain, save, save up, stash away, stockpile, warehouse

strategy *n.* angle, approach, design, game, management plan, maneuvering, method, plan, plot, policy, procedure, program, scenario, scheme, tactics

strike *n.* job action, organized work stoppage, sitdown, slowdown, walkout, work stoppage

structure *n.* anatomy, architecture, arrangement, build, building, collection, collection of arrays, composition, configuration, conformation, construction, design, edifice, erection, exterior, fabric, figure, form, format, frame, framework, infrastructure, makeup, network, order, organization, pattern, shape, system

study *n.* analysis, application, attention, concentration, consideration, deliberation, examination, exploration, inquiry, inspection, investigation, learning, meditation, musing, pondering, probe, questioning, reading, reasoning, reflection, research, reverie, review, rumination, scrutiny, subject, thought

study *v.* analyze, apply oneself, consider, contemplate, deliberate, do research, examine, explore, figure, inquire into, inspect, investigate, learn, meditate, muse, peruse, ponder, probe, read, reason, reflect, research, review, ruminate, scrutinize, think out, think over, weigh

style *n.* **1.** approach, behavior, characteristic, custom, design, fashion, form, habit, kind, look, manner, method, mode, pattern, practice, quality, shape, sort, spirit, system, technique, texture, tone, trend, type, variety, vein, vogue, way **2.** capitalization, dialect, diction, expression, language, phraseology, phrasing, pronunciation, punctuation, speech, spelling, treatment of words, vocabulary, way of speaking, way of writing, word choice, wording

subdivision *n.* category, class, development, part, piece, portion, section, segment, share, subcategory, subclass, subgroup, subsection, subsegment

subject *n.* **1.** area of study, argument, business, case, course, course of study, discipline, discussion, gist, idea, item, material, matter, motif, motive, object, plot, point, problem, question, story, study, subject matter, substance, text, theme, thesis, thought, topic **2.** case, citizen, client, customer, dependent, inhabitant, national, patient, resident, subordinate

submission *n.* acceptance, acquiescence, allegiance, assent, capitulation, compliance, conformity, deference, giving in, malleability, nonresistance, obedience, observance, passivism, passivity, pliability, prostration, resignation, servility, subjection, submissiveness, submitting, subservience, surrender, tractability, unassertiveness, yielding

submit *v.* **1.** advance, apply, argue, assert, bid, claim, contend, enter, hand in, introduce, move, offer, present, proffer, propose, propound, put forth, put forward, state, suggest, tender, theorize, turn in, volunteer **2.** abide by, accede, accept, acknowledge, acquiesce, agree to, be malleable, be passive, be submissive to, be tractable, capitulate, cease struggle, cede, comply with, concede, consent to, defer to, do not resist, endure, fall, fold, give away, give ground, give in, give way to, grant, humor, indulge, lay down arms, obey, observe, relent, resign self to, succumb to, surrender, tolerate, withstand, yield

subordinate *n.* aide, assistant, attendant, deputy, employee, helper, hired help, inferior, junior, second, servant, staff, underling

subordinate *adj.* accessory, ancillary, auxiliary, inferior, junior, lower, lower-rank, satellite, secondary, smaller, submissive, subservient, subsidiary, tributary

subscribe *v.* **1.** accept, buy, contract for, contribute to, donate to, enroll in, invest in, pay to use, pledge to, promise to, purchase, register for, sign for, support, take, undertake **2.** accede to, acquiesce in, advocate, agree, allow, approve, assent, attest to, authorize, back up, believe in, condone, consent to, co-sign for, countersign for, endorse, give permission for, guarantee, have confidence in, have faith in, help, permit, recommend, sanction, second, sign for, support, testify to, underwrite

subsidiary *adj.* accessory, additional, adjuvant, aiding, ancillary, assistant, assisting, auxiliary, branch, contributory, extra, lesser, minor, secondary, subordinate, supplemental, supplementary, tributary

subsidize *v.* aid, back, contribute to, endow, finance, fund, give money to, help, invest in, maintain, pay for, put up money for, sponsor, support, underwrite

subsidy *n.* aid, allotment, allowance, assistance, assistantship, award, backing, contribution, endowment, fellowship, financial aid, gift, grant, help, payment, provision, scholarship, sponsorship, subsidization, subsistence, support, welfare

substantiate *v.* affirm, attest to, authenticate, back up, bear out, confirm, corroborate, demonstrate, document, establish, justify, manifest, prove, ratify, show clearly, support, sustain, validate, verify

substitute *n.* agent, alternate, auxiliary, backup, deputy, double, fill-in, ghostwriter, proxy, relief, replacement, representative, stand-by, stand-in, surrogate, temporary expedient, temporary help, understudy

substitute *v.* act for, alternate, back up, change, cover for, delegate, deputize, do work of, double for, exchange, fill in for, interchange, relieve, replace, serve in another's place, stand in for, supplant, take another's place, take place of, understudy

subtract *v.* decrease, deduct, diminish, discount, remove, take away, take from, take off, take out, withdraw

succeed *v.* **1.** accomplish, achieve, acquire, advance, arrive at, attain, attain success, become successful, become wealthy, be fortunate, benefit, be successful, be victorious, carry out, complete, conquer, do well, fare well, flourish, gain, get ahead, grow, impress favorably, obtain, prevail over, profit, progress, prosper, reach, reach goal, realize, surmount, thrive, triumph, triumph over, win, win out over, work out **2.** become heir to, come after, come next, ensue, follow, follow after, go next, inherit, replace, supersede, supervene, supplant, take over, take place of

success *n.* accomplishment, achievement, affluence, attainment, being successful, benefit, doing well, fame, fortune, gain, good fortune, profit, progress, prosperity, realization, reward, triumph, victory, wealth, winning

successful *adj.* advantageous, best-selling, booming, flourishing, fortuitous, fortunate, fruitful, gainful, lucky, lucrative, moneymaking, noteworthy, paying, productive, profitable, prospering, prosperous, rewarding, thriving, triumphant, undefeated, victorious, wealthy, well-paying, winning

sue *v.* accuse, appeal, bring an action, bring charges against, bring suit, bring to court, bring to justice, bring to trial, charge, enter plea, entreat, file claim, file suit, implore, indict, institute legal proceedings, litigate, petition, plead for, prefer charges against, prosecute, solicit, summon, supplicate, take to court

suggest *v.* **1.** advance, advise, advocate, bring up, conjecture, counsel, give advice, introduce, move, offer, offer opinion, offer plan, offer suggestion, pose, proffer, propose, propound, put forward, recommend, submit **2.** allude to, bring to mind, evoke image of, hint, imply, indicate, insinuate, intimate, lead to believe, point in direction of, point to, put in mind of, signify, symbolize

suggestion *n.* **1.** advancement, advice, counsel, idea, invitation, motion, opinion, plan, pointer, presentation, proposal, recommendation, submission, tip **2.** allusion, hint, implication, indication, innuendo, insinuation, intimation, notion, suspicion, symbol, thought

suit *n.*   case, cause, lawsuit, legal action, litigation, proceeding, prosecution, trial

sum *n.*   **1.** aggregate, all, amount, entirety, gross, gross amount, quantity, score, summation, tally, total, totality, value, whole   **2.** conclusion, overview, recapitulation, review, summary, summing up, synopsis

summarize *v.*   abstract, condense, digest, encapsulate, epitomize, give main points, give summary, outline, recapitulate, review, sketch, sum up, synopsize

summary *n.*   abstract, brief, capitulation, compendium, condensation, digest, epitome, extract, outline, précis, prospectus, recapitulation, review, short statement, sketch, summation, synopsis

superintendent *n.*   administrator, caretaker, curator, custodian, director, maintenance person, manager, overseer, supervisor

superior *n.*   boss, chief, dignitary, director, executive, head, leader, manager, notable, principal, senior person, supervisor

supervise *v.*   administer, be responsible for, conduct, control, direct, govern, guide, handle, look after, manage, manage people, monitor, oversee, pilot, preside over, superintend, take care of, watch over

supervision *n.*   administration, care, conduct, control, direction, governance, guidance, handling, looking after, management, management of people, monitoring, oversight, presiding over, superintendence, taking care of, watching over

supervisor *n.*   administrator, boss, caretaker, chairperson, chief, custodian, director, executive, guide, manager, monitor, overseer, superintendent

supplement *n.*   accessory, addendum, addition, additive, adjunct, appendix, attachment, codicil, complement, epilog, extension, extra, insert, postscript, rider, sequel, subsidiary, suffix

supply *v.*   afford, cater, contribute, deliver, dispense, endow, equip, feed, fill, furnish, give, grant, hand over, outfit, produce, provide, replenish, satisfy, stock, transfer, turn over, yield

support *n.*   **1.** advocacy, aid, approval, assistance, backing, encouragement, espousal, furtherance, help, lift, patronage, protection, provision, relief, sponsorship, succor, sustenance, upkeep, welfare **2.** abutment, base, bed, brace, buttress, column, cornerstone, footing, foundation, frame, fulcrum, groundwork, joist, pillar, pole, post, prop, reinforcement, substructure, underpinning

support *v.* **1.** advance, advocate belief in, agree with, aid, approve of, assist, back, care for, champion, defend, encourage, endorse, espouse, finance, foster, further, justify, keep up, look after, maintain, nourish, patronize, pay expenses of, pay for, promote, protect, provide for, provide welfare, side with, sponsor, stand behind, subsidize, substantiate, sustain, take care of, underwrite, uphold **2.** base, bolster, brace, buttress, cradle, hold, hold up, keep up, prop up, reinforce, shore up, sustain, undergird, uphold

supporter *n.* advocate, aide, ally, backer, benefactor, champion, coworker, defender, exponent, expounder, fan, follower, helper, patron, proponent, second, sponsor, subscriber, sustainer

surplus *n.* balance, excess, extra, overage, overflow, overrun, overstock, oversupply, plethora, remainder, residue, superabundance

surroundings *n.* ambience, area, atmosphere, background, climate, environment, environs, habitat, locale, location, milieu, neighborhood, setting, vicinity

suspend *v.* adjourn, arrest, bar, break off, cease, check, cut short, debar, defer, delay, discontinue, dismiss, eliminate, end, exclude, halt, hold off, hold up, interrupt, lay aside, lay over, postpone, put off, quit, reject, retard, shelve, stop, table, withhold

symbol *n.* brand, character, characters, character string, crest, emblem, figure, glyph, graphic representation, hieroglyph, letter, likeness, logo, logotype, mark, representation, string of characters, trademark

symmetry *n.* agreement, balance, conformity, congruence, consistency, consonance, correspondence, evenness, parallelism, regularity, sameness, similarity, uniformity

symposium *n.* assembly, conference, congress, convocation, debate, panel discussion, round table, synod

synchronism *n.* chronological arrangement, coexistence, coincidence, concurrence, concurrency, coordination, isochronism, simultaneousness

synchronous   *adj.*   coexistent, concurrent, coterminous, isochronal, simultaneous, synchronal

synonymous   *adj.*   comparable, compatible, correspondent, corresponding, equal, equivalent, exact, identical, interchangeable, like, parallel, same, similar

synopsis   *n.*   abstract, brief, capsule, condensation, conspectus, digest, epitome, extract, outline, précis, prospectus, recapitulation, review, sketch, summary

system   *n.*   collection, combination of components, course, design, guidelines, method, methodology, mode, operation, outline, pattern, plan, policy, practice, procedure, process, program, rule, scheme, strategy, structure, systematization, tactics, technique, way

systematize   *v.*   arrange, array, methodize, order, organize, put in order, regulate, standardize, systemize

T

table *v.* defer, delay, hold off, hold up, lay aside, postpone, put aside, put off, put on hold, shelve

tabulate *v.* alphabetize, arrange, catalog, categorize, chart, codify, enumerate, grade, group, index, inventory, list, methodize, order, organize, range, systematize

tact *n.* acumen, adroitness, care, common sense, consideration, control, courtesy, diplomacy, discernment, discretion, discrimination, finesse, judgment, perception, poise, prudence, refinement, sensitivity, skill, subtlety, tactfulness, thoughtfulness, understanding

tactics *n.* approach, campaign, course, defense, design, generalship, logistics, maneuvers, maneuvering, means, method, move, plan, plot, ploy, policy, procedure, scheme, short-term methods, stratagems, strategic moves, strategy, technique

takeover *n.* acquisition, bid, change in controlling interest, change of interest, change of control, change of ownership, merger, merging, taking over

talent *n.* ability, aptitude, aptness, artistic ability, capability, capacity, craft, endowment, expertise, expertness, facility, faculty, flair, forte, genius, gift, inventiveness, power, skill

tangible *adj.* actual, appreciable, concrete, corporeal, definite, detectable, discernible, distinct, embodied, evident, existent, existing, manifest, material, observable, obvious, palpable, patent, perceivable, perceptible, physical, real, sensible, solid, substantial, tactile, touchable, visible

tape *v.* **1.** audiotape, dub, make record, make tape, record, register, tape-record, videotape **2.** bind, bond, close, fasten, hold together, mend, seal, secure, stick together, wrap

target *n.* aim, ambition, destination, end, goal, idea, intent, intention, mark, object, objective, point, purpose, pursuit, quarry

tariff *n.* ad valorem tax, assessment, charge, cost, duty, exaction, excise, export tax, federal tax, fee, import tax, impost, levy, payment, rate, schedule of charges, surcharge, system of charges, tax, toll, value-added tax

task *n.* assigned work, assignment, burden, charge, chore, commission, duty, effort, engagement, enterprise, errand, exercise, function, job, labor, lesson, mission, occupation, operation, process, project, quest, responsibility, strain, undertaking, work, work element

tax *n.* **1.** assessment, charge, contribution, custom, duty, exaction, excise, fee, fine, impost, levy, rate, tariff, taxation, taxing, toll **2.** burden, charge, demand, drain, duty, encumbrance, exertion, imposition, load, obligation, onus, pressure, responsibility, strain, weight

tax *v.* **1.** assess, charge, demand, exact, fix, impose, lay impost, lay on, levy, put on, rate, require **2.** burden, charge, drain, drive, encumber, exhaust, load, make demands on, oppress, overburden, overload, overwork, push, put pressure on, strain, stress, tire, wear out, weigh down

teach *v.* advise, brief, catechize, clarify, coach, demonstrate, direct, drill, edify, educate, elucidate, enlighten, explain, explicate, expound, give information, give instruction, give lessons, gloss, ground, guide, hold forth, illustrate, impart, implant, inculcate, indoctrinate, inform, infuse, initiate, instill, instruct, lecture, nurture, point out, prepare, propound, school, show, train, tutor

teamwork *n.* collaboration, combined action, combined effort, concert, concord, cooperation, coordination, harmony, interaction, joint action, joint effort, mutual cooperation, pooling resources, reciprocity, synergy, union

technical *adj.* industrial, mechanical, methodological, scholarly, scientific, specialized, technological, vocational

technician *n.* adept worker, authority, expert, maven, proficient worker, skilled worker, specialist

technique *n.* approach, artistry, capability, course, craft, custom, execution, facility, fashion, manner, means, method, methodology, mode, pattern, procedure, proficiency, routine, skill, style, system, tactics, technical skill, way

technology *n.* application of science, applications, applied knowledge, developed applications, engineering, scientific method, use of applied science, use of technical knowledge, use of technical methods, use of technical processes

temperament *n.* attitude, bent, character, constitution, disposition, emotions, humor, idiosyncrasy, inclination, makeup, mentality, mettle, mood, nature, outlook, personality, predilection, predisposition, propensity, quality, spirit, temper, tendency

tempo *n.*   beat, cadence, intermittence, measure, meter, momentum, motion, movement, pace, periodicity, progress, pulse, rate, recurrence, rhythm, speed, time, velocity

temporary *adj.*   acting, ad hoc, ad interim, backup, brief, ephemeral, evanescent, fleeting, impermanent, interim, limited, momentary, mortal, passing, perishable, provisional, short, short-lived, short-term, stopgap, substitute, transient, transitory

tenant *n.*   addressee, boarder, inhabitant, landholder, leaseholder, lessee, lodger, occupant, renter, resident, roomer

tendency *n.*   bent, bias, custom, disposition, habit, impulse, inclination, inclining, leaning, liability, likeliness, partiality, penchant, predilection, predisposition, proclivity, proneness, propensity, slant, susceptibility, trend, turn

tenet *n.*   article of faith, assumption, axiom, belief, canon, conviction, credo, creed, doctrine, dogma, faith, hypothesis, ideology, maxim, opinion, persuasion, position, postulation, precept, presumption, principle, rule, theory, thesis, view

term *n.*   **1.** appellation, denomination, description, designation, entry head, expression, head, locution, name, phrase, terminology, title, word   **2.** course, coverage period, cycle, duration, interval, length of time, limitation, period, phase, season, semester, sentence, session, space, span, spell, stretch, time

terminal *n.*   **1.** communicating device, computer area, computer device, computer work area, computer workstation, input-output device, personal computer, point of data entry, video display unit   **2.** carrier, depot, facilities, freight station, passenger station, station   **3.** boundary, end, end of line, end of road, extremity, limit, termination, terminus

terminology *n.*   language, locution, nomenclature, phraseology, phrasing, terms, vocabulary, wording

terms *n.*   agreement, assumptions, clauses, conditions, demands, details, particulars, points, premises, provisions, provisos, qualifications, specifications, stipulations, suppositions, understanding

test *v.*   analyze, appraise, assay, assess, check, check out, determine, evaluate, examine, experiment with, explore, inspect, interrogate, investigate, judge, measure, probe, prove, put to test, question, quiz, scrutinize, try, try out, verify

testify *v.* acknowledge, affirm, assert, assure, attest, authenticate, back up, bear witness, certify, confirm, corroborate, declare, demonstrate, depose, endorse, establish, give evidence, give testimony, give word, make evident, make promise, offer assurance, pledge, profess, promise, prove, show, stand behind, state under oath, substantiate, swear to, uphold, validate, verify, vouch for, vow, warrant, witness

testimonial *n.* commemoration, commendation, endorsement, favorable mention, homage, honor, honorable mention, letter of recommendation, memorial, memorialization, ovation, recommendation, reference, referral, remembrance, salute, testament, testimony, tribute, voucher

testimony *n.* affirmation, assertion, attestation, avowal, confirmation, corroboration, declaration, demonstration, deposition, documentation, evidence, grounds, information, proclamation, profession, statement, substantiation, support, sworn statement, testament, verification, witness

text *n.* **1.** body, contents, context, data, essence, focus, fundamentals, gist, idea, information, issue, main body, matter, point, printed matter, subject, subject matter, substance, theme, thesis, topic, wording, words **2.** book, handbook, manual, primer, reader, reference, reference book, schoolbook, textbook, workbook

theme *n.* **1.** argument, background information, concept, gist, idea, issue, keynote, main idea, motif, point, problem, proposition, question, recurrent pattern, subject, subject matter, text, thesis, topic **2.** article, commentary, composition, criticism, dissertation, essay, exposition, manuscript, monograph, paper, piece, report, research paper, study, thesis, treatise, written composition

theorem *n.* assumption, axiom, belief, concept, conclusion, dictum, formula, hypothesis, law, postulate, principle, proposition, provable statement, rule, theoretical proposition, theoretical statement, theory, thesis

theory *n.* assumption, belief, concept, conjecture, doctrine, dogma, hypothesis, idea, philosophy, postulate, premise, presumption, rationale, speculation, supposition, surmise, theorem, thesis

thesis *n.* **1.** argument, assertion, assumption, axiom, belief, conjecture, contention, hypothesis, idea, opinion, point, position, postulate, postulation, premise, presumption, principle, proposition, statement, subject, supposition, surmise, theme, theory, topic, view   **2.** composition, discourse, disquisition, dissertation, essay, investigation, master's thesis, monograph, paper, research paper, study, tract, treatise

thought *n.*   **1.** apprehending, attention, cogitation, cognition, concentration, consideration, considering, contemplation, deducing, deduction, deliberation, discerning, focusing, inducing, induction, inference, inferring, introspection, intuition, meditation, musing, perceiving, rationalization, rationalizing, realizing, reasoning, recall, recollection, reflection, reminiscence, retrospection, review, rumination, scrutiny, speculation, theorization, thinking, understanding, using logic   **2.** appraisal, aspiration, assessment, assumption, belief, calculation, concept, conception, concern, conclusion, conjecture, conviction, dream, estimation, expectation, feeling, guess, hope, hypothesis, idea, image, judgment, notion, opinion, premise, prospect, sentiment, supposition, surmise, theory, view

threshold *n.*   **1.** beginning, birth, bottom, brink, commencement, conception, dawn, debut, edge, entry level, genesis, inception, onset, origin, outset, point of departure, source, start, starting point, top, verge   **2.** door, doorsill, doorstep, doorway, entrance, entryway, gate, ground plate, opening, portal, sill

thrift *n.*   austerity, conservation, conserving, economizing, economy, frugality, parsimony, prevention of waste, prudence, saving, scrimping, skimping, stinginess, thriftiness, thrifty management

throughput *n.*   computer performance, output, processing rate, processing time, production, system efficiency, system performance, transmission rate, work rate

tier *n.*   band, belt, category, class, floor, grouping, layer, level, line, order, rank, row, story, stratification, stratum, zone

time *n.*   age, break, chronology, date, day, duration, epoch, era, extent, future, hour, instant, interim, interlude, intermission, interval, juncture, length, lifetime, minute, moment, month, occasion, past, pause, period, point, present, season, second, shift, span, spell, stretch, tempo, tenure, term, tide, tour, turn, week, while, year

timely *adj.*   appropriate, auspicious, convenient, favorable, fitting, fortunate, opportune, prompt, proper, propitious, punctual, ripe, seasonable, suitable, up-to-date, up-to-the-minute, well-timed

title *n.* **1.** article name, banner, book name, caption, document name, head, headline, inscription, legend, rubric, sign, story name, streamer, subhead, subtitle **2.** alias, anonym, appellation, assumed name, denomination, designation, epithet, form of address, honorific, label, name, pen name, pseudonym, stage name, style, term, term of respect **3.** claim, deed, entitlement, evidence of ownership, evidence of possession, holding, license, ownership, possession, privilege, proof of ownership, property deed, right

token *n.* badge, evidence, expression, favor, gift, indicia, indication, keepsake, mark, memento, memorial, note, proof, remembrance, reminder, representation, sign, souvenir, symbol, testimony, trophy

tolerance *n.* acceptance, allowance, benevolence, endurance, forbearance, fortitude, immunity, indulgence, kindliness, lack of prejudice, leeway for variation, open-mindedness, permissible deviation, resistance, stamina, strength, sympathy, toleration, unresponsiveness

toll *n.* assessment, charge, consideration, cost, duty, exaction, fee, impost, levy, payment, price, rate, tariff, tax, tribute, usage charge

tone *n.* accent, attitude, color quality, color value, emphasis, expression, force, inflection, intonation, manner, manner of expression, mode, modulation, mood, musical sound, pitch, resonance, sound quality, spirit, stress, style, style of expression, temper, timbre, tonality, vibration

tool *n.* **1.** apparatus, appliance, contrivance, device, gadget, icon, implement, instrument, machine, mechanism, object, utensil **2.** accessory, accomplice, agency, agent, auxiliary, dupe, intermediary, medium, messenger, pawn, puppet

topic *n.* area of activity, case, concept, field of inquiry, idea, issue, main idea, matter, notion, point, point in question, problem, proposition, question, resolution, subject, subject matter, text, theme, thesis

total *n.* accumulation, aggregate, amount, bulk, entire amount, entirety, full amount, gross amount, mass, quantity, result, sum, totality, whole

total *v.* add, add up, amount to, calculate, cipher, comprise, compute, consist of, count, enumerate, equal, figure, number, reach, result in, sum up, yield

toxic *adj.* contagious, contaminating, dangerous, deadly, harmful, infectious, infective, injurious, lethal, noxious, pestilent, poisonous, venomous, virulent

track *v.* apprehend, ascertain, detect, determine, discover, expose, find, find out, follow, go after, hunt for, look for, pursue, run down, search out, trace, trail, uncover, unearth

trade *n.* **1.** bargaining, barter, business, buying and selling, commerce, commercialism, dealing, enterprise, exchange, interchange, market competitors, marketing, merchandising, negotiating, negotiation, sales, swap, traffic, transactions, truck **2.** business, calling, career, craft, employment, enterprise, handicraft, job, lifework, line of work, livelihood, occupation, profession, pursuit, skill, vocation, work

trademark *n.* brand, brand name, device, emblem, hallmark, identification, label, legal protection, logo, logotype, mark, name, representation, sign, symbol, stamp, tag, word

tradition *n.* convention, custom, customs, established form, established practice, fashion, folklore, form, habit, lore, observance, practice, praxis, ritual, unwritten law, usage, way

traffic *n.* barter, business, business activity, business connection, buying and selling, commerce, communication, connection, dealing, exchange, interchange, marketing, merchandising, trade, transactions, truck, volume, volume of activity, volume of business

traffic *v.* bargain, barter, buy and sell, deal, do business, exchange, handle, interchange, make deals, market, merchandise, negotiate, sell, swap, trade, transact, truck

train *v.* accustom, break in, coach, develop skills, direct, discipline, drill, educate, enlighten, equip, exercise, familiarize, give lessons, ground, guide, improve, inculcate, indoctrinate, inform, instruct, make ready, practice, prepare, prime, qualify, school, season, shape, study, teach, tutor

training *n.* apprenticeship, background, basics, coaching, demonstrating, development, direction, discipline, drilling, education, grounding, guidance, indoctrination, instruction, learning, practice, preparation, readying, schooling, seasoning, teaching, tutelage

trait *n.* attribute, character, characteristic, distinguishing feature, feature, habit, idiosyncrasy, manner, mannerism, mark, oddity, peculiarity, property, quality, quirk, virtue

transact *v.* accomplish, carry on, carry out, close deal, complete, conclude, conduct, contract, discharge, do business, enact, execute, exercise, handle, manage, negotiate, perform, prosecute, purchase, sell, settle

transaction *n.* accomplishment, action, agreement, bargain, business deal, carrying on, carrying out, closing of a deal, completion, concluding, conducting, contract, deal, discharge, doing business, enactment, event, execution, exercising, handling, managing, negotiation, performance, proceeding, prosecution, purchase, purchasing, realization, sale, selling, settling, trade, undertaking

transfer *n.* assignment, bequeathal, bestowal, change of location, consignment, conveyance, conveying, displacement, disposition, move, relocation, removal, sale, shipment, transferal, transference, transit, transmission, transmittal, transportation

transfer *v.* assign, bequeath, bestow, carry, cart, cede, change location, consign, convey, deed, delegate, deliver, dispatch, dispense, displace, dispose of, express, ferry, forward, give away, grant, hand over, haul, mail, move, remove, pass, pass on, relegate, relocate, remove, sell, send, ship, sign over, take, transmit, transplant, transport, turn over

transit *n.* carriage, carrying, conveyance, crossing, freightage, motion, movement, passage, passing, portage, shipment, transfer, transference, transport, transportation, transporting, travel

translation *n.* decoding, conversion, elucidation, explanation, interpretation, paraphrase, rendering, rendition, rephrasing, restatement, transcription, translated version, transliteration

transmit *v.* bequeath, broadcast, carry, communicate, convey, diffuse, dispatch, disseminate, forward, hand down, impart, issue, mail, pass on, radio, relay, remit, route, send, send out, ship, spread, take, telecast, televise, transfer, transport

transport *v.* bring, carry, convey, deliver, ferry, forward, move, send, ship, take, transfer, truck

travel *n.* See **trip**

treasury *n.* **1.** archive, bank, cache, depository, exchequer, repository, storage, vault **2.** assets, bonds, capital, currency, finances, funds, holdings, money, resources, revenue, savings, securities, shares, stocks

treatise *n.* commentary, composition, critique, discourse, discussion, disquisition, dissertation, essay, exposition, monograph, paper, review, study, thesis, tract

treatment *n.* angle, application, approach, care, conduct, dealing, direction, execution, exercise, management, manipulation, manner, method, mode, practice, procedure, proceeding, processing, reception, strategy, usage, way

trend *n.* **1.** aim, bearing, bent, course, current, direction, drift, general direction, general movement, inclination, leaning, movement, orientation, progression, stream, swing, tendency, tenor, tone **2.** craze, fad, fashion, look, mode, rage, style, taste, vogue

tribute *n.* acclaim, acclamation, accolades, acknowledgment, appreciation, citation, commendation, compliment, eulogy, honor, laudation, panegyric, praise, recognition, respect, testimonial

trip *n.* cruise, drive, excursion, expedition, flight, journey, mission, outing, passage, pilgrimage, tour, travel, trek, voyage

troubleshooter *n.* arbitrator, diplomat, mediator, negotiator, peacemaker, repairperson, serviceperson

truck *n.* **1.** barter, business, buying and selling, commerce, commercial goods, commodities, dealings, exchange, merchandise, stock, trade, traffic **2.** panel, pickup, semi, semitrailor, stationwagon, van, vehicle

truck *v.* bargain, barter, buy and sell, carry, convey, deal, deliver, do business, exchange, handle, haul, negotiate, ship, swap, trade, traffic, transfer, transport

true *adj.* **1.** absolute, accurate, actual, authentic, certain, confirmed, correct, dependable, earnest, exact, factual, genuine, honest, lawful, legal, legitimate, licit, natural, perfect, precise, proper, pure, real, right, rightful, sincere, straight, sure, truthful, unadulterated, undeniable, unerring, unimaginary, unquestionable, valid, veracious **2.** allegiant, conscientious, constant, dedicated, dependable, devoted, dutiful, faithful, fast, firm, honest, honorable, incorruptible, loyal, reliable, scrupulous, sincere, stable, staunch, steadfast, steady, true-hearted, trusted, trustworthy, unswerving, unwavering, upright

trust *n.* **1.** business, business combination, combination, combine, conglomerate, corporation, group, institution, large company, monopoly, organization **2.** agreement, care, charge, custody, duty, fiduciary relationship, guardianship, keeping, protection, responsibility, safekeeping, superintendence, supervision, trusteeship, tutelage, ward **3.** anticipation, assurance, belief, certainty, certitude, confidence, conviction, dependence, expectation, faith, hope, reliance, sureness

trustworthy *adj.* believable, credible, dependable, ethical, faithful, honest, honorable, loyal, principled, reliable, responsible, steadfast, true, trusted, unfailing, upright, veracious

turmoil *n.* agitation, bedlam, chaos, commotion, confusion, demonstration, disorder, disquiet, distress, disturbance, ferment, fuss, mix-up, noise, pandemonium, protest, protest march, revolt, riot, row, strife, strike, trouble, tumult, turbulence, unrest, upheaval, uproar

turnaround *n.* economic improvement, favorable reversal, improvement, receipt-to-return time, reversal, time spent, total time, turnabout

turning point *n.* change, crisis, critical moment, critical period, crossroads, crucial moment, crucial occurrence, culmination, decisive moment, decisive point, development, juncture, new direction, shift, transition

turnout *n.* **1.** aggregate, amount, amount produced, output, product, production, quota, total produced, volume, yield **2.** assemblage, assembled group, assembly, attendance, attendees, audience, congregation, crowd, gathering, number, spectators, throng, viewers

turn out *v.* appoint, bring out, build, equip, fabricate, finish, fit, furnish, make, manufacture, outfit, process, produce, put out

turnover *n.* employee losses, movement out, number of replacements, overturning, ratio of sales to net worth, reorganization, replacement frequency, reversal, rotation, shakeup, shift, trading volume, upset

type *n.* character, face, font, letter, print, printed character, printed output, printing, symbol, typeface

typical *adj.* average, characteristic, classic, common, commonplace, conventional, customary, emblematic, everyday, expected, general, habitual, illustrative, indicative, model, natural, normal, ordinary, paradigmatic, prevalent, quintessential, regular, regulation, representative, sample, standard, stock, suggestive, symbolic, unexceptional, usual

U

unabridged *n.* all-inclusive, complete, comprehensive, entire, full-length, intact, total, unabbreviated, uncondensed, uncut, unshortened, whole

unacceptable *adj.* below-par, improper, inadmissible, insupportable, objectionable, unappealing, undesirable, unsatisfactory, unsuitable, unwanted, unwelcome

unanimous *adj.* agreed, collective, combined, common, concerted, concordant, consonant, harmonious, like-minded, shared, solid, undisputed, undivided, unified, united

unauthorized *adj.* illegal, illegitimate, outlawed, prohibited, unallowed, unapproved, uncertified, unlawful, unofficial, unsanctioned, unwarranted, wrongful

unconditional *adj.* absolute, categorical, certain, complete, conclusive, decisive, definite, incontestable, indisputable, indubitable, open, outright, positive, total, unconstrained, undisputed, unequivocal, unlimited, unmistakable, unqualified, unquestionable, unreserved, unrestricted

unconventional *adj.* atypical, bizarre, curious, eccentric, idiosyncratic, individual, irregular, nonconformist, odd, offbeat, original, peculiar, rare, uncommon, unfamiliar, unique, unorthodox, unparalleled, unusual

undecided *adj.* ambivalent, debatable, doubtful, dubious, hesitant, indecisive, indefinite, irresolute, open, pending, tentative, uncertain, uncommitted, undetermined, unresolved, unsettled, unsure, wavering

underestimate *v.* depreciate, disparage, minimize, miscalculate, misjudge, rate too low, slight, underrate, undervalue

underline *v.* accent, accentuate, call attention to, draw attention to, emphasize, feature, give emphasis to, give prominence to, highlight, italicize, mark, punctuate, stress, underscore

underscore *v.* See **underline**

understand *v.* **1.** apprehend, be acquainted with, be aware of, be cognizant of, be conscious of, comprehend, discern, fathom, figure out, glean, grasp, have knowledge of, infer, interpret, know, learn, penetrate, perceive, realize, recognize, see, seize, sympathize **2.** accept, assume, believe, conceive, conclude, conjecture, consider, deduce, fancy, guess, imagine, infer, presume, suppose, surmise, suspect, take for granted, take it, think

understanding *n.* **1.** acquaintance, apprehension, awareness, cognizance, comprehension, consciousness, discernment, fathoming, figuring out, gleaning, grasp, inference, insight, interpretation, intuition, knowing, knowledge, learning, penetration, perception, perceptiveness, realization, recognition, seeing, seizing, sympathy **2.** acceptance, assumption, belief, conception, conclusion, conjecture, consideration, deduction, fancy, guess, imagining, impression, inference, interpretation, judgment, opinion, presumption, surmise, thinking, view, viewpoint **3.** accord, arrangement, common view, compact, concord, contract, covenant, deal, informal agreement, pact, truce

undertake *v.* agree to, assume responsibility for, attempt, begin, commence, commit to, contract for, embark on, endeavor, engage in, enter upon, guarantee, initiate, launch, pledge, promise, set about, set out, start, take on, try, try out, venture, volunteer for

undertaking *n.* agreement, assignment, campaign, commission, commitment, contract, covenant, deal, effort, endeavor, enterprise, game, job, obligation, operation, pact, pledge, program, project, promise, proposition, pursuit, quest, task, venture, work

undervalue *v.* depreciate, disparage, minimize, miscalculate, misjudge, rate too low, sell short, underestimate, underrate

underwrite *v.* accede, agree to, aid, approve, assume risk, back, consent, cosign, countersign, endorse, finance, fund, guarantee, help, initial, insure, maintain, promote, provide financing, sanction, seal, sign, sponsor, subscribe to, subsidize, support, uphold, validate

undo *v.* abolish, abrogate, annul, cancel, counteract, countermand, cut out, defeat, destroy, disengage, dispense with, do away with, eliminate, eradicate, free, invalidate, make void, negate, neutralize, nullify, offset, overthrow, overturn, put end to, quash, reinstate, remove, repeal, rescind, restore, retract, return, return to previous state, reverse, reverse previous action, revoke, subvert, undermine, unlock, vitiate

unemployed *adj.* disengaged, fired, free, idle, inactive, inoperative, jobless, laid off, nonfunctioning, out-of-work, unengaged

unethical *adj.* corrupt, deceitful, dishonorable, dishonest, disreputable, illegal, immoral, improper, unconscionable, underhanded, unlawful, unprincipled, unprofessional, unscrupulous, wrong

unfair *adj.* biased, deceitful, discriminatory, dishonest, dishonorable, disproportionate, illegal, immoral, improper, inequitable, injurious, one-sided, partisan, unconscionable, undue, unethical, unjust, unjustifiable, unlawful, unprincipled, unreasonable, unscrupulous, unsporting, unwarranted, wrong

unfamiliar *adj.* **1.** ignorant, inexperienced, unaccustomed, unacquainted, unaware, unconversant, uninformed, uninitiated, uninstructed, unknowing, unpracticed, unskilled, unversed **2.** bizarre, curious, different, exotic, foreign, new, novel, obscure, original, peculiar, remote, strange, uncommon, unconventional, unexpected, unexplored, uninvestigated, unique, unknown, unorthodox, unparalleled, unusual, weird

uniform *adj.* **1.** compatible, congruous, consonant, established, fixed, formalized, harmonious, homogeneous, invariable, measured, methodical, ordered, orderly, regimented, regular, regulated, stable, standard, symmetrical, unalterable, unchangeable, unchanging, undeviating, undiversified, unfluctuating, unvaried, unvarying, well-balanced, well-proportioned **2.** analogous, comparable, consistent, consonant, correspondent, double, equal, equivalent, exact, identical, like, mated, same, selfsame, similar, undifferentiated, unvaried, unvarying

unimportant *adj.* frivolous, inferior, immaterial, inconsequential, inconsiderable, insignificant, irrelevant, little, meaningless, minor, negligible, nonessential, petty, slight, trifling, trivial, unnecessary, useless, worthless

union *n.* **1.** alliance, association, coalition, confederacy, congress, consortium, federation, guild, labor union, league, local, order, society, syndicate, trade union **2.** accord, agreement, amalgam, amalgamation, blend, combination, commixture, compound, concord, congregation, consolidation, fusion, harmony, joining, meeting, melding, merger, merging, mix, mixture, symbiosis, synthesis, unanimity, unification, unison, uniting, unity

unit *n.* arm, assemblage, assembly, complement, component, constituent, detachment, division, element, entity, group, ingredient, item, link, member, module, outfit, part, piece, portion, product, product line, section, segment, subassembly, subdivision, subsidiary, system, totality, wing

unite *v.*   affiliate, ally, amalgamate, associate, band together, blend, bring together, coalesce, combine, commingle, confederate, conjoin, connect, consolidate, cooperate, fuse, gather together, homogenize, incorporate, intertwine, join, join forces, join together, league, link, merge, mix, pool, pull together, solidify, strengthen, syndicate, unify, weld, work together

united *adj.*   affiliated, allied, amalgamated, associated, banded together, blended, coalesced, commingled, confederated, conjoined, connected, consolidated, cooperative, fused, gathered together, homogeneous, incorporated, integrated, intertwined, joined together, merged, mixed, pooled, solidified, strengthened, syndicated, undivided, unified, welded, working together

unity *n.*   accord, agreement, alliance, combination, compatibility, concert, concord, confederation, congruity, consensus, federation, harmony, homogeneity, identity, individuality, likemindedness, oneness, sameness, similarity, singularity, totality, unanimity, unification, uniformity, union, unison, wholeness

universal *adj.*   all-embracing, all-inclusive, boundless, broad, catholic, common, comprehensive, ecumenical, endless, extensive, general, generic, global, multinational, omnipresent, preponderant, total, ubiquitous, unlimited, unrestricted, widespread, worldwide

unlawful *adj.*   banned, criminal, felonious, forbidden, illegal, illicit, larcenous, outlawed, prohibited, unauthorized, unconstitutional, unlicensed, wrongful

unload *v.*   alleviate, discard, discharge, dispose of, dump, empty, free, get rid of, move out, remove, sell, sell off, take profit, transfer, unburden

unnecessary *adj.*   additional, dispensable, excess, expendable, extraneous, gratuitous, irrelevant, needless, noncompulsory, nonessential, optional, random, redundant, superfluous, surplus, undesirable, unessential, unneeded, unrequired, useless, worthless

unpaid *adj.*   **1.** delinquent, due, mature, outstanding, overdue, past due, payable, unsettled   **2.** contributed, donated, free, gratuitous, honorary, unsalaried, voluntary, volunteer

unprofessional *adj.* amateurish, improper, inadequate, incompetent, inefficient, inexperienced, inexpert, lax, neglectful, negligent, unbusinesslike, undignified, unethical, unfitting, unprincipled, unskilled, unsuitable, untrained

unqualified *adj.* **1.** amateur, ill-equipped, inadequate, incapable, incompetent, ineligible, inexperienced, unable, unequipped, unfit, unprepared, unskilled, unsuited **2.** absolute, categorical, certain, clear, complete, consummate, downright, explicit, outright, perfect, positive, thorough, thoroughgoing, total, unadulterated, unconditional, unequivocal, unlimited, unmitigated, unreserved, unrestrained, unrestricted, utter, wholehearted

unreasonable *adj.* **1.** absurd, biased, erratic, far-fetched, foolish, illogical, impossible, incongruous, incredible, invalid, irrational, meaningless, mindless, nonsensical, opinionated, preposterous, reckless, senseless, shortsighted, silly, thoughtless, untenable, wrong **2.** excessive, exorbitant, extreme, immoderate, inordinate, outrageous, overpriced, prohibitive, undue, unfair, unjust, unwarranted, wrongful

unreliable *adj.* capricious, deceptive, delusive, disreputable, dubious, erratic, erroneous, fallible, false, fickle, frivolous, implausible, inaccurate, inconstant, irresponsible, questionable, uncertain, unconvincing, undependable, unfaithful, unsound, unstable, unsure, untrue, untrustworthy, vacillating, wavering

unsafe *adj.* chancy, dangerous, explosive, hazardous, insecure, menacing, ominous, perilous, precarious, risky, threatening, treacherous, uncertain, undependable, unreliable, unsound, unstable, unsteady, untrustworthy

unsatisfactory *adj.* defective, deficient, disappointing, displeasing, imperfect, inadequate, inappropriate, inferior, insufficient, lacking, mediocre, objectionable, poor, troublesome, unacceptable, undesirable, unfit, unsuitable, unwelcome, unworthy, wanting

unsound *adj.* ailing, bankrupt, dangerous, defective, delicate, deranged, diseased, encumbered, erroneous, fallacious, faulty, flawed, flimsy, frail, illogical, inaccurate, incorrect, indebted, infirm, insecure, insolvent, invalid, mad, shaky, unbalanced, unhealthy, unreliable, unsafe, unstable, unsteady, unsubstantial

unsuitable *adj.* disproportionate, ill-suited, improper, inadequate, inadmissible, inappropriate, incompatible, incongruous, inconsistent, ineligible, inharmonious, unacceptable, unbecoming, unfit, unfitting, unseasonable, unseemly, unsuited

untimely *adj.*   abortive, anachronistic, awkward, early, ill-timed, inappropriate, inconvenient, inexpedient, inopportune, mistimed, out-of-date, premature, unfortunate, unlucky, unpropitious, unseasonable, unseemly, unsuitable, unsuited, wrong

unusual *adj.*   abnormal, atypical, bizarre, curious, different, exceptional, extraordinary, infrequent, irregular, odd, peculiar, phenomenal, queer, rare, remarkable, scarce, strange, surprising, uncommon, unconventional, unexpected, unfamiliar, unique, unorthodox, unparalleled, unprecedented

unwarranted *adj.*   baseless, groundless, inappropriate, indefensible, inexcusable, unconscionable, undeserved, unfair, unfounded, ungrounded, unjust, unjustified, unreasonable, unwarrantable, wrong

update *v.*   amend, bring up to date, make current, make modern, make new, modernize, modify, provide current information, refurbish, rejuvenate, renew, renovate, revise

upgrade *v.*   better, correct, expand, expand capabilities, fix up, improve, improve performance, improve quality, modernize, purchase new release, purchase new version, refurbish, replace

upkeep *n.*   care, conservation, expenses, keep, maintenance, management, overhead, preservation, repair, subsistence, support, sustenance

up-to-date *adj.*   contemporary, current, modern, popular, present, present-day, state-of-the-art, stylish, timely, trendy, up-to-the-minute

urban *adj.*   central, city, civic, developed, downtown, inner-city, intensively developed, metropolitan, municipal, town

usable *adj.*   accessible, available, consumable, convenient, employable, functional, helpful, operative, practicable, practical, ready, running, serviceable, useful, working

usage *n.*   application, convention, custom, employment, expression, form, formality, habit, handling, language, locution, management, manner, method, mode, observance, operation, policy, practice, procedure, regulation, routine, rule, speech, tradition, treatment, use, way, wording

use *v.* apply, avail oneself of, capitalize, consume, control, employ, exercise, exert, exhaust, expend, exploit, find use for, handle, make use of, manage, maneuver, manipulate, operate, practice, profit by, put into action, put to use, put to work, regulate, set in motion, spend, utilize, wield, work with

useful *adj.* advantageous, beneficial, commodious, convenient, effective, effectual, favorable, functional, handy, helpful, instrumental, practicable, practical, pragmatic, profitable, rewarding, serviceable, suitable, usable, utilitarian, valuable, worthwhile

usual *adj.* accustomed, average, common, commonplace, conventional, customary, established, everyday, expected, familiar, fixed, frequent, general, habitual, mainstream, natural, normal, ordinary, prevailing, prevalent, regular, routine, standard, stock, typical

utility *n.* advantage, applicability, avail, benefit, convenience, favorableness, fitness, functionalism, point, practicality, profitability, service, serviceability, usability, use, usefulness

V

vacancy *n.* available position, available room, chance, emptiness, gap, hiatus, job opening, opening, opportunity, rental, space, vacuousness, vacuum, void

vacate *v.* abandon, annul, avoid, depart from, discharge, dissolve, empty, evacuate, give up, go away, hand over, leave, leave empty, let go, move out, quit, relinquish, render void, renounce, resign, retire from, set aside, turn over, void, withdraw

valid *adj.* accurate, attested, authenticated, authoritative, believable, binding, certified, cogent, conclusive, confirmed, convincing, correct, credible, determinative, factual, genuine, just, lawful, legal, legally binding, legitimate, logical, official, operationally acceptable, permissible, persuasive, powerful, proven, reasonable, right, solid, sound, strong, substantial, tested, trustworthy, truthful, weighty, well-founded, well-grounded

validate *v.* approve, attest to, authenticate, authorize, certify, confirm, corroborate, empower, entitle, establish, legalize, legitimize, license, make legal, notarize, permit, prove, qualify, ratify, sanction, set seal to, substantiate, verify, warrant

validity *n.* accuracy, authority, cogency, correctness, effectiveness, force, genuineness, lawfulness, legality, legitimacy, persuasiveness, potency, power, right, soundness, strength, weight

valuable *adj.* appreciated, beneficial, cherished, costly, dear, estimable, expensive, helpful, high-priced, important, inestimable, invaluable, precious, priceless, prized, profitable, rare, respected, scarce, serviceable, treasured, useful, valued, very important, worthwhile, worthy

value *n.* **1.** appraisal, assessment, charge, cost, evaluation, expense, financial worth, market price, monetary worth, price, rate, valuable consideration, valuation **2.** advantage, benefit, consequence, desirability, estimation, excellence, gain, goodness, help, implication, import, importance, marketability, meaning, merit, profit, purpose, quality, sense, significance, stature, superiority, use, usefulness, utility, valuation, worth

variable *adj.* changing, changeable, flexible, fluctuating, fluid, inconstant, irregular, protean, random, uncertain, unsettled, unstable, unsteady, vacillating, variant, varying, wavering

variety *n.* **1.** assortment, collection, conglomeration, difference, disparity, divergency, diversification, diversity, heterogeneity, intermixture, medley, miscellany, mixture, multifariousness, potpourri, variance, variation **2.** brand, breed, category, class, classification, denomination, description, division, genre, grade, kind, lot, make, order, race, sort, strain, subdivision, type

various *adj.* assorted, different, differing, disparate, distinct, diverse, diversified, heterogeneous, individual, manifold, many, miscellaneous, mixed, multifarious, multiple, numerous, separate, several, sundry, unequal, unlike, variant, varied, variegated

vault *n.* basement, box, cellar, crypt, depository, hold, mausoleum, repository, safe, safe-deposit box, sepulcher, storeroom, strongbox, strong room, tomb

vehicle *n.* **1.** agency, agent, channel, conduit, expedient, implement, instrument, intermediary, means, mechanism, medium, method, ministry, organ, route, tool, way **2.** automobile, bus, car, carrier, conveyance, machine, tractor, transportation, truck, van

vendor *n.* businessperson, dealer, importer, manufacturer, merchant, salesperson, seller, supplier, trader, wholesale distributor

venture *n.* adventure, chance, deal, enterprise, experiment, gamble, hazard, investment, mission, project, pursuit, risk, speculation, undertaking

verbal *adj.* conversational, exact, expressed, literal, oral, precise, rhetorical, spoken, stated, vocal, unwritten, verbatim

verbatim *adj.* accurate, exact, explicit, faithful, letter-for-letter, line-for-line, literal, precise, strict, undeviating, word-for-word

verify *v.* acknowledge, affirm, assure, attest to, authenticate, back up, bear out, bear witness to, certify, check, confirm, corroborate, demonstrate, determine, document, double-check, establish, guarantee, identify, justify, make certain, make sure, prove, substantiate, support, testify to, underwrite, validate, vouch for, warrant

versatile *adj.* adaptable, all-around, all-purpose, changeable, many-sided, multifaceted, multipurpose, resourceful, variable

version *n.* account, adaptation, clarification, condensation, copy, enactment, execution, form, interpretation, paraphrase, portrayal, production, reading, rendering, rendition, reproduction, restatement, rewording, sketch, story, transcription, translation, understanding, variant

viewpoint *n.* angle, attitude, feeling, opinion, outlook, perspective, point of view, position, posture, sentiment, slant, stance, stand, standpoint, vantage point, view

violation *n.* abuse, breach, contravention, crime, delinquency, dereliction, disruption, encroachment, felony, illegality, infraction, infringement, misbehavior, misdemeanor, negligence, offense, transgression, trespass, violating, wrong

vision *n.* concept, conception, discernment, dream, envisioning, fancy, farsightedness, foresight, idea, ideal, insight, mental image, mental picture, outlook, perspective, point of view, slant, standpoint, understanding, view, visualization

visual display *n.* See **monitor**

vocabulary *n.* dictionary, glossary, language, lexicon, terminology, thesaurus, wordbook, word inventory, words, word stock

vocation *n.* art, business, calling, career, craft, employment, field, job, lifework, line of work, livelihood, occupation, position, post, profession, pursuit, situation, trade, undertaking, work

volunteer *v.* advance, bestow, come forward, give, grant, offer, offer services, present, present self, proffer, propose, put forward, say, sign up, step forward, submit, suggest, tell, tender

vouch for *v.* affirm, answer for, assure, attest to, authenticate, avow, back, back up, bear witness, be responsible for, certify, confirm, corroborate, cosign, ensure, give assurance, guarantee, indemnify, profess, promise, sign for, sponsor, stand behind, substantiate, support, swear to, uphold, verify, vow, warrant, witness

W

wages *n.* allowance, compensation, earnings, fee, income, pay, payment, recompense, remuneration, reward, salary, stipend

waive *v.* abandon, avoid, cede, defer, delay, disclaim, dismiss, dispense with, disregard, eliminate, forgo, forsake, give up, hold off, postpone, prorogue, put aside, put off, refrain from, relinquish, remove, renounce, set aside, shelve, stay, surrender, suspend, table, turn over, yield

waiver *n.* abandonment, avoidance, deferral, delay, disclaimer, dismissal, elimination, forsaking, giving up, postponement, putting aside, refusal, relinquishment, removal, setting aside, surrender, tabling

walkout *n.* See **strike**

warehouse *n.* depository, depot, distribution center, hold, repository, stockpile, stockroom, storage place, storehouse, storeroom

wares *n.* articles, commodities, goods, line of merchandise, manufactured goods, manufactured items, manufactures, merchandise, produce, products, stock, supplies, vendibles

warrant *n.* accreditation, assurance, authentication, authority, authorization, certificate, certification, commission, credential, credentials, guarantee, justification, license, pass, permission, permit, pledge, right, sanction, security, support, validation, verification, warranty, word

warrant *v.* accredit, affirm, approve, assure, attest to, authenticate, authorize, back, certify, commission, defend, endorse, ensure, give word, guarantee, justify, license, permit, pledge, promise, provide warranty, sanction, secure, stand behind, stipulate, support, swear to, take oath, underwrite, uphold, verify, vouch for, vow

warranty *n.* assurance, authorization, binding promise, certificate, collateral, covenant, guarantee, pledge, promise, protection, sanction, security, support, surety, written guarantee, written promise

wasteful *adj.* careless, excessive, extravagant, immoderate, improvident, lavish, liberal, overgenerous, overindulgent, prodigal, profligate, profuse, reckless, spendthrift, thriftless, uneconomical, wanton

wealth *n.* abundance, affluence, assets, bounty, capital, cash, fortune, funds, gold, holdings, luxury, means, money, opulence, plenitude, plenty, profusion, property, prosperity, resources, riches, richness, securities, treasure, worth

weigh *v.* analyze, consider, contemplate, deliberate, evaluate, examine, give attention to, give thought to, meditate on, mull over, ponder, reflect on, ruminate, study, think about, think over

well-known *adj.* acclaimed, celebrated, common, conventional, customary, eminent, established, famed, familiar, famous, illustrious, important, known, notable, noted, notorious, popular, preeminent, prominent, recognized, renowned, traditional, widely known

widespread *adj.* boundless, broad, common, comprehensive, diffuse, extensive, far-ranging, far-reaching, general, outspread, pervasive, popular, prevalent, rampant, sweeping, universal, unlimited, unrestricted

will *v.* bequeath, bequest, confer, devise, give, hand down, leave, pass down, pass on, probate, transfer

withdraw *v.* **1.** abolish, abrogate, annul, call off, declare void, disavow, disclaim, dissolve, invalidate, nullify, quash, recall, recant, renege, repudiate, rescind, retract, reverse, revoke, take back **2.** back out, bow out, check out, depart, disengage, draw away, draw back, drop out, ease out, ebb, exit, fall back, get away, give ground, give way, go, keep apart, leave, move back, phase out, pull back, pull out, quit, recede, recoil, remove, retire, retreat, shrink back, take leave, take off, take out, vacate

withhold *v.* abstain, arrest, check, conceal, constrain, contain, curb, deny, detain, disallow, hide, hold back, hold in, inhibit, keep back, keep from, keep in check, keep secret, keep under control, refrain from giving, repress, restrain, retain, suppress

witness *n.* attester, beholder, bystander, corroborator, deponent, eyewitness, observer, onlooker, signatory, signer, spectator, testifier, viewer, watcher

witness *v.* **1.** affirm, attest, authenticate, bear out, bear witness, be witness, certify, confirm, corroborate, depose, endorse, give evidence, give testimony, say under oath, sign, substantiate, swear to, testify, verify, vouch for, warrant **2.** be witness to, be present at, follow, look at, look on, mark, note, notice, observe, see, take in, view, watch

word processing *n.* composition, computer preparation, document creation, document preparation, document processing, information processing, keyboarding, text creation, text manipulation, text editing, text preparation, text processing, typing

work *n.* **1.** art, assignment, business, calling, capacity, career, charge, commission, contract, craft, duty, employment, endeavor, engagement, field, handicraft, job, line of business, line of work, livelihood, mission, occupation, office, position, post, practice, profession, pursuit, responsibility, role, service, situation, skill, specialization, station, task, trade, vocation **2.** activity, chore, current task, drudgery, effort, endeavor, exercise, exertion, functioning, industry, labor, obligation, performance, production, striving, struggle, trouble, workout

work *v.* **1.** be employed, be gainfully employed, do business, do job, earn livelihood, follow trade, freelance, have job, hold job, practice profession, pursue activity, specialize in, undertake **2.** accomplish, achieve, act, carry out, cause, control, create, direct, drive, effect, execute, function, handle, implement, manage, maneuver, manipulate, move, operate, perform, run, serve, use, wield

worker *n.* apprentice, artisan, craftsperson, employed person, employee, laborer, operative, operator, tradesperson, wage earner, working person

workstation *n.* See **terminal 1**

worldwide *adj.* all-encompassing, all-inclusive, catholic, comprehensive, ecumenical, extensive, far-reaching, general, global, international, pandemic, universal, wide-ranging, widespread

worth *n.* **1.** appraisal, asking price, assessment, credit, estimation, evaluation, market price, price, profit, rate, valuation, value **2.** advantage, benefit, good, help, importance, merit, quality, significance, trustworthiness, usefulness, utility, virtue, weight

wrongful *adj.* corrupt, criminal, dishonest, felonious, illegal, illegitimate, illicit, larcenous, unethical, unjust, unlawful, wrong

X

x *n.* big question, mystery, puzzle, question, question mark, riddle, unknown, unknown factor, unknown quantity, variable

Xerox *v.* See **copy**

Y

yield *v.* **1.** accrue, afford, bear, blossom, bring forth, bring in, earn, engender, furnish, generate, give, give rise to, net, pay, pay back, produce, proffer, provide, render, return, sell for, supply, tender, turn out   **2.** abdicate, accede, accept, acquiesce, admit defeat, agree, allow, assent, back down, capitulate, cede, comply, concede, defer, deliver, disclaim, give in, give over, give up, go along with, hand in, hand over, let go, part with, permit, release, relent, relinquish, remit, resign, submit, succumb to, suffer defeat, surrender, transfer, turn over, waive

Z

zenith *n.*   acme, apex, apogee, cap, capstone, climax, crest, crown, culmination, height, high point, meridian, peak, pinnacle, summit, tip, vertex

zone *n.*   area, arena, band, belt, department, district, locale, quarter, realm, region, section, sector, sphere, territory, tract

More selected BARRON'S titles:

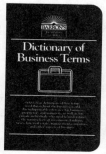

Dictionary of Accounting Terms
(1918-0) $11.95, Canada $19.95
Dictionary of Banking Terms
(1530-4) $11.95, Canada $15.95
Dictionary of Business Terms
(1833-8) $11.95, Canada $15.95
Dictionary of Computer Terms
(9023-3) $9.95, Canada $12.95
**Dictionary of Finance &
Investment Terms**
(9035-7) $11.95, Canada $15.95
Dictionary of Insurance Terms
(3379) $10.95, Canada $14.50

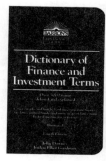

Dictionary of Marketing Terms
(1783-8) $11.95, Canada $15.95
Dictionary of Real Estate Terms
(1434-0) $11.95, Canada $15.95
Dictionary of Tax Terms
(1780-3) $9.95, Canada $12.95

BARRON'S FOREIGN LANGUAGE BUSINESS DICTIONARIES

Seven bilingual dictionaries translate about
3000 business terms not found in most foreign phrasebooks.

French for The Business Traveler
(1768-4) $9.95, Canada $12.95
German for The Business Traveler
(1769-2) $9.95, Canada $12.95
Italian for The Business Traveler
(1771-4) $9.95, Canada $12.95
Japanese for The Business Traveler
(1770-6) $11.95, Canada $15.95
Korean for The Business Traveler
(1772-2) $11.95, Canada $15.95
Russian for The Business Traveler
(1784-6) $11.95, Canada $15.95
Spanish for The Business Traveler
(1773-0) $9.95, Canada $12.95

All prices are in U.S. and Canadian dollars and subject to change without notice. At your
bookseller, or order direct adding 10% postage (minimum charge $3.75, Canada $4.00)
N.Y. state residents add sales tax. All books are paperback editions.   ISBN PREFIX 0-8120

Barron's Educational Series, Inc.
250 Wireless Boulevard, Hauppauge, NY 11788
In Canada: Georgetown Book Warehouse
34 Armstrong Ave., Georgetown, Ontario L7G 4R   (#12) R 4/95

More selected BARRON'S titles:

BARRON'S ACCOUNTING HANDBOOK, 2nd EDITION,
Joel G. Siegel and Jae K. Shim
Provides accounting rules, guidelines, formulas and techniques etc. to help students and business professionals work out accounting problems.
Hardcover: $29.95, Canada $38.95/ ISBN 6449-6, 880 pages

REAL ESTATE HANDBOOK, 3rd EDITION,
Jack P. Freidman and Jack C. Harris
A dictionary/reference for everyone in real estate. Defines over 1500 legal, financial, and architectural terms. Hardcover, $29.95, Canada $39.95/ ISBN 6330-9, 810 pages

HOW TO PREPARE FOR THE REAL ESTATE LICENSING EXAMINATIONS SALESPERSON AND BROKER, 5th EDITION,
Bruce Lindeman and Jack P. Freidman
Reviews current exam topics and features updated model exams and supplemental exams, all with explained answers. Paperback, $12.95, Canada $16.95/ ISBN 2994-1, 340 pages

BARRON'S FINANCE AND INVESTMENT HANDBOOK, 4th EDITION,
John Downes and Jordan Goodman
This hard-working handbook of essential information defines more than 3000 key terms, and explores 30 basic investment opportunities. The investment information is thoroughly up-to-date. Hardcover $35.00, Canada $45.50/ ISBN 6465-8, approx. 1200 pages

FINANCIAL TABLES FOR MONEY MANAGEMENT
Stephen S. Solomon, Dr. Clifford Marshall, Martin Pepper, Jack P. Freidman and Jack C. Harris
Pocket-sized handbooks of interest and investment rate tables used easily by average investors and mortgage holders. Paperback

Real Estate Loans, 2nd Ed., $6.95, Canada $8.95/ISBN 1618-1, 336 pages
Mortgage Payments, 2nd Ed., $5.95, Canada $7.95/ISBN 1386-7, 304 pages
Bonds, 2nd Ed., $5.95, Canada $7.50/ISBN 4995-0, 256 pages
Canadian Mortgage Payments, 2nd Ed., Canada $8.95/ISBN 1617-3, 336 pages
Adjustable Rate Mortgages, 2nd Ed., $6.95, Canada $8.50/ISBN 1529-0, 288 pages

Barron's Educational Series, Inc.
250 Wireless Blvd., Hauppauge, NY 11788
In Canada: Georgetown Book Warehouse
34 Armstrong Ave., Georgetown, Ontario L7G 4R9

(#11) R6/95

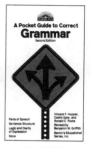

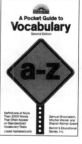